Praise for Teaching Wi[tchcraft]

"What I love about *Teaching Witchcraft* is its very inten[...] and the teacher. Miles knows his subject, but he also und[...] mation which does not insult the intelligence but is at the same time very accessible. We are long beyond the time of guarding the Craft with a cloak of deep secrecy. As the author says, this is the textbook he wished (we all wished) had been available so many years ago. Bravo!" —**Holli S. Emore, M.Div., Cherry Hill Seminary**

"There is a beautiful fantasy in the Pagan communities about studying with a seasoned teacher, preferably in a cottage garden. The reality is that few people actually learn magic at all—they read and read but rarely have the nerve to practice. This exquisite book reminds us that ours is—as all crafts are—an experiential journey, filled with trial and error. We are reminded that the learning is in the doing and that cottage garden simply isn't available to many people. Let this book be your cottage garden and let this wise author be your teacher. You have much to gain from its pages and from his experience. Highly recommended." —**H. Byron Ballard, village Witch and author of *Roots, Branches & Spirits***

"In Miles's revised edition of *Teaching Witchcraft*, seekers can find their way back home to the Old Religion of nature that our souls long to remember. Divine love, reverence, and beauty are found within these pages, served with a hearty helping of Miles's signature mirth! Complex concepts unfold like a conversation with a trusted mentor. Arranged into easy-to-understand teaching modules, this guide to the history, ideals, and magickal practices of Wicca provides a much-needed structure for formal coven classrooms and book clubs among solitary practitioners alike. Just as the first edition was a foundational text for the Sojourner Tradition of Modern Witchcraft, the revised edition remains on our recommended reading list for all students and teachers of Witchcraft." —**Heron Michelle, High Priestess and author of *Elemental Witchcraft***

"This is a much-needed manual—not just for students, but specifically for teachers of the Craft. In a field where the vast majority of books are intended for neophytes, Miles has created the most comprehensive compilation I've ever seen on all aspects of the Craft— history, philosophy, ethics, tools, liturgy practice, and magickal theory—all organized as a course of lessons, from introductory to advanced, with brief quizzes at the end of each. As both a teacher and a perpetual student, I am pleased to give this work my highest recommendation!" —**Oberon Zell, founder and headmaster of Grey School of Wizardry**

Teaching
Witchcraft

About the Author

Miles Batty (United Kingdom) has been studying Witchcraft since 1974 and has been active in the Pagan community since 1985. He is ordained clergy in the Wiccan faith and has served as coven Priest, author, and director and coordinator of various Pagan events and organizations. He has lived in England, Wales, the United States, Canada, and Scotland. Miles is well-known in both the United States and United Kingdom.

Teaching Witchcraft

UPDATED & REVISED

A Guide for Students &
Teachers of Wicca

MILES BATTY

LLEWELLYN PUBLICATIONS | WOODBURY, MINNESOTA

First Edition
First Printing, 2023

Book design by Christine Ha
Cover design by Cassie Willett
Interior art by the Llewellyn Art Department
    Figures 1–20, 22 by the Llewellyn Art Department
    Figure 21 (chakra figure, page 289) by Mary Ann Zapalac

Llewellyn is a registered trademark of Llewellyn Worldwide Ltd.

Library of Congress Cataloging-in-Publication Data (Pending)
ISBN: 978-0-7387-7242-4

Llewellyn Worldwide Ltd. does not participate in, endorse, or have any authority or responsibility concerning private business transactions between our authors and the public.
    All mail addressed to the author is forwarded, but the publisher cannot, unless specifically instructed by the author, give out an address or phone number.
    Any internet references contained in this work are current at publication time, but the publisher cannot guarantee that a specific location will continue to be maintained. Please refer to the publisher's website for links to authors' websites and other sources.

Llewellyn Publications
A Division of Llewellyn Worldwide Ltd.
2143 Wooddale Drive
Woodbury, MN 55125-2989
www.llewellyn.com

Printed in the United States of America

Other Books by Miles Batty

Teaching Witchcraft: A Guide for Teachers and Students of the Old Religion (2006)

The Green Prince's Father (2007)

Dedication

This book is dedicated to three remarkable people:

To Heron Michelle: Witch, Priestess, mother, entrepreneur, Pagan dynamo, author, and dear friend. Thank you for your endless friendship and support. You really may never know how deeply your wisdom and kindness have touched me.

And to my friend Marilyn Dillon, who published the first edition of *Teaching Witchcraft*. We wouldn't be here now if it wasn't for you—thank you for taking a chance.

And to my brother Philip, who introduced me to Witchcraft in the first place. I doubt either of us realized it at the time, but you started me on a path that has defined the rest of my life.

Acknowledgements

I wish to thank, in no particular order, Ariana Lightningstorm, Nybor and Elspeth, Heron Michelle, Amber K, Janet and Stewart Farrar, Snooze Hamilton, River Higginbotham, Isaac Bonewits, Magistra Abigail Blackwell, Ron "Stonemage" Taylor, Marilyn Dillon, Byron Ballard, Oberon Zell-Ravenheart, Heather Greene, Marysa Storm, Jamie Hendrickx, Professor Ronald Hutton, members of Free Spirit Festival, Pagan Spirit Gathering, and Dragonfest, and all the Witches of history who contributed to the tapestry of our path.

May the Lord and Lady bless you all.

Disclaimer

The publisher and author assume no liability for any injuries caused to the reader that may result from the reader's use of content contained in this publication and recommend common sense when contemplating the practices described in the work. In the following pages you will find recommendations for the use of certain essential oils, incense blends, and ritual items. If you are allergic to any items used in the rituals, please refrain from use. Magickal work is not meant to replace the care of qualified medical professionals.

Contents

Foreword

Comprehensive does not begin to describe the material contained in this book. If you are a teacher looking for a resource for Wicca 101 and 102, look no further! This well-written, logically organized work contains the essentials and many often omitted details every student should know. It is organized as lessons complete with study questions and exams. This truly takes a lot of the work out of teaching a Wicca 101 and 102 class. I am a math teacher by profession and know a well-organized curriculum when I see one. This is a work of art!

Before I found Miles Batty's book, I wrote my own first- and second-year curriculums. When I discovered his book, which is truly written for teachers of the Craft, I switched to his curriculum and only included parts of mine that were particular to our tradition. His work is far more organized, clear, and professional than my own. His study questions are thought-provoking and well worded. He is able to explain complicated concepts and even esoteric intricacies on a level that allows beginner students to achieve an appropriate level of understanding. (After all, we shall not seek to overwhelm a dedicant's senses with the full workings of the LBRP or break their brains with all of the Kabbalah at once. Small steps are required on this path of knowledge.) Miles finds a way to impart vast amounts of knowledge without speaking over the heads of the students while not talking down to them. It is a fine line to walk, and he walks it well.

As a teacher, I love that he gives me suggestions on class discussions (a.k.a. his classroom modules). It helps me easily start a discussion about the lessons with my students and show them how to apply the lesson we have just finished. The provided study questions help me determine if my students understand the material. He lists additional recommended reading at the end of each lesson and a thorough bibliography at the end of the book.

I will continue to use Miles's work in my classes and strongly recommend his work to anyone seeking to teach Wicca. He will make your experiences and your students' experiences richer and deeper. As a classroom tool, this is absolutely ideal and unique.

Thank you for writing such an amazing curriculum!

—**Jamie Hendrickx**
a.k.a. Lady Amayuladi Disa
High Priestess, Serenity Coven

Introduction

You've probably picked up this book because you're either a student of Wicca wishing to learn more or a teacher hoping to present information to a group of people new to the Craft.

This book is not intended to be an in-depth analysis of every aspect of Witchcraft. That would require at least six dozen books this size! Instead, it was created to provide an understanding of the different facets of the Craft and hopefully to inspire the student to look further. It should be noted that this book covers many facets of Wiccan ethics and perspective; it is not dedicated to a single path or tradition. Indeed, many of the opinions presented are mine and not necessarily those of the Wiccan community as a whole.

This book consists of two parts, Wicca 101 and Wicca 102, but is collectively known as Wicca 101, the generic term for a Wicca studies class. The Wicca 101 section delves into the history of Witchcraft and examines the philosophies and ethics of the Craft. In the Wicca 102 section, we'll examine the inner workings of a typical Witch's coven, examine the procedure of a ritual, and study spells and spellcrafting.

There are a few subjects discussed that you may feel uncomfortable teaching—or just plain disagree with. Topics such as abortion, suicide, death, and the afterlife are explored from a Wiccan perspective. If you feel that such topics are inappropriate for your class, feel free to leave them out. After all, this is your Wicca 101 class, not mine.

Unless noted as historical figures or actual deities, all names and groups mentioned within this book are fictitious and used to illustrate the lesson. Any resemblance to actual persons or groups is purely coincidental.

The invocations, charges, rituals, and spell verse presented in this book are my own composition unless a specific author is cited or noted.

Within these lessons, you may encounter uncredited anecdotes or references that you might have seen or heard elsewhere. I wish I could give due credit for every illustrative example or shred of wisdom that found its way into this book. Snippets of wisdom shared around a campfire, moments in ritual that resonated with me, or discussions with friends at a gathering—these were the roots of what grew into the writing of this book. My heartfelt gratitude and blessings go out to those who have helped make this book what it is today. Whether by personal input, well-received advice, or inspired madness, you all have a hand in the creation of this volume.

Advice for Teachers

Apparently you've taken a major leave of your senses and decided to teach Witchcraft to a group of neophytes. You have two choices here:

1) Put this book down and find a small hole to hide in until the feeling goes away.

Or

2) Read through each section carefully before you begin the lesson.

Every so often, a coven Priestess decides it's time to open the door to seekers and teach the mysteries of the Craft to a group of would-be Witches. If the individual is lucky, they assemble a fairly coherent group of students, and they search through their books for a selection of topics that they can compile into a good class curriculum. The Priestess opens books like *Wicca: A Guide for the Solitary Practitioner* by Scott Cunningham, *Elemental Witchcraft: A Guide to Living a Magickal Life through the Elements* by Heron Michelle, and *Buckland's Complete Book of Witchcraft*.

Many people freeze up at this point. "What topics do I teach? What comes first? What do I put emphasis on?"

And if it's anything like many first-time Wicca 101 classes, at the end of the first meeting the students have learned (a) whose house they're meeting at next time and (b) who's bringing the Doritos. My coven was no different when we decided to host such a class. We had a substantial library of metaphysical books but lacked a classroom format, a teacher's resource. We found that in Amber K's book *CovenCraft*. In it, she offered a rudimentary structure for a class on Wicca, and that was the catalyst for this book. I started with her framework and expanded it. Amber K is, to be fair, this book's godmother.

Advice for Students

If you're a student, whether studying alone or with a group, I hope this information is clear, useful, and informative. Read through the book, answer the study questions if you like, and with luck the information I've presented here will broaden your understanding of Wicca and Witchcraft.

At the rear of the book, I've included a selection of teaching supplements; you may use these as you like.

How to Use This Book

The lessons provided here are divided into two categories: Wicca 101 and Wicca 102.

Wicca 101 is a sixteen-lesson course, and Wicca 102 is a twenty-three-lesson course. These are usually presented once a week, making a total of thirty-nine weeks. Allowing for holidays, delayed classes, and a short break between 101 and 102, these lessons should easily fit into a one-year initiation program.

If you are a teacher with a group of students, the lessons in this book can be read "as is" by the instructor, although personal variation and input is always welcomed. Each lesson, as presented, is relatively short, usually no more than nine or ten pages. It is assumed that at each class there will be a period of getting organized and a review of the previous lesson. The reading of the lesson follows, then comes a discussion period to deepen the understanding of the subject matter. Allow approximately two to three hours from start to finish for each class. There are study questions accompanying each lesson, but it is recommended that the study questions are not used until the end of class. If the questions are handed out as class begins, students will simply fill them out as class progresses. All too often the information travels in the ear, out the hand, and is instantly forgotten. If the students are urged to reflect on the lessons and answer the questions later, more information stays where it belongs.

At the back of the book, you'll find a selection of teacher's resources, including classroom modules and suggestions for additional exercises.

Keep in mind that simply reading from this book is not enough; doing so will merely teach you somebody else's (namely, my own) view of the Craft. Each lesson should combine three parts: reading from the book, the instructor's personal experience, and student input. And if you disagree with the information presented and wish to deviate, please do!

Wicca 101 covers the basic history, fundamentals, and ethics of the Craft. There is no magickal practice taught in the first section; that is discussed in Wicca 102. After completing the 101 section, you should have a good idea of who to accept into Wicca 102 and who to turn away. People who are getting into the Craft for the wrong reasons (greed, selfishness, lust, etc.) or those who just don't get it will probably have drifted away before the completion of the Wicca 101 lessons anyway. If not, this is a good time to "weed out the deadwood."

If you are teaching for a coven, upon the completion of the Wicca 101 class, neophytes may be awarded the status of coven dedicant. They have shown an acceptable degree of dedication, sincerity, and enthusiasm and can begin serious study of the practice of Witchcraft. A sample dedication ritual is presented in appendix 3.

Wicca 102 teaches coven structure and protocol, ritual construction and etiquette, spellcrafting, divination, the uses of ritual tools, and the themes and practices of magick.

After completing Wicca 102, a Priest and Priestess can welcome young Witches into the formal coven and award them the first-degree initiation if such a degree system is used. A sample initiation ritual is offered for this purpose. If you are a Solitary (non-coven-affiliated) Witch, whether studying alone or with a group, you'll find a possible self-initiation ritual here too.

Beyond the Classroom

After finishing these lessons and attaining first-degree status, students will hopefully want to go further in their exploration of and involvement in the world of Witchcraft.

If the degree system is used, it would go something like this:

The second degree is awarded to Witches only after they have sufficient talent and dedication to apply the teaching of the Craft themselves, have made a life-altering decision, or have overcome a deep phobia. Whether it is getting out of an abusive relationship, learning to walk after months of paralysis, bungee jumping, or speaking before a crowd, a significant personal accomplishment is usually regarded as sufficient dedication to be awarded the second degree. Stepping outside of your comfort zone—that's the key. Teaching the Craft to others is another good way to earn second-degree status.

Finally, the coven elders can award third degree to those who have shown advanced insight, understanding, and application of the Craft principles and practices.

In writing this book, I tried to avoid tailoring the lessons to any particular path or tradition. Instead, I present a general overview of Witchcraft and Wicca and allow the students to develop their own perspectives. After all, every individual is their own person with their own way of connecting with the Divine. I did, however, put some emphasis on the difference between "Old Craft," such as the Gardnerian tradition, and contemporary Wicca. Witchcraft has—and we know this—a rather checkered heritage. It's a hodgepodge of folk traditions, metaphysics, seasonal observances, archaeological research, pantheistic worship, and ancestor veneration. I don't try to pretend it's squeaky clean and perfect, nor that it has all the answers.

The roots of Witchcraft—from its earliest Neolithic beginnings to modern influences—come from all over the globe, but the formative history started in Britain and northern Europe. I present the history in that light to keep it as short as possible. If I included every thread of our diverse tapestry, we'd be here for ages!

While the lessons presented offer a fair amount of insight and understanding of the Craft, it is by no means the end-all and be-all of Craft knowledge. Students are encouraged to go further in their research and to read and learn as much as possible. There are countless books, articles, and websites on the history of the Craft, the meanings of the sabbats, ritual and spell construction, and Wiccan ethics. Please, go read!

Introduction to the Llewellyn Edition (or, the author's dirty little secret)

"What inspired you to write this book?" I've been asked that many times. The short answer is: Somebody had to.

The book you're reading now originally started life as *Teaching Witchcraft: A Guide for Teachers and Students of the Old Religion,* a classroom-designed textbook/workbook published in 2006.

Other than *Buckland's Complete Book of Witchcraft,* nobody as far as I knew had written a comprehensive classroom textbook designed for a teacher to use as a Wicca 101 guide. I'd sat in on loads of Wicca 101 classes at festivals and in people's living rooms, and what many of them lacked was structure or a class syllabus to follow.

I originally wrote *Teaching Witchcraft* over several months in 2004 and 2005, using notes and anecdotes I'd compiled from years of workshops and conversations, casual research, and observing Witches just being themselves at home, in rituals, and at Pagan festivals.

Once I had the basic outline in mind, something like a framework to follow, the book came together relatively quickly. I developed a class outline, penciled in the lesson subject matter for each one, and wrote the lessons I knew already. The procedure of ritual. The ethics of spellcasting. I dug into my Pagan library and started flipping through books, adding information that I thought the classes needed. Esbats. The Ardanes. The Principles of Wiccan Belief.

By the end of 2005, I had the book in a reasonably finished form and ready to send to a publisher. And I was lucky; it only took two rejections before I stumbled across a private direct-to-print company called Three Moons Media, and the first edition of *Teaching Witchcraft* was available in 2006.

But there's a sort of dark secret behind that old first edition, which I haven't told anyone until now. A couple of people guessed it. Isaac Bonewits guessed it.

Remember when I said I'd sat in on many Wicca 101 classes?

I was a student, eager to learn. *I didn't write the book as a teacher sharing knowledge. I wrote it as a student looking for answers.* This was the textbook I wished *I'd* had when I was first learning all this stuff.

And I was delighted when it became reasonably popular.

Then, as more people come to me with observations about the information I'd presented, I began to realize that I hadn't known as much as I thought I did. I got a lot of the information right, but I got some of it wrong too. I'm not ashamed to say it—some parts of the first edition were almost laughably inaccurate. (If you ask me nicely, I'll tell you which parts.)

As I write this, that first edition was published fifteen years ago, and I often found myself reexamining my work. I was aware of what information I'd included and where the mistakes were, and I started keeping a mental list of corrections I'd want to put in a second edition. And a lot had changed in the Pagan community! My old book was desperately outdated.

I tried to start a revised edition several times, but it just never flowed. The magick wasn't there. I kept on second-guessing myself. I knew it would happen; I just didn't know when.

Fast-forward to the summer of 2021. A dear friend of mine is published by Llewellyn Worldwide, who contacted me with a desire to release a revised edition of *Teaching Witchcraft*. I dug out my old manuscript and a printed copy, collected my notes, and went through each chapter and made those corrections I'd been saving up. Fifteen years is a long time, but suddenly it was all coming together. Working together with the editors at Llewellyn, I finally accomplished what I'd been trying to do for so long.

So here, in *Teaching Witchcraft: A Guide for Students and Teachers of Wicca*, is the book that *Teaching Witchcraft* should have been all along. Whether you use it as a classroom textbook or for personal study, hail, and welcome! I hope it does what you want it to do.

WICCA 101
The History, Philosophy, and Ethics of Witchcraft

LESSON 1
An Introduction to Witchcraft

Welcome to Wicca 101!

Over the next few lessons, we will explore the meanings, philosophies, history, and practices of the Craft. Think of this first lesson as the icebreaker. Here we will discuss what Witchcraft is and is not, what words like *Witch* and *Wicca* really mean, and what you can expect from this course.

This course is not designed as the absolute sum of Craft knowledge. It merely gives you enough information to provide a basic understanding of the subject matter and hopefully inspires you to seek further.

After each lesson, you will find study questions, which are intended to help you deepen your understanding of the topic and should help to further your progress in the Craft. If you are studying with a teacher or mentor, after all sixteen lessons in Wicca 101, you may receive a final exam, and your teacher will review your performance and progress in the course. Students showing enough aptitude, dedication, and enthusiasm will be encouraged to proceed with Wicca 102.

What Is Witchcraft?

To be blunt, Witchcraft is many things. It is a religious principle, a collection of folkways and customs, and a lifestyle and philosophy. It is not a religion per se, and this will make more sense as we continue. Its earliest roots can be traced back more than twenty thousand years, but it would be inaccurate to say that Witchcraft itself is that old. It is better to say that what we call Witchcraft today is derived from a collection of practices and beliefs that evolved over time. It's easier to think of it as a tapestry made from a diverse weave of threads that combine to create a common belief system.

Witchcraft is as much a way of life, a philosophy, and a belief system as it is an actual religion. Witches strive to protect the earth and her inhabitants and to live in harmony with others.

Witches usually meet in religious groups called covens, which are like small families or church groups. While Christians identify themselves as belonging to different denominations, such as Catholic or Baptist, many Witches belong to different traditions, such as Gardnerian or Stregheria. Just as many practitioners claim to be Solitary Witches, not belonging to any tradition or coven.

Witches worship the "old gods," or pre-Christian deities, such as Apollo, Freyja, and Isis as well as archetypal divinities known as the Lord and Lady, or the god and the goddess.

Witches celebrate the changing seasons of the year in rituals called sabbats. Seen collectively, the eight sabbats represent the changing seasons, the love and vitality of the goddess and the god, the goddess's enduring care of the world, and the god's cycle of life, sacrifice, and rebirth. Some Witches and covens also honour the full moon with rituals called esbats.

Most Witches cast spells; a spell is a kind of "interactive prayer." Spells should never be used for harm, nor ever without the express permission of the spell recipient or target.

Now let's take a look at something that is probably even more important to understand this early on.

What Is Witchcraft Not?

There are a lot of preconceptions and misconceptions about the Craft. Here I will attempt to separate fact from fiction or, worse, vicious rumor. The word *Witch* carries with it many connotations. To some, a Witch is a beautiful, mysterious woman. To others, a Witch is a shrivelled, cruel hag. Still others might see a Witch as a servant of Satan. Unfortunately unscrupulous people have been known to use the word unethically, for self-promotion, or to harm others.

You might know people who use or misuse the word. Here are a few of the misconceptions people have about Witches.

Devil Worship or Satanism

Wiccans do not worship Satan. That fallacy exists because of a medieval Christian misconception, wherein anyone not dedicated to Jesus must, of course, be a servant of Satan. There *are* Satanists who call themselves Witches, but they are not the goddess worshippers of the Craft. We'll take a brief look at who Satanists are and why such confusion exists in lesson 4.

A Sure-Fire Road to Success

Witchcraft is not a way to win the lottery, succeed in business without really trying, or make people fall in love with you. Witchcraft has been grossly misrepresented by Hollywood and scores of bad novels. Many movies would have you believe that Witches are either ugly, manipulative old women, teenagers on a power trip, or demons disguised as everyday humans.

Orgies

Witches' sabbats are not mass orgies or festivals of wanton debauchery. Sometimes sexually focused acts with consenting participants do occur, but they are not the "reason for the season." If anyone tries to use sex as a ploy to manipulate others or claims it's part of a "coven initiation," they are just engaging in or trying to promote abusive and potentially illegal behavior. Those who exhibit predatory behavior will certainly be judged accordingly by others in the coven or the community. Such behavior is not tolerated. Ever. Consent is paramount. I will talk about free will in later lessons, and free will and consent go hand in hand.

Death Spells

Witches do not use magick to kill. Spells designed to kill others are simply fictitious. While magick can be used for harm, there will always be repercussions and unforeseen consequences.

Creative Drug Use

While some Witches, like people of any faith, might occasionally partake in recreational drug usage, the use of drugs is not ever required in covens or magickal events. Indeed, many covens prohibit recreational drug use or excessive drinking before participating in ritual. Entering a magickal environment under the influence of mind-altering substances could have disastrous effects! Even alcohol, popular at the closing of many rituals, is consumed in moderation.

Evangelism

A coven that works too hard to recruit members or to proselytize their beliefs has an entirely different focus than working magick, recognizing the sabbats, or honouring the gods.

Cult Mentality or Coercion

You may have heard about people using religion to promote a cult status for themselves. Witchcraft is not a cult, and Witches are not cultists. Any coven leader or elder who tries to coerce others through subliminal manipulation, bullying, or hazing rituals should be reported to the authorities. A mystical or magnetic personality does not necessarily reflect the principles of perfect love and perfect trust. Nobody has the right to treat others like puppets or pawns, nor demand that they do anything that makes them uncomfortable. Loyalty to a coven does not imply subjugation or servitude. Take a moment to consider some of the accusations ascribed to religious cults or other unethical spiritual practices. As you learn more, compare them with Witchcraft.

Other Red Flags to Watch Out For

You may find yourself seeking other Witches or covens to study or worship with. Here are a few more red flags to avoid as you search:

- Any leader or elder who tries to manipulate or coerce you against your will or uses sex as a come-on.
- Any physical abuse within the Craft.
- Required use of hallucinogenic drugs for "enhanced magickal development."
- Any leader or elder who is evasive, vague, or inconsistent about their training and background. If they claim to have credentials, they should be able to show them.
- Covens that promote evangelizing and proselytizing. Witches do not go knocking on doors to drum up business. If a person is meant to find Witchcraft, they will do so in their own time and on their own terms.
- Any leader or elder who charges exorbitant amounts of money for training. Asking for reimbursement for supplies or travel expenses is acceptable, but coven membership should not have a tuition.
- Any coven that spends more energy and time on politics and bickering than on magickal growth and worship.
- Any leader or elder who lives off the coven funds.

Who's Who and What's What?

As you move through these lessons, many words will come up over and over again. Let's take a look at some major ones here.

Pagan

There are two possible definitions for Pagan. (Okay, three if you count definitions made by non-Pagans.)

1) One who lives in accordance with the cycles of nature and the changing seasons, or one for whom reverence for nature is an important part of life.
2) One who follows a non-Abrahamic (Christianity, Judaism, Islam) religion, such as Ásatrú/Norse heathenry or the worship of Hellenic or ancient Greek or Egyptian pantheons or Celtic deities.
3) Anyone who is not a Christian could be considered Pagan or Heathen. Buddhists and Hindus, however, do not regard themselves as "Pagan" even though gods like Shiva, Brahma, and Parvati are indeed honoured by Pagans.

Witch

A Witch is a person of any gender who uses Witchcraft or follows its principles. While a Pagan is one who lives in harmony with nature or honours old gods, a Witch is a Pagan who uses Witchcraft. You can be a Pagan without being a Witch, but you generally cannot be a Witch without being Pagan. (Generally? We'll get into that in lesson 4. Like herding cats, this, let me tell you.)

Witchcraft

Witchcraft is the practice and religion employed by Witches. Witchcraft, really, is many things. It is a philosophy, a religion, and a lifestyle. It would be nearly impossible to say that Witchcraft is *this* but not *that* because it is a tapestry composed of so many different threads. A reverence for nature, goddess worship, the use of spells, and an understanding of Pagan cosmology are all parts of what we know as Witchcraft.

Witchcraft can trace its earliest roots back more than twenty thousand years, but it is in no means a direct lineage. Rather, Witchcraft grew and evolved over time, piece by piece, from a wide range of sources. What we know as Witchcraft today was only brought together within the last few decades.

It's also known as the Craft, which is merely an abbreviation of Witchcraft.

The Old Religion

The Old Religion is another term for Witchcraft. This is something of a misnomer because Witchcraft was only recently defined by its own members as a true religion. The term was adopted early in the twentieth century when Margaret Murray proposed that Witchcraft had a direct lineage back to Neolithic European "goddess cults." Her research was later found to be inaccurate, but the term remained.[1]

Wicca

According to Gerald Gardner (if you don't recognize that name, you will later), the word *Wicca* is derived from *Wica*, which he said was the original name for Witches.[2]

Today, Wicca is sort of an offshoot from the older, established traditions such as Gardnerian. While many Witchcraft traditions have an established liturgy, eclectic Wiccan traditions incorporate practices from several disciplines and pantheons, including even technological references, fantasy, science fiction, and folk magick, as well as Witchcraft itself. The practice of adopting aspects of other cultures can come under scrutiny as cultural appropriation, and care must be taken to avoid cultural appropriation.

Magick

Unlike magic (spelled with no *k*), magick is the art or science of focusing will to alter one's immediate reality. Magic is parlor tricks, sleight of hand, and pulling rabbits out of a hat. This is a spelling distinction that Aleister Crowley made popular, and many Pagans use it.

Before we go any further, let's make one very important clarification. There is no such thing as "black" or "white" magick, or "evil" or "good" magick. Magick is a neutral force, like electricity. How it's used depends on the user. Let's look at it this way: Think of a chair. If I say to you, "You look tired; have a seat." Does that make it a "good" or "white" chair? Or if I pick up that same chair and beat you with it, is it then an "evil" or "black" chair? The chair, like electricity or magick, is neutral. It's how it's used that counts.

Not every Pagan uses magick, but many do.

---

1. Hutton, *The Triumph of the Moon*, 362.
2. Doyle White, "The Meaning of 'Wicca,'" 185–207.

Coven

A coven is like a magickal family or a church group. It is a small group of dedicated Witches who join together for mutual support, strength, and growth. Covens are usually led by a High Priestess and/or Priest, there is usually an established hierarchy, and members have specific tasks within the coven.

Grove

A grove is like a minor coven. Groves are often teaching or study groups. There may or may not be a Priest and Priestess, and grove members need not be dedicated Witches.

Tradition

Similar to Christian denominations, Craft traditions follow established systems of worship and practice. Gardnerian, for example, is the tradition created by Gerald Gardner, and the feminist Dianic tradition was named after Diana, Greek goddess of the moon.

Sabbats

Eight times a year, Witches celebrate the sabbats, which are rituals honouring the changing seasons of the year. Sabbats reflect the seasons, the cycle of life, and the union between the goddess and the god. These celebrations can be joyous or solemn, depending upon the occasion.

Lesson 1: Study Prompts and Questions

What Is Witchcraft?
- What does the word *Witch* mean to you? What images did it evoke when you were younger?
- What do you hope to learn from these lessons?

What Is Witchcraft Not?
- Why do you think so much negativity is associated with Witchcraft?
- Why do you think people are willing to believe those negative things?

Who's Who and What's What?
- Offer definitions of these words or phrases: *Witch*, *Wiccan*, *Pagan*, *coven*, and *magick*.

Lesson 1: Recommended Reading

- *Paganism: An Introduction to Earth-Centered Religions* by Joyce Higginbotham and River Higginbotham
- *Paganism: An Introductory Guide: Pagan Holidays, Beliefs, Gods and Goddesses, Symbols, Rituals, Practices, and Much More!* by Riley Star

The History of the Craft: From the Birth of Religion to the Ancient Empires

"In order to appreciate where you are," my father once told me, "it's important to know where you've been."

We continue our Wicca 101 studies over the next three lessons with a look at the history of Witchcraft from the dawn of history to the present day. To begin, we'll examine the earliest roots of Witchcraft, which to some extent mirror the birth of Western civilization. While Wicca has its roots in many different cultures and civilizations, we'll focus on the influence of people from Britain, northern Europe, Greece, and Rome in these lessons.

As a note, my analysis of prehistory is highly speculative and should not be taken as factual. The best archaeological research can only hope to understand what early people thought or believed, based on scant evidence.

Religion in Paleolithic Times

The year is 25,000 BCE.

The last Ice Age is retreating, and humankind—whether Neanderthal or early Homo sapiens—has learned the use of fire, organized hunting, and rudimentary language. The wheel is still more than twenty thousand years away. Loose tribes of nomads roam the plains that will one day be known as Europe, Africa, and Asia. Still at the mercy of the whims of nature, humans must make sense of this world to survive. Early humans worked hard to stay alive. They fashioned bone, wood, and stone into simple tools; they learned the cycle of the seasons, the ways of animals, and the nature of plants.[3]

---

3. Cunliffe, *The Oxford Illustrated History of Prehistoric Europe*, 79.

Archaeological evidence suggests ancestor worship in which bodies were either ritu-alistically buried or cannibalistically consumed. Some believed that to take in the flesh of another was to gain their strengths, whether the flesh was from a bear, an ox, or a grand-father. Ancestor veneration led to ancestor worship and the possibility that the ancestor's spirit was still alive in another world.[4]

Gradually, the idea of a spirit world developed into the presence of beings—whether human, animal, or hybrid—who could influence life in the physical world or could be called upon to help in that world. This slowly grew into the concept of divine beings.[5]

Over the course of thousands of years of the Neolithic, many diverse spiritual con-cepts and practices developed. There was never a single, homogeneous faith, but rather different clans in different regions developed their own spiritual "language." Toward the north, the focus was more on a kinship with the seasonal changes and alignment of the stars, whereas farther south a more dualistic interpretation developed, focusing on the roles of male and female. In the area that would become Turkey, small clay figurines of female figures, usually seen pregnant, were being fashioned. It is possible that these were created to ensure successful birth or as goddess images, which suggested a femi-nine divinity.[6]

By around 10,000 BCE, people in the northern areas of Europe, the remnants of Neanderthal and the more prominent Homo sapiens, were creating a spiritual landscape that involved an awareness of the changing seasons and cycles of growth, an animistic connection with beasts such as the aurochs and the stag, and veneration of ancestral spirits. They had learned the paths of the sun and the moon, recognized the patterns of stars and planets in the sky, and had learned to distinguish and cultivate different herbs. They had observed the migratory patterns of birds before seasonal changes and how animals reacted to changes in the weather before they became apparent. Animals were thought to hold the key to the spirit world, which is why shamans and others with spiri-tual authority sought to connect with the different animals to bridge that gap.[7]

As clans of people grew and developed, they stopped roaming and remained in areas where they could prosper. Clans became farming communities, and communities

---

4. Thomas, "Eating People Is Wrong."
    Narr, "Prehistoric Religion."
5. Tylor, *Primitive Culture*, 420–22.
6. Kark, "Archaeologists from Stanford Find an 8,000-Year-Old 'Goddess Figurine' in Central Turkey," *Stanford News*.
7. Barnard, *Genesis of Symbolic Thought*, 63.

became the first villages. Regions slowly developed spiritual identities.[8] Stone circles were erected on the British Isles and in Europe. It is understood that their positions and orientations were carefully chosen to correspond to solar and lunar positions. What roles the stone circles played in people's everyday lives is still largely speculative, but they remained vital to the people of the area for thousands of years.

The Birth of the Wicce

Stone and Iron Age communities around the British Isles and northern Europe were still dependent on the natural world around them and had a developing awareness of the spirit world. A hierarchy of sorts gradually emerged. Those with a greater capacity to communicate with the spirit world developed into a priesthood, and stratifications within the community were not unknown.[9] Even Neolithic people expressed a bias of one gender over another—graves of males often had more ornate grave goods than those of females (that have been found so far, anyway)—and the more adept warriors had a greater abundance of grave goods, or things buried with them to take to the afterlife. People buried with more jewelry and beads often bore tattoos and scarification that we can assume to have been spiritually significant.[10] This tells us that Priests were regarded as a separate class within the community, distinct from the common villagers. These Priests were a select few who were more able to produce the desired results when directing the rituals and more able to offer sage advice when needed.

We can speculate that these ritual leaders, or Priests and Priestesses, would become known as the Wicce (WI-ki), or "Wise Ones." (The problem with relying on historical or archaeological analysis is that you are frequently trying to work backward, using what you know to fill in the blanks of what you don't know without letting any presumed bias taint your research. Do we know for certain that our Neolithic Priests were actually Wicce? Not at all. But linguistic experts can trace the origins of words backward as well, and the etymological roots of *Wicce/Wica/Wika* are appropriate for the period.[11] We can call our shamans or Priests *Wicce* with some reliability that we aren't completely off the mark.)

---

8. Balter, "The Seeds of Civilization," *Smithsonian Magazine.*
9. Mark, "Religion in the Ancient World."
10. Robb et al., "Social "Status" and Biological "Status": A Comparison of Grave Goods and Skeletal Indicators from Pontecagnano," *American Journal of Physical Anthropology.*
11. Doyle White, "The Meaning of 'Wicca,'" 185–207.

As time progressed, some of the Wise Ones of old became known by another name: Druids. What we assume to know of Britain's ancient Druids comes from reports, ostensibly from Caesar himself, and transcribed by the scholar Diodorus Siculus in 36 BCE and later by the scholar Strabo in 20 CE. He declared that three castes of people in the Gallic lands were held in honour: the *bardoi*, the *ovateis*, and the *druidai*. The Druids were a revered caste of priests, both male and female, who oversaw much of the spiritual and cultural welfare of early Britain. They were held in such regard to be as important as nobles, and a Druid, it was said, could stop two warring factions from fighting.[12]

The scholar Pliny the Elder gave a more detailed account of them in around 75 CE. They were poets, scholars, scientists, mathematicians, and lawgivers. They had the authority to deny people from attending religious service, to advise on matters of government, and to perform augury and prediction. Druids recited an oral tradition—nothing was written down—and Caesar estimated that it could take twenty years for a young person to memorize everything they needed to know to join the order.[13] They studied the movement of the stars in the cosmos and the behavior of birds on the wing. They studied the anatomy of the human body and acted as surgeons when needed. Whether or not they performed human sacrifice is conjectural. They may have, but this is not confirmed. If they did, it would not have been any evil act but a release of the spirit from one body to inhabit another.[14]

The practice of Druidry was actively suppressed by the Romans, and what had been an elite order of Priests in the first century CE was reduced to maligned fortune tellers and herbalists by the third. Still, their early prestige is remembered throughout history in the writing of contemporary scholars, and the Druids were an integral part of the history of the Celtic civilization.[15]

It wasn't until the eighteenth century that a serious interest in Druidry resurfaced, thanks to historians like William Stukeley, who fostered a fascination with the ancient practice that has flourished in recent decades.[16]

The word *Druid*, incidentally, has several possible origins. It could have originated, as Pliny suggested, from the Greek *drui-ides*, which means "oak-tree-wise," or from the

---

12. Hutton, *Blood and Mistletoe*, 5–7.
13. "Druids."
14. Hutton, *Blood and Mistletoe*, 5–7.
15. Hutton, *Blood and Mistletoe*, 14.
16. Piggot, *William Stukeley*, 51.

early Welsh word *drwi*, or "wren-wise," which noted their use of the habits of birds as a form of augury.[17]

Vikings, Norse Mythology, and the Eddas

Much of what we know of the Vikings comes from historical record of raids and pillages at sites like Lindisfarne in 793 CE and York in 866. But the Norse people are so much more than just a bunch of Viking raiders, and it would be a gross injustice to ignore what we know of the ancient Norse. Our knowledge of early Norse mythology comes from two sources, the *Poetic Edda* and the *Prose Edda*.

The *Poetic Edda* is a series of poems, written by authors whose names we'll never know, from 800 to 1100 CE that were transcribed from oral tradition around 1200 CE. They recount the philosophy and legends of the Icelandic people. The *Prose Edda* is composed mostly of stories, mostly transcribed by Snorri Sturluson around 1220 CE. Within the *Prose Edda*, the prologue introduces the Norse gods, and subsequent books tell of Norse mythology and delve into the importance and format of storytelling.[18]

One portion of the *Poetic Edda*, the "Hávamál," is dedicated to Odin and offers advice on living, conduct, and wisdom. It describes some of Odin's exploits, including how he acquired the knowledge of the runes, and explores old Norse philosophy. The runes, or futhark, date from the second century CE and are as much a system of divination as they are a mere alphabet. It is also from the "Hávamál" that modern Norse scholars introduced the Nine Noble Virtues and the Aesir and the Vanir, two families, or clans, of gods.[19] The Aesir were gods such as Odin and Thor, and they were regarded as "principal" gods. The Vanir included gods such as Frey and Freyja, gods of marriage, childbirth, and fortune telling, and nature spirits.

Magickal practitioners among the Norse were the male *gothi* (GO-dee) and the female *githya*, who served as community religious leaders, and the *seidr* (SAY-thr), who dealt in soothsaying and fortune telling. *Seidr* was actually the name of both the practitioner and the practice itself.[20]

---

17. Piggot, *William Stukeley*, 89.
18. Sturtluson, *EDDA*, xii–x.
19. Price, *The Viking Way*, 94.
20. Price, *The Viking Way*, 108.

The Anglo-Saxons and the Wyrd

The Roman Empire collapsed around 430 CE, and with it went the Roman occupation of Britain and northern Europe. This led to a period that was labeled the "Dark Ages" under the assumption that there was no learning or advance of civilization from the Roman Empire to the Renaissance.

To call this period uneducated or uncivilized is a gross injustice to the people who lived there. The Romans had left, leaving the Celts to rule in Britain, and the Norse were making inroads from the north, bringing gods such as Odin and Thor with them. Britain became a true melting pot of culture and religion, and by 800 CE the Anglo-Saxon people were increasing in prominence.[21]

Anglo-Saxon is a hybrid of two cultures. Well, actually three. It is a mix of the Aengli, from which we get the word *England*, the Saxons, who came from the Saxony region of France and Germany, and the Jutes, a Germanic tribe already occupying what would become Britain. These cultures merged to create the Anglo-Saxon, which filled the void left by the Romans. This allowed the melding of the Celtic people with the Saxons and the Norse. Gods, as we will learn later, morph, changing names and appearances, as the people worshipping them evolve. Just as the Greek gods adopted Roman names—Zeus became Jupiter and Aphrodite became Venus—the Norse gods adopted Anglo-Saxon names. Odin became Woden, Thor became Thunor, which also gives us the word *thunder*, and Tyr became Tiw. The Pagan Anglo-Saxon pantheon also gives us the days of the week. Wednesday is Woden's day and Thursday is Thunor's day.[22]

The Anglo-Saxons saw the amalgamation of the Druids, the Celts, and the Norse, and the religious and magick systems began to evolve. This syncretic development paved the way for much of what happened later.

Another vital contribution of Anglo-Saxon spirituality is the concept of wyrd. The wyrd (pronounced like *wear* with a *d* at the end) was seen as the guiding force of life—yet not really a controlling force. Think of it this way: The wyrd is like a rushing river, the current of life. A person in a small boat can ride the current, going wherever it takes them, or the person can row and steer, guiding their own path along the river but not fighting it. Sometimes the person must negotiate eddies and swift currents, and surpassing them makes the individual a better oarsperson for their efforts. If they try to fight the

---

21. Brugmann, "Migration and Endogenous Change," 30–45.
22. Welch, "Pre-Christian Practices in the Anglo-Saxon World."

river, or row against the current, they will exhaust themself, getting nowhere. The river—the wyrd—affects all who touch it. If a person tries to dam up or redirect the river, they affect the lives of every plant and animal along its course. The wyrd feeds, supports, and guides all living things. There also are two other perceptions of the wyrd.

In the first, wyrd is not seen as a linear progression, like time. Rather, it is all-encompassing. Eternal yet instant. Chronological perception of the wyrd is not "yesterday, today, and tomorrow" but a state of constant "now." ("What time is it?" "It is now.")

In the second, the wyrd is a guiding but not controlling force of a person's destiny. If a person abandons a well-paying job to fight forest fires because they feel it is their "calling," that is their wyrd. Likewise, a person who flies to Nepal on a whim is also following their wyrd. It is a calling that cannot be denied; to deny it would likely cause sickness and depression.[23]

Modern Witches use the wisdom of the Anglo-Saxon wyrd to better understand the flow of magick in their lives and recognize their place in the cosmos. Incidentally, there is an excellent modern interpretation of the wyrd. In George Lucas's *Star Wars* saga, Jedi Knights call it the Force.

Religions of Other Cultures

Raising huge monuments along the banks of the Nile, the people of ancient Egypt lived in the blazing heat of the sun and survived annual floodings, drought, and famine, and their pantheon reflected their lifestyle. To be fair, the Egyptian civilization was more than six thousand years old, and the gods we know—Ra, Isis, Osiris, and others—were relatively new in its history. Ra, the sun god, watched over all; Isis, goddess of life, was the provider; and Osiris judged one's soul upon death. Bastet and Sekhmet were goddesses represented by cats. Bastet was a gentle, caring aspect, and Sekhmet was more defiant and aggressive.

While the Egyptian culture had no real influence over northern European Wicce of that period, the spirituality and mysteries have left an impression on people for centuries. Many mystics and magickal practitioners have studied, emulated, and adopted aspects of the Egyptian religions. From the latter half of the nineteenth century, ancient Egypt has awed and inspired people the world over, and many modern Wiccans have adopted their gods as readily as any other.

---

23. Bates, *The Way of Wyrd*, 4–7.

The Grecian civilization began in the fields and hills overlooking the Aegean Sea, and from 3000 to 1000 BCE they grew and prospered in a (mostly) peaceful nature. They waged war upon neighbours only when negotiation was impossible and to defend Grecian lands and interests, and the Greek pantheon reflects this. They had many gods and goddesses of wisdom, music, wine, motherhood, and so on, but only one, Ares, was devoted specifically to warfare. Athena, mother of Athens, is known for her military strategy and tactics and emphasizes the intellectual aspects of warfare as opposed to the brutality of combat. By 500 BCE, Athens was regarded as the center of the civilized world, and the Grecian influence spread from Spain to India. While the Greek city-state of Sparta became known for its military strength and well-trained soldiers, Athens and much of Greece regarded philosophy, reason, and revelry as the order of the day, and the Greek pantheon was revered and honoured across the Aegean Sea. Astrology was an accepted science at this time, and people knew the ways of the world and understood their place in the cosmos. They developed laws and customs for the betterment of the people, and both men and women held the title of philosophers, statesmen, teachers, and so on. The Athenian system of democratic government became the foundation for most legal systems in the Western world.[24]

On the eastern shores of the Mediterranean, Hebrew scholars began putting together a magickal system known as the Kabbalah. Essentially a combination of philosophy, science, magick, and mysticism, it has been evolving over the centuries. The Kabbalah, Hebrew for "doctrines received from tradition," employs secret knowledge and philosophies not revealed to the masses. According to legend, the framework of the Kabbalah was taught by Jehovah to a group of angels who then gave it to humans after their fall from grace. Moses is said to have taught the Kabbalah to seventy elders during the Exodus, and it was passed down as an oral tradition until the eighth century when it was finally written down.

The Kabbalah states that God is all things: good, evil, day, night, male, female, within, and without. It represents the organized pattern of the universe, which can be deciphered through the mysteries of letters and numbers. It is a road map, in a sense, of the path by which God created the universe and the three pillars by which humans can achieve divinity. The pillars represent masculine, or mercy; spirit, or gentleness; and feminine, or

---

24. "Classical Greek Culture."

judgment. Other interconnecting lines exist as well, and together the seventy-two combinations represent the mysteries of the universe.[25]

Through the Middle Ages, the Kabbalah was studied by alchemists hoping to unlock the secrets of life and by mystics hoping to reach divinity. Because of its Hebrew origin and its use of magick and esoteric philosophies, the medieval church often assumed it to be evil, and it was thus associated with heathen Jews and Witches. Many Witches use the Kabbalah and incorporate its patterns into their own studies. Indeed, the tarot and the Kabbalah complement each other quite nicely.[26]

Lesson 2: Study Prompts and Questions

Religions in Paleolithic Times
- Why did early civilizations envision deific forces in nature?
- What spiritual changes developed as civilization advanced?

The Birth of the Wicce
- What prompted the development of the first Priests, or Wicce?
- What roles do we think the Wicce played among the people?
- How do we know the Priests were treated with respect and reverence?
- Why did the ancient Romans want to suppress the Druids' influence in early Celtic society?
- Briefly explain the possible origin and meanings of the word *Druid*.

Vikings, Norse Mythology, and the Eddas
- What literary sources taught us about early Norse mythology?
- What is the difference between the Aesir and the Vanir?
- Explain the difference between gothi/githya and seidr.

The Anglo-Saxons and the Wyrd
- Why are the Anglo-Saxons important to the history of Witchcraft?
- Explain the concept of the wyrd.
- How can the idea of the wyrd be applied to magick?

---

25. Huss, Pasi, and von Stuckrad, "Introduction. Kabbalah and Modernity."
26. Román, "Season of the Jewitch: The Occultists Reviving Jewish Witchcraft and Folklore."

Religions of Other Cultures
- Explain how environmental changes can affect the evolution of religion.
- What influence has the ancient Greek civilization had on the modern world?
- What is the mythology behind the Kabbalah?
- Why was the Kabbalah associated with Witchcraft?

Lesson 2: Recommended Reading

- *Blood and Mistletoe: The History of the Druids in Britain* by Ronald Hutton
- *The Magical History of Britain* by Martin Wall
- *The Magical World of the Anglo-Saxons* by Tylluan Penry

LESSON 3
The History of the Craft:
The Dark Ages and the Inquisition

This lesson continues the history of Witchcraft from the rise of Christianity into the Middle Ages. It's a popular misconception among some young Witches that the pre-Christian world was an idyllic, goddess-oriented nirvana where the women ruled, everyone was a Witch, and the world was at peace. Then men arrived with their swords and penises and their patriarchy and messed everything up. Another misconception is that the Witchcraft that began there has followed a direct matriarchal lineage down through the centuries. Sadly there was no ancient lesbian paradise nor a direct lineage of Witches through history, but there was a patriarchy. Well, you can't have everything…

The Rise of Monotheism and the Patriarchy

As early as 4000 BCE, a paradigm shift began to occur in societies around the Mediterranean. Where social roles and structure had been more egalitarian, an interesting change began to occur. As more and more people congregated in growing communities, towns and cities developed, and with them came finance, housing, and law enforcement. The men, long the protectors of the community, took it upon themselves to organize and defend the growing towns. Their roles changed from protectors of family and clan to protectors of the community, regional defenders, and, finally, to leaders of the cities. Laws were written, intricate political structures grew, and taxation and regulation became more prominent. The male role had changed from hunter and protector to soldier and politician.

Under male law, however, the role of the female was greatly reduced to family caregiver, cook, and baby maker. She became a second-class citizen. Along with the decline in the status of women, the seers and wisewomen gradually lost importance in metropolitan areas, and in some cases, they were banished altogether.

Men continued to give themselves more power. The concept of a single male ruler, such as a king or emperor, appeased the desire for power, and after a single male ruler, the next logical step was a single male deity. Consider the Egyptians: around 1340 BCE, Pharaoh Akhenaton abandoned polytheism and declared that Aten—the Sun—was the only deity. The Pharaoh Tutankhamen later reversed that declaration, but such concepts were the foundation of monotheism, which was revived later when the early Abrahamic faiths, Christianity and Judaism, become prominent.[27] Islam is the third Abrahamic faith, but it wasn't created until much later.

The Fall and Rise (and Fall) of the Roman Empire

In lesson 2, we saw how Athenian philosophy and politics influenced much of the Mediterranean world. This was most evident in Rome, where they adopted not only Athenian politics but their gods as well. Zeus became Jupiter, Athena became Minerva, and Ares became Mars, just to name a few. Rome was adept at incorporating elements of other cultures into their own to become a stronger, more viable force. They took the religion and politics of Athens, the fighting fury of the Huns, and the military strategy of the Turks and grew into the strongest empire the world had seen thus far. From roughly 700 BCE to 350 CE, the Roman Empire held the world in its grasp. It conquered nations, built roads, and carried Roman rule and culture as far as northern Germany, the coast of Ireland, and the southern tip of Africa.[28]

A by-product of war and colonization is the spread of religion, and the Roman gods saw altars erected in many areas that Roman legions traveled. There were temples to Minerva in England, sacred groves to Bacchus in France, and altars to Jupiter along the Euphrates, some of which can still be seen today. The Roman Empire controlled the ancient world for centuries. By about 150 CE, the light of Rome covered almost a quarter of the earth's surface.[29]

As we have seen, religions, forms of worship, and even gods change over time; the rise of monotheism was no different. It wasn't that someone just woke up one day with a new idea. From polytheism, the worship of many gods, grew henotheism, the idea that while there are many gods—all equally valid—the believer reserves their devotion for a

---

27. Ridley, *Akhenaten*, 13–15.
28. Southern, *The Roman Empire*, 14–16.
29. Huskinson, *Experiencing Rome*, 261.

single deity, and from henotheism grew monotheism, the denial of the existence of any other gods but the one.

Within the walls and council chambers of Rome, greed and corruption were eating away at the empire's foundation. The Pagan Roman Empire was crumbling, and a new faith was emerging. Led by the Priests of this new monotheistic faith, the people of Rome revolted against the ancient, now corrupt regime. The tide was slowly beginning to turn. By 200 CE many Roman citizens, tired of the endless greed and depravity of the emperors, followed the will of the new Priests and joined in the worship of a single deity, spurred on by the promise of change.[30]

Early Christianity, which had started as an offshoot of Judaism, promoted a single deity and his chosen avatar in human form. Naturally, though, many different people took the idea and ran with it, so by 200 CE there were hundreds of different sects and cults all calling themselves Christian but with different ideas about doctrine, the nature of Jesus's divinity, and the methodology of worship. The First Council of Nicaea, held in 325 CE and overseen by Emperor Constantine the Great, was an ecumenical conference designed to bring all the different Christian sects into one agreement. They wrote and adopted the Nicene Creed, which laid out the fundamental concepts of Christianity as they are understood today.[31]

Constantine never condemned Paganism; he had been born Pagan and maintained a policy of henotheism even as the spread of Christianity widened and he himself was baptized. He died in 337 CE, and the subsequent rulers of the Empire were less forgiving as the religion grew in scope and influence.[32]

Paganism and the Rise of Christianity

In 380 CE Theodosius I passed the Edict of Thessalonica, which declared Christianity the "official" religion of the Empire. In direct opposition to the henotheistic nature of Constantine, Theodosius used his position to actively banish Paganism. He tore down Pagan temples across the Empire and declared Pagan worship illegal.

---

30. Esler, *The Early Christian World*, 24–25.
31. The Editors of Encyclopaedia Britannica, "First Council of Nicaea."
32. "Constantine," *Christianity Today*.

By 429 CE the *Codex Theodosianus*, a book compiling Theodosius's laws and edicts, was being used as justification for the persecution of Pagans and, indeed, of anyone guilty of heresy.[33]

This wave of conversion was met with resistance, and many Pagan gods were "rebranded" as Christian figures. Now people could still worship as they had, but the church could still claim dominance. This is evident in the date on which the birth of Christ is honoured. In Pagan Rome, December 25 marked the date of Sol Invictus, or the "Unconquerable Sun." Constantine had declared that December 25 was, what a surprise, also the date of the birth of Jesus Christ.[34]

During the time of Pope Gregory I, 590 to 604 CE, it was ordered that "the caverns, grottoes, crags and glens that had once been used for worship of the Pagan gods (be) now appropriated by Christianity: Let altars be built and relics be placed there, so the Pagans have to change from the worship of their demons to the one true God."[35]

Pagan shrines and temples were either destroyed outright, rebranded, or built over to force people to adopt the new faith. Anyone who resisted was labeled a heretic and punished. This became a handy tool to convince people to convert; the punishment for heresy was often death.

In 1198 Pope Innocent III stated that the pope is God in flesh. Therefore, any act against God was an act against the pope and thus an act of treason.[36]

In the thirteenth century, things got a little uglier. Two key figures in the church's stance on Witchcraft were the Dominican friars Albertus Magnus and Thomas Aquinas. Magnus, the more lenient of the two, read Aristotle and Plato and studied zoology, botany, astrology, astronomy, medicine, and philosophy. He had declared that Witches fell into one of two categories. Either they practiced harmful magick, for which the penalty was death, or they were experiencing "spiritual apostasy." Apostasy is the intentional denial or renunciation of a religion, and spiritual apostasy is the idea that this denial exists because the person has been deceived by spiritual or diabolical forces. These Witches, Magnus had reasoned, had no power of their own and had merely been deceived by demons. They simply needed salvation.[37]

---

33. Mango, *The Oxford History of Byzantium*, 105.
34. "History of Christmas."
35. MacMullen, *Christianity and Paganism in the Fourth to Eighth Centuries*, 74.
36. Pennington, "Innocent III."
37. Cunningham, *Reclaiming Moral Agency*, 93.

Thomas Aquinas, however, combined the two arguments, saying that Witches performed harmful magick *and* were under the influence of diabolical forces. He said that Witches were guilty of causing harm to members of the church, which was heresy and punishable by death, and that apostasy was blasphemy, which was also punishable by death.[38]

The writings of Thomas Aquinas were frequently used as an argument against anyone who the church decided was "inconvenient." Consider the fate of the Knights Templar. Originally created in 1119, the Knights were given the divine purpose of liberating the Holy Land, the alleged birthplace of Christ, from the Muslims, and making it a Christian land.[39] The Crusades raged for years, during which time the Templars faced mounting accusations of becoming rich, corrupt, and greedy.[40] Their greed and their growing reputation of corruption put them in conflict with the interests of the church, so Pope Clement V, King Philip IV of France, and King Edward II of England collaborated to have the Templars defamed. They were accused of Witchcraft, and in a mock trial, they were found guilty of diabolism, perverse acts of Witchery, and making pacts with Baphomet. In 1314 the Knights Templar were executed en masse. They actually had nothing to do with Witchcraft, but it was a convenient accusation, and it added fuel the notion that Witchcraft was synonymous with devil worship.[41]

The Inquisition

The Inquisition was never handled by a single, central authority, and it was not created specifically to hunt Witches. It began in 1184 with the Episcopal Inquisition in Languedoc, France, with the intention of weeding out heretics and apostates within the Catholic church. The Spanish Inquisition was created in 1478, and the Roman Inquisition soon followed in 1542.

Heretics and apostates were the first to be tried, but the scope soon widened to include bigamists, Jews, Muslims, blasphemers, adulterers, homosexuals, and eventually Pagans and those thought to be practicing Witchcraft, and when anyone was found guilty, their property suddenly belonged to the church. Handy, that.

---

38. Gibbons, *George Lincoln Burr*, 173–74.
    Aquinas, "Question 11, Article 3."
39. Barber, *The New Knighthood*, xxi–xxii.
40. Burman, *The Templars*, 45.
41. Barber, *The Trial of the Templars*, 202–16.

In 1484 Pope Innocent VIII issued the papal bull entitled *Summis desiderantes affectibus*, or "Wishings of the utmost concern," which gave full papal support to the Witch hunt, and commanded that an organized inquisition be established. Witches were regarded as heretics to Christianity, which became the greatest of their crimes and sins. Within continental and Roman law, Witchcraft was *crimen exceptum*, a crime so foul that all normal legal procedures were superseded. Because the devil himself was not going to confess, it was necessary to gain a confession from his human agents.[42]

In 1486 two German scholars, Heinrich Kraemer and James Sprenger, wrote a book called the *Malleus Maleficarum*, or "Hammer of Witches." Endorsed by the Roman Catholic Church, the *Malleus* gave "evidence and testimony" that Witches were in league with the devil and that their mission was to destroy all that is good and holy in the world.[43] It listed detailed instructions for the trial, judgment, and punishment of Witches, and for almost two centuries, it was used as the "instruction manual" for the Inquisition. Judges, Witchfinders, and inquisitors used a wide range of torture methods to prove a Witch's allegiance to the devil or to drive evil spirits out of the accused.

Here are a few examples of methods used:

- The accused was "swum," or bound so they were unable to move and thrown into a pond. If the accused floated, it proved that the devil was causing them to behave unnaturally, and they were given further tortures. If the accused sank (and drowned) then they were saved.
- A "boot," or a hard wooden frame with holes for spikes, was placed around the leg. During questioning, iron spikes were pounded through the holes and into the accused's leg, crushing bone and muscle beyond repair.
- Red-hot pincers were often used to tear and shed flesh from bone.
- A "pear," or a metal, pear-shaped device with segments that unfolded like flower petals when unscrewed, was used. Inserted into the mouth, anus, or vagina, it would rend and destroy internal tissues.
- The use of the "Judas cradle" was particularly cruel. This torture device was simply a large wooden spike. The victim was hoisted up and lowered onto it, and the accused's own body weight would drive the spike deeper into their body.[44]

---

42. Halsall, "Medieval Sourcebook."
43. Summers, *The Malleus Maleficarum*, xi.
44. Abbott, *Execution*, 213.

The inquisitors believed that their actions were valid. Their justification for these gruesome acts was that if you were possessed, Satan would depart, not wanting a ruined body, and your soul would be saved. If you were guilty, they could force a confession out of you, and your soul would be saved. And if you were innocent, you would, of course, comply with the will of the church, and your soul would be saved. More often than not, the tortures resulted in death—either immediately or in lingering agony.

Of course, hanging was always popular, as was being burned at the stake, and the exact number of people tortured and executed during the Inquisition can never be known. Some sources say as many as nine million died, but it was probably closer to forty or sixty thousand.[45]

We know the sequence of events within the church that led to the Inquisition, but do we know anything about the victims of persecution or what they actually practiced? Most were very likely not Witches at all. Quite a few names and trial records exist, along with their accusations or confessions.

Just to give you an idea, here is a *very* short list of some of the victims who were executed for the crime of Witchcraft.[46]

Name	Location	Date of Death	Death
Matteuccia de Francesco	Papal State	1428	burned alive
Guirandana de Lay	France	1461	burned alive
Gentile Budrioli	Italy	1498	burned alive
Gyde Spandemager	Denmark	1543	burned alive
Lasses Birgitta	Sweden	1550	beheaded
Ursula Kemp	England	1582	hanged
The Pappenheimer Family	Bavaria	1600	burned alive
Alice Nutter	England	1612	hanged
Elizabeth Clarke	England	1645	hanged
Adrienne d'Heur	France	1646	burned alive

In the year 1611, a new English translation of the Bible was published. It wasn't the first English version, nor did King James I commission it himself. It only later became known as the "King James Version" because it happened during his reign. However, he

---

45. Rapley, *A Case of Witchcraft*, 99.
46. Barstow, *Witchcraze*, 227–43.

did authorize some edits of his own in the final manuscript. Among these was changing Exodus 22:18 to read: "Thou shalt not suffer a Witch to live."

The Old Testament, which Exodus is part of, was originally written in several languages, including Hebrew and Greek, and had been rewritten many times by many different scholars over the centuries. In the original version, Exodus 22:18 said that a *kashaph* (Hebrew for *sorcerer*) who interfered with local affairs must be put to death. A lot of Old Testament laws demanded executions. Latin scholars had translated *kashaph* to *maleficos* (meaning "evil person"; i.e., a sorcerer, criminal, or political dissident). By the time the Bible got to King James, he saw an opportunity to secure his place in history. By changing *maleficos* to *Witch*, he had ordered a death sentence against all alleged or accused Witches, Druids, magicians, peasant midwives, and wisewomen. This new version of the Word of God fanned the flames of the anti-Witch craze.[47]

By the year 1600, accused Witches had been hunted, tried, and persecuted for more than four centuries, and the Inquisition had ravaged Europe for many decades. People were known to accuse their enemies of Witchcraft just to get them out of the way. Old, homeless women were often suspect, and any strangers, physically disabled people, or unpopular people were often marked as Witches and killed too.

The Politics of Witch-Hunting and the Decline of the Inquisition

In March of 1644, Matthew Hopkins of England became "Witchfinder General." This was largely a self-appointed title, although he claimed to have been appointed by Parliament. He would ride into town with a list of accusations against Witches and charge the local council a hefty sum while he examined the accused. The trials were held not by any religious authority but by the local justices of the peace. He only served as Witchfinder for three years before dying of tuberculosis at age twenty-eight, but in those three years, more women were hanged for Witchcraft than in the entire previous century.[48]

Hopkin's 1647 book, *The Discovery of Witches*, proved very popular with similarly minded people in the New World, including Puritan ministers Increase Mather and his son Cotton, in Salem, Massachusetts, some forty-five years later.

---

47. Kondratiev, "Thou Shalt Not Suffer a Witch to Live."
48. Robbins, *The Encyclopedia of Witchcraft and Demonology*, 252.

The events of the Salem Witch trials are well known, but here's a very quick summary:

In Salem Village in January 1692, two young girls, Betty Parris and Abigail Williams, began acting strangely, screaming, thrashing about, and tearing at their clothes. They claimed to have been pinched and pricked by unseen forces. Why they behaved this way is still unknown. Some say it was just to get attention. Others say that they had eaten contaminated bread. But other girls mimicked their behavior, and people suspected Witchcraft. Three people were quickly accused, including Tituba, an enslaved woman from Barbados who was owned by the Parris family, who used to tell the girls stories from home. She confessed to the accusations and named others as Witches. As more and more people were named, horror and confusion gripped the town. Among the accused were Sarah Good, a woman who was named a Witch simply because she rebuked Puritan values, and Giles Corey, a churchgoing man who proclaimed his innocence even while he was sentenced to death. Tituba later admitted that her owner, Samuel Parris, had coached her on what to say during her trial.

By the time the panic ended a year later, more than two hundred people had been accused and nineteen were executed.[49]

The hysteria caused by the Salem Witch trials—and indeed by Matthew Hopkin's methods in England—undermined the authority held by Witch trials and inquisitions on both sides of the Atlantic. People questioned the methods and validity of torture and examination, and the Inquisition finally began to lose favor.

By the early 1800s, after the execution of tens of thousands of people, the Inquisition was all but ended. Witches were still despised and exiled but not always murdered. Meanwhile, people still practiced folkways or village traditions, including dancing the maypole, blessing the first grains and harvest loaf, Yule logs, and the Mari Lwyd. Pagan traditions with centuries of history were still relevant, even as the church's persecution of Witches was losing steam.

Between the rift between Protestants and Catholics and the advances in science and medicine, such as the smallpox vaccination in the early 1800s, the church was losing its dominion over people's everyday lives. The Inquisition was becoming little more than posturing, and the Spanish Inquisition was finally abolished in 1834.[50]

---

49. Demos, *Entertaining Satan*, 11, 401–9.
50. Kamen, *The Spanish Inquisition*, 273–75.

Lesson 3: Study Prompts and Questions

The Rise of Monotheism and the Patriarchy

- Explain how the roles of men and women changed so radically as civilization became more complex.
- Why do you suppose Ramses wanted to proclaim himself "Ra incarnate"?

The Fall and Rise (and Fall) of the Roman Empire

- Explain the difference between monotheism and henotheism.
- Why did people take to the new faith? What did it offer?

Paganism and the Rise of Christianity

- What was the purpose of the Council of Nicaea?
- What compromise did the church make to ensure that they were not rivaled by other gods?

The Inquisition

- Who were the Knights Templar, and why were they accused of Witchcraft?
- Explain the Roman Catholic Church's justification for arresting non-Christians.

The Politics of Witch-Hunting and the Decline of the Inquisition

- What changes were made to the King James Version of the Bible?
- What triggered the Salem Witch trials?

Lesson 3: Recommended Reading

- *A History of Witchcraft: Sorcerers, Heretics & Pagans* by Jeffrey B. Russell and Brooks Alexander
- *Witchcraze: A New History of the European Witch Hunts* by Anne Llewellyn Barstow

The History of the Craft: The Rebirth of Witchcraft

The Dark Ages is the period of history from the collapse of the Roman Empire to the Renaissance. It lasted about six hundred years, give or take. During the Dark Ages and the early Renaissance, the Inquisition swept across Europe and touched the Americas until the late seventeenth century. It was a devastating period in history not just for Witches but for humanity as a whole. Something had to change.

The Age of Enlightenment

German philosopher Martin Heidegger stated in 1938 that the start of the Age of Enlightenment can be credited to René Descartes's 1637 quote "*Cogito, ergo sum,*" or "I think, therefore I am," and fifty years later to Isaac Newton's publication of his *Philosophiæ Naturalis Principia Mathematica (Mathematical Principles of Natural Philosophy)*. Newton explained that the laws of nature, such as gravity, were definable, measurable principles that were not subject to divine intervention. These heralded a new way of thinking where people valued humanism, liberty, tolerance, progress, the sciences, and the separation of church and state.[51]

New studies in science and medicine were proving that germs and bacteria, not diabolical forces, spread disease. Witches had been blamed for the bubonic plague, or the Black Death, of the 1340s, but examinations in the 1800s proved that the bacterium *Yersinia pestis*, spread by fleas, had been the real culprit.

Witches, or people accused of Witchcraft, were still generally mistrusted in the eyes of the "modern human" of the 1800s, but they soon fell into one of three categories. Were they indeed agents of Satan and best avoided? Were they peculiar old women who lived alone and kept strange but effective medicines? Or were they fictional characters

---

51. Duignan, "Enlightenment."

appearing in Shakespeare's plays or Grimm's fairy tales? Whichever it was, they certainly weren't responsible for all the evils for which they had been accused.[52]

The English Witchcraft and Conjuration Act of 1736 is a good example. It allowed for the prosecution of those who "pretend to exercise or use any kind of Witchcraft, Sorcery, Inchantment (sic), or Conjuration, or undertake to tell Fortunes." The punishment was one year's imprisonment, quarterly stints in the pillory for one hour, and the payment of sureties for good behavior. There's an important distinction—it didn't say you couldn't be a Witch, it said you couldn't pretend to be a Witch. Because Witches weren't real.[53]

Oddly, as the Age of Enlightenment became more and more the age of rational thinking, another trend was emerging: an interest in fantasy and make-believe. As the Imperialist expansion spread, it introduced people to new lands, people, and customs, stirring the imagination. Enter authors like Edgar Allan Poe, Bram Stoker, and J. M. Barrie and a renewed interest in esoteric mysteries and practices such as the practices of ancient Egyptians, the Kabbalah, and tales of Witchcraft and Pagan rites from Italy.

Aradia *and* The Golden Bough

Two books were published in the late nineteenth century that were pivotal in the cultural understanding and reevaluation of Witchcraft and Paganism: Charles Godfrey Leland's *Aradia, or the Gospel of the Witches* and James Frazer's *The Golden Bough.*

Aradia, published in 1899, is a collection of texts allegedly given to the author by Maddalena, Leland's Italian Witch informant. Its fifteen chapters portray the origins, beliefs, rituals, and spells of an Italian Pagan Witchcraft tradition. The central figure of that religion is the goddess Aradia, or Diana, who came to Earth to teach Witchcraft to the local peasants so they could resist their feudal oppressors and the Catholic church. It caused a stir when it was first published because it offered a view of Witchcraft far different from what the church had been saying for five hundred years and because it claimed that Lucifer appeared as the counterpart to Aradia. He was portrayed not as an evil figure but as a Pagan deity.

Aradia has been influential in the modern Witchcraft revival since the 1950s, even though some people question its validity. Some claim it is authentic, others claim that it is a compilation of research from many different sources, and others say Leland just

---

52. Davies and Blécourt, *Beyond the Witch Trials*, 187–91.
53. Davis, *Witchcraft, Magic, and Culture*, 1–2.

made the whole thing up, including the figure of Maddalena herself. Doreen Valiente, an influential Wiccan Priestess and author who wrote much of today's Wiccan liturgy, stated that the *Aradia* was influential in inspiring her Charge of the Goddess from 1953.[54]

In 1890 Scottish anthropologist James Frazer published *The Golden Bough: A Study in Magic and Religion*. It is a comparative analysis of religious narratives that finds many similarities in religious figures and practices. *The Golden Bough* was the first published work that listed Jesus Christ as merely one of several sacrificial deity figures without exalting him. This alone caused controversy, along with the notion that Pagan worship had existed alongside Christianity and was not the work of Satan.[55]

Some critics of Frazer said that he had preestablished conclusions and used his ethnographic evidence to justify them, or that he had created a Darwinian timeline of cultural evolution with little substance. Still, many people, including Joseph Campbell and Gerald Gardner, said that Frazer's work was influential in their understanding of religious diversity. Two people inspired by Frazer's work were the anthropologist Margaret Murray and a wealthy occultist named Aleister Crowley.

Of Anthropologists and Occultists

Earlier I mentioned that the spread of Imperialist expansion saw a growing interest in the ways and cultures of other people and civilizations. Along with merely studying them came the desire to learn more about their roots, which led to the growing interest in the fields of archaeology and sociology.

Margaret Murray

Margaret Murray was born in India in 1863 to a missionary family. She worked as a nurse before majoring in Egyptology in university, and in 1898 she became a lecturer on Egyptology and a leading archaeologist. Murray was part of the team that excavated the site of Osireion in 1903, and she was respected for her academia and known for her work with the feminist movement.

She worked as a field nurse in France during the First World War until she became ill and recuperated in a hospital near Glastonbury. It was there that she developed an interest in English folklore and the history of Paganism, both before and during the Christianization of Britain.

---

54. Mathiesen, "Charles G. Leland and the Witches of Italy," 50.
55. Leach, "Kingship and Divinity."

Murray saw correlations between ancient Pagan practices, modern folkways, and the traditions and rituals described in Leland's *Aradia*, and in 1921 she published *The Witch-Cult in Western Europe*. In her book, she described Pagan practices that had been practiced in pre-Christian England and maintained by Pagan Britons even as the church became more influential. She told of covens of thirteen members, initiation rites, and observances celebrating May Eve, November Eve, midsummer, and midwinter. She described worship of a fertility goddess and of a horned male deity, who may have been misinterpreted as Lucifer. She wrote of a matriarchal hereditary lineage within the covens and of the Pagan sacrifices of animals and children. She described how Witches kept their secrets in a coven book and that neophytes signed their names in menstrual blood.

Her assertations were almost immediately criticized. Critics said she was influenced by church pamphlets on demonology and her own work as a feminist, as well as seeing similarities between ancient and modern practices and assuming there was a direct link between the two. While Murray defended her analysis for years, her work on Witchcraft has since been largely discredited. Nonetheless, much of what she described—minus the sacrifices—found its way into Gerald Gardner's treatment of Wicca a few decades later. He often claimed that she was the "grandmother of Wicca."[56]

Aleister Crowley

Edward Alexander "Aleister" Crowley was born into a wealthy Christian family in Warwickshire, England, in 1875. In his teens he rejected his family's Christian upbringing and studied Western mysticism, and in 1898 he joined the Hermetic Order of the Golden Dawn. Crowley fancied himself a mountaineer, poet, and playwright, and in 1912 he joined the Ordo Templi Orientis, or the OTO. Over the next several years he traveled the world and experimented with drugs, and in 1904 he claimed that he had been contacted by Aiwass, a disembodied voice that gave him secret knowledge. It was then that he founded the religion of Thelema, which he described as an "esoteric, occult, and spiritual philosophy, and a religious movement."[57] It was while creating Thelema that Crowley wrote the passages for which he is best known: "Do what thou wilt, shall be the whole of the law" and "love is the law, love under will."[58] He would later claim that

---

56. Noble, "From Fact to Fallacy."
57. Sutin, *Do What Thou Wilt*, 228.
58. Crowley, *The Book of the Law*, 7.

Aiwass was also known as Satan, Lucifer, or the emblem of Baphomet, the androgynous deity symbolizing arcane perfection.

Crowley never identified as a Witch; he was a ceremonial magician, an occultist, a mystic, and a hedonist. He wrote voluminously, writing such works as *Liber 777* (1909) and *Magick in Theory and Practice* (1929). He designed the Thoth tarot deck, painted by Lady Freida Harris, and created the spiritual organization A∴A∴, whose members seek human perfection through a blend of yoga and ceremonial magick.

Crowley died in 1947 of bronchitis, but his writings and his practices, while controversial and often illegal, paved the way for many future occultists, mystics, and magicians, including Gerald Gardner.

The Birth of Modern Witchcraft

The works of Leland, Frazer, Crowley, and Murray captivated the mind of Gerald Gardner, a civil servant and amateur anthropologist. Gardner was born in Lancashire, England, in 1884 to a moderately wealthy family who traveled frequently to the South of France, Portugal, and coastal West Africa. It was while he was in West Africa that he developed a lifelong interest in both weapons and the study of native cultures.

He lived in the Far East, in Ceylon (now Sri Lanka) and Singapore, and worked as a civil servant before retiring and returning to England in 1936. He maintained his interest in native traditions and customs and wrote frequently about his findings in the Far East. On the advice of a friend, he became a practicing nudist and often visited nudism clubs in the 1930s. Gardner joined the Rosicrucian Order Crotona Fellowship in 1939. It was through the order, later that year, that he met what he claimed to be an ancestral Witch's coven, similar to what Murray had described, in the New Forest of England.

A lot of what Gardner claimed to be true may or may not be accurate; he was known for falsifying information and offering fraudulent credentials to win people over. Gardner was, so he claims, initiated into this ancient coven in September 1939 by Dorothy Clutterbuck. It was during his initiation ceremony that he heard the words *Wicca* and *Wicce*, terms that according to Murray had died out centuries earlier. It was then that he decided to revive this lost religion.[59]

Gardner spent the next few years compiling information for his new religion. He took the works of Murray, ceremonies based on those of the Rosicrucian Order, and

---

59. Hutton, *The Triumph of the Moon*, 207–8.

rituals from the New Forest coven, as well as information acquired from Aleister Crowley, and from this melting pot of sources he created a religion he called Wicca. In 1949, under the pseudonym Scire, he published *High Magic's Aid*. It was published as fiction, but it was his first attempt to publicly define modern Wicca. In 1951 England repealed the Witchcraft Act, which had been law since 1542. With newfound freedom, Gardner published *Witchcraft Today*. In it he first openly described himself as a Witch.[60]

In 1952 Gardner met Doreen Valiente, a young woman who eventually became High Priestess of his Bricket Wood coven. While she helped him edit his Book of Shadows, which he said was copied from the New Forest coven and dating back centuries, she was dubious of his claims and wondered if he hadn't just written the whole thing himself.

Gardner died in 1964. He had been an amateur anthropologist, professed nudist, and Witch, and he may have been something of a charlatan. But whether or not he found a legitimate, hereditary coven or cobbled something together from a mishmash of different sources, he is responsible for introducing the religion of Wicca, and he is widely regarded as the father of modern Witchcraft.

When Gardner died, Valiente joined Robert Cochrane in his coven Clan of Tubal Cain. She admired many of his philosophies about Witchcraft, including the desire to live closer to nature, and incorporated much of his philosophy into her later writing. But Cochrane was openly dismissive of Gardner and Gardnerian Witchcraft and frequently belittled them, which forced Valiente to leave his coven. Cochrane died by suicide in 1966. Cochrane, though he is frequently forgotten, remains an important figure in the development of Witchcraft through the 1960s.[61]

The Renaissance of the Craft

The 1960s were an amazing decade for modern Witches. The feminist movement, counterculture, and growing environmental concerns all carried the message that a new awareness was blossoming, and these changes were embraced by the newfound religion of Wicca. There was still suspicion, resentment, and hatred toward Witches, but many people were beginning to see the nature-oriented path as a safe and peaceful alternative to the monotheistic faiths. In the early 1960s, author Raymond Buckland was initiated into the Craft by Gardner, and he quickly became an outspoken figure in the revival of Witchcraft. Others

---

60. Hutton, *The Triumph of the Moon*, 201.
61. Hutton, *The Triumph of the Moon*, 313–18.

borrowed from his ideas and started groups and practices of their own, including Sybil Leek, Stewart and Janet Farrar, Laurie Cabot, Timothy Zell, and many more.

Along with the growing interest in Wicca, there was a growing diversity of offshoots from Gardnerian Wicca as people took the basic formula and added their own touches to it. Let's briefly look at a few:

Alexandrian Wicca

Founded by Alex and Maxine Sanders in the 1960s, this tradition bears a lot of similarities to Gardnerian, emphasizing gender polarity in roles and ceremonial magick in practice, but with more emphasis on inspired and improvised ritual and less on rote and liturgy.

Dianic Wicca

In 1971 Zsuzsanna Budapest combined Wiccan practices with feminist ideology to create Dianic Wicca, a goddess-centered version of Witchcraft. Dianic Wicca was designed to be a women-only tradition, although some have let men join their groups. Some have criticized it as a return to monotheism.

The Reclaiming Tradition

Miriam Simos, better known as Starhawk, started as a Dianic Witch but sought to reconcile Gardnerian and Dianic Wicca. She published *The Spiral Dance* in 1979, which combined elements of the two, and created a new tradition known as Reclaiming.

Feri Wicca

Originating in California in the late 1960s, Feri Wicca combines Wicca with elements of the Kabbalah, Hoodoo, Gnosticism, and sensual/sexual mysticism.

British Traditional Wicca (BTW)

This tradition exists primarily in North America and is an umbrella term for Gardnerian and similar "foundation" traditions such as Alexandrian and Blue Star Wicca.

Seax-Wica

Created by Buckland, Seax-Wica combines Gardnerian Wicca with aspects of Anglo-Saxon spirituality, such as replacing the goddess and Horned God with Freyja and Woden.

Many traditions are self-initiatory, meaning that one does not need to be initiated by an elder member of that tradition. Seax-Wica is one such tradition, and an individual can recite the ceremony as offered in Buckland's *The Tree*, published in 1973, and proclaim oneself a member of the tradition.

By the 1980s Wicca was becoming a well-known and respected alternative faith, and in the United States the court case of *Dettmer v. Landon* resulted in Wicca being officially acknowledged as a religion.[62] It was this case that recognized that incarcerated Wiccans cannot be denied the right to practice their faith, nor the access to ritual tools while in prison, just like members of any other established religion.

With the introduction of the internet, Witchcraft has become more accessible than ever. Of course, there is still lingering resentment. There are—and always will be—those who mistrust and misunderstand Witches, and those who doubt the legitimacy of the Craft. Some try to deny Witches the right to practice their faith, and others simply refuse to believe that Witches aren't satanic—and act accordingly.

In the year 2000, Pope John Paul II issued a public apology for the centuries of hatred and violence the Catholic church has waged upon other faiths. While he did not specifically mention Witches or the Inquisition, he made it clear that the church will no longer stand in the way of each person's right to connect with the Divine in their own way.[63]

The Return of Who's Who and What's What

In the very first lesson, we took a look at the words *Witch*, *Wicca*, and *coven*. Now that we've come to the end of the history lesson, let's reexamine some of these words in a bit more detail.

Ásatrú

This is a Nordic-based, noninitiatory tradition. The Ásatrú wear Norse garb and honour the Aesir and the Vanir. Rather than holding sabbats to honour the seasons, Ásatrú hold celebrations called althings to honour growth and achievement.

---

62. "Herbert Daniel Dettmer."
63. Stourton, *John Paul II*, 1.

Coven

A close-knit magickal family, similar to a church group, composed of Witches, Wiccans, or Pagans. Covens come together to form a more powerful bond, for magickal working, for support, and for friendship.

Druid

Modern Druids consider themselves stewards of nature and keepers of wisdom. Unlike Wiccans, most Druids don't honour the god or goddess in their ceremonies, but they revere the elements, seen as aspects of the Divine in nature, and the ancestors or the ancients. Druids meet in groups called groves and honour the eight sabbats, the earth, and the ancestors. They don't cast spells or use magick in that sense, but they believe in awen, which can be perceived as divine inspiration or an inspirational flow of energy.

Awen

There are several principal groups dedicated to Druidry, although Druids don't need to belong to any. In 1964 Ross Nichols founded the Order of Bards, Ovates & Druids, or OBOD. OBOD is an English organization that promotes the principles of nature conservancy, education, and harmony. In America Ár nDraíocht Féin, or ADF, founded in 1983 by Isaac Bonewits, pursues the same goals with an emphasis on Celtic studies. Unlike traditional Druids, the neo-Druids of ADF recognize three realms of divinity: the gods, the ancestors, and nature.

Eclectic Witches

Eclectic Witches borrow from multiple Pagan traditions and practices to enrich their own. Eclectic covens take what works for them and discard what doesn't, building their own system layer by layer.

Pagan

Pagan is a generally accepted term for any non-Abrahamic religion. Witches, Buddhists, and even Hindus might be considered Pagan, although Hindus, and certainly Buddhists, would refute that. To most Witches, though, a Pagan is a follower of any nature-oriented belief system, whether they work magick or not. Thus, a Witch is Pagan, but a Pagan is not necessarily a Witch.

Self-Initiatory Tradition

A self-initiatory Witchcraft tradition in which anyone can claim to be a member of that tradition and be a Witch just by saying so. Nobody else has to welcome them in.

Solitary or Solitaire

A Solitary Witch is one who has not joined a coven and prefers to practice alone. They may or may not have been coven members in the past. Many Solitaries are self-initiated.

Tradition

Similar to a denomination in Christianity, a tradition has its own ideology and established set of protocols and ritual practices. Gardnerian, Alexandrian, Seax-Wica, and Feri are all traditions.

Wiccan

A Wiccan is a follower of the religion of Wicca, which is not quite the same as Witchcraft. Wicca is rooted in Witchcraft, but it also embraces many twentieth- and twenty-first-century elements. Wicca often borrows from Zen Buddhism, spirituality from various Native American cultures, fantasy fiction, and other sources and combines them into a modern syncretism that does not exist solely on outdated concepts. Some Old Craft Witches say that Wiccans are too fluffy, that they ignore the darker elements of both Witchcraft and human nature, the possibility that using harmful magick can be justified, and the hardships the victims faced during the Inquisition. Of course, many Wiccans claim that theirs is the next evolution of the Craft, acknowledging the past but living in today and looking to tomorrow.

Witch and Witchcraft

A Witch is a person who practices Witchcraft. Well, that was easy. Just to muddle it up a bit, try this:

Witchcraft is a philosophy, a practice or a skill set, and a way of life but not necessarily a religion. It is a reverence for nature, a connection with magickal forces, and a belief in the innate worth of all living things. Witches believe that magick is a universal force that anyone can harness. Witches are usually Pagans who honour the old gods, or pre-Christian deities, in rituals and ceremonies, but some believe that the power comes from within, and one does not need the gods' favor to call oneself a Witch. Witchcraft is often referred to as the Old Religion, borrowing a term coined by Margaret Murray even though (1) she's been largely discredited in her research on Witchcraft, (2) Witchcraft is not inherently a religious practice, and (3) there are religions older than that.

Other Groups Associated with Witchcraft

There are three other types of practitioners often associated with Witchcraft. They are included here simply to understand the differences.

Satanists

If you're a Witch, someone somewhere has probably asked you if that means you worship Satan. Who are Satanists, and why do they call themselves Witches?

First off, Satanists are not goddess worshippers, and there are actually two kinds of Satanists: traditional and modern. Traditional Satanists see Satan as a benevolent pre-Christian (possibly Roman) deity known as Satan, Lucifer, or Baphomet. The name *Lucifer*, or "Light bringer" in Latin, heralds the planet Venus, which appears in the sky just before dawn. According to legend, Lucifer wanted to rule the heavens but was banished by Ba'al, so he shines just before the coming of the light.

Modern Satanism was created by Anton LaVey, a Californian circus performer and photographer, in 1966. Modern, or LaVeyan, Satanism believes that Satan is more of a concept or an inspiration than an actual deity. (You know the phrase "If you see the Buddha on the road, you must kill the Buddha"? Same thing.) LaVey took the literary "noble rebel" aspect of Satan from such sources as Baudelaire's poem "The Litanies of Satan" and combined them with humanism, occult theory, and the writings of Ayn Rand and Nietzsche to create a new hybrid of religion and psychology. Most modern Satanists focus on seeking happiness in the material realm rather than the spiritual. The Church of Satan follows LaVeyan Satanism.

In both cases, female Satanists are called Witches and males are called warlocks, which merely adds to the layperson's confusion regarding the Craft. And, yes, there are people who call themselves Satanists who worship the anti-Christ with all the Hollywood trappings.

So why call themselves Witches? Well, Satanists argue that Witchcraft is just that—the craft, or skill, of the wise, not the religion of the wise. Anyone who uses magick is using the skill of Witchery; it's an ability, not a faith. A psychic healer who cures ills is using Witchcraft and so is a telephone tarot card reader. Why not, then, use the term *Witch* with that definition?

Warlocks

Warlocks, by literal definition, are oath-breakers, deceivers, and ones who have betrayed a sacred oath. The term comes from the Middle English *waerloga* around 1000 CE, when its original definition was similar to apostate, or one who has renounced the faith.[64] Within traditional Witchcraft, a warlock is one who has betrayed the coven or broken the oath of initiation and is considered outcast.

Some people are reclaiming the word and using it to define a male Witch, but the generally understood definition is oath-breaker and is not often used.

Cowan

A cowan, though the word is almost never used anymore, is anyone who is not of the Craft. You could say that the word *muggle* is a modern equivalent.

Lesson 4: Study Prompts and Questions

The Age of Enlightenment
- Why do you suppose people were willing to embrace science, philosophy, and reason over church doctrine?
- Why did an interest in fantasy and make-believe become popular?

---

64. Online Etymology Dictionary, "Warlock," accessed October 15, 2022, https://www.etymonline.com /word/warlock/.

Aradia and the Golden Bough

- What was Leland describing in his book *Aradia, or the Gospel of the Witches*?
- Why was James Frazer's *The Golden Bough* seen as controversial?

Of Anthropologists and Occultists

- In your own words, explain why you think Margaret Murray's views on Witchcraft were so widely criticized.
- What are two passages for which Aleister Crowley is widely remembered?
- Name one of the religious organizations with which Crowley is associated.

The Birth of Modern Witchcraft

- Gerald Gardner is regarded as the "father of modern Witchcraft." Do you think this title is accurate? Why or why not?
- Choose one name from this list, and explain why you think it is important: the Crotona Fellowship, the New Forest coven, Doreen Valiente, and Scire.
- Gardner constructed Wicca with contributions from several different belief systems, philosophical schools of thought, and folkways. Does Wicca's aspect of being a modern reimagining of older systems affect its validity or effectiveness? Why or why not?

The Renaissance of the Craft

- In your own words, explain why the movements of the 1960s share some similar ideologies with Wicca.
- Explain why so many different traditions emerged in the 1960s and 1970s.

The Return of Who's Who and What's What?

- Briefly explain the following terms: Ásatrú, coven, Druid, eclectic, and Solitary Witch.

Lesson 4: Recommended Reading

- *A History of Witchcraft: Sorcerers, Heretics & Pagans* by Jeffrey B. Russell and Brooks Alexander
- *The Triumph of the Moon: A History of Modern Pagan Witchcraft* by Ronald Hutton

LESSON 5
Facets of Spirituality and Divinity

In the last three lessons, we studied the history of Witchcraft from its Neolithic origins to today. Now let's change gears slightly; the next few lessons will focus on humankind's perception of divinity. What is God? Who or where is God? Throughout these lessons you'll encounter the goddess, the Earth Mother, the Green Man, and many other archetypes, as well as specific deities such as Brigit, Odin, Athena, and Hecate. Where did the idea of a divine presence come from? Such has been the focus of theological debate for millennia. I can't answer all those questions here, but we'll have a look.

The Humanized Face of Divinity

Humanity, for all we have accomplished with science and intellect, is still basically a simple beast. As much as we might be able to conceptualize the idea of a divine force, we need a way to bring that force into a form that we can understand and deal with. We need to be able to grasp a concept before we can understand it; comprehending the Divine is the same way.

Look at it this way: There is a sort of ritual that occurs whenever a small child is taken to the ocean for the first time. They are led by the hand to the shore where they stand and look out at the unending water from surf to horizon. They see but cannot comprehend what they are seeing. They blink a couple of times, then turn around and dig a little hole in the sand. Water fills the hole, and the child plays with that. The child has just created a reflection of the unknowable in manageable form—something they can get their mind around.

This same concept, the recreation of the unknowable, is why early humans gave a face to the immense forces of nature. In order to understand it, they had to be able to identify it. Those early humans, who painted on cave walls with mud and feared the lightning, called the womb-like cave "mother" and the fierce lightning "father." This understanding of the forces of nature was the beginning of the concept of a god and a goddess. Fierce,

powerful, and frightening things, such as lightning and rutting stags, were seen as masculine, and nurturing, protective things, such as mother animals and caves, were seen as
feminine. Oh, there were crossovers, such as gentle spring breezes or angry mother bears
with cubs, but the general association was that masculine forces were harsh or offensive,
and feminine forces were defensive and protecting.

From this simple understanding of the duality of nature arose the concept of a balanced divinity—a father and mother of all life. The god aspect of nature is fierce, vir-
ile, protective, loving, and strong. He is the crash of thunder, the howling wolf, and the
mighty oak. He guards against attack, hunts for the tribe, and supports or protects the
goddess.

The goddess aspect is nurturing, strong, protective, and teaching. She is the rush
of the river, the supple willow, and the fierce mountain lion. She provides shelter and
warmth, she guides and teaches, and she is the mother of all things.

With these ideals as aspects for the different faces of the Divine, our ancestors had
the ability to comprehend and connect with the immeasurable forces of life. These were
the humanized faces of divinity.

Immanent versus Transcendent Deities

If the god and goddess are seen as humanized aspects of nature, or masks upon the
unknowable, then we must ask: what—or where—is the Divine? Theologians have con-
jectured that gods exist in two possible modes: immanent or transcendent.[65] Let's examine these.

Immanence, as commonly used when talking about the Divine, refers to a deity that
exists within everything. The Divine is part of everything, and everything is part of the
Divine. The Green Man is an example of an immanent deity.

Transcendent refers to a deity being "above and beyond." They may have created the
world, but they exist separate from it—apart from the creation. Jehovah is an example of
a transcendent deity.

Protranscendent arguments state that, like a parent to their child, the transcendent deity guides and nurtures but is a separate entity. A common expression is that a
benevolent ruler watches over all. In this belief, it is the same with God and the world.
Arguments against transcendent deities include the notion that any deity able to create

---

65. Relton, *Studies in Christian Doctrine*, 57.

a world would not be so cruel as to abandon it to random chance, watching for mere amusement, and that if a god takes a hand in the affairs of the world, they are no longer "above and beyond."

The argument against immanence is that when a lion kills a gazelle, they are killing part of themselves. Or that god created humans, who created nuclear waste, so god, in turn, brought about the creation of their own poisons. A god would not, it is reasoned, be self-destructive.

The argument for immanence is that life exists in darkness as well as light—that the gazelle recognizes its own demise as part of the continuous circle of life and that human's poisons are, like a child playing with fire, part of learning one's own limitations. Witches, as a rule, follow that the god and goddess are immanent deities.

Monotheism, Polytheism, Animism, and Pantheism

Let's look at divinity another way. Not only can gods be perceived as male and female and within and without, but they can be perceived in other forms as well: monotheistic, polytheistic, animistic, and pantheistic. First, here is a quick definition of each term:

Monotheism

Monotheism is the concept that there is a singular deity who is responsible for the creation, maintenance, and judgment of all things. The Divine exists as a single entity from which all things came. Think of an extended big bang theory. All matter and energy in the universe existed in a single molecule, and that molecule was God. From that burst of life began the infinite cycle that continues today.

Polytheism

Polytheism is the concept that there are many different gods who all exist as a collective. Fire, love, reason, night, day, warfare, death, and music are all governed by specific deities. Together they compose the wholeness of life. Many cultures, such as Greek, Roman, and Aztec, honour polytheistic divinities.

Animism

Animism is the belief that all natural forces, objects, and phenomena are individual spirits. The animistic concept allows that a stone has a soul, as does a tree, a badger, and a waterfall. The crashing sound of the water is the voice within the soul of the waterfall.

Volcanoes, wind, and even the night sky each possess a soul. Rather than assign deific names to aspects of life, the animist says that the aspect itself is a living thing.

Pantheism

Pantheism has two possible definitions. They could be called Eastern and Western pantheism.

Eastern pantheism states that the material world is an extension of the transcendent god. All we have, all we are, and all we know are only manifestations of an unknowable Divine. To the Eastern pantheist, humankind is to god as laughter is to emotion.

Western pantheism, easier for many to grasp, states that since *pan* means "all," pantheists honour all gods regardless of culture or origin. The Unitarian Church is an excellent example of Western pantheism.

Regarding Western pantheism, some people feel that the word *pantheism* is misused. Since theology is the study of religion, and *pan* means "all," pantheism implies following all religions. The principle of following all named deities would be called *pandeism*. Pantheist or pandeist? You decide.

Creation Myths

Where did we come from?

This question has been the source of wonder and examination since people first thought to ask it. Religions all over the world have creation myths, and a few are examined here. Creation myths are stories, in myth and parable, that tell the story of how the universe, the world, or people began. They reflect the culture and cosmology of the region.

Christians say that everything began with the Word, and the Word was God.

According to Greek mythology, in the beginning was Chaos, dark and formless. Out of Chaos grew Gaea, the many-bosomed earth. Chaos gave birth to night and water, and Gaea gave birth to air and daylight. Together Gaea and her son, lover, and husband Uranus created the Titans, who were the predecessors of the gods.

In Hindu mythology, we are told that the universe began as Chaos. The god Vishnu, formed from will, separated the heavens from the body of Earth. The sun rose from a great pillar at the navel of the world, which divided the cosmos into three parts: Earth below, heavens above, and air between. Much later, Purusha, the first man, was sacrificed, and his four limbs became the four castes of society.

The origin of the universe according to the Japanese is that three nameless beings arose from the body of a carp that slept in the chaotic ocean. The beings gave birth to the first gods and goddesses, among whom were the twins Izanagi and Izanami. The brother and sister came down from the heavens on a rainbow but found no land. Izanagi stirred the waters with his spear and formed the island Onogoro.

In Navajo legend, there was only darkness and silence. Far off to the north, a little cloud awoke and wandered south in search of light. The small cloud discovered a larger, darker cloud that was the keeper of secrets. The clouds fought, making the rains fall, which opened up a hole in the ground and released all the animals. The small cloud then gave the animals the task of finding light and peace, which is why animals wander.

There are hundreds of other myths. Tibetan myths claim the world came from an egg. Egyptian tales speak of a scarab beetle that swam out of the waters of the goddess Nut. Nut created the primordial essence, and the beetle created all the lands and life. These are only a few of the myriad legends of creation.

What of the Wiccan creation myth? Where do Witches say we came from?

Most Witches believe that billions of years ago the universe was formed in an event called the big bang. In it, interstellar particles flew out in all directions. Some particles cooled, coalesced, and developed into swirling galaxies and stars, and debris from stars formed into planets. On one of those little planets, just the right amount of heat hitting just the right combination of protein molecules in just the right amount of water developed into microscopic bacteria. They grew and diversified into simple aquatic plant and animal life. Millions of years later, some little fish were left gasping in the shallows when the tides rolled out, and they gradually evolved a way to survive out of the water. Leap ahead another few millennia, and a small apelike primate picked up a stick to dig grubs out of a tree root…

"Wait, hold up," I hear you say. "That's not a creation myth. That's scientific fact."

Yup, sure is.

And that's where most Witches believe we came from.

And we can also believe in gods and goddesses. Weird, huh?

"But don't Witches have a *real* creation myth?" you ask. "A story with mystical elements and parable. Something besides exploding galaxies and fish with a poor sense of timing?"

Well, yes and no. Just like the Witch's ancestral family tree is a mismatched tapestry woven together from a hundred different threads, there is no single Wiccan creation myth we can look back on.

Or there wasn't until Pagan author Starhawk wrote one for her book *The Spiral Dance*, first published in 1979. It's not universally accepted canon, but it's a decent offering.

> *Alone, awesome, complete within Herself, the Goddess, She whose name cannot be spoken, floated in the abyss of the outer darkness, before the beginning of all things. As She looked into the curved mirror of black space, She saw by her own light her radiant reflection, and fell in love with it. She drew it forth by the power that was in Her and made love to Herself, and called Her "Miria, the Wonderful."*
>
> *Their ecstasy burst forth in the single song of all that is, was, or ever shall be, and with the song came motion, waves that poured outward and became all the spheres and circles of the worlds. The Goddess became filled with love, swollen with love, and She gave birth to a rain of bright spirits that filled the worlds and became all beings.*
>
> *But in that great movement, Miria was swept away, and as She moved out from the Goddess She became more masculine. First She became the Blue God, the gentle, laughing god of love. Then She became the Green One, vine-covered, rooted in the earth, the spirit of all growing things. At last She became the Horned God, the Hunter whose face is the ruddy sun and yet dark as Death. But always desire draws Him back toward the Goddess, so that He circles Her eternally, seeking to return in love.*
>
> *All began in love; all seeks to return to love. Love is the law, the teacher of wisdom, and the great revealer of mysteries.*[66]

Unlike older creation myths, which reflect the culture and cosmology of the region, Starhawk's version is based more on Wiccan philosophy. In the years since the book's publication, it has become recognized as valid as any other, and many Witches have embraced it. You can too. Or you could read creation myths from other cultures for inspiration and education. There are many. Funny thing is that Witches accept them all as valid.

Why?

---

66. Starhawk, *The Spiral Dance*, 19.

Because we know that creation myths—no matter who wrote them or what they say—are cosmological reflections of humanity. They justify why we are us. That's all creation myths are meant to do, really. They do more than explain how we began; they justify why we are us.

God and Goddess Origin Myths

While the mythologies of creation vary greatly, a surprising amount of deity origin myths follow similar lines. You will find that in most cases the type of birth reflects the role they play in the world. Universally there are five distinct origin myths of the gods. They are:

- Anthropomorphic birth, or born from animals
- Astral birth, or born from the cosmos or the stars
- Elemental birth, or born from elements of air, water, fire, or earth
- Extraction birth, or being physically removed, fully grown, from a parent
- Parthenogenic birth, or having no parents or fertilization

Normal "born from a mother and father" births of gods are actually quite rare. Here are more details and a few examples for the five standard birth myths:

Anthropomorphic Births

Gods born of animals or born with animal forms or features naturally govern those animals to which they are related. Mehuret, a provider goddess of Egypt, was born from a cow. She was depicted with a cow's head and multiple breasts. Vasila, of Russia, protector goddess of horses, was born from a mare and has a horse's head. Meztli, an Aztec moon god, was hatched from a butterfly cocoon. He resembles a small, old man with shining butterfly wings.

Astral Births

Deities of astral birth often govern the stars, the cosmos, or the heavens. Gaea, the Greek "Mother of All," was born from the stars. Her story is a close parallel to the Witches' creation myth. Aditi, in the Hindu faith, was born from the void and willed herself into being, then birthed the universe. Ra, the Egyptian sun god, formed himself out of sunlight when the universal mother, Nut, was not looking.

Elemental Births

Elemental births reflect deities who govern the element to which they were born, and there are many myths of elemental births. Pele, of Hawai'i, was born of a volcano. The Greek Aphrodite was born of sea-foam; Japan's Iwanaga-hime, who protected sailors from crashing into the rocks, was born of stone; and the Graeco-Roman god Mithras was born from a stone, carrying a torch and dagger.

Extraction Births

Violent and bloody extraction births are quite prevalent, and they often involve goddesses of death and rebirth. The Hindu goddess Kali is a prime example. When demons threatened to conquer the earth, Durga, a warrior goddess, fought them viciously. She took a cut to the head (or sweated drops of blood), and Kali sprung fully formed from her brow, taking her side in battle. In Greek myths, Zeus was stricken with a headache and begged Hephaestus to remove his head. Hephaestus only cut his brow open, and Athena sprung out fully grown and fully armored, shaking her spear.

Parthenogenic Births

Of births without fertilization, the most famous is Jesus, who came from a virgin birth. Others include Amaterasu of Japan. Her father, Izanagi, gave birth to her all by himself. In Sumerian myths, Sadarnuna, goddess of the new moon, was born of the crone moon, Ularnuna, with no male assistance of any kind.

Thealogy and Reality

First, let's examine the word *thealogy*. It differs from the word *theology*, with an *o*, which is the study of religion primarily from a masculine viewpoint. Most theological studies concentrate on the Christian perspective. *Thealogy*, with an *a*, is the study of the whole scope of spirituality—masculine, feminine, and beyond. Every aspect of life and cosmology must be explored to fully understand the importance of religion in our lives.

Gods are more than just a way of explaining the creation of the universe, the habits of animals, or the cycles of the moon and seasons. Gods play a greater role in human's awareness. The gods' interactions with humankind gives people an active role in the world around them and a feeling of importance and self-worth. Not only are humans one of the beasts, but their reasoning mind gives them the ability to see the universe as a whole. The scope of reality, from the pattern of the stars to the ceaseless toil of ants, is all part of a greater picture. Every deity plays a part in the unfolding universe. Birth, death, poverty, love, war, trees, horses, fish, baking, and rainbows are all governed by some divine force.

The myriad divine forces reflect human's way of understanding the myriad facets of life, the universe, and their search for the answers.

Lesson 5: Study Prompts and Questions

The Humanized Face of Divinity

- Describe two ways early humans perceived invisible forces in the world around them.

Immanent versus Transcendent Deities

- What does it mean for a deity to be immanent or transcendent? Briefly describe each term.

Monotheism, Polytheism, Animism, and Pantheism

- Define and offer examples of each concept: monotheism, polytheism, animism, Western pantheism, and Eastern pantheism.

Creation Myths

- Explain the importance of creation myths, and why we need them.
- If a culture's creation myths are reflections of the people of that culture, do you think that Starhawk's creation myth is a reflection of Wicca or Witchcraft? Why or why not?

God and Goddess Origin Myths

- List and define the five prominent classes of deity origin myth.
- Why do you think similar origin myths carry across different cultures and nations?

Thealogy and Reality

- Explain the difference between thealogy and theology.
- What role do gods play in the lives of humans?
- What role do humans play in the lives of gods?

Lesson 5: Recommended Reading

- *The Great Cosmic Mother: Rediscovering the Religions of the Earth* by Monica Sjöö and Barbara Mor
- *The Masks of God* by Joseph Campbell

LESSON 6
The Many Faces of the Goddess

The goddess, by any name, is a central figure in most Wiccan worship. In her myriad faces she is the Earth Mother, life and death, birth and rebirth, and the source of magick and inspiration. In this lesson we'll look at the goddess in her different forms: Earth Mother; Maiden, Mother, and Crone; goddesses of love and fertility; sun and moon goddesses; warrior goddesses; and goddesses of death.

The Earth Mother

In her most primal form, the goddess is perceived as the Earth Mother and the living embodiment of the spirit of the planet. She represents the most basic aspects of the feminine: mother, protector, healer, and provider. The Earth Mother is seen as the immanent soul of the world, the living womb. She is the all-knowing, all-caring, and all-loving creator, nurturer, teacher, and destroyer of all. She is the source of all life. Everything we know, everything we use, and everything we touch, smell, hear, and taste comes from the earth. The Earth Mother is the embodiment of our material growth.

According to James Lovelock's "Gaia Hypothesis," planet Earth is technically alive in that the living organisms of the world interact with their surroundings to form a synergistic, self-regulating, and complex system that maintains and perpetuates life on the planet.[67]

The Earth Mother, perceived as a living entity, is the ultimate immanent deity. When we pollute the oceans, we hurt her. When we chop down a forest, we feel her weep. When we heal a bird's broken wing, we hear her sigh. She is part of us, and we are part of her. The Earth Mother is the personification of the interconnected spirits of all that lives and grows upon the earth. Images of the Earth Mother often portray a naked, rotund woman who sometimes has leaves or vines for hair.

---

67. Lovelock, *The Vanishing Face of Gaia*, 163.

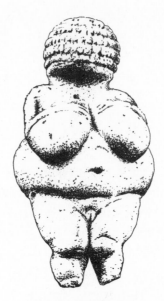

Venus of Willendorf

The Triple Goddess

The goddess is often seen in three parts: Maiden, Mother, and Crone. These are the three phases, or faces, of the divine feminine aspect and are comparable to the waxing, full, and waning phases of the moon. The most common image representing the Triple Goddess is the triple moon pentagram, which shows two reversed crescent moons on either side of a pentagram. Let's examine each of the three faces.

The Maiden

The Maiden, or virgin, Goddess is the embodiment of youth, vitality, sexuality, purity, and innocence. She is the young girl, the dreamer, the idealist, and the hopeful. With her young face turned to the wind, she is the essence of youth and unlimited potential.

Images of the Maiden Goddess include Persephone, Greek goddess of youth; Eir, Scandinavian goddess of protection or mercy; and Zorya, the Slavic goddess of the dawn who opens the gates for the sun to start its daily journey.

Keep in mind, however, that *virgin* does not mean "one who is sexually pure" in this context. Originally a virgin was a woman complete within herself. This could mean a young girl, a woman who has never borne children, or an unmarried woman, childless or otherwise. The Maiden Goddess can be youthful, flirtatious, and eager but also determined and capable.

The Mother

As the center of the Triple Goddess, the Mother Goddess represents the middle years of a woman's life; the bright, magickally empowered fullness of the moon; and the wise, nurturing aspect of the feminine divinity. She is the caring mother, the loving provider, the wise teacher, and the source of abundance and joy. The Mother Goddess is seen as the embodiment of female maturity. She understands the ways of the world; she knows the joys and pains of childbirth, the delight and frustration of raising children, and the bittersweet sorrow of watching her children grow and leave the nest. She is the living heart of motherhood.

Images of the Mother Goddess include Demeter of Greek mythology, whose grief over the loss of Persephone brought winter's cold hand across the land. Another is Cybele the Anatolian goddess and mother of the mountains. In Latvian mythology, the Mahte is a collective of seventy or so individual mother goddesses, each of whom governs a different aspect of life. There is Mieza Mahte, mother of barley; Pirts Mahte, mother of the bathhouse; and Sniega Mahte, mother of snow.

The Crone

The Crone Goddess, the final face of the Triple Goddess, is the old, wise woman, the grandmother, and the hag. She is the final stage of life. She can be cruel but is usually seen as an older, loving woman, now past childbearing age, who has experienced all the joys and sorrows of the world. Her children are grown, she has outlived her husbands, and she lives to share her knowledge and wisdom with the world. Since she is old enough to know all, she cannot be fooled. She sees through illusion, knows the truth behind the mask of humankind, and has tasted the bitter kiss of death. To some, the Crone Goddess is the reaper, the bringer of death and solace. To others, she is the bringer of wisdom.

Images of the Crone Goddess include the Ereshkigal, Sumerian goddess of the underworld; Hecate, Greek goddess of magick, spells, and the dark moon; and Cailleach, Celtic goddess of disease, death, wisdom, and winter.

Maiden, Mother, and Crone

Goddesses of Love and Fertility

Stepping outside the image of the Triple Goddess, we see that there are some archetypes that transcend the triad. They can embody two or even all three phases in one form. A good example of this would be goddesses of love and fertility. Aphrodite is probably the goddess that comes to mind most readily. She is youthful, sexual, and vibrant, but she is also a caring mother, a harsh teacher, and ageless in her wisdom and mystery.

Goddesses of love, sexuality, passion, and fertility know many faces. Besides Aphrodite, there is Branwen, the Celtic goddess of love and beauty; Freyja, the lusty and passionate warrior goddess of Norse mythology; and the Egyptian Hathor, goddess of love, beauty, and music.

All these goddesses share some commonalities. As a goddess of love, they are the givers of passion, romance, lust, creativity, and desire. As a goddess of fertility, they fill wombs, grant healthy offspring, and urge abundant crops to grow. They do have a dark side as well. If they are spurned or rejected, the unfortunate will know loneliness, heartbreak, starvation, and sorrow.

Moon and Sun Goddesses

From shifting clouds to the changing moon and the stars above, the sky has always held a deep fascination for humankind. For many millennia, humans have looked into the sky with awe and wonderment. It is no surprise, then, that goddess images were bestowed upon both faces—the welcoming, vibrant warmth of the sun and the cold, mysterious, shadowed face of the moon.

In Western culture, the moon as a feminine aspect is generally more prevalent. The sun as masculine, however, is a far more widespread concept, and the moon as masculine is relatively rare.

The moon is often perceived as a goddess, and the goddess is usually one who governs death and rebirth. Here's why: It did not take long for people to realize that the twenty-eight-day lunar cycle mirrored the woman's twenty-eight-day menstrual cycle. They don't specifically align for every woman—that is, of course, a myth—but menstrual cycles have intrigued and frightened people for many years. The moon also affects the tides, and so the changing phases of the moon, coinciding with the menstrual cycle, could easily be perceived as a divine mystery of death and renewal. The Morrigan, Hecate, and the Iberian goddess Ataegina are representations of moon goddesses of death and rebirth.

Images of the goddess as a female aspect of the sun are rather rare in Europe but for a few notable exceptions. In Celtic lore, Brigit is a triple sun goddess with her three faces of morning, noon, and dusk. She is the principal goddess of the Celts and the lover-mother-teacher who brought fire down from the sky to her people. She is the goddess of the hearth and the forge, poetry, and inspiration and motherhood. Amaterasu is a major figure in the Japanese pantheon, and she represents the fullness of life, warmth, security, and vitality. She is also the goddess of divine inspiration, and her sorrow brings about the darkness of night. In Egypt both Sekhmet and Hathor are goddesses of the sun. As a sun goddess archetype, Sekhmet takes the heat of the sun to an extreme. She is the protective lioness and the furious, enraged mother whose searing truth burns away all lies and facades. The sun goddess archetype gives us light and warmth as well as inspiration and protection.

Warrior Goddesses

As much as the goddess represents a nurturing, healing figure, she may also be seen as a proud warrior, strong and unafraid. The mother bear defending her cubs, the protective mare with her foal, and the matriarchal elephants who will aggressively defend their calves are all natural examples of the warrior goddess figure. In Greek mythology, the Amazons define the warrior goddess archetype as sensual, fierce, proud, and defiant. Artemis, the huntress, is both a strong warrior with bow and arrow and a coy maiden with dancing eyes and an air of mystery. She embodies the wide scope of feminine potential and ability.

There are some who feel that the warrior goddess icon belongs as a fourth aspect of the Triple Goddess. Between Maiden and Mother, a woman can be a defiant, strong-willed force capable of great fury and passion. Full of drive and determination, she has outgrown childhood but is not inclined to assume the responsibilities of motherhood.

Goddesses of Death

The sight of Kali, with her blazing eyes and necklace of skulls, is a sobering visage. Likewise, the midnight-skinned and lion-headed Ereshkigal evokes a nervous glance from even the most stoic of onlookers. But goddesses of death do not represent finality and oblivion. Yes, Kali is widely recognized as a goddess of death and terror, but she is revered in India as a figure of death and rebirth. She represents not the end but a new beginning. Ereshkigal is seen as taking souls into her belly where they go from her back into the earth to begin anew.

While possibly frightening, no goddess of death is to be feared. They are the Crone aspect personified, bringing wisdom and enlightenment at the end of the day and carrying you through the night into a new tomorrow.

Lesson 6: Study Prompts and Questions

The Earth Mother
- Briefly define the ancient meaning of the Earth Mother.
- Using James Lovelock's "Gaia Hypothesis," offer two examples of the physical reality of the goddess.

The Triple Goddess

- List the three aspects of the Triple Goddess, and briefly explain each one.
- Offer examples of two goddesses that define each aspect.

Goddesses of Love and Fertility

- List three aspects commonly attributed to a fertility goddess as opposed to a love goddess.
- Is the goddess of love restricted only to physical pleasure? Explain and justify your answer.

Moon and Sun Goddesses

- What physical event is closely associated with the moon goddess and why?
- Name two moon goddesses, and briefly define their spheres of influence.
- Name two sun goddesses, and briefly describe their spheres of influence.

Warrior Goddesses

- Justify the female warrior goddess archetype, and offer two examples.
- Can a goddess of war also be a goddess of love? Explain.
- Do you agree that the warrior goddess could be perceived as a fourth aspect of the Triple Goddess? Explain and justify your answer.

Goddesses of Death

- Define the full meaning of the goddess of death archetype, and offer two examples.

Lesson 6: Recommended Reading

- *The New Book of Goddesses and Heroines* by Patricia Monaghan
- *The Twelve Faces of the Goddess: Transform Your Life with Astrology, Magick, and the Sacred Feminine* by Danielle Blackwood

LESSON 7
The Many Faces of the God

Wicca is a religion of dualities—light and dark, day and night, life and death, and goddess and god. In the last lesson, we examined different aspects of the goddess archetype, from Earth Mother to Crone Goddess. So here, naturally, we flip the coin and examine the masculine god archetypes, from the Green Man to the Oak and Holly Kings. As the counterpart to the goddess, the god represents strength, vitality, passion, and courage. He is the embodiment of the divine male: strong, caring, loving, protective, and honourable.

The Horned God

The most primal image of the archetypal male deity is the Horned God. Seen in ancient etchings as an anthropomorphic stag, he embodies both the wisdom and spirituality of humankind and the stamina and agility of the stag. He is the sage, the mystic, the lover, the dancer, and the dreamer. To many of our earliest ancestors, he was the essence of the masculine. He granted the people healthy babies, successful hunts, and prolific growth. As one of the most vivid images of Pagan divinity, he personifies the essence of vitality, courage, and compassion.

The Horned God

In Gallo-Roman Europe, he was known as Cernunnos. He was seen in the rich soil, the turbulent sky, and the rushing waters. He was the tall tree, the howling wolf, and the soaring eagle. To some, he is also known as Herne the Hunter. There is some doubt, however, as to whether Herne was an actual deity or merely a tenth-century figure who was revered for providing for his community in a Robin Hoodesque manner.

The Horned God is born of the Mother Goddess. He is said to have no father because he is his own father. Throughout the year, he remains in close relationship with the goddess and the cycle of the seasons. As he matures, he will impregnate her again, ensuring his rebirth into the coming year.

The Horned God represents the powerful, positive male qualities that derive from a deeper understanding of masculine self than the stereotypical male ideal of today. When a person strives to emulate the Horned God, they allow themself to be "Free to be wild without being violent, angry without being cruel, sexual without being coercive, spiritual without being chaste, and able to truly love."[68]

For many Pagans, the Horned God is an image of inner power and of a potency that is more than merely sexual. He is the Undivided (or Unified) Self in which the mind is not split from the body, nor the spirit from the flesh. United, both can function at the peak of creative and emotional power. The Horned God is not subservient to the goddess, nor is he seen as above her. They are equal—two halves of the same mystery. The symbology of the Horned God, like that of the goddess, is both internal and external. Through the Horned God and the goddess alike, both men and women can learn the balance of strength, courage, compassion, and empowerment.

The Green Man

Like the Mother Goddess, the Green Man is an enduring and powerful archetype. He embodies the cyclical flow of nature and assures us (and the goddess) that he is never far away. The Green Man represents fortitude, resilience, fertility, and luck. The Green Man offers a connection to the deep wisdom of the earth: the cycle of death and rebirth, the continuous renewal of the living universe. He appears in many forms, and he can be seen as a man with hair of leaves, a man wearing a cloak of leaves, or a disembodied face surrounded by leaves and vines that flow from his mouth. This last image is the most popular. A distinctly Pagan symbol, images of the Green Man are prevalent in many medieval churches and abbeys. The small leafy face is often tucked away in small carvings on the ceiling or lurking behind fountains.

The Green Man is the son of the goddess, and he is the benevolent, youthful guise of the loving god. He is a symbol of fertility and luck and has enjoyed a popularity undiminished through the centuries. He is Tammuz, Dionysus, and Cernunnos. In Rome, he was known as Bacchus, god of vegetation, wine, and divine rapture. He appears in many European countries in various guises. In Germany he is known as Blattgesicht, and in France he is Le Feuillou. This Pagan icon, symbolizing nature's cycle of rebirth and hope, has metamorphosed across cultures and been adopted more readily than most other pre-Christian archetypes. Many fairy tales portray him as a friendly talking tree who imparts wisdom and guidance. In America, a giant green man represents a line of canned and frozen vegetables.

---

68. Vawr, Gawr, and Gawr, *The Word*, 303.

The Green Man is still popular today as human's awareness of their connection with the living ecosystem grows, and the smiling verdant deity offers guidance to those who want to live in harmony with nature and the earth.

The Green Man

The Oak King and the Holly King

The Oak and Holly Kings are another of the male divinity archetypes of modern Witchcraft, although they are more prevalent in England and Europe than in the Americas. They are twin gods who battle each other at Litha and at Yule. They are two sides of the same coin, and neither can exist without the other.

At both Litha (midsummer) and Yule (midwinter), the Oak and Holly Kings do battle to rule over the seasons. Each time, one is ritually slain and lies in state until he returns to battle his twin at the other half of the year. Two themes run throughout the kings' saga. The first, of course, is the seasonal shift of winter into summer and back again. The other is the ritualistic mating and sacrificial death of each in his season.

Here is how the saga runs:

As summer becomes autumn and the season flows into the chill of winter, the Holly King reigns. His rule brings the turning of the trees and the cold touch of frost. At Yule, the shortest day of the year, the Oak King rises and challenges his brother. They duel, and the Holly King falls. Under the Oak King's reign, the days grow longer, trees bloom, and warmth returns to the land. The Oak King rules until midsummer, the longest day of the year, when the Holly King returns to battle him. As each is in his prime—that is, Spring Equinox for the Oak King and Autumn Equinox for the Holly King—they mate with the goddess, giving her their seed. As each king ages, he gives his strength back to the land and awaits his demise.

The Oak King, the Lord of the Greenwood and golden twin of the waxing year, represents the innocence, growth, and vitality of the growing world. The Holly King is the Lord of the Winterwood and the darksome twin of the waning year. He represents the wisdom of age and the maturity of the season. The twin gods together reflect the cycle of nature, the immortal dance of the seasons. They are gods of growth, sacrifice, and rebirth—themes reflected in many cultural pantheons.

The Sacrificial God

If there is one common theme running through many of the god mythos, it is one of sacrifice. While the Crone Goddess frequently represents the gateway to the underworld, a good number of gods give of themselves, all or in part, for the benefit of the world.

Some gods are harvest deities who die with the reaping of the grain. Others die as an act of atonement or to fulfill an obligation, and some sacrifice only part of themselves as payment for something gained. Here are but a few:

Jesus was nailed to the cross, itself an extension of the Tree of Life in the Garden of Eden. Through his sacrifice, the sins of Adam and Eve, and thus all humankind, were absolved.

The Sumerian god Tammuz and his sister Geshtinanna each spend six months of the year in the underworld in a cycle, similar to the Oak and Holly Kings.

Odin, of Norse mythology, was bound to the Yggdrasil, the Tree of Life, for nine nights. He sacrificed his right eye so humans could learn the mystery of the runes.

Tyr, also of Norse mythology, sacrifices his right hand to the Fenris wolf so humankind will learn justice and order.

The Hindu's Shiva, husband—sort of—to Kali, sacrificed himself to her ferocious hunger so her wrath would not destroy the earth.

The Egyptian god Osiris is possibly not a sacrificial god per se. He was killed and dismembered by his brother Set, and Isis found all the parts and revived him. The scattering of his body reflects the casting of seeds at planting season, and his death and resurrection mirrors the flooding of the Nile valley.

There is some criticism that equating a deity that dies and is reborn with the vegetative cycle is an oversimplification of the mythology and that not every resurrected deity has to represent agriculture. In his book *The Gardens of Adonis*, Marcel Detienne argues that judging all resurrected deity mythos by one rule risks equating every dying god with the sacrifice of Jesus.[69]

Sun and Moon Gods

Ask any Pagan to name a sun god, and the first answer you'll get will probably be the Egyptian god Ra or the Greek Apollo. These are probably two of the most widely known sun gods.

Malakbel, from the Syrian city of Palmyra, was one of a triad of deities. Malakbel was the sun, Aglibol the moon, and Baalshamin the sky.

The Vedic-era Hindu deity Surya is the god of the sun, and he was seen riding a chariot pulled by seven horses, which represent the seven colours of light in the visible spectrum.

Koyah, of the Turks, is a sun god whose solar rays represent strings connecting the spirits of plants, animals, and people.

Sun god archetypes are regarded universally as beneficial; they are fathers, teachers, leaders, and sources of divine inspiration. Ancient civilizations recognized that without the sun, all life would perish, so sun gods also became gods of birth, fertility, and creation itself and the chasers and protectors of mystery's deep shadows.

Many cultures also recognize gods of the moon. While moon goddesses are more prevalent, the cultures that regard the moon as masculine are often nomadic or hold fishing and trading as a prime concern. Here the moon becomes the protector, guide, and guardian of the traveler. The moon's wandering path and changing face offers solace to those whose lives are measured in miles. Its silvery light guides them on their way and gives them reprieve from the bright light of the sun. Let's examine a few examples of moon gods.

Khonsu, of Egypt, lost a game of *senet*, or passage, to Thoth. As part of his wager, he lost his light. He had to constantly wax and wane, only showing his true face one night out of the month.

---

69. Detienne, *The Gardens of Adonis*, iv–xi.

Coyote, a well-known trickster god of the Navajo nation, stole a bag of dark crystals from the Great Mystery and blew them into the heavens, causing the stars to twinkle in the sky.

Chandra is the Hindu god of the moon and is associated with Navagrahas, the nine planets, and the Dikpalas, the guardians of the directions.

The Aztec moon god Tecciztecatl is an interesting one. It was believed that the sun and the moon periodically died, and a new sun and moon were chosen. The gods built a bonfire, and both Nanahuatzin and Tecciztecatl were chosen as sacrifices. Nanahuatzin leaped into the fire and became the sun. Proud and boastful Tecciztecatl wanted to be the sun as well, but he hesitated too long and became the moon. The gods threw a rabbit at him in jest, which is why there is an image of a rabbit on the moon's face, and it never shines as bright as the sun.

Trickster Gods

Not all gods (or goddesses, for that matter) are friendly. Although all gods have lessons to teach, some are mischievous, cruel, or downright evil. Many cultures have trickster gods who fool humans—or other gods—to learn from their own folly.

In many cultures, the trickster god doubles as a messenger god. Hermes is one such example; Cupid, with his tiny arrows, is another.

Coyote leads people astray to let them learn from their own mistakes.

Loki, of Norse mythology, tricks humans and gods alike. He was a catalyst in the sequence of events leading to Ragnarok, the demise of the gods and rebirth of the world.

Kokopelli is revered throughout many southwestern American regions known among the Aztecs and the Hopi. He is often shown hunchbacked or with a pack on his back and playing a flute. Kokopelli is a storyteller, a traveler, and a god of trickery and weaving.

Gods of Death

Earlier we discussed sacrificial gods like Tammuz and Odin. Here we look at those gods who govern the death of others. Unlike many death goddesses, who represent rebirth and transformation, most male death-related deities have two "offices." They either rule over the judgment and progress of the soul in the afterlife, or they represent the terror and trauma of death.

Hades is well known as the god of the dead and king of the underworld; he watches over the souls of the departed. His relationship with Persephone gives us the changing seasons.

The Roman god Orcus punishes evildoers in the afterlife to ensure purification before rebirth. He is also the punisher of broken promises.

Yama is the Chinese god of the dead. His image appears on hell money, or nonlegal bank notes, which can be burned to win the favor of one's ancestors.

Baron Samedi is one of the lwa of Voudou. He is seen as a well-dressed skeleton in a top hat and tuxedo, smoking cigars and drinking rum. Baron Samedi greets the deceased as they enter his realm, but he also protects children and whispers cures to doctors.

Charon, of Greek mythology, isn't a god per se but a psychopomp who ferries the souls of the departed across the river Styx.

There are many more deities associated with the terror of death, such as Ahriman of Persia, also known as the Prince of Demons, and Arawn, the Celtic god of death and war.

The Hero

Sometimes the difference between human and god is vague; some people were born mortal and became gods. In classical mythology, a hero was a person with exceptional abilities who undertook a series of challenges and was often honoured as a divine figure in their own right.

Hercules, King Arthur, and Cu Chulainn are all examples of mythic heroes. While they are not archetypal gods, the heroes of mythology bridge the gap between human and the Divine, bringing humans closer to spiritual reality.

Many heroes were sent on valiant quests to retrieve treasures or overcome a series of obstacles. These are usually storytellers' renderings of older myths, which themselves are renditions of natural events. Among the stories of King Arthur, for example, is the search for Mabon. Arthur searches high and low for the missing son of the Lady of Winter Frost. Assisted by symbolic Celtic animals, they find him in a cave at Yule, and his return brings the light back to the land. And did you know that the twelve labors of Hercules represent the twelve zodiac signs and, thus, the cycle of the year?

Please remember that not all heroes are male! Two prominent heroines that come to mind are Boudicca and Hypatia. Rather than mythic or literary figures, these were both real, historical figures.

Boudicca was the queen of the Iceni tribe in Anglo-Saxon England. When the Romans invaded her lands in 60 CE, she raised an army and fought back, defeating Rome's forces in Londinium and Cirencester. She was finally captured, and she took her own life before she could be executed.

Hypatia was a teacher in Alexandria in 415 CE and the first recorded female philosopher and astronomer. When fanatical Christians attacked and burned the Library of Alexandria, she was dragged into the street, stripped bare, and flayed alive.

History remembers both these women as vital, vibrant, and defiant heroines.

Another form of myth cycle, the hero's journey, depicts the growth of a child into an adult. This allegorical tale can be used to depict a person's rise to defeat a foe, seasonal cycles, or the growth of an entire civilization. Pop culture figures who use the hero's journey mythic arc include Luke Skywalker, Harry Potter, Sarah Williams from *Labyrinth*, and Janet Weiss from *The Rocky Horror Picture Show*.

A really simplified example of the hero's journey can be seen in the riddle: "What walks on four legs at dawn, two at noon, and three at dusk?" Answer: a human.

Lesson 7: Study Prompts and Questions

The Horned God
- Why is it said that the Horned God has no father?
- Give two examples of a person's intentions in emulating the Horned God.

The Green Man
- Describe two popular images of the Green Man.
- What lessons does the Green Man teach that can benefit both ancient and modern humankind?

The Oak and Holly Kings
- What are the seasons of each king?
- Briefly explain the meaning of the duels of the twin gods.

The Sacrificial God
- Why do you suppose so many sacrificial deities are male?

Sun and Moon Gods

- Name two sun gods and describe their purpose.
- Identify two masculine lunar deities.
- What aspects of life does the moon god archetype govern?

Trickster Gods

- What two roles does the trickster god commonly take?
- Name three trickster gods, and identify their cultural origins.
- In what way do trickster and messenger gods benefit humankind?

Gods of Death

- Why do you suppose many goddesses of death represent transformation, whereas gods of death serve as stewards of departed souls?

The Hero

- What is the mythic symbology of the hero?
- Name three heroic figures, and briefly describe their deeds.

Lesson 7: Recommended Reading

- *The Hero with a Thousand Faces* by Joseph Campbell
- *The Witches' God* by Stewart and Janet Farrar

LESSON 8
Charges of the Goddess and the God

Do Wiccans pray? How do we commune with our gods? Are there special prayers or passages to recite?

In general, no, but we do have the charges. A charge is part prayer, part invocation, and part divine message; it is a way of connecting with the Divine. Excerpts from charges can be read aloud during initiations, used as meditative inspiration, or read as part of a daily motivation. Personally I find the charges to be a window into the meaning and intention of the god and goddess archetypes.

The four charges presented here are the ones most commonly encountered. Over time, covens and traditions have made revisions to the charges, adapting them as need or poetic preference dictate.

The Charge of the Goddess

The original Charge of the Goddess was presented in the 1899 book *Aradia, or the Gospel of the Witches* by Charles Leland. Many versions have been created since, and the version offered here is one of the most common. Written in 1964 by Doreen Valiente, it borrows from Leland and reflects some of the practices of the Gardnerian Tradition. If any single work could be considered canonical liturgy by Witches across the board, this is it.

Listen to the words of the Great Mother, she who of old has been called Artemis, Astarte, Dione, Melusine, Cerridwen, Diana, and by many other names:

Whenever you have need of anything, once in the month, and better it be when the moon is full, then shall ye assemble in some secret place to adore the spirit of Me, who am Queen of all the Wise. You shall be free from slavery, and as a sign that ye be free, you shall be naked in your rites. Sing, dance, feast, make music and love, all in My praise. For Mine is the ecstasy of the spirit, but Mine also is joy on Earth. My law is love unto all beings. Mine is the secret door that opens upon the land of youth, and Mine is the cup of the wine of life, that is the Cauldron of Cerridwen, that is the Holy Grail of Immortality. I give the knowledge of the spirit eternal, and beyond death, I give peace, freedom and reunion with those who have gone before. Nor do I demand aught in sacrifice, for behold, I am the Mother of all things, and My love is poured out upon the Earth.

Hear now the words of the Star Goddess, the dust of whose feet are the hosts of Heaven, whose body encircles the universe:

I who am the beauty of the green earth, and the white moon among the stars, do call upon your souls… arise, and come unto Me. For I am the soul of nature that gives life to the universe. From Me all things proceed, and unto Me they must return. Let My worship be in the heart that rejoiceth, for behold—all acts of love and pleasure are My rituals. Let there be beauty and strength, power and compassion, honour and humility, mirth and reverence within you. And you who seek to know Me, know that thy seeking and yearning will avail thee not, unless thou knowest this mystery: that if that which you seek you findest not within thee, you will never find it without, for behold—I have been with thee from the beginning, and I am that which is attained at the end of desire.[70]

The Charge of the God

While the Charge of the Goddess as just presented is considered canonical liturgy, there is not a single god-oriented charge as broadly accepted. There are many versions one can easily find in a quick web search, and this one, whose author is unknown, is widely recognized. Similar in construction to the Charge of the Goddess, this version highlights the god's role in his relationship to the Lady and his duties to the world.

Listen to the words of the Great Father, who of old was called Osiris, Adonis, Zeus, Thor, Pan, Cernunnos, Herne, Lugh, and by many other names:

My Law is Harmony with all things. Mine is the secret that opens the gates of life and mine is the dish of salt of the earth that is the body of Cernunnos that is the eternal circle of rebirth. I give the knowledge of life everlasting, and beyond death I give the promise of regeneration and renewal. I am the sacrifice, the father of all things, and my protection blankets the earth.

---

70. Valiente, "The Charge of the Goddess."

Hear the words of the dancing God, the music of whose laughter stirs the winds, whose voice calls the seasons:

I who am the Lord of the Hunt and the Power of the Light, sun among the clouds and the secret of the flame, I call upon your bodies to arise and come unto me. For I am the flesh of the earth and all its beings. Through me all things must die and with me are reborn. Let my worship be in the body that sings, for behold all acts of willing sacrifice are my rituals. Let there be desire and fear, anger and weakness, joy and peace, awe and longing within you. For these too are part of the mysteries found within yourself, within me, all beginnings have endings, and all endings have beginnings.[71]

The Charge of the Dark Goddess

Of all four charges presented here, this version is thought by many to be the most powerful. More than just inspirational, the Charge of the Dark Goddess offers empowerment and a sense of purpose. This charge also embraces what many "Old Craft" Witches feel is missing from Wicca—the sense that everyone has both light and dark aspects to their personality and that the use of one's dark side for beneficial ends is not contradictory.

Wisdom and Empowerment are gifts of the Dark Goddess of Transformation. She is known to us as Kali, Hecate, Cerridwen, Lilith, Persephone, Fata, Morgana, Ereshkigal, Arianrhod, Durga, Inanna, Tiamat, and by a million, million other names:

Hear Me child, and know Me for who I am. I have been with you since you were born, and I will stay with you until you return to Me at the final dusk. I am the passionate and seductive lover who inspires the poet to dream. I am the One who calls to you at the end of your journey. After the day is done, My children find their blessed rest in My embrace. I am the womb from which all things are born. I am the shadowy, still tomb; all things must come to Me and bare their breasts to die and be reborn to the Whole. I am the Sorceress that will not be ruled, the Weaver of Time, the Teacher of Mysteries. I snip the threads that bring My children home to Me. I slit the throats of the cruel and drink the blood of the heartless. Swallow your fear and come to Me, and you will discover true beauty, strength, and courage. I am the fury which rips the flesh from injustice. I am

---

71. Batty, *Teaching Witchcraft*, 69. (Original author unknown.)

the glowing forge that transforms your inner demons into tools of power. Open yourself to My embrace and overcome. I am the glinting sword that protects you from harm. I am the crucible in which all the aspects of yourself merge together in a rainbow of union. I am the velvet depths of the night sky, the swirling mists of midnight, shrouded in mystery. I am the chrysalis in which you will face that which terrifies you and from which you will blossom forth, vibrant and renewed.

Seek me at the crossroads, and you shall be transformed, for once you look upon my face, there is no return. I am the fire that kisses the shackles away. I am the cauldron in which all opposites grow to know each other in Truth. I am the web which connects all things. I am the Healer of all wounds, the Warrior who rights all wrongs in their Time. I make the weak strong. I make the arrogant humble. I raise up the oppressed and empower the disenfranchised. I am Justice tempered with Mercy. Most importantly, child, I am you. I am part of you, and I am within you. Seek Me within and without, and you will be strong. Know Me.

Venture into the dark so that you may awaken to Balance, Illumination, and Wholeness. Take My Love with you everywhere and find the Power within to be who you wish.[72]

The Charge of the Dark God

This charge, unlike that of the dark goddess, speaks not of empowerment but of acceptance. Death inevitably follows life; all that lives must die to be reborn. Embracing this truth, one knows strength and conviction born of wisdom.

Listen to the words of the Dark God, who was of old called Lakchos, Donn, Anubis, Hades, Setesh, Hoder, and by many other names.

I am the shadow in the bright day; I am the reminder of mortality at the height of living. I am the never-ending veil of Night where the Star Goddess dances. I am the Death that may be so that Life may continue, for behold, Life is immortal because the living must die. I am the strength that protects, that limits; I am the power that says No, and No Further, and That Is Enough. I am the things that cannot be spoken of, I am the laughter at the edge of Death. Come with me into the warm enfolding dark; feel my caresses in the hands, in the mouth, in the body of one you love, and be transformed. Blow me a kiss when

---

72. Batty, *Teaching Witchcraft*, 70. (Original author unknown.)

the sky is dark, and I will smile, but no kiss return, for my kiss is the final one for all mortal flesh.[73]

Mirrors of the Gods

The four charges presented in this lesson are by no means the only ones used. Different people perceive the gods in different ways, so, of course, no two charges need be the same. Each charge offers a perspective into the relationship between the Witch and the gods. Here are a few excerpts from different charges I've written over the years:

Of the Goddess

Think not that I am distant. I am with you always. I am the crash of the waves, the whisper of the wind. I am the stones beneath your feet and the stars in the sky. I have been here since time began and I shall remain long after the world you know has gone to dust. I am the Goddess Immortal. I am part of you.

Of the God

Seek me when you need me, though I am never far away. I am the life of the forest and the vitality of the moonlit night. I am the dream of possibility and the fleeting glimpse of desire. I beckon you to stand proud, urge you to strive, inspire you to believe. I am the source of your will and the crucible of your intention. Look within yourself and I am ever there.

Of the Dark Goddess

When your world seems its darkest, when all hope seems lost, look to the night sky to see my face. Darkness and despair are not the final breath of today, but the first whisper of tomorrow.

I am the strength to persevere, I am the sword that challenges the demons and the shield that defends the innocent. I am the wind of change, the fire of conviction, the fountain of hope and the foundation of belief. Look to me to find the path through the darkest hour, for I walk unafraid of the unknown. Join me and face the darkness, for together we triumph.

---

73. Batty, *Teaching Witchcraft*, 71. (Original author unknown.)

Individual Gods and Goddesses

Charges can also be written to individual deities. Here is an excerpt from my own charge to Pan:

> *Mine is the dance of life, the song of celebration. Mine is the way of natural passion, ecstasy, and earthly delights. Come together at my place of worship, to sing, to dance, feast, make merry and make love. If at morning, noon, or dark of night, drink from my cup of festive delight.*
>
> *I am your protector, your lover, your guide, and your light. I am the flame of desire, the dance of delight. My music brings joy and laughter to the world. Keep my song in your heart throughout the year. As the fields ripen, as the flocks grow, I shall ever be with you.*

Elements of the Charge

All charges share common elements. They offer insight into what the deity provides, what one can expect of the deity, and what the person must face in encountering the deity. A standard charge consists of the following elements:

- Invocation: The deity's name or names are given, as well as a brief mention of the deity's "office." Usually only the invocation is in third person (they, them); the rest of the charge, and in some cases the whole thing, is presented in first person (I, me).
- Promise: The deity assures the person what they can expect. Here the deity's office is defined more clearly, and a pledge of guidance or counsel is made to the reader.
- Challenge: The deity explains what is expected of the reader. Often known as stepping up to the plate, the challenge often requires that the reader explore their own doubts or fears.
- Conclusion: The deity speaks to the reader one-to-one and allows a resolution to be reached.

Lesson 8: Study Prompts and Questions

Charges of the Goddess and the God

- Review each of the charges and summarize each charge in a single concept, writing a paragraph or two.
- Different parts of the charges affect people in different ways. What parts spoke to you and why?

Lesson 8: Recommended Reading

- *Aradia, or the Gospel of the Witches* by Charles Leland
- *The Charge of the Goddess: The Poetry of Doreen Valiente* by Doreen Valiente

LESSON 9
The Wheel of the Year and the Eight Sabbats

The term *Wheel of the Year* has come up occasionally in these lessons, but what does it mean? The common calendar is twelve months long, running from January 1 to December 31, and the astrological calendar begins on the Winter Solstice. But what about the Witches' calendar? In this lesson, we'll take a look at the eight sabbats that compose the Wheel of the Year.

An Overview of the Witches' Calendar

The Witches' calendar is divided up into eight holidays, which are called sabbats. They are spaced evenly, approximately six weeks apart. There are two types: greater sabbats and lesser sabbats. The greater sabbats reflect the life cycle of the goddess and the god, and the lesser sabbats are the solstices and equinoxes. It is important to note that while all sabbats are listed on a specific calendar date, the actual astronomical occurrence might be up to three days away from the date of observance.

The Witches' calendar is as follows:

Samhain	October 31	greater sabbat
Yule	December 21 (Winter Solstice)	lesser sabbat
Imbolc	February 2	greater sabbat
Ostara	March 21 (Spring Equinox)	lesser sabbat
Beltane	May 1	greater sabbat
Litha	June 21 (Summer Solstice)	lesser sabbat
Lughnassadh or Lammas	August 1 or 2	greater sabbat
Mabon	September 21 (Autumn Equinox)	lesser sabbat

As you can see from this list, the year begins at Samhain. It might seem, then, that Mabon is the end of the year, but in fact, the year both begins and ends at Samhain. It is not really a beginning or an ending; it is an eternal process. It's called the Wheel of the Year for a reason. Within each section, we'll examine the sabbat's cultural history and the Pagan mythological significance.

Wheel of the Year

Samhain, October 31

Samhain (SOW-en) marks both the beginning and the end of the Witches' calendar year. It was originally a Celtic festival that marked the end of the harvest season and the start of the dark of the year. Variations of the festival have been observed in both Celtic and Gaelic cultures, and the Samhain we know today includes a lot of crossovers between the two.

A quick note that the words *Celtic* and *Gaelic* are going to crop up a lot. *Celtic* refers to most of the British Isles and the northwestern region of France. *Gaelic* originate froms the Gaels of Scotland. Samhain's name comes from the Celtic region and is thought to mean "summer's end." It's known as Samhuinn in Scotland and Samain in Ireland. There is some debate as to the legitimacy of this definition, as the Celtic summer actually ended in August. It's possible that the name comes from the proto-Celtic *Samani*, meaning "assembly."

Samhain had several purposes. For some, it was the beginning of winter, and people would leave offerings of food on their doorsteps overnight to appease the winter spirits, so they would lighten the burden of the coming months. For others, it was the third harvest (the first two being Lammas and Mabon) when the final provisions before winter were stored and livestock was brought down from the summer pastures. Any animals not expected to survive the winter were put down for food. With people gathering and a bounty suddenly available, feasting, celebration, and games became the order of the day, and once every three years, a council would decide upon new laws to be enacted. For yet others, it was the time that the veil between the worlds was at its thinnest, so the Fae or departed loved ones could cross into this world.

All these different customs and traditions became integrated over the centuries, and the Samhain we know today involves aspects of all of those purposes.

Mythologically, Samhain is when the Green Man, or the Horned God, or possibly Cernunnos, crosses the veil himself and dies. His death is the end of the growing year and the start of winter. The goddess goes into mourning until Yule, when he is reborn.

Popular customs at Samhain include setting lanterns in the windows to welcome departed souls home and leaving an extra space at the dinner table. Magickal rites performed at Samhain could include banishings and other "getting rid ofs."

What is the deal with pumpkins at Samhain? Other than the fact that they look all neat and spooky, carved and lit with candles, what are they really for? Samhain is the time that the dead can communicate with the living. Houses that would welcome back deceased relatives and loved ones would guide them home with a burning candle, but sometimes the visitors wouldn't be departed souls. They'd be Fae or malignant spirits. Gourds, turnips, or pumpkins would be carved with grotesque faces and placed on the doorstep to keep the unfriendly spirits at bay and protect the house. Sometimes lanterns were carved with runes, the names of the departed, or talismans of luck.

Finally, while Samhain is traditionally observed on October 31, the actual celebration can be held on any day between the 31st and the astrological date, which occurs during the first week of November. Many astrological websites will have these dates listed.

Yule, December 21

The Winter Solstice marks the longest night of the year and, come the sunrise, a time of renewal. The word *Yule* comes from the Norse *Jul*, meaning "wheel," and indeed the turning of the Wheel of the Year is most obvious at Yule. In the Northern Hemisphere, the Winter Solstice is the shortest day and longest night of the year before the reawakening of the year and the days start getting longer again. The word *solstice*, by the way, comes from the Latin *sol*, or "sun" (you knew that one already), and *stitium*, or "stopping." It is at the at solstices that the sun stands still.

In Wiccan mythology, the goddess gives birth to the young god at Yule, and with him comes the promise of a new year. (Sound vaguely familiar? A lot of religions have major deities born at Yule.) To celebrate this renewal, people exchange gifts and offer blessings and good will to one another.

Another popular event at Yule is one half of the battle that takes place twice a year: the battle of the Oak King and the Holly King, who each represent one half of the year. The Oak King, who represents the warmth of the year, always wins at Yule, so he can influence the coming months, and the Holly King always wins at Litha, so he can bring the cold months back.

If so much is happening at Yule—new births, Winter Solstice, and all that—then why is Samhain regarded as the Witches' New Year and not Yule? Because by Celtic reckoning, the new day begins at midnight, not at dawn. It's the new day when you go to sleep, not when you wake up.

A popular image around Yule, the Winter Solstice, and Christmas (there's a lot happening here) is a jolly, fat man in a red suit. But what does a big guy in a red suit have to do with Yule, a pregnant goddess, or the baby Jesus? Well, actually, he has very little to do with Christianity but a lot to do with Pagans. In third-century Greece, Nicholas was a bishop who saved three young sisters from prostitution by leaving them enough coins to pay their dowry. He was too humble to meet the family directly, so he'd toss bags of coins into their windows at night. He also resurrected three children who had been murdered, and this miraculous act led to his canonization. He became known as Saint Nicholas, the patron saint of children, and Saint Nicholas's Day is December 6. Meanwhile in Norway, legends abound of a benevolent winter spirit with white hair who rides a flying reindeer (or a goat or horse) and leads a procession of spirits across the night sky. He is known as Sinterklaas, and he brings luck to all who need it during the winter months. His day, likewise, is December 6. Of course, the legend of the bearded, flying winter spirit began with Odin astride his eight-legged horse, Sleipnir.

If both Sinterklaas and Saint Nicholas's days are December 6, why do we celebrate Christmas on December 25? That's the date of the Winter Solstice as observed on the Roman Julian calendar—before the Gregorian calendar was adopted. When Constantine made Christianity the official state religion, declaring the solstice as the presumed date of the birth of Jesus was easy. The rest, as they say, is history.

Imbolc, February 2

Imbolc is when the world really starts coming back to life. Ewes are pregnant with lambs (indeed the Celtic origin of the word *imbolg* means "in the belly"), and cows, ewes, and other animals are heavy with milk (which gives us the Gaelic translation *oimelc*, or "mother's milk").

Imbolc is closely associated with one specific deity, Brigid, and she is also known as Saint Bridget. Brigid is, among other things, the Celtic goddess of birth, fertility, inspiration, forge craft and metalsmithing, and domestic arts like cooking and healing. With her guidance, it is possible to begin anew as the world reawakens.

Imbolc is also believed to be when the Cailleach, the divine hag of Gaelic tradition, gathers her firewood for the rest of the winter. Legend has it that if she wishes to make the winter last a good while longer, she will make sure the weather on Imbolc is bright and sunny, so she can gather plenty of firewood. Therefore, people would be relieved if Imbolc was a day of foul weather, as it means the Cailleach is asleep and winter is almost over. This is reflected in many other means of weather prognostication, including an irascible little rodent in Pennsylvania. If he sees his shadow, it's said that there will be six more weeks of winter. But if you look at the calendar, you'll notice that the first day of spring is March 21—six weeks away—so you're getting six more weeks of winter no matter what you do!

The Imbolc revival cycle can also be seen in the Greek myth of Persephone. The virgin goddess was abducted by Hades in the autumn, and Demeter, goddess of the earth, mourns for the loss of her daughter. Her sorrow brings the cold touch of winter, and she threatens never to allow warmth to return until her daughter is returned. Persephone's return from the underworld is celebrated at Imbolc.

Magickal rites performed at Imbolc include purification, reaffirmation and rededication, and picking up those New Year's resolutions you dropped. Some Witches honour Imbolc by going on a fast, eating no meat until Ostara.

The Wiccan myth cycle, I'm sure you've already guessed, is that the young Lord and Lady are reawakening with the revival of the year. There's much to do!

Ostara, March 21

Ostara, the Spring Equinox, marks the beginning of spring. The days have been gradually getting longer since Yule, and now the world stands at the point of equal night and equal day, and the air is charged with the promise of fertility and abundance, bringing alive promises made at Imbolc. According to sociologist J. P. Mallory, Ostara and Easter are both named after Eostre, the Germanic goddess of the dawn, whose presence signifies the return of life and vitality to the world.[74] Like many of the sabbats, it shares a date and some similarities with a Christian equivalent, and as in most of those scenarios, the Christianized version borrows heavily from the Pagan. This is especially obvious with Ostara and Easter. Both Easter and Ostara celebrate rebirth and rejuvenation. The world is coming back to life, and Christians believe that Jesus is resurrected after his sacrificial crucifixion.

Incidentally if Christmas, the alleged day of Christ's birth, is always December 25, then why does Easter, the date of his crucifixion and resurrection, hop all over the calendar? The answer to that is another clue to the Pagan origins of Easter. Ostara is celebrated on the Spring Equinox, and many times the celebrations would continue until the next full moon. During the Council of Nicaea in 325 CE, it was decided that Easter should always held on the first Sunday after the first full moon following the Spring Equinox. Go check the calendar!

If Easter is the time of Christ's resurrection, then what's with all the Easter eggs and bunnies and chicks? Well, they, of course, are ancient fertility symbols. Eggs because they hold new life in their fragile shells and the yolk resembles a little shining sun, and rabbits because the rabbit is one of very few animals that can conceive while already pregnant!

---

74. Mallory and Adams, *Encyclopedia of Indo-European Culture*, 148–49.

Magicks performed at Ostara include spells of renewal, balance, and fertility.

Within the Wiccan goddess and god myth cycle, the young goddess and the young god are both blossoming into their vibrant selves as the Wheel of the Year continues to turn.

Beltane, May 1

Beltane, one of the greater sabbats, is also known as May Eve, Walpurgisnacht, or Baltein. It has been observed since ancient times with great bonfires. Beltane rites celebrate fertility, love, and the blossoming of life as personified in the passions of the Lord and Lady. Children conceived at Beltane are said to be "goddess blessed." Traditionally celebrations began at dusk on Beltane Eve and lasted twenty-four hours. This is the sabbat of blossoming powers and awakened fertility. Beltane is one of the oldest sabbats (some call it the "original" sabbat) and the counterpart to Samhain. Beltane is named for Ba'al, the Mesopotamian god of fire, and celebrates heat, passion, cleansing, and flame. Large bale fires were burned in his honour, and the word *bale*, as in *hay bale*, comes from his name.

One common activity at Beltane celebrations is the maypole dance. A tall pole has dozens of colourful ribbons hanging from the top, and people hold them and dance around the pole in two directions, deosil (clockwise) and widdershins (counterclockwise). They alternate as they pass, over and under each other, and a complex web of colour is woven around the pole. In rural European villages, the decorated maypole was carried with great fanfare to the village or town square where it was joyfully erected. The maypole has much deeper symbolism than just a children's game. The maypole represents the lingam, or phallus, of the god thrust into the goddess. The dance is a raising of magick and spirit—and heart rates—as the web of life is spun around the spirit of the gods. It should be noted that the judges and scribes of the Inquisition found no fault in such "heathen acts." After all, such customs were established tradition!

Litha, June 21

Litha takes place on the Summer Solstice, the longest day of the year. The powers and vitality of nature are at their peak. On this day the Lord and Lady consummate their marriage (although some traditions see this as a Beltane observance), and the earth is saturated with their embrace.

Litha is a popular festival and a day of sun worship in many parts of the Northern Hemisphere. The peak of power of the sun god is manifested in flourishing crops and livestock, participants enjoy a great feast, and bonfires burn well into the night to celebrate the world's vitality.

Litha is a good time to work on emotional or dream-related magick and spells devoted to the fulfillment of life. Life-altering decisions are not to be ignored, and spells devoted to such changes are best started at Litha. The faerie realm is said to be very active at Litha; if you notice keys missing or pets behaving abnormally or strangely, elfin spirits are active in your home. You might appease them by offering simple gifts of shiny or playful objects left on the doorstep.

The name Litha, incidentally, is relatively new. It has been known for centuries as midsummer or midsommar, but German Neopagans borrowed the name from an account by Anglo-Saxon scholar Bede.[75]

A popular midsummer chant comes from Rudyard Kipling's book *Puck of Pook's Hill*:

Oh, do not tell the Priest of our Art,
For he would call it sin;
But we shall be out in the woods all night,
A' conjuring summer in.
And we bring you news, by word of mouth,
For women, cattle and corn,
Now is the Sun come up from the South,
With Oak and Ash and Thorn![76]

Lughnassadh or Lammas, August 1 or 2

The word *Lughnassadh* (LOO-nah-sad) comes from the ancient Gaelic. Lugh was a Gaelic sun god, and the leader of the Irish fey people, the Danaan. The term *Tuatha de Danaan* means "people of Danaan."

Lughnassadh began, according to legend, as a celebration honouring Tailtiu, Lugh's mother. She had exhausted herself preparing the grain for harvest season, so this festival—the first of three—honours her and her sacrifice. Lughnassadh would be a time of feasting, celebration, games of athletic competition, and drinking.

Lughnassadh is traditionally the time of the first harvest, when the first fruits are brought in and the first grain harvested. These were often regarded as offerings to

---

75. Cantrell, *Wiccan Belief and Practices*, 104.
76. Kipling, *Puck of Pook's Hill*, 29.

Lugh. Even though the bounty was enjoyed by all, the spirit of the harvest was his tithe. The time of first harvest is also when the first loaves are baked from the harvested grains. These first loaves are regarded as magickal, containing the full potency of the Lord and Lady. A piece of each loaf is customarily broken off and dropped on the ground or buried.

This sabbat is commonly known as either Lughnassadh or Lammas, but really the two are separate events. Lammas is a Christian harvest observance held at the same time. The name comes from the Middle English words for *loaf* and *mass*.

Mabon, September 21

Mabon, or the second harvest, is held on the Autumn Equinox, when the days and nights are again equally balanced. The Horned God is still with us, but his strength is diminishing. Older now, he looks to Samhain, which will be when he crosses through the veil until his rebirth at Yule.

Mabon is the time of the completion of magickal workings begun at Litha and the winding down of the year. The equal opposite of Ostara, Mabon is the time of settling old debts and obligations and of making peace with oneself. Mabon is the time of earth-related magick, taking long walks in the woods, and devoting time to reflection and self-examination. Decorations for the Mabon sabbat include leaves in their changing colours, flint corn, and sheaves of wheat.

The name Mabon is very new; the sabbat was named after the Welsh legendary figure Mabon ap Modron by Aidan Kelly in 1970.[77]

And, so, we return to Samhain one year later.

The Witches' Calendar Today

The Wheel of the Year and its sabbats are a poetic representation of the changing seasons and the growth, courtship, and love of the Lord and Lady. The sabbats are often presented as agricultural festivals with harvests, plantings, and fertility celebrations, and the Wheel of the Year is a mirror of the creative cycle of the world, which is manifest in all living things. Trees flourish in the spring and lose their leaves in the fall, and many animals give birth, mate, and hibernate at specific times during the year. Likewise, ideas and plans are best started in the summer when the creative spirit is at its peak. Litha, it

---

77. Zell-Ravenheart and Zell-Ravenheart, *Creating Circles & Ceremonies*, 227.

is said, is the best time to begin works of high magick, and Mabon is the best time to resolve them. It is unwise to start any major plans between Samhain and Yule. This is when the ebb and flow of the creative spirit is at its lowest. Despite the seemingly appropriate image of initiating Witches into a coven at Samhain, this is best left until Beltane, when the world's vitality is bursting forth.

Observant students will by now have commented that the seasons are reversed in the Southern Hemisphere with Yule at midsummer. They're not wrong.

With a little introspection and imagination, the Wheel of the Year can easily be applied to life today. We may not all be farmers or hunters, but we are all part of the living world, with dreams, ideas, and goals. The sabbats are as real as the world around you.

Lesson 9: Study Prompts and Questions

An Overview of the Witches' Calendar
- List the eight sabbats in order with the appropriate dates.
- What is the difference between greater and lesser sabbats, and which is which?

Samhain
- What is the significance of Samhain?
- Explain the concept behind the "veil between the worlds" and the importance of honouring the dead.

Yule
- Describe the meaning of Yule.
- Who are the Oak King and the Holly King? Why do they fight?
- If Yule is so close to the customary New Year's Eve, then why is Samhain seen as the Witches' New Year?

Imbolc
- What is the meaning of Imbolc?
- Name two other observances that take place at this time.

Ostara
- Why is dawn significant at Ostara?
- Who is Ostara/Easter allegedly named after?
- If Christmas is always December 25, why does the date of Easter observance hop all over the calendar?

Beltane
- What is the origin of the name Beltane?
- Why are Beltane observances like the maypole dances significant?

Litha
- What aspect of the god's life cycle is recognized at this sabbat?
- What mythical battle is reenacted in some traditions, and what does it mean?

Lughnassadh or Lammas
- Who is this sabbat named after and why?
- What is the symbolism of "first harvest"? Why is this important?
- Provide another name often given to this sabbat and the significance behind that name.

Mabon
- Mabon is known as "second harvest." Explain what this means.
- What personal obligations are commonly observed at this time?

The Witches' Calendar Today
- Do you think observing the sabbats is important in the twenty-first-century world? Why or why not?
- How can the meanings of the sabbats be applied to making plans and decisions?

Lesson 9: Recommended Reading
- *Eight Sabbats for Witches* by Janet and Stewart Farrar
- *Witch's Wheel of the Year: Rituals for Circles, Solitaries & Covens* by Jason Mankey

LESSON 10
The Esbats and Other Lunar Mysteries

We've gone through the Wheel of the Year and learned about the sabbats. But there's another wheel of sorts, and it's that of the thirteen named moons of the year. Here we'll learn the different names of the moon and look at some possible lunar-centric meditations.

The Thirteen Esbats

Traditionally esbats are the Witches' full moon celebrations. Whereas the sabbats honour the Lord and Lady through the seasons of the year, the esbats focus on the Witches' connection with the world, magick, and each other, and they are held for two reasons: to honour the gods, especially goddesses attributed to the moon, such as Hecate or Diana, and to celebrate and explore the life, magick, and mystery of the Craft. The word *esbat* comes from the French *s'esbattre*, which loosely translates to "frolic joyfully."

Alert students will recall this line from the Charge of the Goddess: Whenever you have need of anything, once in the month, and better it be when the moon is full, then shall ye assemble in some secret place to adore the spirit of Me, who am Queen of all the Wise.[78] Today esbats need not be in "some secret place," and usually the Priestess's home is acceptable. Meeting on the night of the full moon, however, is preferable, and meeting outside is best, weather permitting.

If meeting on the exact night of the full moon is impossible, most Witches prefer to meet before the full moon and as close to the specific date as possible. Some Witches celebrate twice a month—on both the full and the new moons.

---

78. Valiente, "The Charge of the Goddess."

Witches' esbats are dedicated to the thirteen full moons of the year, which are:

Moon Month	Craft Name[79]	Farmer's Almanac Name[80]	Goddess
January	wolf	wolf	Inanna
February	chaste	snow	Februa
March	seed	worm	Persephone
April	hare	pink	Isis
May	dyad	flower	Sappha
June	mead	strawberry	Hera
July	wort	buck	Cybele
August	barley	sturgeon	Selene
September	wine	corn	Demeter
October	blood	hunter's	Artemi
November	snow	beaver	Hecate
December	oak	cold	Minerva
thirteenth	Witches'	(no name)	(no name)

The phrase *blue moon* has two meanings. It can either mean the thirteenth moon of the year or the second full moon in a single month. A black moon, by contrast, is the second new moon in a single month. In such cases, the esbat is often dedicated to life's deeper mysteries rather than a simple celebration.

Moon Phases and Meditations

Many of the world's cultures share a common belief that rituals held during different phases of the moon can have significant results. Rituals for gain or benefit are best performed during the waxing moon, as it grows from new to full, and rituals for banishment or reduction should be performed when the moon goes from full to new. Naturally full moon rituals, performed when the moon is at its brightest, would benefit taking control of oneself or a situation or adding "oomph" to a spell.

---

79. Moura, *Grimoire of the Green Witch*, 68.
80. K, *CovenCraft*, 148.

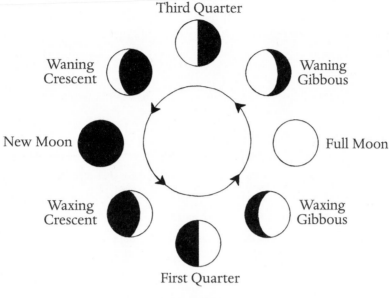

Moon Phases

Beyond rituals, simple meditative exercises during different phases of the moon can have similar benefits. Here are a few possible exercises one might perform:

Full Moon Meditations
- To realize one's potential
- To welcome change and new possibilities

Waning Moon Meditations
- To rid oneself of unwanted emotional burdens or stress
- To change or overcome a bad habit

New Moon Meditations
- To accept or come to terms with a loss, such as the passing of a loved one
- To start anew

Waxing Moon Meditations
- To find the courage to move forward with a plan or commitment
- To accept a positive change; if you're generally apprehensive about believing that good things could come to you, this could be quite a rewarding exercise.

In all of these, the meditation procedure is basically the same even though the desired results could be dramatically different.

First, find a spot where you can relax and lie back undisturbed. If possible, it should be somewhere that the moon shines on you. An open window is good; being outside is better. Get comfy.

Light a white candle, and let it burn for a moment. Make sure that the candle is somewhere safe should it tip over.

Close your eyes, relax, and breathe deeply and slowly for a minute or two. Whisper to yourself or say out loud, "Mother Moon, goddess of magick, let me be one with you. Let me accept these changes I desire. Let the magick flow through me."

Spend a few moments contemplating the result you're looking for. In your mind's eye, see it already happening. Be comfortable with what you visualize.

When you are ready, give thanks, and open your eyes.

Be sure to put your candle out. We'll be looking at candle magick in lesson 35.

The Moon and Magick

The moon has always had a remarkable effect on people and animals. Many pet owners comment on their pets' odd behavior during full moons, and many a Witch experiences heightened magickal awareness when the moon is in its prime. If the moon has such an effect on humans, life, and the earth itself, it's easy to see why it plays such an important role in magick. The moon is a principal aspect of Witchcraft, from denoting when spells and rituals should be performed to enacting rites of divination and communing with the gods themselves. As a rule, spells for prosperity, luck, and other positive goals are best performed when the moon is going from new to full. The closer to a full moon, the better. Spells for banishment and to overcome bad habits are best performed when the moon is growing darker.

Moon-mirrors are often used in divination. A moon-mirror, or scrying mirror, can be any dark, reflective surface, such as a still pool of water or a black or copper disk. As with a crystal ball, you don't actually see anything "in" the mirror, but by watching the mirror and nothing else, you can allow your gaze to unfocus so images from your subconscious are allowed to appear. The art of scrying will be studied later, in lesson 21, but in general it's the ability to focus beyond sight, letting your subconscious show what your eyes often fail to see.

There is a ritual performed at full moon rites known as Drawing Down the Moon. In such ceremonies, the High Priestess stands ready and receptive as a coven member guides the power and energy of the moon goddess into her, allowing the wisdom of the deity to flow through her words. In a way, it's similar to some Christian rites in which people start "speaking in tongues." Since the Priestess draws the goddess into her, not merely into a ritual setting, this is not recommended for anyone without proper training and control. The experience can leave some people disoriented, dazed, or nauseous. You'll learn how to ground and center in lesson 29.

Mysteries of the Moon

What do we know about the moon? While its origin is only theorized, we do know quite a lot about it. It is roughly one-quarter the size of the earth, and it has one-sixth the gravity. The moon's orbit affects the earth, and the ocean's tides are dictated by the moon's position. It has no light of its own. The moon's radiance is merely reflected from the sun. The earth's position between the sun and the moon defines its phase, and the moon's position between the earth and the sun defines the eclipses.

For many millennia, the changing face of the moon has fascinated and intrigued people in every part of the world. It was once thought that looking into the face of the moon would drive one mad; from *lunar* we get the words *lunacy* and *lunatic*. Schizophrenic behavior was often blamed on the moon, and medieval scientists even went so far as to dissect the human brain to see if its twin lobes matched the light and dark moons.

Although studies haven't found any reliable and significant correlation, it does often seem that there are more violent crimes committed by people and aberrant behavior exhibited by animals during the full moon.

Lesson 10: Study Prompts and Questions

The Thirteen Esbats
- List the names of the thirteen esbats in Craft and common terms.
- In what way do esbats differ from sabbats?
- What is a blue moon?

Moon Phases and Meditations
- What moon phases are beneficial to what sort of meditation or spellwork?

The Moon and Magick

- Briefly explain why the moon's phase is important in planning spells.
- Describe what a moon-mirror is and how it works.
- Why is a Drawing Down the Moon ritual best left to qualified experts?

Mysteries of the Moon

- Explain how the full moon seems to affect some people.

Lesson 10: Recommended Reading

- *Many Moons: The Myth and Magic, Fact and Fantasy of Our Nearest Heavenly Body* by Diana Brueton
- *Moon Magic: A Handbook of Lunar Cycles, Lore, and Mystical Energies* by Aurora Kane

LESSON 11
Principles of Wiccan Belief

In the 1960s Wicca and the Craft enjoyed unprecedented growth, acceptance, and popularity. It was as if shaking off the shackles of history had breathed new life into the Old Religion. People were coming together from a myriad of different paths and traditions, celebrating their differences and similarities, but at the same time, gross misunderstandings about the Craft threatened to weaken its newfound freedom, and glory seekers threatened to undermine its legitimacy.

Obviously something had to be done. In April 1974 the self-appointed Council of American Witches convened to discuss and establish a list of fundamental guidelines for the Craft. They were careful to clarify this as "American" Witchcraft, as such guidelines might be rebuffed by Italian Strega or English family covens who had practiced in secrecy and followed their own guidelines.

The Council, which was hosted by Carl Weschcke, founder of Llewellyn Worldwide, ran from April 11 to 14 in Minneapolis, Minnesota.

In this lesson, I will list each article, as written in Chas Clifton's *Witchcraft Today, Book One*, in italics followed by my own interpretation and analysis.[81]

Part 1: The Preamble

The Council of American Witches finds it necessary to define modern Witchcraft in terms of the American experience and needs.

We are not bound by traditions from other times and other cultures, and owe no allegiance to any person or power greater than the Divinity manifest through our own being.

As American Witches we welcome and respect all teachings and traditions and seek to learn from all and to contribute our learning to all who may seek it.

---

81. Clifton, *Witchcraft Today, Book One*, 19–20.

It is in this spirit of welcome and cooperation that we adopt these few principles of Wiccan belief. In seeking to be inclusive, we do not wish to open ourselves to the destruction of our group by those on self-serving power trips, or to philosophies and practices contradictory to those principles. In seeking to exclude those whose ways are contradictory to ours, we do not want to deny participation with us to any who are sincerely interested in our knowledge or beliefs.

We therefore ask only that those who seek to identify with us accept those few basic principles.

The Articles and an Analysis

1) *We practice rites to attune ourselves with the natural rhythm of life forces marked by the full of the Moon and the seasonal quarters and cross-quarters.*

    As Witches we live in harmony with the cycle of nature and observe the seasonal changes with rituals and celebrations.

2) *We recognize that our intelligence gives us a unique responsibility toward our environment. We seek to live in harmony with Nature, in ecological balance offering fulfilment to life and consciousness within an evolutionary concept.*

    As sentient beings we realize that humankind, in its common greed and corruption, poses a threat to the balance of nature. As Witches we realize that it is our duty to our Mother to strive to maintain that balance. As humans, we seek fulfillment in our lives and a purpose to our future.

3) *We acknowledge a depth of power far greater than that apparent to the average person. Because it is far greater than ordinary, it is sometimes called "supernatural," but we see it as lying within that which is naturally potential to us all.*

    We recognize the existence of a power, manifest in every living thing, which some consider as "supernatural" or "otherworldly." We see it as a factor of our everyday lives.

4) *We conceive of the Creative Power in the Universe as manifesting through polarity—as masculine and feminine—and that this same Creative Power lives in all people, and functions through the masculine and feminine. We value neither above the other.*

Life, in all forms, exists in a balance. The polarity of male and female and light and dark is integral to this balance. None is greater than the other.

5) *We value sexuality as pleasure, as the symbol and embodiment of life, and as the interaction source of energies used in magical practice and religious worship.*

Sexuality is neither taboo nor frowned upon. Rather, it is seen as an act of love, pleasure, and divine grace. To some, sex can be used for magickal power raising. To others, sex should be special, intimate, and shared with loved ones, not used to further one's magickal prowess. Sex used as a form of religious worship is acceptable as long as all parties concerned recognize the intent and purpose within which the act is performed.

6) *We recognize both an outer and an inner, or psychological world—sometimes known as the Spiritual World, the Collective Unconscious, The Inner Planes, etc.—and we see in the interaction of these two dimensions the basis for paranormal phenomena and magical exercises. We neglect neither dimension for the other, seeing both as necessary for our fulfilment.*

As magickally aware beings we recognize the existence of a spiritual or a collective unconscious world, which exists hand in hand with the material world. Neither can supersede the other, and we should not focus on one to the extent of ignoring the other. The harmonic balance and interrelationship of these two planes of existence is integral to the working of magick and of other metaphysical events. Neither plane can exist without the other. This, again, shows the balance of all things in life.

7) *We do not recognize any authoritarian hierarchy, but do honor those who teach, respect those who share their greater knowledge and wisdom, and acknowledge those who courageously give of themselves in leadership.*

As Witches we do not follow an organized religion; ours is an ancient, primarily oral tradition without a specific hierarchy or chain of command. While we do have laws and codes of conduct and roles within the coven, we do not have a specific corporate infrastructure. There are those in the Craft who have more experience and more knowledge to offer; we acknowledge their wisdom and cherish their teachings, but they are no more powerful than any other members of the Craft.

8) *We see religion, magic, and wisdom in living as being united in the way one views the world and lives within it—a world view and philosophy of life which we identify as Witchcraft, the Wiccan Way.*

Our religion is not separate from our everyday lives; it is an integral part of our lives from everyday actions to specific acts of worship. We strive to live and share our talents and gifts in a way that is harmonious to all and in accordance with the teachings and philosophies of the Craft.

9) *Calling oneself "Witch" does not make a Witch—but neither does heredity itself nor the collecting of titles, degrees, and initiations. A Witch seeks to control the forces within her/himself that make life possible in order to live wisely and well, without harm to others and in harmony with Nature.*

One cannot become a Witch by simply deciding "Today I am a Witch." Neither does claiming a hereditary lineage or having a collection of titles and degrees make one a Witch. While being initiated into the Craft is recognized as an achievement, it does not imply that we have truly learned to live the Craft of the Wise. Living as a Witch is an ongoing process with occasional moments of merit and recognition. Being a Witch means being able to live in harmony with nature, to cherish the gifts the goddess gives us, and to harness and wisely use the magickal forces within us. Ours is not always an easy road and one not traveled lightly.

10) *We believe in the affirmation and fulfilment of life in a continuation of evolution and development of consciousness giving meaning to the Universe we know and our personal role within it.*

Life's a journey, not a destination.

11) *Our only animosity towards Christianity, or towards any other religion or philosophy of life, is to the extent that its institutions have claimed to be "the only way" and have sought to deny freedom to others and to suppress other ways of religious practices and belief.*

The Christian church is not our enemy. We recognize all life-affirming faiths as valid, and we support everyone's right to find their own spiritual path, whether it mirrors ours or not. The only argument we have with the Christian church is the idea that theirs is the "only way" and that unless we forgo our spiritual path to follow theirs, we are judged wrong and must suffer the same fate as their wrongdoers.

12) *As American Witches we are not threatened by debates on the history of the Craft, the origins of various terms, the legitimacy of various aspects of different traditions. We are concerned only with our present and our future.*

As the documented evidence of the origins of our faith has been (a) lost in the sands of time or (b) intentionally destroyed by malicious forces, we cannot completely vouch for the accuracy of our practices as compared with ancient tradition. Therefore, we see no point in arguing over the origins of our ways or the legitimacy of different traditions. Rather, we strive to share and cherish our differences and look together to the future.

13) *We do not accept the concept of absolute evil nor do we worship any entity known as "Satan" or "the Devil" as defined by the Christian tradition. We do not seek power through the suffering of others nor accept that personal benefit can be derived only by denial to another.*

Despite what the Christian church tries to say about us, we do not follow any personification of evil. Witches do not perceive evil as a force or entity. We tend not worship any Christian figures, either malevolent or benign. Witches do not seek the domination of others, the subjugation of other races or faiths, or the pursuit of personal benefit through the denial or oppression of others.

14) *We believe that we should seek within Nature that which is contributory to our health and well-being.*

    We ascribe to that radical notion that exercise, fresh air and sunshine might actually be good for you. Take a walk along the beach. Dance in the rain. Salads are better for you than gummi bears. You are part of nature—embrace that.

Individual Application and Interpretation

Since Witches place great value on individual freedom and thought, it is only appropriate that each be allowed to interpret the Principles of Wiccan Belief in their own way. Therefore, you should be allowed to create your own interpretation of the articles and determine how they can be applied to your own life. As long as the original meaning and intent of the principles are not compromised, individual interpretation is welcomed.

Lesson 11: Study Prompts and Questions

The Articles and Analysis

- According to the Principles of Wiccan Belief, Wiccans hold rites to attune themselves with what events?
- What do the principles say about an authoritarian hierarchy?
- According to the principles, can one become a Witch simply by saying that they are one?
- According to the principles, what is the Wiccan view of "absolute evil"?
- Compare and contrast the goals of the Council of Nicaea with the goals of the Council of American Witches. What similarities do you see?

Lesson 11: Recommended Reading

- *Drawing Down the Moon: Witches, Druids, Goddess-Worshippers, and Other Pagans in America Today* by Margot Adler
- *Witchcraft Today, Book One: The Modern Craft Movement* edited by Chas Clifton

LESSON 12
The Wiccan Rede, Ethics, and the Magickal Life

The next few lessons in Wicca 101 will focus on the question of ethics and behavior as they relate to various aspects within the Craft. We'll look at ethical considerations regarding love, sexuality, interacting with others, and more.

Introducing the Rede (Short Version)

To start, let's examine a poem by Doreen Valiente that has become fundamental to Wiccan philosophy.

> *Bide the Wiccan Law ye must,*
> *In perfect love, in perfect trust.*
> *Eight words the Wiccan Rede fulfill:*
> *An ye harm none, do what ye will.*
> *Lest in self-defense it be,*
> *Ever mind the Rule of Three:*
> *What ye send out, comes back to thee.*
> *Follow this with mind and heart,*
> *And merry ye meet and merry ye part.*[82]

There is much confusion regarding the origin of the rede; fragments have been ascribed to Aleister Crowley, Doreen Valiente, and Gwen Thompson, among others. The line "An ye harm none, do what ye will" is often attributed to Crowley, who wrote, "An ye harm none, do what thou wilt" in 1904, and the Rule of Three is often regarded as a Wiccan perception of balance, or a Law of Return.[83] The origin of a Rule of Three osten-

---

82. The Doreen Valiente Foundation, *The Wiccan Rede*.
83. Crowley, *The Equinox*, 3.

sibly comes from Rudolf Steiner, who wrote—also in 1904—"For every one step that you take in the pursuit of higher knowledge, take three steps in the perfection of your own character."[84] Although, Steiner's observation is more about personal development than karmic return. The word *rede*, by the way, comes from the Old English word *roedan*, which is the origin of the words *road* and *route*. It translates roughly to "path" or "direction" as well as "advice."[85]

Wherever the threads originated, it is generally accepted that the Wiccan Rede in its current form was first offered by Valiente in 1964.

There are two versions of the rede—one long and one short. The shorter one, a simple poem, is accepted by many as the "Ten Commandments," for lack of a better term, of the Craft. The longer version will be examined later in this lesson.

An Analysis of the Wiccan Rede

In this next section, I'll break the rede down line by line and see how it all fits together.

"Bide the Wiccan Law ye must,"

First of all, the rede is a poem. Unless you're talking about specific legal terminology, poetry sees words like *law*, *creed*, and *vow* as kind of interchangeable as line scheme and rhyme dictate. Wiccans don't think it's really talking about a "law" that you "must" follow. The rede is a poetic presentation of a Wiccan pledge. It's a recommended course of action. It just scans better the way it's written. Besides, the author had to make *must* rhyme with *trust* in line 2.

"In perfect love, in perfect trust."

These words are essentially one of the fundamental guidelines of Wiccan philosophy. They are quoted at initiation, used in ritual, and have become so recognized and accepted as to escape analysis. But since we're here, let's have a look. "Perfect love" is not an easy concept for many; love is often conditional—a compromise. "In perfect love" asks that one's love—to self and to others—be without flaw. Both totally giving and receiving. "Perfect trust" is even harder to grasp. Trust, especially in this day and age, is a hard-won prize. Here it is an understanding that honesty and responsibility can be well

---

84. Steiner, *Knowledge of the Higher Worlds and Its Attainment*, 74.
85. Online Etymology Dictionary, "Rede," accessed October 15, 2022, https://www.etymonline.com/word /rede.

given and well received. Trust is like a two-way street. Or, if you like, a two-edged sword. Can they trust you?

"Eight words the Wiccan Rede fulfill:"

Again, poetic license. The rede is not "fulfilled" in eight words, the rede is merely "established" in eight words. In the final analysis of a Witch's life, the rede might never have been fulfilled—but it was presented to them in this poem.

"An ye harm none, do what ye will."

Many people have a problem with this line. In Craft reckoning, all things deserve respect, and all things have their place in life. To harm "none" means to not harm, hurt, grieve, beset, annoy, badger, harass, disturb, exasperate, bother, worry, vex, torment, ire, anger, or in any way upset any living thing. This is, in normal, everyday life, unavoidable. Here are some examples:

- You do a spellworking to land a cushy job. It works; you get the job. But in so doing, you have denied the job to another, someone you don't even know, who also has bills to pay.
- You inhale and, with every breath, murder thousands of viable airborne microbes. You cad!
- The person behind you in traffic reads your bumper sticker and laughs so hard he spills his coffee in his lap, causing mild burns.
- You get out of the shower. Walking from the bathroom to the bedroom, you cross in front of a window where an old lady happens to glance up and see you naked. She suffers from a weak heart anyway, and the sight of your naked bod puts her over the edge.

In all four examples, you are unaware of the harm you caused, and it's obvious that living a life in which you harm absolutely nobody is impossible. It seems, therefore, that the rede here refers to causing "intentional" harm. Hacking up your neighbour's shrubbery with an axe. Running somebody off the road. Spreading dishonest rumors about a rival coworker. These are harmful acts that can—and should—be avoided. There are also established laws that need to be observed. But as long as you can live your life and be honest with yourself about your intentions, then all is well. You can do whatever you like, as long as you are not breaking laws or intentionally harming others by your actions.

"Lest in self-defense it be,"

Okay, sometimes you have to cause a little harm in self-defense. If you are being attacked by a mugger or other assailant, a blast of pepper spray in their face will cause them harm, but it is for your own protection, and many judges will agree with you. Likewise, if you are being harassed or stalked at work, notifying your superiors might endanger that person's job, but it's for your own protection and, ultimately, theirs.

"Ever mind the Rule of Three:"

The Rule of Three relates to the principle of cause and effect. Materialistically many people regard the ethical perception of cause and effect as "an eye for an eye, a tooth for a tooth." You steal a neighbour's shovel, they steal one back. But that's the rule of one, not three. Look at it this way: if you throw a stone into a pond, ripples spread out from the splash in ever widening circles. Likewise, if you cause harm, the harm affects not just your target but other people they interact with—their friends, family, etc. If you tell a lie and the lie is repeated, other people are affected by your dishonesty, and you could be responsible for the effect it has on all of them. The reverse is also true; if you help others, the rewards are more than compensatory. It could also be considered that the Rule of Three affects you—and others—on multiple levels. It could have an effect on your psyche, your well-being, and your demeanor. The "three" here is a poetic way of describing the ripple effect. It rhymes well with the next line, and the following line is a continuation of this one in more than just rhyme.

"What ye send out, comes back to thee."

This is the essence of the Rule of Three, or the Law of Return, mentioned above. Whatever you do, whatever act or thought you manifest, will return to you "threefold." Do somebody a favor, and you will be rewarded well. You may not be rewarded by material gains but perhaps by reputation or suddenly finding yourself in a less stressful situation. Cause harm to another, and you will ultimately find yourself a recipient of greater harm.

"Follow this with mind and heart,"

The meaning of the rede, not the exact wording, should be followed in word, thought, and action. As written, it is unfeasible, but to follow the meaning and the intent of the rede is a path upon which to safely walk.

"And merry ye meet and merry ye part."

If you live in according to the rede, you may find that others welcome your presence, enjoy your company, and encourage you to return. This is another example of the "What ye send out" line. If you are a likable person, people will like you. In a magickal setting, you will find that working magick is easier if you are of a clear and calm disposition. And of course, "merry meet and merry part" is a standard greeting in almost every Wiccan setting. We greet each other as friends and part ways as friends.

In Summary

All in all, the rede is not a bad poem. Take it with a grain of salt, examine and analyze the words within, and you'll find it offers fair guidance to those of the Craft: live in harmony with yourself and your surroundings, bring joy to those you meet, strive not to do real harm, nurture growth within yourself and others, and you can do anything!

Incidentally some modern Wiccan versions of the rede omit the "self-defense" line. Read it again without that line. Does it change the meaning of the rede?

The Wiccan Rede (Long Version)

Here is the "extended" version of the Wiccan Rede, which was first published in *Green Egg Magazine* in 1975. Author Gwen Thompson attributed it to her grandmother, although that claim has been questioned. This longer version, also called the "Rede of the Wiccae," is a fanciful way of remembering some details of Wiccan lore.

Bide within the Law ye must, in perfect Love and perfect Trust.
Live you must and let to live, fairly take and fairly give.
For tread the Circle thrice about, to keep unwelcome spirits out.
To bind the spell well every time, let the spell be said in rhyme.
Light of eye and soft of touch, speak you little, listen much.
Honor the Old Ones in deed and name, let love and light be our guides again.
Deosil go by the waxing moon, chanting out the joyful tune.
Widdershins go when the moon doth wane, and the werewolf howls by the
*   dread wolfsbane.*
When the Lady's moon is new, kiss the hand to Her times two.
When the moon rides at Her peak, then your heart's desire seek.

Heed the North wind's mighty gale, lock the door and trim the sail.
When the wind blows from the East, expect the new and set the feast.
When the wind comes from the South, love will kiss you on the mouth.
When the wind whispers from the West, all hearts will find peace and rest.

Nine woods in the Cauldron go, burn them fast and burn them slow.
Birch in the fire goes, to reveal what the Lady knows.
Oak in the forest towers with might, in the fire it brings the God's insight.
Rowan is a tree of power, causing life and magick to flower.
Willows at the waterside stand, ready to help us to the Summerland.
Hawthorn is burned to purify, and to draw faerie to your eye.
Hazel, the tree of wisdom and learning, adds its strength to the bright fire burning.
White are the flowers of Apple tree, that brings us fruits of fertility.
Grapes grow upon the vine, giving us both joy and wine.
Fir does mark the evergreen, to represent immortality seen.
Elder is the Lady's tree, burn it not or cursed you'll be.

Four times the Major Sabbats mark, in the light and in the dark.
As the old year starts to wane, the new begins, it's now Samhain.
When the time for Imbolc shows, watch for flowers through the snows.
When the wheel begins to turn, soon the Beltane fires will burn.
As the wheel turns to Lammas night, power is brought to magick rite.
Four times the Minor Sabbats fall, use the Sun to mark them all.
When the wheel has turned to Yule, light the log the Horned One rules.
In the spring, when night equals day, time for Ostara to come our way.
When the Sun has reached its height, time for Oak and Holly to fight.
Harvesting comes to one and all, when the Autumn Equinox does fall.

Heed the flower, bush, and tree, and by the Lady blessed you'll be.
Where the rippling waters go, cast a stone, the truth you'll know.
When you have and hold a need, harken not to others' greed.
With a fool no season spend, or be counted as his friend.
Merry Meet and Merry Part, bright the cheeks and warm the heart.
Mind the Three-fold Law you should, three times bad and three times good.

When misfortune is enow, wear the star upon your brow.
Be true in love this you must do, unless your love is false to you.
These eight words the Rede fulfill: An ye harm none, do what ye will.[86]

Ethics and the Magickal Life

Now that you've read the rede, you might be thinking, "What about those ethics you mentioned?" or "What do ethics and knowing right from wrong mean to a Witch?"

First off, honesty is a major concern. A good Witch must be willing to be honest with themselves first. Shakespeare said it best: "This above all: to thine own self be true." If you are not willing to be honest with yourself, how can you hope to work magick for others or face the gods? Witches should not be selfish or vain and should not enter the Craft looking for free sex, an ego boost, or a way to manipulate others. The Craft is not a get-rich-quick scheme and should not be used for fun. Being a Witch—and having the knowledge of magick, metaphysics, and parapsychology that Witches do—means having enough of a sense of responsibility and self-control not to abuse it. It is a gift or a talent—certainly not a publicity stunt.

Also remember that a Witch is held responsible for every action taken. In many Christian denominations a person has to atone for their actions after their death. For many Witches, the repercussions can seem immediate. For example, a Witch steals something expensive from work, and on the way home, their car breaks down. Or the Witch fakes an illness to get a day off work, and they then lose two more days because they really did get sick. For many Witches, the honesty factor is almost palpable. Given the opportunity to take advantage of an unethical situation, many Witches claim to feel almost physically nauseous when acting on it or even when contemplating the action. If a Witch buys something from a shop and notices that the cashier has given them too much change back, they will usually correct the cashier's mistake rather than take the extra money. They will do this for two reasons. One, the idea of taking the money gives them that funky, nauseous feeling. Two, they know that if they take it, Loki, Coyote, or somebody else is going to have fun with them later to teach them a lesson. Better safe than sorry.

How should a Witch or Wiccan behave? Let's look at a couple of hypothetical situations and see how Craft ethics can be applied:

---

86. Thompson, *The Wiccan Rede*.

- A close friend asks your opinion of her new dress. Your first reaction is: "It makes you look like a couch!" But do you tell her this? How well do you know her? Will she accept such an answer? Honesty is always the preferred policy but so is tact, and brutal honesty might cause more harm than any good. You might say: "That's a good colour for you." or "It really complements your eyes."

- A friend asks you for a love spell; she has met a man that she wants to seduce. Love spells or spells to influence a third party are a big issue in the Wiccan community; Witches value personal freedom and free will very highly. After so many years of persecution and subjugation, free will is a prime concern, and to put a spell on another person without their permission is a violation of their free will. "Harm none." The honest Witch will refuse to aid her friend. Instead, you could cast a love spell of a different sort. Rather than putting a spell on some guy to fall for your friend, you could cast a spell on her—with her permission—to make her more receptive to love. She may even wind up meeting a better person than the one she had an eye for.

- You are loading several heavy boxes onto the back of a truck. A friend offers to help. You know that he is rather clumsy and accident prone. He might slip and drop a box, hurting himself or damaging the contents of the box. But to refuse his help will hurt his feelings. This is a case where you simply must be honest. "I don't want to hurt your feelings, but I'm worried you might get hurt." Both he and the boxes will survive unscathed.

In all these situations, a choice had to be made. Ethics questions can run the gamut from critiquing a friend's dress sense to aiding in life-and-death situations. Try to determine where and when help is appropriate, and if you don't know, don't help.

On a slightly more serious note, consider the following applications. Note that these subjects are very personal and controversial for many people, and you may wish to skip over these altogether. That's quite all right.

The following situations are very real aspects of modern life that almost everyone has an opinion about. Should a murderer, for example, be put to death? Is it right to aid another's intentional demise? And is it wrong to end a pregnancy? Let's examine these one at a time and look at the common Wiccan perspective. Your opinion may differ; that's okay.

Murder and Capital Punishment

Should a killer be killed? A lot of people oppose capital punishment. "You're killing people to show that killing people is wrong." Many Witches feel it depends on the circumstances. A man gets drunk in a bar, a fight gets out of hand, and the night ends with a body in the parking lot. That's nowhere near as bad as a serial killer who murders two dozen people and sexually violates the bodies. The man from the bar did not deserve to die, but neither does his drunken attacker. The serial killer, however, has stepped so far beyond normal behavior that he has violated the sacred trust in him as a living being.

What about a woman who accidentally kills someone who threatened her children? Here, her behavior mirrors natural behavior and what a mother bear might do to protect her cubs. It was defensive.

How about a soldier who kills in the line of duty? Ironically, many Witches, who respect and revere life, would not voluntarily join any armed forces in the first place. For those who do, they see their sense of duty as part of their wyrd. Still, many Witches in the armed forces prefer noncombat roles, such as medical support or supply. Witches who do face the possibility of combat recognize two things. They understand that the possibility of taking another person's life could arise and that the divine essence in the other person's life is immortal and that just the body, the physical shell, is taken. Besides, the Witch also knows that the other person understood the risks involved before joining *their* own armed forces.

Suicide

When it comes to suicide, is it your right to take your own life? Is it right to aid another in doing the same? Most people disapprove of suicide; it is a betrayal of that divine trust. An honest Witch will say that unless an irreversible medical condition is involved, suicide should not be considered an option. Depression, financial woes, an abusive marriage—these are all things that can be overcome. In the matter of medically assisted suicide, every case so far has involved some terminal illness with physical anguish that medical science can offer no relief from.[87] Rather than just fading away slowly and painfully, most Witches support the idea of facing death on one's own terms with knowledge and forethought. It's not seen as "giving up." Instead, it is an honourable, courageous decision to cross the veil.

---

87. "The Right to Die with Dignity."

Abortion

The topic of abortion is a difficult one for almost every religion. Many followers of the Craft, who revere the life in all things, see it this way: just as the goddess first became aware of the presence of the god in her womb at Yule, so do Witches recognize the spirit of life in theirs. For Witches, life does not begin at conception, nor at birth, but at a crucial point in between. You see, the question of abortion ties very closely with the concept of reincarnation, which almost every Witch holds as being self-evident. (We will study the concept of reincarnation, and its relevance to the Craft, in lesson 15.) And remember, Witches do not shy away from the concept of psychic awareness; we embrace it.

On the subject of abortion, the important question to ask is this: Has the new incarnate soul "moved in" yet? If it has, then the occupant of the individual's womb is a living being and should be protected. If not, then the fetus is still just a "vessel," and the pregnant person has the right to decide what to do with it. Granted, there are some who cannot tell when a soul has taken residence, and in those cases, a line should be drawn. Even if the individual is not consciously aware of the arrival of the soul, you can often hear how their reaction to the pregnancy changes. This is usually most obvious when they are explaining it to children. One week, the expecting individual might say, "I'm going to have a baby," and the next, they say, "There's a little person growing inside me." Whether they realize it or not, they have subconsciously become aware of another presence in their womb. If the expecting individual cannot tell whether the fetus has received a soul yet, it is generally accepted by the medical community that any time up to eleven weeks after the last period, an abortion is safe. Any later than that and there exists the possibility of harm to the pregnant person. It is also possible that complications of the pregnancy itself could put the pregnant person at risk, and aborting the fetus would save their life rather than risk losing both.

Eating Meat

And finally, here is one that many will vehemently disagree on. Is it ethical or does it cause harm to eat meat? Some will say that the animal was, of course, harmed; it is dead now. Others will argue that plants have as much feeling, emotion, and right to exist as animals do and that vegetarians or vegans are no better. Who is right? The human digestive system is designed—normally—to process both plant and animal matter, so it's usually not a question of diet, but a personal, moral choice. This is one only you can answer for yourself.

In Summary

I want to state again, the opinions as stated above are the general consensus, not absolutes. You are welcome to disagree if your gut tells you to.

Now on to a lighter topic.

Manifesting Divinity Within and Without

Let's take a look at how to live a spiritual life. To start, here's a quote I'm very fond of from Pierre Teilhard de Chardin:

> *"We are not material beings living a spiritual life,*
> *we are spiritual beings living a material life."* [88]

If we are indeed spiritual beings living a material life, how do we relate to the world around us or within us? How do we relate to the gods that live within us?

We know that every culture in human history has, at some point, worshipped and revered gods, and gods influence every aspect of our lives. How does one manifest a god within? In polytheistic terms, each god has specific realms of influence. The Egyptian goddess Bastet, for example, is the protector of cats and embodies the nurturing aspects of motherhood. Dagda is a strong Celtic warrior god and a vibrant father figure. Every deity is a multifaceted being and has wisdom and lessons to offer us. While many monotheists may deny it, many a Witch will tell you that the spirit of every deity exists in every living thing. A tree may not look very feline, but the spirit of Bastet can be found in its living energy, and even though a televangelist may ardently deny it, they can work with the wisdom of Hecate, the goddess of magick and Witchcraft. The wisdom of the gods is available to us if we merely acknowledge it. The trick is to tap into that part of them within ourselves.

We are the gods made manifest, and our actions reflect their presence within us. When I need courage, I call upon Tyr. When I need compassion, I call upon Kuan Yin. When I need to stop a moment and remember to laugh at myself, I call upon Ganesha.

On a deeper level, every person embodies aspects both masculine and feminine. In the modern world, we are often taught that people are all one gender or the other, and some people claim that aspects like homosexuality are merely aberrant behavior. Most Witches embrace the full realm of humanity and recognize both the male and female within every living thing. Every human has feminine aspects and masculine aspects. An

---

88. Furey, *The Joy of Kindness*, 138.

important lesson for men studying the Craft to remember is to embrace their feminine side, not shun it. Aphrodite has as much to teach about life as Thor and vice versa. To fully taste the waters of life, we must be willing to embrace every aspect of ourselves—male and female, god and goddess, warrior, healer, trickster, muse, and faery—and not ignore those facets of our spirit that others might think odd.

If we honour the gods within ourselves, we must also honour them in others. Every living thing is a vibrant, magickal being with energy and vitality, and it is only right to respect them as such. By this reason, no one individual is better than any other. While it may seem that a Hollywood celebrity or an elected official has more to offer than the average person, all are living entities that are worthy of love and compassion. The divine spirit exists within all living things. Some religions say that God exists as a separate entity in another place, and our goal as humans is to reach that place. In the Craft, it is understood that the gods exist in all places, at all times, and in every living thing. We are ourselves little gods and goddesses, growing into our full potential. To harm another is to harm that divine spark inside.

Lesson 12: Study Prompts and Questions

Wiccan Rede
- Who originally wrote the Wiccan Rede?
- What eight-word line is the foundation of the rede?

An Analysis of the Wiccan Rede
- Write your own analysis of the rede. You can break it down line by line or paraphrase the whole thing in your own words.
- How would you explain the rede to a Christian, a Muslim, or an atheist? Give examples of what you might say.

The Wiccan Rede (Long Version)
- The long rede speaks of many different things. What does it say to do on the different phases of the moon?
- What are the different woods mentioned, and how should they be used? Which one do you not burn? Why?
- How would you mark the sabbats?
- What does "merry meet and merry part" mean to you?

Ethics and the Magickal Life

- How should honesty be applied in situations where an honest answer might hurt someone's feelings?
- What would you say if someone asked you for a love spell?
- Offer another situation where the Wiccan perspective of ethics could be applied and how you'd handle it.
- Do you agree with the opinions presented on capital punishment, medically assisted suicide, and abortion? Why or why not?

Manifesting Divinity Within and Without

- "We are not material beings living a spiritual life; we are spiritual beings living a material life." Explain what this means.
- What gods would you call upon if you wanted to summon courage? Humility? Compassion?

Lesson 12: Recommended Reading

- *The Rede of the Wiccae: Adriana Porter, Gwen Thompson, and the Birth of a Tradition of Witchcraft* by Robert Mathiesen and Theitic
- *Witchcraft for Tomorrow* by Doreen Valiente

LESSON 13
The Language of Love

We continue our study of the Wiccan perception of ethics with a look at something near and dear to everyone's hearts: love.

Love, simply put, can be defined as the warm and personal feeling of attachment or affection one feels for another or the act of expressing that affection. Let's have a look at how many Wiccans and Witches view love in its myriad forms. This lesson covers several aspects of love that may seem disconnected, but they—from romantic relationships to connection to animals and the earth—are part of the same sentiment.

All Acts of Love and Pleasure Are My Rituals

It should be obvious by now, to anyone who's been paying attention, that the driving force of the universe, the union of the god and goddess, and the ultimate bond of humanity is love.

Remember the Charge of the Goddess? One of the most often quoted lines is "All acts of love and pleasure are My rituals."[89] Some people immediately infer that to be a permission of promiscuity, but the ramifications are far deeper. An expression of love is so much more than just an excuse to play hide-the-salami.

Love is more than just an emotion; it is the principal force of life. Witches see it as an expression of life itself. While all emotions are recognized and respected, none is more important than love. Love is the language of the goddess, and Witches speak in her language.

Unfortunately, love is often misunderstood and misused. As vital an emotion as it is, love scares some people and confuses others. It has been said that you cannot love others if you cannot love yourself first. In the Charge of the Goddess, we are also told

---

89. Valiente, "The Charge of the Goddess."

that "if that which you seek you findest not within thee, you will never find it without."[90] Therefore, Witches often try to come to terms with their emotions, so they can embrace love openly and honestly.

Love, honestly given and received, is a vital force. Abused and misused, it hurts everyone it touches. Therefore, Witches don't—or at least shouldn't—use the emotion foolishly. There are some who abuse love; they use it as a ploy, a tool, or a weapon. Love's deception and deceit will ultimately only hurt everyone involved.

Many Witches' views of love do not mirror the accepted social values. Rather than a standard nuclear family with heterosexual values, a husband and wife, and 2.5 kids, many Witches do not shy away from the possibility of loving others of the same sex or of loving more than one partner. The emotion of love is not something to be easily dismissed.

Witches have individual thoughts, feelings, opinions, and free will. Some people express love for all genders, emotionally and/or physically. Each Witch is their own person, and the feelings of each are—or should be—respected and honoured. If one's desire to love another is not returned, it is not pursued, nor is revenge sought. Recognize consent and harm none.

While I'm on the subject of "all" aspects of love and pleasure, I should mention that there are sometimes boundaries that should be observed. Just because it says "all," it is not carte blanche to do what you want. Always observe respect, consent, and honour. Respect each other's requests or boundaries, never offer love without consent, and honour each other's rights and sanctity. Even if you consider yourself a hugger, some people do not want to be touched without express permission. Do not assume that when the coven Priestess says she welcomes the love of the god, she means you. I'll touch on this again in the next lesson, Witchcraft and Sacred Sex.

Aspects of Love

Love is a multifaceted beast, and the emotion can be expressed in more ways than just affection for others. It can be shown in our thoughts, words, and deeds. Love has been categorized into seven different aspects, which are:

- *Agape:* The universal love, consisting of love for strangers, nature, or the gods
- *Eros:* Sexual or passionate love, or a modern perspective of romantic love

---

90. Valiente, "The Charge of the Goddess."

- *Ludus:* Playful and uncommitted love, intended for fun with no resulting consequences
- *Philautia:* Self-love, healthy or unhealthy; unhealthy if one places oneself above the gods, to the point of hubris, and healthy if it is used to build self-esteem and confidence.
- *Philia:* The love of friendship or goodwill; it is often met with mutual benefits that can also be formed by companionship, dependability, and trust.
- *Pragma:* Love founded on duty and reason and on one's long-term interests
- *Storge:* Love found between parents and children; it is often a unilateral love.[91]

Using these distinctions, love can be expressed as a desire for fulfillment. Following one's dream, or one's wyrd, whether it is to become a teacher or a veterinarian or to run a marathon, is an expression of love. Volunteering one's time to work with handicapped children, interpreting for the deaf, or shoveling the snow off your seventy-eight-year-old neighbour's walkway are all expressions of love. There are many different kinds of love, which are expressed in a variety of ways. For example, a firefighter saves lives because they love their work and the satisfaction it brings. A teacher loves having the ability to shape and build young minds. A man might love his wife but not in the same way he loves his son and not in the same way he loves watching hockey games on TV.

Incidentally, children grow up watching and mirroring their parents. If you teach your children the value of love and compassion, they will honour those values. If they grow up in an environment of mistrust and bigotry, those are the values they will come to understand.

You are probably familiar with the phrase "Practice random kindness and senseless acts of beauty." It is a delightful sentiment! Giving flowers to a total stranger, helping your new neighbours move in, or stopping traffic so a mother duck and her five babies can waddle across the road are excellent examples of random kindness—random acts of love. Some people are distrustful and paranoid and might believe your kindness masks nefarious intent, but that should not deter you from spreading kindness and beauty.

---

91. Lee, *Colours of Love*, 15.

Here are a few questions and concerns that may arise, especially among those new to the Craft, concerning Witches, love, and the world at large.

"How Will I Tell My Parents/Friends/Teachers that I'm Studying Witchcraft?"

A lot of people have concerns and misunderstandings about the Craft. "Is it evil? Will they make you worship Satan? Aren't you scared?" Well, um, no, no, and hopefully not. This is the thirteenth lesson in the class. Surely you know by now if this is where you want to be. Telling people who might misunderstand Witchcraft is best done gently. You might say you're in a nature-oriented study group or that it's an alternative religion class. If they press the issue, yes, be honest; don't flat out lie. You shouldn't be deceitful or shady, and here's why: For centuries people have been told that Witchcraft is evil, wrong, and so on. If they are not shown the truth about Witchcraft, that suspicion will only continue. They'll have no reason to believe otherwise. Tell the truth, be honest, and do so with love.

"Will Jesus Still Love Me If I Become a Witch?"

This is a common concern among young Wiccans who are considering converting to the Craft from Christianity. There are two parts to the answer here:

One, even though the Bible says again and again that it is a sin to turn away from God, you must remember that the Bible was written by men, not gods. It is hoped that Jesus and God are more compassionate than the men who penned the Bible. Would Jesus still love you? That's a very personal question, which only you can answer. Old Testament Jehovah might not be, but Jesus is more understanding. Some of his followers aren't, but he is.

And two, nobody demands that you abandon your old faith to follow the Craft. The old gods are more understanding than that. (Remember from lesson 1 that Witchcraft is a more of a philosophy, a lifestyle, and a skill set than an actual religion. Wicca is a religion. Witchcraft, technically, is not.) You can pursue the Craft in conjunction with other faiths if you are comfortable with that. Witches can honour Isis, Apollo, and Thor in ritual, so why not Jesus as well?

"Can I Marry Someone Who's Not a Witch?"

Of course! As long as they are accepting of your spiritual path there is no dilemma at all. Some religions forbid marrying outside the faith; the Craft is not one of them. Just be sure to respect their religious observances as much as they should respect yours.

"Will Being a Witch Make Me Better in Bed?"
Um, no. That's up to you. Becoming a Witch will (hopefully) give you a better understanding of yourself and your own spirituality, not your sexual prowess.

Love and the Wiccan Family

Witches today enjoy a liberty undreamed of in centuries past—the opportunity to live and to raise a child openly as a Pagan family. Wiccan families today have an unprecedented freedom of faith and devotion.

What is the best way to raise a child in the Craft? What should a parent watch out for? First and foremost, children need to be aware of the existing biases and phobias the ordinary people may have about the Craft. There is—and possibly always will be—deep misunderstanding and mistrust of Witches and Wiccans and how we practice our faith. Children love to share their experiences with others, but if little nine-year-old Travis blurts out to classmates and teachers that his family participated in a Pagan ritual, the repercussions could be devastating. Teach children the value of tact and decorum and knowing when not to share. If the child's teachers or friends start coming to the parents with questions, be polite, be honest, be tactful, and be respectful—of both their misgivings and their intelligence.

Even though Wiccan parents may want to raise their children in the Craft, I believe that such views should not be enforced as rigid dogma. When the child is old enough to understand, they should be allowed to explore other possibilities of faith and spirituality, and if they seem drawn to Buddhism or Judaism or some other path, the parents shouldn't prevent this spiritual exploration. It's a very real possibility that the child may follow a different calling than the parents. Of course, if the child is being drawn in by a potentially dangerous fringe cult, wise judgment and intervention may be needed. Raise children in love and peace and do everything possible to nurture their respect for life, an awareness and tolerance of people's differences and diversity, and a love and awe of the beauty of the world around them.

When you hold your child and touch their tiny hands and feel their tiny spirit, look into their eyes. Remind yourself that you are holding a tiny little god who has within them the promise of all the world and all the infinite tomorrows.

A Potpourri of Love

As we close out this lesson, let's examine a few other important facets of meaningful relationships and love—everything from pets, familiars, and totem animals to taking care of the world. This is sort of a mixed bag of topics in one section, and it is much like the emotions we carry every day.

Polyamory

Polyamory is the concept of being in a committed, loving relationship with more than one partner. Triads are not unusual in Pagan communities, regardless of the genders of the participants. Not all polyamorous relationships are sexual, and many remain committed for the emotional strength and support. When a polyamorous group chooses to keep their sexual activity exclusively to their partners, it's known as polyfidelity.

Our Relationship with Pets, Guardians, and Familiars

Lots of people keep pets. They can be anything from cats and dogs to horses, snakes, or tarantulas. Pets provide companionship and affection, and they offer people someone to care for. Many Witches, often devout animal lovers, keep an abundance of pets. The names they give their pets are often as colourful as the pets themselves, and names of gods and mythical figures are common names for Witches' pets. In some medieval illustrations, Witches were shown with familiars, usually cats or toads, which were said to be demonic assistants or imps who worked the Witch's evil. They bore names like Grymalkin, Grizelda, and Pyewacket, and such names are still common among Wiccan pet owners. While such fanciful names were often amusing, the accusations were not. Many an innocent was accused and killed for merely having a pet with an unusual name or for talking to it in a kind and loving manner.

Many people keep service animals, such as a seeing-eye dog or a seizure-alert dog, and feel lost without them. Guardians could be seen in a similar vein. If a person comes into your home and the dog or cat reacts strangely around them, pay attention to that. Your pet can sense things we cannot. A guardian is a pet, yes, but special attention is paid to how it reacts to certain situations or people. "If you come into my house and my dog doesn't trust you, I'm not going to trust you either."

What is a familiar? What makes a familiar different from a pet? Some would say that a familiar is a spirit guardian in animal form. Others argue that the familiar is empathetically bonded to its owner and that the Witch is more powerful and adept when the familiar is close at hand. Whichever it is, there is no doubt that Witches are fiercely loyal to their familiars and treat them as equals within the family.

Power Animals

Many people feel a strong connection to certain kinds of animals, such as the spirit of the wolf, bear, or eagle. You can't have a lion or a golden eagle as a pet, but you might have one tattooed on your arm or stamped on a piece of jewelry. This connection with a power animal can be a direct conduit to the strength of the animal itself.

Loving and Healing the Earth

It is no lie that this planet has been injured by humankind's greed and corruption; the scars and poisons of war and ignorance wound Earth more every day. Witches revere the goddess, respect nature, and love animals. But aside from simple spells, what else can they do for the earth? Many feel that it is their sacred duty to do what they can to heal the planet. While spells and magickal workings are good, every act is honoured. A healing work for the planet is a valid act of love and is, therefore, a ritual of the goddess. Contributions to earth-conscious charities are sacred acts, as are simple things like recycling newspapers, picking up trash from the side of the road, or mending a bird's broken wing.

The earth, in a Witch's eyes, is a living deity; she is the earth, mother, lover, friend, and spirit of every living thing. As such, she deserves protection, love, and attention. Every act—every word of compassion and healing—gives back what humankind has taken.

Here is a tale that seems appropriate: A traveling man passes a stranger by the side of the road. The stranger is planting a tree. The traveling man asks the stranger why he is planting a tree in such an odd place.

"Well, as I see it," says the man, "I'm giving back to the earth. It's my way of saying thanks for the privilege of living on this planet."

"Oh, so the tree represents your gift?" asks the traveler.

"No, think of it as paying rent," is the reply.

Lesson 13: Study Prompts and Questions

All Acts of Love and Pleasure Are My Rituals

- Explain the meaning of the line "All acts of love and pleasure are my rituals" from the Charge of the Goddess.
- Some Witches' views of love differ from mainstream society's views. Why do you think this is?

Aspects of Love

- Briefly define each of the seven aspects of love and provide examples for any two: agape, eros, ludus, philautia, philia, pragma, and storge.

Love and the Wiccan Family

- Do you think there are right and wrong ways to raise a child in a Wiccan family? Give some examples.

A Potpourri of Love

- What is polyamory, and why do many Wiccans and Witches accept it as a valid relationship model?
- In your own words, describe the difference between pets, guardians, and familiars.
- What is a power animal? Do you have one? If so, why do you think your power animal is that creature?
- Give three examples of ways one can help to heal the earth.

Lesson 13: Recommended Reading

- *Animal Speak: The Spiritual & Magical Powers of Creatures Great & Small* by Ted Andrews
- *The Urban Pagan: Magical Living in a 9-to-5 World* by Trish Telesco
- *When, Why…If: An Ethics Workbook* by Robin Wood

LESSON 14
Witchcraft and Sacred Sex

In the last lesson, we examined several aspects of love from lines in the Charge of the Goddess to aspects and expressions of love to healing the planet. This time we'll switch gears and go from love to sex in order to understand the Craft's perspective on sacred sexuality.

Sex, whether real or implied, is central to Wiccan mythology. The god and goddess consummate their marriage at Beltane (or Litha), and their union is reflected in the vitality of the natural world. And every person you've ever met is alive because someone, somewhere, had sex. Sex is a fundamental aspect of life, and it is a foundation of the Wiccan religion.

As a warning, this lesson addresses many adult topics. If children or minors are allowed to participate in these lessons, you may wish to review the subject matter with parents before continuing.

Sex and the Craft

If you put the love quote from the Charge of the Goddess together with the harm none line from the rede, it should be easy to see how Witches view sexual expression as a valid extension of love. Also remember this line from the Principles of Wiccan Belief: "We value sex as pleasure, as the symbol and embodiment of life, and as the interaction source of energies used in magical practice and religious worship."[92] As stated above, it is central to Wicca, and the union of the god and goddess is a fundamental theme in Wicca.

Sex can be used in many ways. It can be part of a spellworking, whether alone or with a partner; reenacted, whether real or implied, in ritual; or used to attain a deeper connection with a deity.

---

92. Clifton, *Witchcraft Today, Book One*, 19–20.

Sex, honestly given and received, is a pure and natural thing, and it doesn't matter what gender the partners involved may be. Misused, as in rape or incest, it is a vile and reprehensible act. Witches are—or should be—law-abiding and ethical citizens, and they should not invite anyone into a sexual situation without express consent. Likewise, honest Witches do not use sex as a tool for advancement in the Craft, nor as a way to influence anyone or win favors.

In the Middle Ages, it was common to assume that Witchcraft was a mass orgy. Many medieval accounts said as much, and such rumor and misinformation have been perpetuated through the centuries. Some people still think Witches eat babies, desecrate churches, and engage in random and promiscuous sex. Witches do indeed have sex and love each other, but desecration and eating babies are not part of the Craft.

Sex and Magick

A sexual act can usually be described in one of two ways: it is either recreational sex and the engaging in sexual acts simply for pleasure and the sharing of passion between partners, or it is procreational sex, which is performed with the specific intent of reproduction. With sex magick, though, a third description is introduced, and it is that of sex as an energy-raising medium or sex as worship. The concept of sex as a form of worship, however, raises a lot of red flags for those who don't understand it. They often perceive recreational sex as sinful, or at least something not to be openly discussed, and the idea of sex as worship is practically blasphemous. Many Witches, however, have no problem with the idea of sex as worship. Both the Wiccan creation myth and the cycle of the sabbats carry heavy sexual references.

To work sex magick, consenting partners cast a circle, using whatever incense or deity invocation work for the purpose, and perform the act with the understanding that the fulfillment of the spellwork is the goal, not personal satisfaction.

The energies within the human body are usually somewhat sluggish and random. A surge of adrenaline can bring them into alignment, but they are generally sort of everywhere. During sex, however, the heartbeat races, the focus shifts, the body directs its attention to the act, and the energy flowing between the participants can be harnessed for spellwork. Witches who practice sex magick typically only do so with their dedicated partners; it's not a free-for-all. The chemistry is much stronger when the participants are committed to each other.

Sex magick is never used between a leader or elder who is "helping" a novice Witch achieve some sort of recognition or plateau or used as any form of coercion or control. There is always clearly understood and informed consent between all participants. And, yes, protection is taken to prevent unwanted pregnancies and disease.

The *Great Rite* is the term for the union of the god and goddess, and it's used when people recreate the act to honour their union. It's more common that the Great Rite is represented symbolically by the Priest holding an athame and lowering it into a chalice, which is held by the Priestess. Indeed, it has been mentioned by many, with tongue firmly placed in cheek, that Wicca's deepest, darkest secret rite is that "the knife goes in the cup." The act can be performed symbolically without the traditional gender designations and roles.

In some communities, the term *Great Rite* has become a euphemism for sexual intercourse between Pagans in any situation.

Skyclad Worship and Nudism

Gerald Gardner was, among other things, a devout nudist, believing that nudity promoted a more natural connection between the Witch and the natural world. Much of his writing reflects this, and he made skyclad worship part of his tradition. Skyclad worship used to be more common than it is today, but some people do still prefer to worship or participate in ritual while naked.

Nudity, to some, is more than just being naked. To stand naked before the goddess—or others—is to be without any disguise, pretense, or false impression. It is the ultimate expression of openness. A line from the Charge of the Goddess states, "You shall be free from slavery, and as a sign that ye be free, you shall be naked in your rites."[93] You wear no shackles, no clothes, or any form of hindrance. This has two meanings. Many Witches feel that ritual nudity symbolizes a connection with nature; there is nothing between the Witch and the goddess. Another perspective is that skyclad refers not only to physical nudity but also to total honesty and a lack of masks, disguises, or false pretenses. All masks are cast aside, and you meet the gods in total honesty and openness.

While many fear nudity, feeling ashamed of their bodies, all people of all shapes and sizes are beautiful as the gods themselves. Overweight? Underweight? Scars? These concerns absolutely do not matter, and your size and shape will not be judged. Indeed, some

93. Valiente, "The Charge of the Goddess."

people who are overcoming such apprehensions or misgivings will find themselves with a renewed level of confidence when they participate in a skyclad event.

Many of the people who do participate will tell you that they not only feel closer to the gods but that the magick flows more freely when it is unencumbered by clothes. In some cases, Witches prefer to wear loose-fitting garments, such as dedicated ritual robes or sarongs, for the same reason. Again, actual nudity is less prevalent than it used to be.

If a coven will be worshipping skyclad, what are the considerations and the pitfalls? First, carefully consider this: Do you allow children to participate in a skyclad ritual? Parents of very young children know that it is sometimes difficult to keep clothes *on* an infant; kids up to about age four often run about the house naked, and many Wiccan parents allow this within the home. Some feel that teaching children to be ashamed of their body only stifles their spiritual development. Combining nudity with religious worship raises a lot of questions in the eyes of authorities, and it is simply the law in many parts of the world that children should not be exposed to nudity, and the legal ramifications on a family can be devastating.

Some Wiccans might argue that since many governments recognize Witchcraft as a legitimate religion, alternative forms of worship are acceptable, including allowing people of all ages to participate in skyclad worship. Maybe, but that argument rarely holds up in court. To avoid the risk of possible legal action, most covens that practice skyclad limit it to adult participation.

What about erections? Many people entering into a clothing-optional situation face the possibility of public arousal. In the Craft, such erections are possible and should be politely ignored; if the person tries to draw attention to it in a lewd or disturbing manner, they should be dismissed from the coven or the event.

Can a person be skyclad in ritual if they're having their period? Skyclad sabbats and esbats do indeed occur, and the goddess does not always check with every person's calendar before the full moon. Coven leaders should understand personal need; if clothing is required for a person to feel comfortable, there is no harm done.

If it is possible, many Witches enjoy skyclad worship outdoors. Indeed, if the ritual includes such things as leaping over a bonfire, being skyclad is safer than wearing a long, flowing robe.

Consider this brief conversation, which you might recognize: "Are those people jumping about naked?" "Of course they're naked. It's dangerous to leap across an open flame with clothes on—they could catch fire!"

Sex and Responsibility

Witches live in a magickal environment with spells, gods, rituals, and so on. But they also live very much in the real world where sexually transmitted diseases, psychological or physical abuse, and awareness and responsibility are major concerns.

How do Witches handle contraceptives? If a condom inhibits pregnancy, is it harming the sperm? Are birth control devices unethical? No, of course not. Contraceptives are a sensible way to avoid unwanted pregnancies, and 99.999 percent of all sperm cells die without fulfilling their purpose anyway. Since the sperm contains only half the DNA required to create an embryo, it is not a living being and is, thus, outside the harm none rule. It is hoped that Witches will have enough sense to use contraceptives if they are not in a position to raise a child in a safe, healthy environment.

I briefly mentioned respect for personal boundaries in the previous lesson, and I want us to examine that again. Some people are natural huggers and openly embrace anyone, but others are not and uninvited or unwelcome physical contact can be a somewhat traumatic experience, tantamount to a violation of personal space.

Respect each other's wishes and boundaries. Honour each other's privacy and identity. Don't ever assume that just because someone might be skyclad that it's an invitation. Their personal connection with their gods doesn't necessarily involve everyone around them.

Witches and Wiccans should never try to use sex as a ploy, coercion, or intimidation. *Respect, consent, honour.* (Have I said that enough yet?)

Lesson 14: Study Prompts and Questions

Sex and the Craft

- In your own words, explain why the Craft's view of sex and nudity is so often misunderstood.
- Explain the message behind "All acts of love and pleasure are my rituals."

Sex and Magick

- Briefly explain the concept of sex as a form of worship.
- How can sex be used in a magickal situation, such as a spellwork?
- What is the Great Rite?

Skyclad Worship and Nudism

- Explain how Gerald Gardner's nudist philosophy influenced his Wiccan practice.
- What are two possible interpretations of the phrase "You should be naked in your rites"?
- When do you think skyclad worship would be inappropriate?

Sex and Responsibility

- Briefly explain why Witches place so much importance on responsible attitudes regarding sexuality.
- Explain why "respect, consent, honour" is a vital concern.

Lesson 14: Recommended Reading

- *The Art of Sexual Ecstasy: The Path of Sacred Sexuality for Western Lovers* by Margot Anand
- *Drawing Down the Moon: Witches, Druids, Goddess-Worshippers, and Other Pagans in American Today* by Margot Adler

LESSON 15
Life, Death, and Beyond

Why are we born? Where do we come from? What is the meaning of life? Where do we go when we die? These and other simple questions will be answered in this lesson.

Keep in mind that the concepts presented in this lesson are not exclusively of the Craft; this is an eclectic mix of Wiccan, Hindu, Christian, and Buddhist principles that together form a cohesive theory on life, death, and beyond.

Much of this lesson is highly subjective; it reflects my opinions and conjectures. You may agree with the concepts discussed here or not; that's your prerogative.

Life

How did life begin? Well, Witches do not believe in the generally accepted Adam-and-Eve-style creation myth. They do not think that the goddess reached down one day and—poof—there was a human looking all confused and hunting fig leaves. The Wiccan perspective generally agrees with scientific theory—that life began as a primordial soup and slowly evolved over millennia. Throughout the centuries, the Lord and Lady were deep within the spirit of every living thing, patiently waiting for us to answer their call.

Why do we exist? What is the meaning of life? Almost any teenager will tell you that people exist because the sperm fertilizes the egg and an embryo develops, growing into a fetus. But that's the how, not the why.

According to the Wiccan creation myth that Starhawk proposed, everything exists because the goddess fell in love with her own image and created a reflection of herself. By the Wiccan philosophy, the meaning of life is that we exist to perpetuate the love created by the goddess.

If that sounds too simplistic, try this: we exist to live, to celebrate every moment, to enjoy every meal, every note in a song, and every cloud in the sky. We were bestowed with the senses to enjoy life, sentience to appreciate it, memory to savor it, and the altruism to share it.

Another answer is that humans, unlike some other animals, have the ability to better themselves and their surroundings. (Some can, yes. Beavers build dams. Birds build nests. But beavers and birds don't study climate change and work to correct it on a global scale.) Humankind's goal—its obligation and its purpose—is to make tomorrow better than yesterday. A person can build a house, open a trust fund for their family, or work to clean up pollution and other environmental hazards.

According to others, the purpose of life is to learn. Every day offers us a new opportunity to experience life and broaden our horizons. Such a path exists beyond lifetimes too. Hindus say that everything we learn in each lifetime adds up, and our total experiences are guiding us toward experiencing divinity.

What separates humans from other animals? Some say sentience, or the ability to think, reason, deduct, and predict. Many animals use tools—otters use stones to crack shells open, monkeys use sticks to dig beetles out of burrows, and birds select appropriate pieces when building a nest—but these are instinctual abilities, not really rational thought. Corvids—crows and ravens—can solve simple puzzles, and octopuses and cuttlefish can pass intelligence tests at a level equal to young children. Many animals exhibit rational thought, comprehension, and problem-solving, but the ability to reflect upon our emotions and learn from them is almost exclusive to humans. Yes, elephants have been known to play pranks on each other just for laughs, and many other animals feel emotion. Animals that mate for life become despondent and moody if their mate dies. Every animal shares psychic awareness to one degree or another too. Everyone knows how dogs, cats, and horses act spooked long before a storm hits. But the complex mix of sentience, memory, emotion, psychic awareness, and empathy makes a rare breed indeed. We can, using these abilities, theorize, plan, and create a material answer to a theoretical problem or, using magick, create a theoretical answer to a material problem.

Humans have all the qualities needed to fully appreciate life. We can savor and enjoy life's experiences, learn from them, and recount the experiences at later dates. That, according to some, is why we exist.

What about the concept of sin? Or karma? How do these relate? Well, sin is essentially a Christian concept and denied by Witches and Wiccans. Indeed, the idea of original sin, that Eve's betrayal of faith cursed humankind for all time, seems ludicrous, as does the notion that after you die you will stand to be judged for your actions, your thoughts, and even your faith. Most Witches recognize that every living thing embodies both dark and light aspects of life—that all things exist in a balance. Everybody has as much capacity to commit harm as to act for good. The trick is to know brevity and self-control.

According to the Hindu philosophy, Karma is the belief that your actions in this life will affect your standing in the next one. It is not really a sort of "instant justice." If you cut someone off in traffic and three blocks later your car breaks down, some would laugh and say, "Well, that's karma for you." No, it isn't. There does appear to be a cosmic system of cause and effect—if you are a positive person, good things tend to come your way—but it would be inaccurate to call that karma.

Death

Most Witches feel that all living things—people, trees, animals, and even rocks—have souls. The soul is the spark of life and the essence inside the body. What happens when we die? Where does the soul go? Do Witches believe in heaven and hell? What is the Craft's perception of the afterlife?

One of the fundamental beliefs in the Craft is that of reincarnation. We mentioned it briefly back in lesson 12. Now let's take a deeper look. It is a widely held belief that while the body, or the material vessel, can die, the soul continues. According to some faiths, including Wicca and Buddhism, the soul returns in a new body to continue learning and experiencing life, heading toward a greater goal. If Witches believe in reincarnation, where do they go in between? Heaven? Well, heaven, as commonly understood, is a Christian concept. It's where God lives and where devout Christians go upon death.

Many Witches, however, believe in the concept of Summerland. Some say it's named after the ancient civilization of Sumer, the first civilization to offer pictographic representations of death and the afterlife. To others it's named for summer, when the Lord and Lady are in their prime. Many Pagans feel that the souls of the departed travel to the lands beyond the west, or beyond the sunset.

Whichever it is, it is commonly held by Witches that after a person dies, their spirit travels to Summerland—into the arms of the goddess—to await a new incarnate existence. While Witches do mourn the dead, they also know that the essence of the person, resting awhile in the lap of the gods, is destined to return in another incarnation.

ArchDruid Isaac Bonewits was interviewed in 1999 and asked about his thoughts on reincarnation. He said, "My beliefs about life after death tend to shift a great deal. I used to believe firmly in reincarnation—but that was 800 years ago, when I was a Buddhist monk at the time. I believe people spend far too much time worrying about life after death and insufficient time worrying about this life … we have to take care of ourselves, our community, and our great, great, great grandchildren. I'll find out what happens when I die; everybody does. And probably for everybody it's a surprise. But I believe that the Gods intend us to do the work now that needs to be done in our lifetimes—and let the next life, if there is one, take care of itself."[94]

Many Pagans dislike the contemporary practice of embalming and burying the deceased in a cement enclosure. They feel that the body should be allowed to decay naturally with its essence returning to the earth. Until recently, this was generally forbidden in Western civilization, but the concept of a natural or green burial does has gained popularity. In such a burial, people lay the unembalmed deceased person in a natural grave and let their body return to the earth. Some green burial cemeteries even plant a tree over the body to let the body's nutrients become the tree. The body then lives on through the many lives supported by the tree.

Beyond

The Hindu idea of a soul traveling through lifetimes is mirrored in the Craft philosophy of reincarnation. But if that's true, are life and death endless, like a cosmic yo-yo? Well, no. It is thought that the soul goes through several lifetimes, learning a little more each time, before eventually ascending beyond this realm.

Have you ever heard of a person described as having an old soul? Such people display a depth of wisdom and clarity that transcends their physical age. Witches often feel that such people have had many past lives and benefited from the ability to retain some of that accumulated wisdom. Some people, but not all, can recall images and feelings from past lives, even recounting dates, names, and faces.

Reincarnation allows the immortal soul a way to learn, evolve, and grow over many lifetimes, and many Witches feel that the more good deeds a person does in their lifetime, the more their soul will have evolved. This ties in nicely with the concept of karma as well. One way or another, the lesson will be learned.

There is some debate on whether a reincarnate soul will always come back human or as a dog, a goldfish, or whatever. Who says souls are restricted to a single species?

---

94. Myth Woodling, "FQA: What Is the Summerland?"

The question is, then, what happens after a soul has learned all it can? What happens next? Do we become as gods? Some feel that the evolved soul becomes another form entirely. Maybe it becomes an angel or spirit guide sent to help developing souls along. And after that? We can only imagine.

Lesson 15: Study Prompts and Questions

Life

- What attributes theoretically separate humans from other animals?
- Three suggestions for the "why" of life are to learn, protect, and enjoy. Can you think of others?
- In your own words, explain the difference between sin and karma.

Death

- Briefly explain the concept of reincarnation and why it applies to Wiccan philosophy.
- What is Summerland?

Beyond

- Do you agree with the idea of an evolving soul? Explain and justify your answer.
- Have you ever encountered an angel or a spirit guide? If you have, please describe the encounter(s).

Lesson 15: Recommended Reading

- *The Pagan Book on Living and Dying: Practical Rituals, Prayers, Blessings, and Meditations on Crossing Over* by Starhawk, M. Macha NightMare, and The Reclaiming Collective
- *The Witches' Way: Principles, Rituals, and Beliefs of Modern Witchcraft* by Janet and Stewart Farrar

LESSON 16
The Web, the Wheel, and the Way

Congratulations, you've made it to the last class of Wicca 101! In this lesson we can let our hair down and relax; this lesson is more about seeing things another way than learning anything substantially new. We'll look at three ways of expressing our Wiccan perspective: the web, the wheel, and the way.

By the way, the notion of the web, the wheel, and the way as a mirror of Wiccan philosophy is entirely my own making. I had several sources and inspirations, but ultimately you can blame me.

The Web

In the nineteenth century there was a man named Chief Seattle, an influential member of the Suquamish Nation, whose words carried weight in both Native American and colonial circles of the area now known as Washington state. In 1854, when the US government purchased several hundred thousand acres of land, he sent a letter to President Franklin Pierce. While there is some doubt as to the legitimacy of that letter, there is no denying the impact of the words. Many people, Witches and Native Americans included, applaud Chief Seattle's sentiments about the world and his perception of humankind's place in it. Here are some excerpts from that letter:

This we know: the earth does not belong to man, man belongs to the earth. All things are connected like the blood that unites us all.

Man did not weave the web of life, he is merely a strand in it. Whatever he does to the web, he does to himself.

We know the sap which courses through the trees as we know the blood that courses through our veins. We are part of the earth, and it is part of us. The perfumed flowers our are sisters; the bear, the deer, the great eagle, these are our

145

brothers. The rocky crests, the dew in the meadow, the body heat of the pony, and man all belong to the same family.[95]

Every living thing is part of a great web of life, interconnected and interdependent. Any educated Witch will tell you that what we do affects everything else—whether we know it or not. That's why it is so important to love and protect the earth, each other, and ourselves. The Wiccan Rede, the principles, and the Charge of the Goddess all establish a foundation of Wiccan doctrine that Wiccans and Witches share the responsibility to protect and heal the earth, to honour her in practice and ritual, and to share the magick and spirituality of the Old Religion.

The Wheel

The Wheel of the Year is a common theme in Wicca and Witchcraft; it defines the passage of the year, the changing seasons, and the life cycle of the Lord and Lady. The year carries us through the seasons and brings us back around again. Samhain to Samhain.

We live, die, and are reborn in a subsequent reincarnation, and the concept of karma says that our behavior in this life will affect our standing in the next one.

The pattern of the wheel can also be applied to Wiccan or Pagan philosophy and the notion that what you send out, comes back to thee. If you spread love, you'll receive love in return, while hostility breeds hostility. This is also the Law of Return.

The Wheel of Fortune is the tenth card in the tarot's major arcana. When drawn, the Wheel of Fortune reminds you that the wheel is always turning and life is in a state of constant change. If you're going through a difficult time, rest assured that it will get better from here. Good luck and good fortune will make their return in time. Similarly, if things are going well, they will change and life may return to "normal" soon. This cycle shows why it is so important to cherish the blissful moments in your life and make the most of them while they are within reach; in a flash, they could be gone.

Circles are a central theme in Wicca and Witchcraft. The pentagram, which we'll examine more closely in lesson 20, is a five-pointed star encompassed by the wheel of life.

Attend any Pagan Pride Day event or festival and you'll probably hear this chant at least once: "We are a circle, within a circle, with no beginning, and never ending."

---

95. Children of the Earth United, "Excerpts from Chief Seattle's Famous Speech."

The Way

There are as many different ways of perceiving the divine essence as there are different people in the world. While there may only be a few dozen spiritual paths, each individual person, ultimately, interprets the Divine in their own way because each person sees in the Divine a reflection of self and vice versa. It can only be assumed that other animals, plants, and stones have their own perception of divinity as well, but for now, we can only guess.

Knowing that, the question could be asked, "Which religion is the one true faith?" The answer is: "All of them." And if we are part of the Divine, and the Divine exists within everything, then everything is part of everything else. God, by any interpretation, is manifest in every molecule, every atom, in existence. A blade of grass is a facet of the Divine, as is a waterfall and the cry of a newborn baby. Everything affects the world around us—whether we know it or not.

Remember the story of a person negotiating the river of the wyrd from lesson 2? We all sail that river, and indeed, we all are that river. If you dam up the bank on one side, that causes the water's flow to alter, which affects others as readily as it affects you.

Some people have adopted a philosophy called the "Trial of Head, Heart, and Hand." It's sort of a WWGD (What Would the Goddess Do?) approach. Any decision should be examined logically (head) and spiritually (heart), and the action taken should not cause harm to others (hand). If the decision agrees with all factors, then it is the appropriate course of action.

As Witches, we have the ability—voluntarily denied by some, seen as irrelevant by others—to shape our destiny in ways beyond the material. It is our right, our heritage, and our gift to use this ability in the most beneficial way possible. Other religions have ways of seeing beyond the veil and lifting the curtain of divine mystery. Buddhists seek enlightenment through meditation. Christians use prayer. Witches, Christians, Buddhists, Jews, Muslims, Hindus, Ásatrú, and all others might see things slightly differently yet, really, we are all the same thing: humans. We are elegant, magnificent, beautiful, clumsy, wise, charming, foolish, and lovable creatures that have come a very long way in a very short time. In the span of time since the universe began, humankind has existed for about a millionth of a second, and as we stand together on the brink of tomorrow, all that really matters is:

Love and honour the spirit within.

Do this, and everything else will fall into place.

Lesson 16: Study Prompts and Questions

The Web

- Who was Chief Seattle?
- Why was Chief Seattle's letter to President Franklin Pierce important?
- Paraphrase the excerpts from the letter in your own words.

The Wheel

- Why is the Wheel of the Year, the Witch's calendar, so important to Wiccan philosophy?
- Explain the principle of the Law of Return.
- What does the Wheel of Fortune tarot card represent?

The Way

- Why do you think there are so many different religions in the world?
- What is "the way"?

Lesson 16: Recommended Reading

- *Transformative Witchcraft* by Jason Mankey
- *When, Why ... If?: An Ethics Workbook* by Robin Wood

WICCA 102
Inside the Coven,
the Meaning of Ritual,
and Magickal Theory

LESSON 17
Inside the Coven

Welcome back to the world of Witches! We go from Wicca 101 studies, which examined the "what" and "why" of the Craft, into Wicca 102, which examines the "how." We begin with an analysis of the coven, what it means, and the roles and obligations of its members, and we'll examine the importance and use of magickal names.

The Origins of the Witch's Coven

The word *coven* has a fascinating origin. In the early Middle Ages, when very few could read, it was common to meet at easily recognizable landmarks such as a tree or crossroads. Landmarks have always been used as common meeting places. This is why we see names like Twin Pines Village or the Bayside Hotel. At such landmarks people would meet, and we got words like *convene, convention, convent,* and *coven.*

The term *coven* as referring to a meeting or council of Witches allegedly first appeared in the trial of Bessie Dunlop in Scotland in 1576. It was reported that the coven was twelve persons, and the devil, addressed in the account as Thom Reid, was the thirteenth member.[96]

There are many accounts from the records of Witch trials that Witches met in covens. According to the accounts, they were exclusively thirteen in number, including the devil, by an assortment of names, who was the officer or in some leadership position.

It is highly unlikely that a Christian symbol of evil appeared at every meeting by any number of Witches, but the judges and witchfinders, fueled by misinformation and paranoia, would certainly want you to think so. It was for this reason that anyone who used folk remedies or had odd birthmarks or gave cats funny names or was a woman simply deemed to be undesirable or a nuisance had to be careful. Being identified as a Witch—whether you actually were one or not—could have devastating repercussions. If one was

---

96. Chambers, *Domestic Annals of Scotland*, 50.

thus accused, anyone they were associated with was suddenly suspect. Coven membership, therefore, would have been a two-edged sword. Yes, the groups offered support and companionship, but if one person was accused, the whole group was at risk.

Now we jump ahead a few hundred years.

When Gerald Gardner was working on his Witchcraft revival, he borrowed extensively from esoteric orders and groups, such as the Golden Dawn and the Freemasons, that always had a defined structure with officers and roles. These were significant in the development of the Witchcraft that he was creating. As for covens, nothing was really known about a coven's structure or hierarchy—besides the questionable descriptions in Charles Leland's *Aradia* or Margaret Murray's research—until Gardner recounted his involvement with a Rosicrucian order called the Fellowship of Crotona and the New Forest Coven in the 1930s. He mentioned a High Priestess of the coven and dedicated initiates, and he included these roles in the description of a working coven in his Gardnerian tradition.

Following the publication of his books in the 1950s and '60s, Gardner worked with Doreen Valiente. As you'll remember, she wrote much of what is considered the foundation of Wicca today.

As more and more people discovered Witchcraft and Wicca and more covens and traditions were created, the specific roles within became more concrete. Covens had an established High Priestess and High Priest, and initiates took on more diverse roles.

The Coven Today

Today's covens are like magickal or spiritual families or study groups. While some prefer solitary practice, a lot of Witches prefer the comfort of a coven. Witches join covens for mutual support, spiritual growth, the opportunity to share in the worship of the gods, and to hold rituals together. Some feel that they offer the sense of bonding and togetherness that their own families lack. Depending on the tradition, being admitted into a coven can be as easy as meeting with the High Priest and Priestess, who decide then and there if you qualify, to enduring a long multistage initiation process—complete with extensive tests and evaluations.

There are two things that today's covens do not do. First, they do not recruit. Witches do not go knocking on doors or passing out pamphlets on college campuses to drum up business. Anyone who is meant to find the Craft will do so on their own terms, in their own time. And second, covens do not have hazing initiation rituals like some college fraternities.

Over the years, one sad truth has stayed with us: People fear what they do not understand and will try to bury or destroy what they fear. All the good publicity in the world can't change what people have been taught for centuries. Witches are still often feared and mistrusted for the simple fact of following a religion so few understand. To some, the risks of being found out as a Witch can be devastating, and secrecy is the best policy. Some have lost their jobs and their homes and had their children taken away by ignorant but well-meaning people who fear that labels like *Witch* and *coven* mean "devil worship." The Biblical reference Exodus 22:18 only furthers the doubt and misinformation; remember the lesson on the Inquisition from Wicca 101.

Still, the Witchcraft of today is one of the fastest growing faiths in the world, and today's covens reflect that growth.[97] They are as diversified as the Witches themselves, following a myriad of different traditions. One standard among today's covens, though, is the duty and obligation a Witch assumes when joining.

Coven Roles and Obligations

Who's who in a coven? What does the degree system mean? What does the High Priestess or a dedicant do? Let's find out.

The Main Roles

To start, let's go over the main roles in a coven.

Seeker

Everyone begins as a seeker—a person looking for answers. The seeker knows that Wicca or the Craft means something special but hasn't yet begun any serious study.

Dedicant

A dedicant is one who has joined a grove or maybe a coven's Wicca 101 class. The dedicant has dedicated themselves to the study of the Craft but has not yet officially joined a coven.

Initiate

After a period of dedication, a Witch may be invited to initiate into a coven. The initiation is a formal ritual where the Witch's magickal name is officially recognized, and they become a welcome member of the coven.

---

97. Mishkov, "Wicca."

High Priestess (HPS)

The High Priestess is the leader of the coven. She acts as the living voice of the goddess and the embodiment of divinity. The HPS is the guiding force behind the coven, leading her coveners in ritual, and is responsible for their teaching, support, and guidance. It is her duty to attend multicoven meetings, representing her coven as a whole. The title of HPS is customarily reserved for third-degree Witches and, usually, women.

High Priest (HP)

As the counterpart to the High Priestess, the High Priest is the voice of the god. He supports and assists her whenever possible, including in ritual and magickal workings. It is his duty to help with the tutelage of the coveners and to act as a guide, counselor, and mentor. He is responsible for overseeing the arrangement and organization of coven tasks and events. Just like the HPS, the High Priest is usually of third degree and is usually a male role. Of course, it is not always necessary that the High Priest be the one to invoke a god, either. Just because Cernunnos is portrayed as masculine figure, the person invoking him is not required to be a male.

Elders

The coven elders are the High Priestess, High Priest, and other third-degree Witches or the founding coven members. In matters of dispute, the coven elders meet to discuss the situation and reach a fair decision.

Witch Queen

The last role a Priestess might hold within a coven is that of Witch Queen. If any coven members leave to form their own covens, their old High Priestess becomes the Crone aspect, as opposed to the Mother or Maiden. If five new covens are formed from the old, the original High Priestess earns the title Witch Queen.

The Three Degrees

Not every coven or tradition uses the degree system; some feel that a progressive level system might show favoritism within the coven. For those who do use the degree system, they say it represents a recognized and accepted progression within the coven. Newly initiated Witches begin at first degree.

First Degree

A first-degree Witch has shown to have a basic understanding of the principles and practices of the Craft and exhibits enough aptitude and enthusiasm to be allowed to advance further within the Craft. Some covens see the title of initiate and that of first degree as identical. Others feel that the initiate has to show themselves worthy to be awarded the degree.

Second Degree

The second degree is awarded to Witches only after they have sufficient talent and dedication to apply the teaching of the Craft, have made a life-altering decision, or have overcome deep fears and obstacles. Whether it is getting out of an abusive situation, learning to walk after months of paralysis, or addressing a fear of public speaking, a significant personal accomplishment is often regarded as sufficient dedication to be awarded the second degree.

Third Degree

Finally, the coven elders can award third degree to those who have shown advanced insight, understanding, and application of the Craft's principles and practices. "Crossing the veil" or coming face-to-face with the gods, whether through ritual or personal meditation, are both signs that a person is ready to receive third degree.

Third-degree Witches can then, if they so choose, "hive off" from the mother coven to form covens of their own. It is understood that any such advancements and degree initiations depend upon the decision of the coven elders. Many covens hold formal rituals of advancement for the up-and-coming Witch. The usual amount of time before progressing further in the Craft is a year and a day.

Other Coven Roles

The following coven duties can be adopted by members of any degree. The only requirement is that the Witch display enough talent and enthusiasm to carry the title well.

Maiden

If the High Priestess could be considered the Mother Goddess of the coven, then the maiden must be the … (can you guess?) Maiden. It is her duty to assist the High Priestess in ritual and coven events, to study under her, and to ultimately assume the role of HPS when the present Priestess steps down. The maiden is also responsible for organizing classes, if the coven uses them, and protecting and maintaining the altar, ritual tools, and supplies. This used to be an exclusively female role, but anyone can serve as maiden; a nonbinary term might be squire.

Summoner

As odd as the name sounds, the summoner is the counterpart to the maiden. He learns from the High Priest to ultimately assume that role when the Priest steps down. The summoner, sometimes also known as the squire, is responsible for maintaining the coven library and acting as courier between local covens. As befits his name, the summoner is responsible for addressing prospective new coven members and arranging their meetings with the High Priest and Priestess. Again, as with the maiden, this used to be a more gender-specific role, but anyone can serve as summoner.

Quarter-Callers

These are not full-time assignments with specific duties and obligations but roles taken during ritual. Part of ritual procedure involves calling upon the four elements—air, fire, water, and earth—which any covener except the High Priest and Priestess can perform. In a pinch, of course, even they can call quarters if necessary.

Additional Roles

The roles of High Priestess and Priest, maiden, summoner, and quarter-callers are essential to any well-organized coven. There are other tasks and responsibilities in a coven, which any qualified person can assume. Of course, any covener can double up on roles if the need arises. These roles include:

Scribe

The scribe keeps the coven Book of Shadows updated and takes minutes during meetings. They also maintain routine coven correspondence.

Bard

Anyone with any singing or musical ability can assume the role of bard. Also called the minstrel, the bard is the musician for the coven. They collect and teach appropriate songs and chants and maintain any musical instruments the coven might use—except those special to the individual owner.

Pursewarden

More commonly known as treasurer, the pursewarden is responsible for keeping track of coven finances. They present the financial report at coven meetings and work with the maiden to arrange possible fundraising events.

Herald

The herald communicates with media services and represents the coven in public situations. If the coven is involved in a newsworthy event, it is the herald's face you'll see on the evening news.

Archivist

The archivist works with the summoner to maintain the coven library. A relatively recent obligation of the archivist is to maintain and update the coven's website or social media presence. In smaller covens, the archivist and the scribe are frequently the same person.

Guardian

The guardian is responsible for protecting the coven members and overseeing security. If a sabbat is held at a public park, for example, the guardian is responsible for keeping curious onlookers at a safe distance and answering the ubiquitous questions. Since such tasks require that the guardian work outside the ritual, the role often goes to a noncoven member, such as a willing spouse or sibling.

The Transformation of Names

Many of these titles seem antiquated. Pursewarden? Scribe? Surely you mean treasurer and secretary. Yes, we do. But Gardner had a flair for the flamboyant, and he liked the medieval-sounding titles. If you'd rather go by treasurer and secretary, please do.

More importantly, the coven roles as just listed were gender-specific when Gardner wrote them. That was decades ago! You do not have to keep to these strictures. If you want a male maiden or a coven with two High Priestesses in it, nobody will stop you. An all-male coven? Absolutely! Gender does not mean today what it meant in 1960. If you'd prefer a nonbinary title other that Priest, which implies male, or Priestess, which implies female, you may opt for Priestan, Ordinant, or Priestex, but most people just use the title Priest with the nod that the word is non-gender-defining.

Coven, Solitary, or Grove?

Even though coven membership seems like an obvious choice, there are many who choose to remain solitary, practicing and worshipping on their own. There is nothing wrong with that; to demand that every Witch join a coven would be a violation of their free will. Witches choose solitary worship for many reasons. They might live where there are no covens nearby or fear exposure and persecution if publicly revealed as a Witch. In some cases, if a coven disbands or members move away, a Witch might worship solitary for a while before seeking out a new coven. Some simply prefer not to mix their energies with others.

When a Solitary Witch, or solitaire, performs a ritual, they act as High Priestess (or Priest) and call the quarters. Naturally, they do everything themself. For example, if a female solitaire is performing a solitary ritual, she can choose to simply omit the Priest's role from ritual procedure, take both duties herself, or envision him as an aspect of the invoked god.

A grove is something like a starter coven that's often created for one of two purposes. It's either to teach the Craft or to simply act as a social gathering of neophytes or solitaires. Grove members are not initiated into the grove, and rituals are not always offered. Some do offer social events, field trips, and similar affairs. Witches can either proceed on to coven status or remain members of the grove. Many Witches are members of a both a coven and a grove.

Increasingly common in the twenty-first century is the practice of meeting online via a social media platform or group conference app. Online meetings and groups can hold discussions and lectures, but rituals, which involve structured, active group participation, often lack cohesion or a satisfactory result. For this reason, most covens or groves that meet online restrict that medium to social interaction.

Many coven-initiated Witches do put a lot of emphasis on lineage. Let's say, for example, a Witch named Lady Ravenstar initiates Grailfire into a coven. Ravenstar herself was initiated by Dorothea Sweetwater. Sweetwater is therefore *upline* from Ravenstar, and Grailfire is two degrees *downline* from Sweetwater. This observation of lineage is only relevant within their social circle.

If Grailfire moves, let's say, from Atlanta to Sacramento, and tries to assert his authority by saying, "I was initiated by Lady Ravenstar," who is unknown to Sacramento Witches, their reaction would likely be, "Yeah, and?" Claims of lineage are only valued if you can trace them back—within a reasonable number of generations—to a name people actually recognize, such as Alex Sanders. Solitaires are self-initiated and must stand on their own two feet without a lineage legacy to fall back on.

If a Witch starts out coven-initiated and chooses to leave to practice solitary, can they still claim hereditary lineage? Yes. It happened; you can't take initiation away. There might be some other reason why they wouldn't want that lineage publicly known, but that's a different matter altogether.

What's in a Name?

Many Witches feel the need to differentiate between their mundane life and their coven or magickal life. One of the most obvious ways to do this is to adopt a special magickal name. Many feel that a magickal name is a reflection of the inner personality. For example, Beth Williams or James Hill could be anybody, but not just anyone is SilverCat or Wyvern.

A Witch's magickal name is special; it creates a separation between the mundane and the magickal, and it manifests a special atmosphere. When the Witch enters into ritual, he is no longer James Hill, bus driver. He is Wyvern, a magickal and vibrant member of the coven. Some Witches never disclose their magickal names to the mundane world and vice versa. To know a person's name is to have some control over them; you cannot command somebody if you don't have a label for them. (Try to ask somebody to do something if you can't get their attention.) Since sharing one's name allows some degree of submission, many Witches keep another secret name, revealing it only to the gods themselves. Of course, you don't have to have a magickal name at all. If you are comfortable using your mundane name in ritual, that is entirely acceptable.

How does one choose a magickal name? There are countless ways. Some people just wake up one day and the name is there, while others meditate for hours to find one. Some draw names from history, mythology, or fiction, such as Gwydion or Vanyel. Many Witches research animal powers, gemstones, or other sources and put two or three elements together to form a composite name. Some draw runes or consult a spirit board and let the magickal alphabet spell out a possible name.

My name, for example, is Miles Batty. When I was first exploring the Pagan community at large, I took the name Valerian. Then, when I became legally ordained clergy, I took the magickal name Satyr Moondancer.

You can choose any name you'd like, really. Gwydion, Dionysus, Oakleaf Silverbranch, Ugly Little Snot-Head Jones, it's up to you.

Lesson 17: Study Prompts and Questions

The Origin of the Witch's Coven

- What did the church think went on in covens in the Middle Ages?
- Explain why knowing members of a coven during the Inquisition could have been beneficial and/or harmful.

The Coven Today

- How do modern covens differ from those described in medieval texts?
- What do today's covens offer their members?

Coven Roles and Obligations

- Give a brief summary of each title: seeker, dedicant, initiate, High Priestess, High Priest, elder, first degree, second degree, third degree, maiden/squire, summoner, quarter-caller, archivist, bard, guardian, herald, purse-warden, scribe, and Witch Queen.

Coven, Solitary, or Grove?

- Give two reasons why a Witch might choose to join a coven. Do the same for solitary practice.
- Explain how a grove differs from a coven.
- What is the purpose of a grove?
- Can solitaires be members of a grove? Explain.

What's in a Name?

- What is the significance of having a magickal name separate from your everyday or mundane name?

Lesson 17: Recommended Reading

- *CovenCraft: Witchcraft for Three or More* by Amber K
- *The Wicca Source Book: A Complete Guide for the Modern Witch* by Gerina Dunwich

LESSON 18
The Laws of the Craft

Witchcraft is not an "organized religion," as there is not a central authority that oversees everyone else. But it's not a "disorganized religion" either. As we've seen already, there are roles and obligations, procedures, and protocols that people generally follow, and in the last lesson, lesson 17, we examined the different roles and obligations within the coven. This time we'll look at another aspect of coven life: the code of laws known as the Ardanes.

The Origin of the Ardanes

Gerald Gardner wrote a list of "Ye Old Laws" that was published in his Book of Shadows in 1961. He used a lot of medieval grammar and spelling, and the laws included frequent admonition to deny any knowledge of Witchcraft, to make any magickal tools from household items to avoid detection, and to keep secret any knowledge of other Witches. Whether these were directly inherited from older laws remains conjectural. Like much of Gardner's writing, they could have been derived from much older work, or he could have invented it. They became known as the Ardanes because Gardner frequently ended each law with the phrase "So it be ardane," or ordained.

The Ardanes is a list of laws for the running of a coven and a Witch's personal behavior and gives advice on conduct in the community. Gardner's original version included advice for Witches who were arrested, persecuted, and tortured. It also included punishments for those who betrayed the goddess or other Witches. Many of these older laws are irrelevant today and have been omitted from later versions of the laws. Doreen Valiente and Alex Sanders both edited and amended them, and the laws have been through several revisions since. Some modern covens and traditions use heavily altered versions or don't use them at all.

The Reading of the Laws

The Laws of the Craft, or Ardanes, presented here are adapted from the laws from *A New Wiccan Book of the Law* by Lady Galadriel, who was High Priestess and founder of the Atlanta-based Grove of the Unicorn, which were reprinted in Amber K's *CovenCraft*. In the preparation of this volume, I have revised them to create what I believe to be a more cohesive whole. They are divided into three sections: personal standards and conduct, within the coven, and within the community.

Personal Standards and Conduct

1) An ye harm none, do what ye will.
2) If you know the rede is being broken, you should work to protect it or repair any damage from its breaking.
3) You should not boast, gossip, or speak ill of others.
4) Be truthful always, save when speaking would lead to a greater harm. Let tact and discretion be your guide. Never lie to yourself, for this is the ultimate act of deceit.
5) Watch, listen, and withhold judgment; in debate let your silences be long, your thoughts be clear, and your words carefully chosen.
6) Deal fairly and honestly in all your transactions with others, following the letter and spirit of any contract you agree to.
7) Should you take a task upon yourself, work hard and well to accomplish it properly and in good time. Always strive to do your best.
8) Keep clean your body and your clothes and your house to the best of your ability.
9) Do not attend any ritual or magickal event while drunk or under the effect of mind-altering substances.
10) Raise your children with kindness. Feed, clothe, and house them as well as you can. Show them love and affection; teach them the value of wisdom and just discipline.
11) Never use magick for show, pride, or vainglory.
12) You may accept payment for the work of your hands but never for magick or work performed in ritual or for the teaching of magick or the Craft within circle.

13) Keep within your Book of Shadows the teachings of your coven and a record of your own rites and learnings. Others may copy from it, but it is not to be borrowed or loaned out.

14) Revere, honour, tend, and heal the earth.

15) Of that which you grow, make, or use, let as much as possible return to the earth as an offering to her to nourish the cycle of life.

Within the Coven

1) Before the coven uses any magick, let them debate its purpose at length; only if all are satisfied that none might be intentionally harmed may the magick be used.

2) Never lie to or deceive others of the Craft.

3) No coven member shall disclose personal information about any other member without the express consent of that person.

4) None but the Craft may see our inner mysteries, but with the consent of the coven, friends and relatives may be invited to witness celebratory rituals.

5) No one may tell cowans where the coven is nor where meetings are held without the consent of the coven.

6) Anyone who condones the breaking of the rede shall be banished from the coven for a year and a day and shall only be reinstated by consensus of the coven.

7) None may come to rituals with those with whom they are at odds. Within ritual, no one may invoke any laws but those of the Craft nor any court but that of the elders of the coven.

8) Remember that neither the coven nor any of its members are above the law of the land.

9) The High Priestess shall guide her coven as a representative of the goddess.

10) In circle the words and wishes of the High Priestess are to be honoured.

11) The High Priestess shall choose whom she will as High Priest, providing that he is of sufficient rank.

12) The High Priest shall support the High Priestess and guide the coven as a representative of the god. The High Priest is due the respect given a counsellor, father, and teacher.

13) If there are disputes within the coven, let the High Priestess convene the elders. They shall hear both sides, first alone and then together, and make a just decision.

14) If the High Priestess and High Priest find it necessary to punish or rebuke a coven member, this should be done in privacy and accepted with grace and humility.

15) Any who have issue with the leadership of the High Priestess or High Priest may leave the coven and, if of high enough rank, form a new coven. They and any coven members who wish to depart with them should not inquire of old coven business until tensions are eased and harmonious relations can resume.

16) If a High Priestess leaves her coven with just cause and notice, the maiden shall assume her role during her absence. If the High Priestess returns within a year and a day, she shall be welcomed back without penalty. However, if her absence exceeds a year and a day, a new High Priestess shall be chosen. This law also applies to the High Priest and summoner.

17) If there is just cause to remove either the High Priestess or High Priest from office, a vote is taken. The ousted Witch shall retire with grace and dignity.

Within the Community

1) Respect others and honour their name and identity.

2) Do not judge those of other faiths, but offer them love and support.

3) Offer friendship and hospitality to strangers who visit among you.

4) Give of your skills, your time, and your learning to the community and to those who work for the benefit of the goddess. Honour those who work willingly for the Lord and Lady without compensation.

5) Never handfast or wed with someone you do not honestly love.

6) Honour relationships and commitments, and do not couple together if it will cause harm to another.

7) Do not steal from human, animal, or spirit. If you have needs you cannot meet, turn to the community for support.

8) Never do anything to disgrace the goddess or the Craft.[98]

An Analysis of the Ardanes

At the start of this lesson, I mentioned that Gardner had written what may have been the first "draft" of the Ardanes and that he claimed to have received them from a much older source. Just to get an idea of how far the Ardanes have been revised, here is an excerpt from his version:

> *To void discovery, let the working tools be as ordinary things that any may have in their houses. Let the Pentacles be of wax, so they may be broken at once. Have no sword unless your rank allows you one. Have no names or signs on anything. Write the names and signs on them in ink before consecrating them and wash it off immediately after. Do not Bigrave them, lest they cause discovery. Let the color of the hilts tell which is which.*[99]

The Ardanes presents a guideline of structure and practice for Witches and Wiccans to follow in their personal lives, within the coven, and in the world at large. Some of the rules may seem irrelevant to some, but as a whole, they present a good outline of behavior and practice.

Lesson 18: Study Prompts and Questions

The Origin of the Ardanes
- Where does the term *Ardanes* come from?

The Reading of the Laws
- Condense the meaning of each section into a paragraph or two: personal standards and conduct, within the coven, and within the community.
- Choose any three laws and describe how they could be applied to your own life, both magickal and mundane.

---

98. K, *CovenCraft*, 357–59.
99. Gardner, "The Old Laws."

Lesson 18: Recommended Reading

- *CovenCraft: Witchcraft for Three or More* by Amber K
- *A New Wiccan Book of the Law: A Manual for the Guidance of Groves, Covens & Individuals* by Lady Galadriel

Elements and Correspondences

One of the first things any new Witch learns is the elements and their correspondences, such as air to east and fire to south, but there is so much more to offer than that. In fact, the lists of correspondences relating to each element could go on for days. The lists presented here are a compilation of information I've been collecting for years, and some more esoteric correspondences come from *The Magician's Companion* by Bill Whitcomb.[100]

The Relevance of Elements

When Witches cast the ritual circle, they call upon the elements to be present as guardians and honoured guests during ritual. Tools, herbs, and the desired results of rituals and spells are all governed by different elements. With the elements playing such an important part in the Craft, it is important to take the time to get in touch with them and gain an understanding of each one, their different correspondent attributes, and their unique qualities. To a proficient Witch, becoming attuned with the elements and enriching an active relationship with them is as important as any other part of the Craft.

How can a Witch work with the elements? That's easy! Suppose you're planning a romantic dinner, and you want to enhance the effect. You'd serve a dish that inspires romance and wear clothes and play music that reflects the element of fire, representing passion. Or if a Witch lives in a hostile neighbourhood, surrounding themself with the calming, grounding aspects of the earth element would make their home a private, soothing sanctuary.

Following each of the lists below, take some time to discuss the attributes and correspondences of each element. You may even think of other categories missing from these lists. There are, of course, some crossover correspondences. Gasoline, for example, is an

---

100. Whitcomb, *The Magician's Companion*, 74–76.

aspect of both fire and water, and it is derived from petroleum, which is extracted from the earth.

Air

Air is the power of movement, freshening, and intelligence. Magickally it represents birth, new beginnings, gateways, and progress. Air is the power of the mind and the force of intellect, insight, and forethought. It is the wind as it tousles your hair and rustles the leaves on the trees. It is the whisper of breath and the force of a hurricane. In ritual, everything begins at east, the position of dawn and the new day.

Basic nature: Flying, freshness, intelligence, moving, sound, suspension
Direction: East
Type of energy: Projective
Colour: Yellow
Places: Airports, cloudy skies, high towers, libraries, mountaintops, offices, schools, travel agencies, and windswept plains
Applications: Breaking bad habits, communications, divination, intellectualism, memory, organizing and organizations, schooling, teaching, tests, thought, travel, and writing
Deities: Aditi, Enlil, Mercury, Nuit, Thoth, and Zeus
Season: Spring (the time of freshness and renewal)
Time: Dawn
Senses: Hearing and smell
Natural symbols: Feathers, fragrant flowers, and incense smoke
Plants: Acacia, almond, bamboo, dandelion, ferns, maple, mistletoe, parsley, rice, and sage
Stones: Aventurine, jasper, mica, and pumice
Metal: Mercury
Creatures: Flying insects, most birds, and spiders
Mythical representatives: Sylphs
Spheres of magick: Divination, concentration, visualization, and wind magick
Magickal tool: Wand (or sword)
Ritual forms of expression: Fanning light objects, positive thinking, thrown objects, and visualization

Musical instruments: Flutes, pipes, and wind instruments

Astrological signs: Aquarius, Gemini, and Libra

Tarot suit: Wands and rods (or swords)

Most people classify the athame and sword as aspects of air and the wand as a fire tool. Some people, though, relate the athame and sword to fire's transmuting aspect and associate the wand with the directional properties of air. Your opinion may differ. This course uses the fire/sword and air/wand association.

Fire

Fire is both the creator and the destroyer. It warms our homes, cooks our food, and fuels our passions. It is the only element that can't exist without destroying something else. Fire transforms objects into new forms; it is a physical expression of energy. Magickally fire represents emotion and volition.

Basic nature: Cleansing, destructive, energetic, forceful, purifying, and sexual

Direction: South (the place of heat)

Type of energy: Projective

Colours: Orange and red

Places: Bedrooms (or other sexually oriented areas), deserts, fireplaces, hot springs, ovens, saunas, volcanoes, and weight rooms

Applications: Authority, banishment of negativity, courage, energy, protection, sex, and strength

Deities: Agni, Hestia, Horus, Loki, Pele, and Vulcan

Season: Summer (the time of heat)

Time: Noon

Sense: Sight

Natural symbols: Flame, heated items, and lava

Plants: Allspice, asafoetida, basil, cashew, fig, holly, marigold, oak, orange, red or black pepper, sunflower, tobacco, and yohimbe

Stones: Agate, amber, carnelian, diamond, garnet, lava, obsidian, pumice, quartz, ruby, sulfur, tiger's eye, and topaz

Metals: Brass and gold

Creatures: Bees, cats of all sizes, crickets, ladybugs, lizards, praying mantises, scorpions, and snakes

Mythical representatives: Salamanders

Spheres of magick: Candles, fire-based magick, stars, storms, and time

Magickal tools: Athame and sword (or wand)

Ritual forms of expression: Burning or smoldering, heating, and red-, yellow-, or gold-coloured banners or clothes

Musical instruments: Guitars and most other stringed instruments

Astrological signs: Aries, Leo, and Sagittarius

Tarot suit: Swords (or wands)

Water

Water is the element of cleansing, healing, psychic awareness, and love. The element of water is vital to our well-being as humans, as it contains within it the essence of life, love, and healing.

Basic nature: Flowing, healing, loving, purifying, and soothing

Direction: West (the place of the setting sun)

Type of energy: Receptive

Colours: Blue and white

Places: Bathtubs, beaches, bedrooms (or other sleep-oriented areas), lakes, oceans, rivers, showers, springs, streams, swimming pools, and wells

Applications: Dreams, friendships, love, marriage, peace, psychic awareness, purification, and sleep

Deities: Aphrodite, Llyr, Mari, and Poseidon

Season: Autumn (the time of harvest)

Time: Dusk

Sense: Taste

Natural symbols: Ice, seashells, and water

Plants: Aloe, avocado, banana, catnip, cucumber, eucalyptus, grape, hibiscus, iris, lilac, patchouli, rose, strawberry, and willow

Stones: Amethyst, aquamarine, lapis lazuli, moonstone, pearl, sapphire, and sugilite

Metals: Copper, mercury, and silver

Creatures: Aquatic birds, mammals, and reptiles and fish of all kinds

Mythical representatives: Undines (water nymphs)

Spheres of magick: Fog, ice, magnets, mirrors, sea, and snow

Magickal tools: Cauldron and chalice
Ritual forms of expression: Bathing, immersion, and showers
Musical instruments: Bells, chimes, harps, and rain sticks
Astrological signs: Cancer, Pisces, and Scorpio
Tarot suit: Cups

Earth

Earth, Gaia, is our fertile and nurturing mother. From fertile, moist soil to sand and stone, it is the densest of all the elements. Earth is the grounding element, used to regain focus and clarity after a particularly stressful—or invigorating—magickal working.

Basic nature: Fertile, grounding, moist, nurturing, and stabilizing
Direction: North
Type of energy: Receptive
Colours: Browns and greens
Places: Canyons, caves, chasms, farms, fields, forests, gardens, groves, marketplaces, nurseries, parks, valleys, and wombs
Applications: Business, conservation, ecology, fertility, growth, health issues, investments, jobs, material wealth and gain, money, progress, and promotions
Deities: Cernunnos, Dagda, Demeter, Gaea, Pan, and Tammuz
Season: Winter (the time of darkness)
Time: Night
Sense: Touch
Natural symbols: Acorns, fresh soil, salt, sheaves of wheat, and stones
Plants: Barley, corn, grains, mugwort, pea, potato, and turnip
Stones: Alum, coal, emerald, hematite, malachite, salt, and turquoise
Metal: Lead
Creatures: Burrowing insects, cattle, dogs, earthworms, and most rodents
Mythical representatives: Gnomes
Spheres of magick: Binding, burial, death and rebirth, gardening, knots, and magnetic
Magickal tool: Pentacle
Ritual forms of expression: Burial, growth, and planting seeds and growing plants

Musical instruments: Drums and percussion
Astrological signs: Capricorn, Taurus, and Virgo
Tarot suit: Pentacles

Spirit

The elements all emerge from spirit, the immutable, changeless source of all energy. It is the topmost point of the pentagram. The primal source of energy that creates and fuels the elements, it is perceived as the ultimate source of all life and energy.

Basic nature: Mystery and unknowable
Directions: Above, below, east, lack of direction, north, south, west, within, and without
Types of energy: Projective and receptive
Colours: Black, clear, and purple
Places: Inner space, outer space vacuums, and the void
Applications: Religious ceremonies
Deities: All
Seasons: All
Time: Eternity
Senses: Psychic
Natural symbols: Dream representations and imagination
Plants: All (or none)
Stones: All (or none)
Metal: Any metal not from this planet, and meteorite
Creatures: Dragons
Mythical representatives: Angels and spirits
Spheres of magick: Divinatory and religious
Magickal tools: All (or none)
Ritual forms of expression: All (or none)
Musical instrument: Voice
Astrological signs: All (or none)
Tarot suit: Major arcana

Why There?

We know that east is air, north is earth, and so on. But why do the elements have those specific associations? Why does west correspond to water?

Remember, the Craft as we know it was primarily based on principles developed over hundreds of years in northern Europe. It is based on the scope of reference available to people from that region, and the elemental attributes reflect that. Think of where countries like France and England are on the map. They have the Atlantic Ocean to the west, the mountains and fjords of Norway to the north, and winds blowing in from the east, and travelers to the south approach the warmer equatorial climate. These four references have been the accepted norm for centuries. Some people have decided to alter that perspective, however, on a coven-by-coven basis. If the early Witches had lived in Alaska, for example, water (the Pacific Ocean) would have been south, earth (mountains) would be east, fire (the Aurora Borealis) would be north, and air (the Bering Strait winds) would have been west. And had the Craft originated in São Paulo or Tokyo, the correspondences would have been different again! Even though every book you're likely to read puts air in the east, keep in mind that some covens may have chosen to rearrange the positions.

Lesson 19: Study Prompts and Questions

The Relevance of Elements

- Explain the significance of the elements, and how they can be harnessed in one's everyday life.
- Collect examples of or write an essay or poem, sing a song, or create a dance about each of the five elements.
- On the following list, label each item or concept with its corresponding element.

    (a)ir, (f)ire, (w)ater, (e)arth, and (s)pirit

__ guitar playing	__ hematite	__ Capricorn	__ hearing
__ Thoth	__ gold	__ north	__ cymbals
__ spring	__ noon	__ earthworms	__ meteorites
__ suspension	__ authority	__ magnets	__ knots
__ east	__ cauldron	__ athame	__ west
__ copper	__ writing	__ south	__ lightning

Why There?

- Explain why the elements are assigned their specific positions.
- Would you classify the sword as fire or air? How about the wand? Explain and justify.
- Think of where you were born. Would the elemental positions remain the same, or would they change? Explain.

Lesson 19: Recommended Reading

- *Earth Power: Techniques of Natural Magic* by Scott Cunningham
- *Elemental Witchcraft: A Guide to Living a Magickal Life through the Elements* by Heron Michelle

LESSON 20
Magickal Signs and Symbols

There's no doubt you've seen the pentacle everywhere in Wicca and Witchcraft. The five-pointed star in a circle is the single most used and obvious symbol of the Craft. But what does it mean? What about the sun wheel or the Norse runes? In our last lesson, we examined the elements and their corresponding attributes and applications. This time we'll apply some of what we learned to magickal symbology and study some of the images commonly used in Witchcraft.

The Pentagram

The pentagram is a radially symmetrical five-armed image that appears throughout nature. You'll find it in the starfish, the sand dollar, and the cross-cut core of an apple. Try it! Five itself is a prevalent number in nature. From the veins of the common leaf to the five digits of the hand to the five extensions of humans (arms, legs, and head), five appears in nature more than any other number.[101]

Pentagram

---

101. Wille, "Evidence for Pentagonal Symmetry in Living and Model Cellular Systems," 866–883.

The overlapping bands of the five-pointed star are surrounded by a circle, and it represents the five elements of life enclosed in the endless wheel of unity. The five elements and their meanings are:

Spirit	topmost point	the all, the Divine, and the mysteries
Fire	lower right-hand point	courage, creativity, and inspiration
Air	upper left-hand point	the arts, communication, and intelligence
Water	upper right-hand point	emotions, intuition, and memory
Earth	lower left-hand point	physical endurance, stability, and strength

In magickal workings, the pentagram is drawn or traced in the air in several different ways. To invoke, or to welcome forces in, it is drawn in a deosil (sunwise) pattern, or clockwise. To banish, or drive away, it is drawn in a widdershins pattern, or counterclockwise. According to some traditions, however, it is always drawn deosil, but invocation starts at the earth position, so the first line goes up, and banishments start at spirit, so the first line goes down.

In the Craft, a pentacle is a round disk inscribed with a pentagram and placed upon the altar. The pentacle can be made of many different materials. It may be drawn on a piece of paper, carved from wood, made from brass, or depicted in ornate stained glass. Pentacles made from silver represent the moon's energy, empowering psychic ability, and those made from gold or copper represent the sun's energy, representing strength and vitality. Many Witches wear a pentacle or pentagram as jewelry on a ring, necklace, or pin, and pentagram tattoos are quite popular. Another style of pentagram, the Triple Goddess, shows the pentagram embraced by two crescent moons on its left and right. Together, these are the Maiden (waxing moon), Mother (full moon), and Crone (waning moon), representing the full cycle of life.

The origin of the pentagram dates far back in history. As far back as pre-Babylonian Sumer, it has been used and venerated by countless cultures and civilizations. To the Jewish faith, it represents the Pentateuch, the first five books of scripture. According to Gnostic texts, it represents the five wounds of Christ upon the cross—a nail in each hand and one in the feet, the crown of thorns, and the spear wound. The pentagram is known by a variety of names, including the Druid's foot, Witch's star, and devil's cross.

Why is the pentagram, a symbol of life, often assumed to represent evil forces? The medieval church wanted to rid the world of anything that did not revere Jesus and Jehovah, so any non-Christian spiritual symbology was automatically branded as evil and heretical. The star of life, which had been a symbol of divine illumination, became stigmatized as something evil and corrupt.

How did it come to be seen as evil? Centuries ago, there was a famous symbol that had been used for ages. The Star of Mendes depicts an inverted pentagram with a goat's head superimposed over the arms of the pentagram. It is not evil at all, and centuries ago it was simply a protective icon for farmers and travelers that had been used for ages. It symbolized the bounty of harvest and livestock and safe travels. The Knights Templar adopted this symbol as their own, and when the Knights were targeted by the church as a heretical force, the accusations of Witchery and devil worship stuck, and the Star of Mendes became synonymous with both devil worshippers and Witches, which further confused the issue.

The inverted pentagram, long associated with Satanism, is not inherently evil either; it merely reflects their view of cosmology. Satanists, you may remember, view material progress as more vital than spiritual growth. By inverting the pentagram, spirit is at the bottom, putting earth (material) and fire (creativity) at the top.

Some Witches use the inverted pentagram to empower a life-changing decision or progress, and it is used in some traditions to represent having achieved second-degree status. To this day, Hollywood continues to misrepresent the pentagram in cheesy horror movies, portraying it as a symbol of evil or malevolent forces.

The Elemental Symbols

The four alchemical symbols have been used since the Middle Ages when alchemists strove to discover the philosopher's stone and the secret of making gold. The first four Greek symbols have been used for centuries; the fifth Greek symbol is a relatively recent addition.

	Air	Fire	Water	Earth	Spirit
Alchemical	△	△	▽	▽	
Greek	☉	○	⊖	⊕	✳

Elemental Symbols

The Symbols of Degree

While some traditions or covens don't use the degree system to recognize advancement within the Craft, many others do. These are the symbols most commonly used to represent degrees:

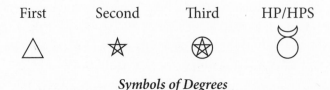

First   Second   Third   HP/HPS

Symbols of Degrees

In some traditions, the second degree is identified by an inverted pentagram. This is falling out of favor due to its association with devil worship.

Other Magickal Symbols

There are hundreds of other symbols used in magick, including the zodiac signs, planetary symbols, and others. We won't examine all of them, but these are a few of the more common signs whose meanings are sometimes ignored or misunderstood.

Ankh

The ankh is widely recognized as an Egyptian symbol of life. It is not, as some Christians will tell you, a modified version of the crucifix. The exact origin of the ankh is unknown. Some say it represents a sheaf of reeds tied in a knot, symbolizing prosperity. To others, it is the phallus of a bull. To even others, it is a representation of a sandal strap, as clothing is symbolic of protection.

Ankh

Triskele

The triskele is a truly ancient symbol. The three-lobed spiral motif can be found in pre-Celtic Iron Age art, circa 3000 BCE, and the three human leg symbol dates from Hellenic Greece, before 300 BCE. The symbol depicts three radial arms, or spokes, and represents the endless wheel of life and progress. Some Wiccans use the triskele as a symbol of dexterity and vitality.

A variation of the triskele is the swastika, showing four arms instead of three. While it once was a valid magickal symbol seen in Sanskrit and Buddhist imagery, it has been permanently tainted by its association with Nazis and the Third Reich.

Triskele

Hexagram

Commonly regarded as a Jewish symbol, the hexagram was not directly associated with the Hebrew faith until the nineteenth century CE. It has appeared in nearly every human culture, from India to the Middle East to Mesoamerica, and has been known as the Star of David, the Star of Solomon, and the elemental knot. This symbol of two identical, interconnected triangles represents balance, equality, and the union between earth and heaven, humankind and god, and the seen and the unseen.

In magick, the hexagram is often seen as a Western counterpart to the yin-yang symbol of balance.

Hexagram

Unicursal Hexagram

Used by ceremonial magicians for centuries, the unicursal hexagram is a stylized version of the hexagram that can be drawn with one line, as the two triangles are connected and interwoven. It can also be seen as two connected pentagrams at east and west. Aleister Crowley used this symbol extensively, adding a five-petaled rose at the center, which unified the Rosicrucian rose, the pentagram, and the macro-cosmic forces of divinity.

Unicursal Hexagram

Om

Originating in India, the om is the foremost Sanskrit symbol of life. Also known as pranava, it represents the "primal voice" of the gods, ultimate consciousness, and the foundation of song and heart. Wiccans use the om as a symbol of life and prosperity.

Om

Udjat

The Eye of Horus, also known as the udjat or wedjat, comes from ancient Egypt. According to myth, Horus's left eye was the sun and his right eye was the moon. Horus's rival god, Set, tore out one (or both) of his eyes, which was healed and returned with the help of Thoth. As such, the symbol represents protection, healing and well-being, and true sight. Sailors would often paint the udjat on their boats in gold on the left and silver on the right.

Udjat

Magickal Writing

One of the major accomplishments of human civilization is the creation of words and letters, the ability to write messages that another person can read and understand. Humankind has created hundreds of writing styles, including the Japanese kanji, the Celtic ogham, and the Egyptian hieroglyphics.

We won't learn to read hieroglyphics here, but we will examine three writing systems popular with modern Witches: the Theban alphabet, futhark, and ogham.

Theban Alphabet

The Theban alphabet was first published in Johannes Trithemius's book *Polygraphia*. There, it is attributed to the scholar Honorius of Thebes, although some modern historians cite Trithemius's student Agrippa as its creator. The alphabet is a direct cipher of the classical Latin alphabet, and as such the letters *J*, *U*, and *W* are absent. The characters themselves are stylized from Hebrew. Francis Barrett included the alphabet in his 1801 book, *Magus*, and it has been popular with occultists and esoteric practitioners ever since.[102]

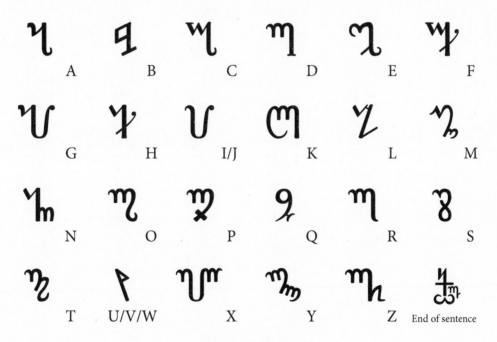

Theban Alphabet

---

102. Barrett, *The Magus*, 64.

Futhark

The futhark gets its name from the first six letters of this Norse runic script, just as alpha and beta, the first two Greek letters, give the alphabet its name. According to Norse mythology, Odin, the All-father, impaled himself with his own spear and hung upside down from Yggdrasil, the Tree of Life, for nine days. In a near-death state, he saw the runes before him, stirring up from the depths of the earth. At the cost of his right eye, Odin was able to give humankind the gift of letters and the ability to speak beyond words. More than just a writing system, the futhark is also a popular divinatory system.

F	U	Th	A	R	K	G	W
ᚠ	ᚢ	ᚦ	ᚨ	ᚱ	ᚲ	ᚷ	ᚹ

H	N	I	J	Ei	P	Z	S
ᚺ	ᚾ	ᛁ	ᛃ	ᛇ	ᛈ	ᛉ	ᛋ

T	B	E	M	L	Ng	D	O
ᛏ	ᛒ	ᛖ	ᛗ	ᛚ	ᛜ	ᛞ	ᛟ

Futhark

Ogham

The ogham (OH-em or OGG-am) script is an early Irish writing system created around the fourth century CE. According to legend, the god Ogma gave the writing system to the people, so they could communicate with each other without alerting invaders—Romans or early Christians. Easily carved into wood or stone, the alphabet follows a central line from which the letters emerge. An ogham sentence, or tree, is usually written vertically from the ground up. Some versions of the ogham show the vowels as small bumps on the tree "trunk," and only consonants appear as branches.

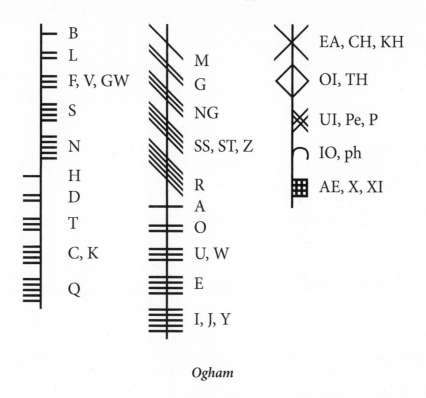

Ogham

In Summary

These are but a few of the hundreds of symbols, writing styles, and magickal imagery available to the Witch. With a little research, you can discover other symbols, their origins, and magickal significance.

Lesson 20: Study Prompts and Questions

The Pentagram

- Draw a pentagram. Then, using your image, identify the five elemental points, and show deosil and widdershins directions.
- What is the symbolism behind the pentagram?
- Offer three examples of naturally occurring pentagrams.
- Satanists and some Witches use an inverted pentagram. What is the significance of this? Is it evil? Explain.

The Elemental Symbols

- Draw the symbols, both Greek and alchemical, for air, fire, water, earth, and spirit.

The Symbols of Degree

- Identify each symbol:

- Why do you think these specific symbols are used?
- Do you agree with the progression from first degree to Priestess? Explain and justify.

Other Magickal Symbols

- Draw and briefly explain the following symbols: ankh, triskele, hexagram, unicursal hexagram, om, and udjat.

Magickal Writing

- On a separate sheet, practice writing with the three alphabets provided.

Lesson 20: Recommended Reading

- *The Magician's Companion: A Practical and Encyclopedic Guide to Magical and Religious Symbolism* by Bill Whitcomb
- *Symbols of the Occult: A Directory of Over 500 Signs, Symbols, and Icons* by Eric Chaline

LESSON 21
The Tools of the Craft

When the average person thinks of a Witch, they may imagine an old hag on a broom or someone holding a wand or peering into a crystal ball. Others may see a person holding an athame or reading from a large book full of mysterious writing.

The tools of a Witch's craft have almost become synonymous with the Craft itself, and you may already have some of these tools of your own. Everyone associates these things with Witchcraft, but what do they really mean? Is an athame just a pretty knife, or is it more than that? Why is a Book of Shadows called that? What's a thurible for? Let's find out.

Altar

Almost every Witch keeps an altar. It is the central material point of the Witch's worship of the Lord and Lady, a meditation area, and the worktable for spells they are casting. As with many aspects of the Craft, there used to be strict rules as to how an altar was set up, what went where, and so on. Now much more free-form expression is allowed. Some traditions maintain that an altar must be "just so," that the goddess statue goes *here*, and the athame is placed *there*.

One commonly accepted guideline is that the altar should be positioned so the Witch faces east when standing at the altar, if possible. This way they are facing the elemental position of the portal, the gateway, new beginnings, and the rising sun. The altar is usually kept in the temple, which can be anything from a specific room in the house to a designated corner of the living room to an outdoor grove. Wherever the temple is, it is commonly entered from the east. Again, it is the position of dawn, portals, and new beginnings. This means that a Witch would enter from the east and walk deosil around the altar so they are facing east. The Witch can then begin their worship, magickal working, or whatever.

Common Altar Items

Here's a short list of some of the things found on a common Witch's altar and what they mean:

- *Goddess image:* Representative of the Lady
- *God image:* Representative of the Lord
- *Chalice:* Symbolic of the feminine aspect
- *Athame:* Symbolic of the masculine aspect
- *Candles:* Symbolic of the "life" of the altar; they are lit to honour the Lord and Lady and burned in spellworking.
- *Pentacle:* The "foundation" of the altar
- *Book of Shadows:* The Witch's diary, journal, and spellbook
- *Salt:* An element of earth; used, along with water, for purification
- *Water:* Usually spring or mineral water; used, along with salt, for purification; it's commonly kept in a small dish or shell of its own, not in the chalice.
- *Incense:* Used to purify the altar and enhance the magick; incense is usually burned in a censer. All forms of incense are acceptable.
- *Feather:* Symbolic of the element of air; often used to "spread" the incense
- *Crystal ball:* Popular scrying tool
- *Assorted stones and crystals:* These might be placed on the altar to add their own energies, to enhance a magickal working in progress, or simply to "charge" them.

Granted, that's a lot of stuff to put on an altar, and depending upon the altar size available, you might simply not have room for everything.

As for the altar itself, it can be set up anywhere, from an available shelf to the top of a dresser in the bedroom to a convenient reading nook. Some altars are portable; they can be quickly packed into a box or luggage for easy travel or storage. A Witch's altar doesn't have to be anything elaborate. It can be made from whatever you have available. A shrine, incidentally, is like an altar dedicated to a specific deity. You'd have an altar for general magickal work and a shrine to Brigit, for example.

Altar

Whatever the items, most are consecrated and personally dedicated to the individual Witch. Some have never even been touched by another person, and to do so is a gross faux pas. Unless you know it's a coven-use item or you have permission, don't touch another Witch's magickal tools. A sample consecration ritual is included in appendix 3 of this book.

For many Witches, the altar is as personal as their wardrobe. Some buy expensive statues of the Lord and Lady, such as gold-plated figures of Isis and Osiris, while others are content with a seashell for the goddess and an acorn or a piece of antler for the god.

Should the goddess statue be to the right of the god or the left? Most people place her at the left, but let's examine both sides. At many wedding ceremonies, the bride stands to the left of the groom, and many feel that the altar should reflect that divine marriage. Of course, at most weddings, the guests are looking at the bride and groom's backs. Look at it from the perspective of the officiant performing the ceremony—or the Witch at the altar. From that viewpoint, the goddess is on the right and the god on the left. Some also say that the goddess should stand on the right because right-handed people, using the left side of the brain, are more material and solid, like the Earth Mother, and left-handers, using the right side of their brain, are more artistic and flightier, like the ever-changing god as he grows through the seasons. Others would argue that Odin, for example, is less flighty than Aphrodite. While general consensus puts the goddess statue to the left of the god, everyone is allowed to be different.

Regarding the altar as a whole, feel free to research altar design and arrangement, but let your resources and creativity flow. It's customary to put the athame near the god and the chalice near the goddess, reflecting the gender association, but again, this is not mandatory. Just as your wardrobe should reflect your personality, your altar should reflect your personal relationship with the Lord and Lady.

Chalice

The chalice is a cup or vessel used to hold water, wine, or other liquids. It can be as ornate or as plain as the Witch desires. Symbolic of the goddess, the chalice is to the female as the athame is male. Representative of the element of water, it is a symbol of life. While every Witch keeps a personalized chalice on their own altar, many covens use a special chalice for group-oriented rituals, which is passed from person to person, each one taking a sip. Of course, if you prefer not to share a drinking vessel, there is no breach of protocol in using your own. You simply hold your chalice up, and the Priest or Priestess pours the chosen liquid into your chalice, and you drink from that. Note that many people like using pewter goblets and chalices. Pewter was originally a blend of tin, copper, and lead, making lead poisoning a risk. Modern pewter, from the 1800s onwards, uses antimony in place of lead and is much safer. Lead-based pewter is much darker in colour.

Athame

The athame (ah-THAH-may or AH-tha-may) is one of the most well-known of the Witch's tools. In magick, the athame is seen as an extension of the Witch's arm, sort of a focusing tool or magickal amplifier. Since the athame is a "power tool," it is usually made from a conductive metal like steel or copper, not inert materials like wood or glass. A conductive element is more beneficial to the magickal flow. Traditionally the athame is a black-handled, double-edged knife with Witch's runes (often in Theban script) carved into the handle. The blade is usually as long as the Witch's hand from wrist to fingertip, and the specific blade length "bonds" the athame to its user. The double-edged blade is a reminder that magick is like a two-edged sword; if misused, it can as easily harm as heal. The handle is black, symbolic of the mysteries inherent in the Craft. Magickally it is perceived as a masculine tool and an aspect of the god.

As times change, so do the laws and customs within the Craft. Many Witches still adhere to the traditional formula for the athame, but others tend to vary. A Witch who honours Freyja might prefer futhark engravings, or a queer Witch might prefer a rainbow-coloured handle. Some prefer to handcraft their own. One athame I have used is carved from willow wood; another has a ten-inch agate blade in a handle of antler bone. Yet another is a simple paring knife from the kitchen with a blue plastic handle, treasured by its owner. The appearance of the athame, like many things, is a question of personal preference. If it works well for you, nobody else has the right to tell you it's wrong.

Every Witch understands that the athame is never used for harm or violence; this rule is inviolate. It must never be perceived as a weapon. Some Witches do, however, disagree on what the athame *can* be used for. To some, it is used in ritual only; essentially its only use is being waved about in the air. To others, the athame can be used for more material applications. For example, it can be used to cut a loaf of Lammas bread in ritual, and some say that any meal cut with such a tool is "blessed." Other Witches use the athame as regularly as a normal kitchen knife. If it is the first thing within reach, the athame is what is used to open the electric bill.

The appearance of the athame—as well as its use—is up to the individual Witch.

Candles

Everyone, whether Craft or not, uses candles. Some light them at romantic dinners, others save them for emergencies. Witches use candles in ritual, to welcome the gods into ritual, for spellworking, or simply for atmosphere. Candles can be made from beeswax, paraffin wax, or synthetic ingredients. Most Witches who can afford them prefer organic beeswax, but of course, paraffin wax is much easier to come by. Some candles are shaped like people or animals, and appropriate figure candles can add to the effect of the spellwork. The colour of candles is important as well; those used for the elements, for example, should be of corresponding colours. The significance of colour in magick and ritual will be discussed in lesson 32.

Some Witches save the candle stubs and melt them down to make new candles.

Pentacle

The pentacle is the central piece of the common Witch's altar. It is usually a round disk inscribed with a pentagram. As a representation of the element of earth, it is usually made of metal or wood. The pentacle can, of course, be as ornate as the Witch desires. Some use a hand-painted clay plate, while others prefer professionally engraved copper disks. One pentacle I have seen is a three-foot circle made of stained glass; another is made from carefully poured salt crystals and replenished at every esbat.

Book of Shadows

It may seem ironic that something so full of enlightening information is called a Book of Shadows, but there is actually a good reason for this. The knowledge of the Craft is often referred to as the mysteries or secrets. A popular and seemingly contradictory quote from beat-generation poet Lew Welch is "Guard the mysteries! Constantly reveal them!"[103] So *shadows* is a variation of *mysteries*, or hidden knowledge. The knowledge found within a Book of Shadows is not to be hidden from view but protected and cherished and revealed through the words or action of the Witch. There is no single book for all Witches, and each Witch should keep their own Book of Shadows, or at least there should be one for the coven. Since the Craft has many different traditions, the sabbats and esbats can be observed in a myriad of different ways. Likewise, no two Witches have identical Books of Shadows. For example, a fifty-eight-year-old Gardnerian grandmother would have a different Book of Shadows than a nineteen-year-old member of a Faerie Wiccan coven.

What exactly is in a Book of Shadows? Pretty much anything the Witch feels is important. There is no set rule as to what it should contain or how it should be organized. Most contain the basics of the Craft, copies of rituals the Witch attended, spell ingredients, and notes from classes and workshops. Other components of a Witch's Book of Shadows might include poetry, recipes, pictures of gods and goddesses, chants, and songs. Some older Witches keep several "volumes" of Shadows that are divided by topic.

Among the older Ardanes is the statement that each Witch should write their Book of Shadows by hand. Some covens adhere to this. Others say that pages copied from books, typed pages, and articles downloaded and printed from websites are fine. Let's examine both sides of the argument:

---

103. Welch, *Ring of Bone*, 114.

On one side, one might say, "Any fool can stuff paper into the printer and push a button or download an app, but to handwrite one's own Book of Shadows is a long and dedicated process. It is a mark of loyalty to the Craft and to the gods. By writing each page by hand, you put your own energies into the work. It is your book and nobody else's."

On the other side, one might argue, "A printed page can have a more professional, magickal look. As the Witch advances in the Craft, their Book of Shadows will likewise grow. A printed Book of Shadows is more organized, easier to read, and easier to edit and update. Handwritten pages, with crossed out words and notes scribbled in the margins, can look sloppy and lazy. Besides, most Witches don't handcraft their own jewelry, they buy it. A Book of Shadows is really no different."

Unless your coven specifies otherwise, this choice is up to you. Books of Shadows can be decorated as the Witch favors too. Some have a medieval tome look, others are decorated with fabrics, feathers, and shells, and some have a more horror-goth look. It's all up to you.

In this digital age, some people don't even have a physical Book of Shadows. Instead, they are quite happy with an App of Shadows.

Wand

The wand is not as widely used as one may think. It's certainly not like using a spell gun and shouting vaguely Latin-sounding words at someone. It is often seen as a counterpart or alternative to the athame. While the athame is a tool of transformation, the wand is a tool of focus used to direct the casting of a spell—not unlike an orchestra conductor's baton. The wand is commonly used for invocations; it is waved through the air as words are spoken or chanted. Wands can be as ornate or plain as the spell—or the Witch—demands.

Common wands are made from wood, such as willow, oak, or ash, or copper, glass, or bone. They can be decorated with ribbons, crystals, and charms.

Other Magickal Tools

There are many other magickal tools available to a Witch; let's examine a few here:

Bell

The bell is used to signify the start or finish of a ritual or to close a spellworking. Since the bell is an element of air, a light, tinselly sound is usually preferred over a heavy, sonorous tone. Some Witches prefer chimes or Tibetan singing bowls.

Boleen (or Boline)

The boleen isn't as widely used as it once was. It is a small sickle-bladed knife used to cut herbs prior to ritual or spellwork. It is generally more associated with Druids than Witches, but many Witches who cultivate their own herb garden prefer to use a consecrated boleen before any other cutting tool.

Broom (or Besom)

Yes, Witches really do use brooms. But no, they don't fly on them. The broom, also called a besom, has many uses. It can be used to clean the circle area before ritual or to banish negative elements from the covenstead. Traditionally a decorated broom is hung over the front door to keep negativity away. The broom represents both the goddess and the god. Whereas the athame is masculine, and the chalice is feminine, the broom is both—it is balanced. It's a long, hard part stuck into a triangular hairy part. No, really.

Cauldron

The cauldron is a metal pot anywhere from a few inches to a few feet across. It has hundreds of uses and can be everything from incense burner to offering bowl. Traditionally the cauldron was a large cooking pot used to prepare meals for the coven or the community. Just as the chalice is symbolic of the goddess, so is the cauldron. It is her womb, symbolizing the mysteries of birth.

Censer

The censer is another type of incense burner. Usually a hanging metal dish, it is carried into ritual by the summoner. A censer can often be seen in formal Catholic masses; it is swung by an altar boy before the procession. Incense is generally popular among Witches, and it is burned in ritual, for meditation, or just for the pleasant aroma. Another form of censer is the thurible, which stands on a solid base as opposed to hanging. Since incense is an element of air, a hanging censer is often more popular.

Cord

Some covens and Witches use the cord, others don't. Cords can be initiatory and presented to a Witch by the coven as they advance in degree. They can also be magickal and used as part of spellwork.

An initiatory cord, also known as a measure or cingulum, is a length of braided cord, about a quarter to half an inch across, that is measured to the Witch's height plus girth or height plus span, from fingertip to fingertip, making them usually between eight and twelve feet long. An initiatory cord can be tied and worn as a belt with the ritual garb or hidden away in some secret place known only to the Witch themself. First-degree cords are often green in colour, representing new beginnings. Second degrees are red for inspiration and creativity, and third are black for a deeper understanding of the mysteries. Upon a Witch's initiation into a coven, the High Priestess presents the Witch with the cord. Some traditions say that knots are ritually tied in the cord as the Witch advances through the ranks, binding them to the Craft.

Cords used in spellwork are a much simpler affair. They can be any colour relevant to the spellwork or the task at hand and made of any material that seems appropriate. Knots are tied in the cord to mark events or decisions made. The cord can also be cut, or ritually severed, to mark the ending of something. Cords used as part of a Witch's initiation are usually braided silk, unless the initiate has a preference.

Crystal Ball

One of the most traditional of "Witchy" things is a crystal ball, which is a scrying tool. By looking into the ball, the Witch's vision turns inward, focusing on the question at hand. The answer or resolution often presents itself in this meditative state. Most crystal balls are actually glass, which is easier to produce, contains fewer impurities, and is much, much cheaper than crystal. Other scrying tools used by Witches include mirrors, shallow pools of water, spirals, or anything else that serves to focus the Witch's attention to a nowhere place while the subconscious or meditative mind gets to work sorting things out.

Drum

Go to any Pagan festival and you'll notice a preponderance of drums. Anything from *djembes* to mushroom-shaped *doumbeks* to Irish *bodhráns* can be found, and a drumming circle is often going from dawn to dusk. On a more personal level, drums are used in coven rituals to mark a heartbeat tempo during meditations, to signify the start or end of rituals, or simply for a spirit-lifting experience.

Garb

Can a Witch's garb be considered a magickal tool? Possibly not, but it is something that the Witch uses in ritual and magickal work. Some Witches work skyclad, making the garb used the Witch's own skin. Some covens insist that all Witches wear matching garb or at least matching accessories like sashes or tabards. Other Witches prefer medieval-looking garb or long, flowing robes. Some might wear saris, kilts, or other cultural dress that reflects their own personal ancestry, or animal hides. Here's a point: a Priest of Herne might wear a deer-hide cloak, which could offend a vegan member of the coven. Consider the reactions and feelings of other coven members when choosing your garb. Whatever the individual Witch chooses to wear is fine as long as no toes are stepped on.

One part of a Witch's garb that used to be widely accepted is the garter. Worn on a female Witch's left thigh, it would denote rank or office, either by colour of band or number of buckles or by number of garters worn. The garter is only used today by Old Craft covens, such as Gardnerians.

Mortar and Pestle

These are the bowl and grinder you see on many pharmacy logos. Used for mixing and powdering herbs and incense, these are a staple of many herbalists. Here's an easy way to remember which part is which: Think of the athame and the chalice. The pestle is masculine, like the athame, and the mortar is feminine, like the chalice. Think *p* for pestle, or papa (god), and *m* for mortar, or mama (goddess).

Staff

Staffs seem to be more popular among male Witches than female. (Think of Gandalf, as opposed to Glenda.) For practical purposes, it can be used as a walking stick or a crutch. Magickally it is regarded as a "wand on steroids" and is consecrated to the specific Witch. The staff is usually the same height as the wearer and decorated with crystals, carved letters, or elemental symbols.

Sword

Some covens use swords in ritual, others don't. They are rarely used by Solitary Witches in ritual, even though many Witches keep swords for decoration. In coven rituals, the Priest walks the perimeter of the circle with the sword, to mark the circle boundary before magick begins. The sword is often referred to as the Master of the Five Elements, a martial arts master once told me, because it is "formed from earth, forged in fire, cooled in water, wielded through air, guided by spirit." Coven swords can be simple fencing épées, elaborate French rapiers with flamboyant basket hilts, or huge Scottish claymores. The shape and use of the sword is, of course, up to the will of the individual Witch or coven. Some traditions use the sword in an initiation ritual, similar to a queen knighting somebody.

And Then There's *That* Guy

What are *not* traditional Witches' tools? Pointy black hats, warty noses, ugly shoes, houses made of candy, that silly, screeching cackle—the list goes on. By the way, have you ever wondered why Witches are often shown wearing pointy black hats? Here's the answer: Anyone of a spiritual nature is said to be in tune with a higher wisdom. A tall hat, such as a stereotypical Witch's or wizard's hat or the pope's miter, represents this attunement; it's like an antenna to the gods. The pope's is white, but since Witches are supposed to be evil, theirs are black. Interestingly enough, the unicorn's horn represents the same thing, as do those little red devil's horns. When Michelangelo carved a statue of Moses, he also gave him two little horns.

Lesson 21: Study Prompts and Questions

- Review the list of tools of the Craft. Write a brief explanation for each and describe how it is used: altar, athame, bell, boleen, Book of Shadows, broom, candles, cauldron, censer, chalice, cord, crystal ball, drum, garb, mortar and pestle, pentacle, staff, sword, and wand.
- Draw an image of an altar and explain why you put the different components where you did.

Lesson 21: Recommended Reading

- *The Witches' Way: Principles, Rituals, and Beliefs of Modern Witchcraft* by Janet and Stewart Farrar
- *The Witch's Altar: The Craft, Lore & Magick of Sacred Space* by Jason Mankey and Laura Tempest Zakroff

LESSON 22
Reality and Magickal Perception

Over the next few lessons, we'll start to develop an understanding of magick and magickal theory. I'll begin with the Witch's view of reality, cosmology, and energy. This is where I explore the correlation between Witchcraft and science. This lesson may seem a little haphazard as I jump around from science to belief to magick to worship to visualization and back again to build a foundation of magickal theory. Like much of the information presented here, this analysis is my own, and it's based on input from dozens of different sources. I'm using science to explain how magick works, but it's going to take a few short side trips to get there. Unlike some belief systems, I believe that the Craft does not try to contradict science but complements it.

Sound odd? Well, get ready. This is pretty heady stuff, so put your thinking caps on!

Reality and Energy

What is reality? How and why do we perceive it the way we do? Reality, simply put, is the state or quality of being real—of existing separately from other things and independent of ideas concerning it. Of course, sometimes the answers you find in the dictionary aren't always enough.

Reality, as we understand it, is existence. You exist. You breathe, pump blood, and think. You are real. You know that a brick is real; you can hold it in your hands and feel its weight. If it falls on your foot, you are suddenly very aware of the reality of the brick! That is a *fundamental reality*. If someone else describes a brick falling on their foot, you are not aware of the reality of this brick but merely the suggestion of it. That is *implied reality*. You are asked to believe that the brick exists without tangible proof.

Now, if enough people believe that this person's implied brick is real, it becomes commonly accepted knowledge that it is a real brick. The more believers this brick has, the more valid it becomes. The suggestion, or implied reality, becomes a *consensual reality*. This is one of the building blocks of magickal theory, which we will get back to a little bit later. Please note that consensual reality has its limits. It cannot turn a lie into a truth.

Scientists have learned that all things vibrate at different frequencies. Light rays are a vibrational frequency of energy. Slow down the frequency, and light becomes sound. Accelerate it, and it becomes ultraviolet, then X-ray, and so on. Matter also vibrates; it is a cohesive dance of atoms that form what we interpret as solid matter. In reality, matter is just another form of energy. The spinning components of the atom create a waveform of quantum energy, which reacts as a physical barrier. You can pick up a glass of water because the quantum waveform of the atoms in the glass creates a physical boundary that the quantum waveform of the water cannot penetrate, and your hand is able to close around the glass and pick it up.

If you could alter the vibrational frequency of your hand, it would be theoretically possible to pass through solid matter. Following that logic, one could become other forms of energy. Matter could become light, sound, and so on if the altered vibrational frequency was attainable. We'll come back to this in a little bit too.

Your living body is an electrochemical battery. Electrons are the power source of atoms, atoms are the building blocks of molecules, and molecules build the cells in the body. Without those minute electrical charges, your body would stop altogether. And within the body, the brain is a chemical factory. It creates molecules that zip along neurons to tell muscles to move, it receives molecular messages about the body, and much like a computer, it stores memory and thought in different combinations of cells and molecules.

Just as the brain is a chemical factory, the less tangible "mind" is an energy nexus, or transmitter. Thought is just a particular sequence of atoms within the brain—just another dance of energy waves. Most people can transmit their thoughts to others via speech or writing and receive others' thoughts via sight or sound. Some people can send and receive data directly from the brain, using an extension of thought-waves we know as psychic ability. For others, the aura exists as a visual manifestation of thought energy, or life energy or ch'i. More intense vibrations create a brighter aura.

In other words, there are different forms of reality: matter, energy, and thought. How does this relate to religion? Well, religion is another perception of consensual reality. Science and religion are like two paths through the woods that both arrive at the center from different directions.

Let's go off on a tangent for just a moment. In Starhawk's Wiccan creation myth, we learned that the goddess created the universe as an expression of love. Accepting that story as a consensual reality, we must ask: if Witchcraft and science are compatible, how does love fit into scientific theory? (Well, it's not that we must, but I want to. So there.)

Love, by any other name, is seen as the principal driving force of the universe. Why do atoms form into molecules? Why does thought exist? Science can peer deeper and deeper into the microspace within the atom, but the "why" of atomic bonding—the basic nucleosynthesis of all matter—is still a mystery. It could be speculated that these events occur and these things exist because of the inherent desire to exist and to continue to exist. Without growth there is entropy, but as long as there is energy and activity, there is growth. Let's call it "subatomic altruism," for lack of a better term. Do atoms say to themselves, "Today I'm going to form a new molecule"? Well, no, but the basic subatomic bonding element of the universe and the drive to grow and exist is beyond physical or chemical analysis. It is inherent in the nature of positive energy to react in a positive manner. Subatomic altruism. This can be explained metaphorically: all energy possesses a desire to grow, and the desire can be defined metaphorically as love.

Energy and Magick

We know that all reality derives from different forms of energy and that energy is mutable. So where do magick and Witchcraft figure into this? Magick, according to Aleister Crowley, is "the Science and Art of causing change to occur in conformity with Will."[104]

By using natural and learned abilities, we can manipulate energies to achieve a desired goal. Magick is an extension of willpower; it is an extension of intent. By expanding that willpower, one can shift energies and alter reality and matter. Witchcraft is one of many frameworks in which magick can be harnessed; it is a spiritual foundation upon which magick and spells can be based.

Remember consensual reality? If enough energy is raised, it can be used to manifest changes upon reality. Magick is the ability to connect with and alter common reality, and a magick spell is the focal point, or the accelerator, of the will. Magickal tools, such as athames and wands, are really just props. The spell does not really need them, but a human can be a weak creature. Tools and props help to enhance the will of the caster. It's

---

104. Crowley, *Magick in Theory and Practice*, xii.

the same reason that churchgoing Christians sing hymns during church services. It's a way to focus the will and raise the energy of the prayer.

Magick and Reality

How does magick "work"? Magick is focused willpower that makes it possible to enact changes upon the vibrational frequency of related forces, which in turn manifest as altered reality. Magickal apparatus and spell components add flavour and focus to the will—to the intent—to enhance the spell's purpose. Spells, then, are that bridge between thought, intent, and reality.

As we saw earlier, consensual reality is a commonly accepted perception of reality. The brick on the foot, for example. Likewise, the reality of principle is a commonly accepted facet of reality.

Legal laws, for example, are not tangible, touchable things, but we understand and accept the reality of them. If you drive much too fast or backward in rush hour traffic, you will face the reality of law when you are ticketed for reckless driving. Laws are a consensually recognized manifest principle.

This concept applies to spellcasting as well. If there is enough conviction that a spell will work, then it will, although not always as the caster intended. If more people are involved, the confidence is increased exponentially. If a spellcaster lacks conviction or confidence, the effectiveness of the spell is, of course, weakened.

Magickal Perception

Magickal perception, also known as astral perception, starlight vision, or metaphysical reality, is a different form of reality. It is the ability to perceive magick as a tangible presence. This is a crucial part of magick—knowing that a spell is working because you can actually see it.

An excellent example of magickal perception involves a man named David Seidler, a British scriptwriter who worked on *The King's Speech* and other films. He'd been diagnosed with bladder cancer in 2006. After years of fighting off the cancer with medications, it returned in 2011, and Seidler was to the point of considering radical surgery or chemotherapy. He started using a technique known as creative visualization. As Seidler put it, "I spent hours visualizing a nice cream-coloured, unblemished bladder lining, and then I went in for the operation, and a week later the doctor called me and his voice was very strange. He said, 'I don't know how to explain it, but there's no cancer there.'" He says the doctor was so confounded he sent the tissue from the presurgical biopsy to four different labs, and all confirmed they were cancerous. Seidler says the doctor couldn't explain how it had happened. But Seidler could. He says he believes the visualizations and a change in his thinking, along with the supplements, were behind what his doctor called a "spontaneous remission." He had stopped feeling sorry for himself because of his cancer and impending divorce.[105] This form of magickal perception is also known as creative visualization, or mind over matter.

Seeing a spell working is as important as the strength of will or power of intent when you cast it.

A good way to see magick is the spark of light exercise. Hold your hands in front of you with the palms facing each other about three inches apart. Now imagine a tiny spark of energy flowing through you in a circle. It should flow from your heart, down one arm, across the gap between your hands, up the other arm, and back around again. When you are comfortable doing that, spin the energy faster and faster until it is a continuous ring. As it crosses the gap, try to see the energy as a glowing crackle of light, arcing from palm to palm.

Eventually the energy will become easy to see. You won't have a physical spark—you can't light your candle with it—but you'll imagine the spark whizzing around, and your creative visualization will empower it. While there is no tangible, glowing light source there, you can see the light you created by sheer force of will. (Even if you didn't "see" the light, did you feel the adrenaline-like crackle of energy in your hands? That's a start!)

Magickal perception is the ability to see magick happening. Despite some people's psychic awareness and astral vision, most people are just base, visually oriented creatures. To see is to know, and to know is to believe. The Witch can visualize the spark of light arcing from palm to palm, so creating it becomes easier. Once the awareness of that ability becomes an accepted reality, the awareness of other forms of perception also become easier. Eventually other vibrational forces will be easier to perceive, to harness, and to manipulate, and the rest of magick and spellcasting will be much easier to achieve. Magickal perception can be applied to other senses as well; one can learn to work with the vibrations and energies of stones, crystals, plants, and animals.

---

105. Cohen, "Can You Imagine Cancer Away?"

Spiritual Reality

What are gods? Is Zeus a big guy with a beard? Did Meztli, the Aztec moon god, really hatch from a butterfly chrysalis? Yes and no. Gods are beings that exist in the astral plane and outside our perception. At this point, you or some bright-eyed students will observe, "But a few lessons back, you said that gods are immanent and not transcendent; they're always everywhere! Now you say they exist in the astral plane!" Yes, but the astral plane is everywhere.

In order to perceive our gods, we need to understand how or why we see them. Let's go back to a passage from lesson 5 for a moment on the facets of spirituality and divinity. I wrote: "Look at it this way: There is a sort of ritual that occurs whenever a small child is taken to the ocean for the first time. They are led by the hand to the shore where they stand and look out at the unending water from surf to horizon. They see but cannot comprehend what they are seeing. They blink a couple of times, then turn around and dig a little hole in the sand. Water fills the hole, and the child plays with that. The child has just created a reflection of the unknowable in manageable form—something they can get their mind around."

When we do that—when we make a little puddle as a reflection of the ocean—we are making a reflection of god's image, and our reflection of the gods is a manifestation of collective consciousness. Created as a way of explaining the mysteries of the universe and to serve as teachers, guides, and protectors, the gods that we imagine exist in the collective mind of humanity as well as in the astral. Each perceived deity exists for a specific purpose, which is empowered by the collective thought and will.

For example, a goddess of love exists as a focus of the thoughts and feelings regarding the emotion of love. A person seeking financial advice would not seek the wisdom of Aphrodite, but someone seeking romantic advice would because the consensual reality image of her—the vibrational frequency of the collective-manifest-will-focus known as Aphrodite—responds favorably to the desires and energies of that seeker. When we pray, invoke deity, or meditate, the image that we manifest serves as a conduit to the actual deity.

Inherent power exists in all things—real and illusory. This is why an image of God, created by the willpower of thousands, can have such power. If enough people believe in the image of Amaterasu, for example, then she exists for us as a cohesive element of that willpower. The more followers a deity has, the more strength, or mana, the deity possesses. The less followers, of course, the weaker the deity. By tapping into the energies and frequencies of different gods, Witches can benefit from the wisdom and challenges offered. Worship is expressed by communicating with a specific deity, and in return, the deity is strengthened by the mana. While some Witches might feel odd sending mana to Jehovah, for example, there is no reason that particular deity should be off limits. However, it is also important to be discerning and respectful when working with deities from living religious cultures. Before working with the gods, connect with the culture and its people in order to determine whether you are welcome and have their blessing.

Here's an allegory to better understand divinity and worship. The internet is a worldwide network supported by millions of users. People access the web for hundreds of reasons, from financial advice to entertainment to counselling. Different websites have different looks, names, and functions, but they all exist for the same purposes—to impart information and guidance, help us manage our lives, and to hopefully help us better ourselves and our surroundings. Gods, or the images of them that we manifest, are like websites. They look different and respond differently, but ultimately they exist to help humanity and all life to learn and grow. Different people and cultures honour different deities, depending upon environment, spiritual focus, and need, but all are visual perceptions of human spirituality and, ultimately, our relationship with the Divine.

Beyond the manifest-will-focus image, Witches also see gods as multifaceted parts of a greater force: the universal divine mystery. What we perceive as gods, such as Zeus, Athena, and Jehovah, are human-made interpretations of different facets of that mystery. It could be said that God created the universe, the universe created humans, and humans created God.

Your UPGs and You

Many people have experienced unverified (or unsubstantiated) personal gnosis, or UPGs, which are a vital part of many people's lives who have an awareness beyond the five senses. It's a divine, spiritual, or religious experience that you swear actually happened to you but cannot scientifically prove. If you absolutely believe that Jesus appeared to you in the scorch marks on a tortilla, that's a UPG experience. If you lost a loved one recently and just for a fleeting second you see them outside the window, that's a UPG. If you're climbing a ladder and your foot slips, but you feel supported by a comforting presence long enough to regain your footing, and you swear your guardian angel just saved your life, that's a UPG.

UPGs are another aspect of creative visualization, however brief. These aren't situations where you are actively trying to see or experience something. Instead, they happen to you and you react to them. Acknowledging that a UPG just happened and accepting it would help open up one's mind to make creative visualization that much easier.

Some people have tried to extrapolate upon the UPG concept with shared personal gnosis (SPG), verified personal gnosis (VPG), and peer-confirmed personal gnosis (PCPG). If you had an experience involving lightning, and you imagined Thor spoke to you, that's a UPG. The fact that lightning is one of Thor's aspects doesn't "verify" the personal gnosis. It just acknowledges that it happened using accepted and understood symbology. Your personal moment is still very much yours!

Lesson 22: Study Prompts and Questions

Reality and Energy

- Compare and contrast fundamental reality and consensual reality.
- In your own words, describe matter and energy.
- How can thought and willpower be applied to energy and vibrational forces?
- Compare and contrast science and religion.
- Explain how love corresponds to theoretical subatomic science.

Energy and Magick

- In your own words, explain what magick is and how it works.
- What purpose do a Witch's tools serve?

Magick and Reality

- Can collective will affect magickal results? Explain and justify.
- Explain the reality of law as opposed to the reality of matter.

Magickal Perception

- Offer an example of your own to explain magickal perception or creative visualization.
- Try the spark of light exercise. Were you successful? Write down an analysis of your results.

Spiritual Reality
- In your own words, explain what gods are and why we need them. (Or why we don't.)
- What is mana? How does worship work?

Your UPGs and You
- Explain what a UPG is.
- Have you ever had a UPG experience? Explain.

Lesson 22: Recommended Reading

- *Creative Visualization: Use the Power of Your Imagination to Create What You Want in Your Life* by Shakti Gawain
- *Magick in Theory and Practice* by Aleister Crowley
- *Real Magic: An Introductory Treatise on the Basic Principles of Yellow Magic* by Philip Emmons Isaac Bonewits

The Four Cornerstones of Magick

We're continuing with our series on understanding the building blocks of magick. In our last lesson, we took a look at quantum physics, the nature of deity, and consensual reality. Now we're going to have a look at the other aspects of magick theory, starting with the four cornerstones, which have been an essential part of magickal theory since 1860.

Understanding the Four Cornerstones

Also known as the Sphinx's Pyramid or the Magician's Pyramid, the cornerstones were first described by Éliphas Lévi, a French occultist and esoteric author, in 1868. More of a principle of understanding than anything else, they are a foundation of magickal discipline. The four cornerstones are to know, to will, to believe (or to dare), and to keep silent.

Knowing how to work with the cornerstones will allow you to create the mental and psychic foundation required to work magick more effectively. Even though there are only four cornerstones, we'll look beyond the material to the understanding and possible applications of the principles in the material world.

In his book *The Great Secret, or, Occultism Unveiled*, Lévi assigned elements; attributes of the sphinx, the keeper of wisdom; and zodiac signs to the cornerstones. They are:

Cornerstone	To know	To will	To believe	To keep silent
Element	Air	Fire	Water	Earth
Attribute	Human	Lion	Eagle	Bull
Zodiac sign	Aquarius	Leo	Scorpio	Taurus[106]

---

106. Huson, *Mastering Witchcraft*, 22.

Some modern practitioners, however, have reassigned the elemental correspondences:

Cornerstone	To know	To will	To believe	To keep silent
Element	Earth	Fire	Water	Air

Some Witches feel the elemental associations and attributes as presented here are appropriate for working with the cornerstones. However, there is a long-standing tradition that reverses two of them. In this case, to know corresponds to earth and to keep silent corresponds to air. Do you see silence, for example, as quiet air or the stillness of earth? Likewise, do you feel that to know echoes the solid foundation of earth or the conviction of the mind?

To Know

In the last lesson, we looked at the power of mind over matter, or creative visualization. That is essentially the basis of the first cornerstone. Knowing the spell will work will give it that extra "oomph" to carry it through. Not just hoping, not wishing, but completely *knowing* it will work. The keystone of magick is intent; that's the key here. You might hope that you hold the winning lottery ticket or believe that your team will win the football game. But to know a spell will work is different. It is a conviction. It is a deep-rooted understanding of the effectiveness of the spell. Besides, you're the one who cast the spell. You're holding all the cards! (But don't let it go to your head—we'll discuss magick and responsibility in a later lesson.) By knowing your spell will work, you are effectively knocking down barriers before they arise.

Lévi described this as an element of air—the breath of intent and willpower. To others, it is the element of earth—the solid, unmoving rock of conviction.

To Will

The second cornerstone is to will. Here you are willing the spell to work, willing change to take effect. Remember the correlation between reality, energy, and magick? That applies here. By force of will, you are manipulating energies and vibrational forces to allow the spell to come to fruition. It is more intuitive than knowing the spell will work; the force of will is the stoking of the fire. It is the drive and the yearning for a successful magickal result. The power of will could be described as the desire or passion of the spellcaster, so will, of course, correlates with the element of fire.

To Believe (or To Dare)

Okay, we have two cornerstones in place, and the third is to believe or, to some, to dare. This is not the same as the first cornerstone, to know. To believe is not about the spell's effectiveness. Instead, it is a belief in yourself and in the strength and ability that you possess as a spellcaster. It's the determination that you have what it takes—the strength within and without—to make a difference. When you're in the middle of ritual or deep in the working of a spell, it is not the time for self-doubt or indecision. Belief in yourself and your own abilities is a basic ingredient of effective spellcasting—or anything else, for that matter. The third cornerstone, sometimes named to dare, corresponds to water, the element of emotion and desire, and it corresponds to the daring and courage to bring a spell to life.

To Keep Silent

Why would a Witch want to remain silent if they're casting a spell? Regarding silence, there are three different levels of sound. There are external sounds, such as other people talking, car horns, and telephones; there are surface sounds, which you make when you move about or talk; and there are internal sounds, which is your internal monologue and the voice of your soul. Silence is the act of going to that quiet space inside yourself and listening to that tiny voice that you generally ignore when it tells you what to do.

First, let's examine different aspects of outside noise. It is, of course, easier to concentrate on magick if you can eliminate outside noises. Don't try to keep silent within the spellworking but outside it. Don't brag about what you're doing—or trying to do— because that might affect the spell's effectiveness. You should also avoid magickal "meddling." Have you ever heard the phrase "too many cooks spoil the broth"? It's like that. The more people you tell, the more chance there is for interference or—even worse— self-doubt and confusion.

Regarding surface sound, a Witch has to make some sound during spellwork. Reciting words, moving objects, lighting candles—everything makes a little sound. But the point is not to make too much sound or work too loudly. It would be unwise to attract attention and possible interruptions during spellcasting.

Ask any experienced Buddhist or Zen mystic what is at the center of the being, and they will tell you it is silence—the song of awareness. One of the reasons for settling and grounding before spellwork is to silence yourself within. Silence is not only essential to the clarity and security of the spellwork but to find the center from which the spell is born.

As you can see, this cornerstone could relate to air and finding the silence and the stillness from which to evoke the spark of magick, or it could relate to earth and finding the foundation within yourself for the same reason.

The Fifth Cornerstone

Huh? Wait up. There are only four cornerstones. Yes, but they all connect at the center. The fifth element, spirit, is the magick itself and the whole reason we're doing this in the first place. Without spirit, it's all for naught. It's the foundation of knowledge, the essence of will, the source of belief, and the sound of silence. If the first four cornerstones are to know, to will, to dare, and to keep silent, the fifth is simply to go. It's on. It's happening.

Spirit is the personal conviction that brings the spell together. It's more than *knowing*, the spirit just *is*. Spirit could also be applied to the divine presence within magick. It's not actively recognized, but without that divine spark, the whole thing falls apart.

The Cone of Power

The pyramid shape has been used for many years, and everyone from the ancient Egyptians to New Age mystics recognize its simple, elegant, effective shape and the power it carries. The pyramidal shape focuses and enhances the energy within, concentrating it at both the peak and the center of the base. Witches also recognize the effectiveness of the pyramid and use a variation of it in ritual and magickal practices. The Witch's cone of power is round at the base as the foundation is a magick circle, although it may still use the four elements in a ritual setting.

When magick is raised, the Witch envisions themself standing inside a magickal circle, and the energy fills the circle, reaching up in a conical shape to a point over the Witch's head. If a group is working together, they stand at the perimeter of the circle, and the apex of the cone is directly over the altar. The more people involved, naturally, the larger and stronger the cone will be. Whether it's a single Witch or a whole coven, the cone of power is a powerful, effective way of manipulating, focusing, and directing magick.

In using the cone, many envision it as a lighthouse. The apex of the cone is the beacon of light, sending the magick out to wherever it's needed. Others see it as a circus big top tent. Bright, colourful, and enchanting, it is filled with wonder and delight. However the cone of power is envisioned, Witches all over the world use it as a way to focus, amplify, and manipulate the magick within.

The Four Cornerstones in Everyday Life

How can the principle of the cornerstones be applied to everyday life? Suppose you are determined to quit smoking. Your goal is to gradually taper down to zero cigarettes within six months. Here's how the cornerstones "fit." You *know* you are going to quit smoking. You *will* yourself to cut back a little more each day. You *believe* that you will reach your goal. And you know that *keeping silent* is important as well. If you tell your friends or coworkers, they may question your resolve and make you doubt yourself.

Lesson 23: Study Prompts and Questions

Understanding the Four Cornerstones

- Explain the significance of the four cornerstones.

To Know

- Explain how knowing a spell's success will affect its outcome.
- Make a comparison between this cornerstone and the elements of air and earth.

To Will

- In your own words, justify the effect of will on ritual magickal working.
- Compare will to the element of fire.

To Believe (or To Dare)

- Explain how one's belief in oneself and self-worth can influence a spell-working.
- Compare belief with the element of water.

To Keep Silent

- Explain the difference between external, surface, and internal noise.
- Justify the importance of silence in spellwork.
- Compare silence to the elements of air and earth.

The Fifth Cornerstone

- Explain how spirit, or to go, connects to the other four cornerstones.
- Justify the importance of honouring spirit in magick and spellcrafting.

The Cone of Power
- Explain why more participants make a stronger cone of power.
- How does a cone of power resemble a lighthouse? What other imagery can you think of to illustrate it?

The Four Cornerstones in Everyday Life
- Offer two examples of how the four cornerstones of magick can be applied to your own life, either magick or mundane.

Lesson 23: Recommended Reading

- *The Great Secret, or, Occultism Unveiled* by Éliphas Lévi
- *The Magician's Companion: A Practical and Encyclopedic Guide to Magical and Religious Symbolism* by Bill Whitcomb

Lesson 24
The Many Faces of Magick

We've looked at magick in a few different ways now—as theoretical quantum physics, as a conduit to the gods, and as cornerstones in building a magickal pyramid, or a foundation from which to cast a spell. Now we'll take a look at magick and spellwork another way: different classifications, or types, of spells. I'll widen the scope a little and look at how music can be perceived as a type of magick too.

Theurgy and Thaumaturgy

Theurgy refers to magick performed with divine assistance, and thaumaturgy is magick performed when the Witch uses themself as their source of power. Ultimately both forms of magick serve to enhance one's life or benefit others, and it could be argued that all magick is, therefore, thaumaturgic, but the process is the principle here, not the result. Look at it this way: If a Witch wants to land a good job, they perform a spell to help the process along. That's thaumaturgy. Another Witch wants to overcome their fear of fire, so they invoke the goddess Feronia to help understand fire and come to terms with its destructive power. That's theurgic magick.

Group or coven rituals can use either form as well. Suppose a coven wants to ensure successful resolution of a court case. The coven's right to use a public park for sabbat rituals is in dispute. The day before the hearing, they invoke Apollo to give them strength, wisdom, and confidence in the courtroom. The ritual is theurgic.

Here's another example: One of the Witches works with a woman whose child is hospitalized with pneumonia. With the mother's permission, the coven works magick to help the child receive the healing they need. The coven could cast a circle and raise a cone of power and send the energy to the child (thaumaturgic), or it could cast a circle and invoke Isis and ask her to help the child (theurgic).

Spell Classification

There are eight essential types of spells that can be used by Witches, Wiccans, or anyone else with an awareness of their own magickal potential. They are:

Abjuration

The word *abjuration* can have two meanings. In legal terminology, to abjure is to renounce, abandon, or repudiate. The word comes from the Latin *abjurare*, which means "to forswear."[107] In magick, abjuration is a type of protective or defensive spell. If you work magick to aid in your defense, such as against malicious gossip, you'd be using abjuration. Carrying a piece of moonstone as a protective amulet or putting up wards or shields in your house are also forms of abjuration. We'll examine these practices again in more detail in lesson 38.

Alteration

These are spells that alter the essential reality of the target. This is nothing as extreme as turning people into frogs, but if you want to make a change or turn over a new leaf, there's alteration. Making a New Year's resolution could be considered a form of alteration. Making the decision to join a twelve-step rehab program and using magick to increase your resolve to stick with it is also alteration. If the spell's target desires a fundamental change, an alteration spell is in order.

Conjuration

Stage magicians perform magic (no *k*) tricks, such as pulling rabbits out of a hat, which they call conjuration. Magickal conjuration is a creative process with tangible results. A spell for financial gain, resulting in getting a raise at work and a bigger paycheck, is conjuration. If you've made your mind up that you need a new car and you cast a spell to make that come true, that's conjuration. You're manifesting something tangible in your life. You know you need the item, and a conjuration spell adds power to making that happen.

Divination

Spells used for problem-solving, guidance, or seeking answers are divination spells. Divination is the art of understanding or foretelling possible upcoming events. Simply put, it is the use of one's own psychic awareness, either alone or assisted by tools such as tarot

---

107. "Abjuration of the Realm Law and Legal Definition."

cards, the futhark, or a pendulum, to uncover hidden knowledge or become aware of possible future paths.

Remember that divination will not tell you what *will* happen but merely what *could* happen if you continue along a specific course of action. There is some argument as to whether divination is theurgic or thaumaturgic. Divination could be thaumaturgic because it harnesses one's own psychic awareness to answer mundane questions, or it could be theurgic because the very word, *divination*, implies communing with the Divine to seek answers to one's questions—or at least to get a glimpse of what's in store. Is divination thaumaturgic or theurgic? You decide.

Divination can be used before or as part of a ritual. Knowing the possible outcome of a ritual or spellworking will make it that much more fulfilling and can empower the Witches involved.

Evocation

When using spells of evocation, a spirit or deity is called into the caster. Just as one can evoke reactions in others, spirits or presences can be evoked in certain situations. Evocation could be regarded as a form of possession. The spirit that is called in temporarily guides the person in manner or actions, and the spirit evoked can assist the Witch or coven in the ritual proceedings. The Witch's ritual of Drawing Down the Moon, in which the moon goddess is drawn into the High Priestess, is an excellent example of evocation. Some Christian churches encourage "speaking in tongues," which is when a participant is filled with the Holy Spirit and flails about the ground; this is also a form of evocation.

Evocations should never be attempted by one who cannot handle the experience. They are usually only performed under strict supervision.

Illusion

Spells of illusion, which are rarely used, are deceptive in nature. A Witch might cast a glamoury, or an illusion spell, upon themselves to avoid being seen by their abusive ex in a crowded room. Illusion spells can also be used to conceal treasured items and to deceive those who would try to find them.

Invocation

Invocative spells are those in which a presence, spirit, or deity is brought to—but not into—the caster. Invoked spirits can be called upon to offer guidance or advice or to

participate in ritual proceedings. An excellent example is the calling of the quarters seg-
ment of ritual, which will be examined in greater detail in lesson 28.

Some people confuse *invocation* with *evocation*. Since *invocation* has the word *in* in
it, it should be bringing something in, but it's the other way around. You bring something into you by *evocation*—just as a favorite smell could *evoke* a happy memory. It's
manifesting that memory inside you. By *invoking* a deity or spirit, you bring them to the
circle, not into a person.

Necromancy

This word often scares people but really it's quite harmless. Necromancy is not about
hacking up dead bodies, performing ritual sacrifices, or raising zombies. The word, as
you can tell from looking at it, is composed of *necro*, or dead, and *mancy*, such as carto-
mancy, or telling the future using cards. Necromancy is somewhere between invocation
and divination and involves asking one's ancestors or spirits for aid.

A séance is an excellent example of necromancy, as is the Samhain ritual of setting
an extra place at the dinner table to honour departed spirits. You'd never kill anything to
perform necromancy, and such harm would only detract from the spellworking.

About spell classification: A spell is defined by its writing and casting, not by its
label. Knowing that a protective spell is abjuration is not as important as the intent that
you put into it, but having that knowledge about your magick makes it a little easier to
bring the spell into focus.

Magick and Music

The history of music predates the history of language. The original musical form was
percussion. Like a heartbeat, it was a rhythmic, recognizable sound. Even before humans
had a spoken language, they understood the urgency or meaning of repetitive drum-
beats. Drumming has remained a principal musical form, and many other instruments
have joined the orchestra. Harps, flutes, organs, violins, and tubas all have a magickal
association.

Magick and music have always gone hand in hand. While not a magickal form in
itself, music can be used to enhance and influence spellworking or to add mood and
atmosphere. Certain songs can affect one's emotions. They can be moving, inspirational,
uplifting, and more. The right music affects the right people. Almost everyone is familiar
with the song "We Will Rock You" (stomp stomp, clap) by the rock group Queen, which

is played before many sporting events to get the audience excited. Witches, however, often prefer soothing, invigorating melodies—something that will calm the nerves and focus the will—prior to ritual or spellcasting. Music from artists such as S. J. Tucker, Tuatha Dea, Wendy Rule, and Faun are popular with Witches to set the mood for meditation or ritual. Of course, if you're happier playing your own music as a way to relax, then absolutely do so!

Chanting

Chanting, or the use of select words or phrases intoned rhythmically, is a powerful magickal tool. Chants can be used in hundreds of different ways, from inspirational and power raising to soothing and calming. Just for fun, try this chant from my own Book of Shadows:

> *Witches dance under a full moon*
> *And we call on magick's boon*
> *As we weave our heart's desire.*
> *Earth and water, air and fire,*
> *Spiral dance, the magick flows,*
> *Spin the spell and let it go!*

Repeat the chant a few times quickly. As the chant progresses, it awakens magick deep within. You might feel a glow that's almost an adrenaline-like rush of energy; that's the power of chanting.

Lesson 24: Study Prompts and Questions

Theurgy and Thaumaturgy
- Define each term and explain the differences between them.

Spell Classification
- List the eight magickal classes, and briefly describe each one.
- Explain, in greater detail, the difference between invocation and evocation.

Magick and Music
- Can music be perceived as a form of language? Explain.
- Explain why chanting is an effective magickal tool.

Lesson 24: Recommended Reading

- *Mastering Witchcraft: A Practical Guide for Witches, Warlocks, and Covens* by Paul Huson
- *Transformative Witchcraft: The Greater Mysteries* by Jason Mankey

LESSON 25
Magick and Responsibility

Before we go any further, I need to cover the basics of magickal safety and responsibility in spellworking. I begin, as all good Witches should, with a look at responsible attitudes regarding magick and spellcrafting. Here are a few pointers one should remember when considering using magick—whether alone or in a group setting. Remember, safe magick is effective magick!

Understanding Magickal Ethics

As with any action, there are ethical situations to consider. We looked at some of these back in lesson 12 of Wicca 101, but let's take some time to take a closer look at the subject of ethics and magick.

Begin No Work until You Have Permission from the Spell's Intended Recipient

Remember, Witches hold the principle of free will as sacred. To work magick on another without their express permission is a violation of magick's prime directive. As with any rule, there are different aspects to consider. If the intended recipient of a healing spell is in a coma, for example, or for whatever reason cannot speak for themselves, then call upon their deity to act on your behalf.

Sometimes what seems obvious might not be. Wishing to heal the earth is a noble and valued concern, but how? If you send healing energy to the Amazon rain forest or Australia's Great Barrier Reef, good. You might want to send energy to aid the fight against global warming, but you'd be sending magick to scientists and lobbyists, and that's where you trip over the consent issue. Likewise, if the intended recipient is a friend's pet, let the friend speak for the pet.

Consider the Appropriate Use of Magick

If the intended work is to protect a victim, such as an abused spouse, you can approach this from two directions: to offer protection for the victim or to "bind" the attacker. Let's look at the free will clause here. By restricting the abusive spouse's actions, you are ensuring that no harm is dealt upon the victim. Is it a violation of free will to bind the attacker, or are you preventing the attacker from violating the victim's free will? There is a line in the rede, "Lest in self-defense it be," that allows for defensive actions if you are in effect protecting your own free will or that of the spell's intended recipient.

Consider the Ramifications of Your Actions

Let's take another look at the abused spouse scenario. It might seem very refreshing to watch the abused spouse's partner drive through a brick wall and end up in the hospital, but that would have other effects as well. The people the wall was built for would be minus a wall, and the crash could hurt innocent bystanders. You don't have any problem with them, do you? (Remember the Threefold Law's ripple effect.)

Do Not Use Magick in Anger or Ill Health

If you have had a bad day at work or faced two hours of road rage, it is not the time to work magick. Not only will your judgment and clarity be tainted, but you will not be focused and centered enough to work magick. Relax, cool off, and wait until you feel refreshed and clearheaded before you even think of lighting a candle or beginning a spell. If you're sick, only attempt a "light" spell for healing. If you're so ill you can't think clearly, wait until you can focus with more clarity. Besides, the energy expended could make you even sicker. You should also remember that spellwork is not a replacement for professional medical care.

Be Mindful of the Weather

This has a simple, common-sense application and a more serious one. First, if you are planning an outdoor ritual, simply be aware of what the meteorologist says. Is it going to rain? Will it snow? Has there been a drought, restricting the use of fires at camps and parks? If the last one is the case, you might think twice about using fire as part of the ritual.

Second, consider that weather patterns are bigger than you are. Here's an excellent example: A large coven plans an outdoor Beltane ritual for May 1, but it's supposed to rain all day. Undaunted, they continue with their plans. Upon arriving at the ritual site, they perform a weather spell, asking for clear skies over the ritual area, and it works. The clouds roll back, and the coven holds the sabbat ritual. After they close the ritual and pack up, the clouds and the rain return, and since the weather pattern in that area had been suppressed for four hours, it returns with greater force than before. The resulting floods cause extended damage, and two people are hospitalized. The moral of this story? It's not nice to fool with Mother Nature.

Don't Brag

Claiming that you are a big, powerful spellcasting hotshot does two things: it makes people think you've watched too many bad movies, and it corrupts your own self-image. Humility leads to clarity; clarity leads to triumph.

Dos and Don'ts of Magick

Let's examine some of the more material limitations of magick. Ethical guidelines are excellent for understanding the "why" and "why not," but now we'll focus on the "how" and "how not."

Understand All the Elements of the Spell

If you try to work magick without understanding every aspect of it, you will have diminished results or none whatsoever. Consider this recipe: "Preheat oven to 350 degrees. Make sure the chicken breast is clean and glabrescent. Add filling, fold over, and batter and bake for twenty-five minutes."

Notice how little made sense after the word *glabrescent* and the whole sentence fell apart? Magick is like that. If you don't understand every aspect of what you're doing, the spell will likewise fall apart. (For the record, *glabrescent* means "smooth, and devoid of hair or feathers.")

Know Your Goal

Before you begin, have a clear idea of what you're doing and what the end result should be. Writing the procedure beforehand is a good idea, so you won't "stray off the path." Employ only qualified participants. While it is safe to assume that you would not ask total strangers to fill roles in a group-oriented spell or ritual, sometimes you have to be particular about who you ask to participate. Inexperienced participants or people who put their own agendas ahead of the spell's objective might resent being left out of the proceedings, but it is in the best interest of the spell and its intended result. Naturally anyone who does not agree with this idea should not be a participant.

Keep the Spell's Focus Clear

Have you ever heard the phrase "too many cooks spoil the broth"? The same is true for magick. Too many outside influences—as well-meaning as they may be—can detract from the effectiveness of the spell. Let the one most qualified direct it, and let everyone else follow their guidance.

Don't Reach Beyond Your Limitations

If you only feel proficient with simple candle-burning spells or energy-raising rituals, don't go attempting to draw down a goddess or invoke departed spirits. You might find yourself trying to handle more than you bargained for. Granted, you should always gently push the envelope of what you can do, otherwise you'll never progress. Don't try to take huge leaps right away, though. Take baby steps at first.

Never Lose the Meaning of the Spell

One of the worst things you can do is to let a spell or ritual become a "mummers' play," or when you are merely going through the motions without feeling any magick or spirit. An "empty" spell or ritual can be as discouraging as a broken doll. (A mummers' play, from Elizabethan England, is performed entirely in mime. Actors wear gaudy clothes and huge, outlandish masks. Unless you know the meaning of the play, it can be confusing, wearisome, and ultimately unfulfilling.)

Don't Use Magick Frivolously

Spells used to heal an injured friend, quit smoking, or overcome obstacles are all acceptable uses of magick. Using magick to make a candle flame dance is not. Using magick to impress friends or perform parlor tricks is foolish and a waste of one's magickal ability. On a deeper level, if you use magick for frivolous or foolish means, not only will the theurgic aspects lose their impact but you will no longer respect your own ability.

Don't Use Magick for Ego Gratification

This closely relates to the previous topic on frivolous magick. If you use magick for "Hey, look what I can do!" thrills or to impress your friends, you will quickly become jaded and disillusioned. Magick is not a toy; like your ritual tools, it should be treated with reverence and respect. If you only use magick selfishly, your greed will get in the way. The magick will quickly pale as your desires exceed your abilities.

Respect the Magick

Spells are special, and so is the magick you're working. A spellcasting, whether alone, in a coven, or in a large ritual, should be treated as an auspicious event. If a spell calls for consecrated water to be poured out over a patch of earth, for example, you should make it a point to pay attention to what you're doing, and pay it the respect it deserves. Don't just walk past and sort of flip a paper cup over so the water pours out as you stroll by. That's disrespectful to the magick, and the spell will suffer because of it.

Don't Take Magick for Granted

Even though magick is around us all the time, it should never be taken for granted. Possessing magickal potential gives you no reason to disrespect it. Acknowledge your abilities just as a surgeon acknowledges their skill on the operating table.

Elect a "Designated Guardian"

This one is rarely used, but you might be asked to participate in a particularly stressful ritual, one which can leave participants physically or psychically drained. In such situations, it's wise to select one person to stay outside the magickal arena. This person, often the coven guardian, can provide refreshments, offer support, and drive people home afterward. Their role is like that of a magickal "designated driver."

Most Important Rules of Magick

Here are the two most vital rules of magick, ethical or otherwise, according to my beliefs:

Always Believe in Yourself

You have within you the potential to move mountains. Self-doubt and insecurity are two of the most daunting barriers faced in magick; don't let insecurity cloud your intentions.

Power Corrupts

Don't let your magickal potential go to your head. Having the ability to work magick does not give you the right to use magick. Think responsibly. Act responsibly.

Practicing Safe Spellcraft

One of the topics we just covered was "Don't Reach Beyond Your Limitations." Going along with that is the admonition that you should not perform any magickal working or work toward any goal that you are not comfortable with.

Don't Bite Off More Than You Can Chew

If you're just getting into energy-raising exercises and reading tarot cards, don't attempt a spell to heal the planet. Your lack of experience will detract from the effectiveness of the spell, and it could have dangerous repercussions. Would you let a ten-year-old drive your car?

Avoid Uncomfortable or Unethical Situations

Are we talking about ethics *again*? Yes, but just long enough to say this: don't attempt any magickal working that you are uncomfortable with or have ethical issues with. Are you unsure about a friend's motives in asking you for a spell? Clarify their intent before you do anything else. Do you fear spiders? Don't try to invoke tarantula energy.

Prevent Interruptions

You're in the middle of a spell, and the phone rings, breaking your concentration. Whether you ignore it and let it ring or break off to answer it, your magickal focus has been broken. Can you pick up where you left off to continue the spell? Should you simply start over? Whatever you do, remember to simply turn your phone off before starting any serious magickal work. During an outdoor ritual, some participants may become sidetracked by outside noises or interruptions, which can affect the outcome of the ritual. This is why a coven guardian is such a useful part of an outdoor or public ritual. Of course, some things, like loud airplanes or barking dogs, simply have to be taken in stride.

Don't Get Impatient

Magick cannot be rushed. If you try to hurry it along, you'll get careless and overlook simple details. Take it slow, take it easy, and get it right. As the saying goes, "The faster you go, the behinder you get."

Avoid Unfinished Business

One of the easiest ways to ruin a spell is to simply forget to finish it. You have an excellent spell planned, everything is in order, but you're so eager to fulfill the magick that you forget to close the spell. This is just like forgetting to turn the stove off after cooking dinner or leaving the car door wide open after a trip. Simply keep your wits about you, and pay attention to detail.

Prevent Magickal Spills

Magick is a funny form of energy. It can "pool" and "sour" like spilled milk. For example, if a Witch raises magick to empower a crystal but fails to ground or earth all the excess energy, some can remain. Just as the charged stone can hold magick long after the spell has been cast, summoned magick can pool where it was raised. This is not unlike spilled grease on the stove top or heartburn. Sour magick can cause uneasiness, loss of concentration, or worse. Animals and children are quite perceptive, and they can usually sense the presence of lingering pools of magick.

How does an energy force like magick "linger" and "sour"? This is a drastic example, but it serves to illustrate the point. A radioactive spill, like the 1986 incident at Chernobyl, causes molecules and atoms to become irradiated, making them behave oddly and affecting anything that comes into contact with the tainted area. Ungrounded magick is essentially the same. Even the physical molecules of the air can become affected, leaving a tainted area that one can physically walk through. When the "excited" molecules begin to slow down, the magickal effect shifts. What once caused a magickal vibration might now only result in a sluggish or disoriented feeling. This is what we call "sour" magick. Eventually the magickal reaction will erode completely, but proficient psychics can detect the presence of magick for years after the effect has passed.

Spilled magick can be cleaned up by raising more magick to reenergize the area and then earthing and grounding the entire area. Since working with this kind of magick can be tricky, it is best left to more experienced practitioners. Don't worry, spilled magick is never as reactive as a radiation or gasoline spill. It won't explode or cause people to develop cancer or an extra nose. At most it might cause ulcers, depression or disorientation, or a temporary loss of psychic ability if one fails to ground and center for too long. Grounding and centering, or releasing excess energy, will be explained in lesson 29.

All Work and No Play?

So far it sounds like the possibility of magick and ritual is bogged down by rules, regulations, and ethical considerations. Can't magick just be fun?

Of course it can! Magick is a lot of fun. While it should always be taken seriously, there is no reason magick cannot also be seen as a pleasurable endeavor. Making candles and incense, drying herbs, and creating new oil blends can be a Witch's hobby, and Witches, just like anybody else, take pride in their work. The sense of pride and accomplishment derived from a job well done or a spell well cast is pleasurable indeed!

When a coven or a group of solitaires get together to raise magick, there is undoubtedly a raising of spirits as well. The feeling of being "giddy with excitement" should be well known to anyone with pulse, and such a feeling can easily be achieved by a cohesive magickal group. When magick is raised, spirits are raised, and where spirits are raised, energy is doubled or even tripled. Harness that energy, celebrate the spirit, and embrace the enjoyment of magick. By channeling that vibrant energy back into the spell, you can make the working of the spell fun. Just don't become so "drunk with laughter" that the spell falls apart. There are limits, after all. Fun, excitement, laughter, and gaiety can be powerful forces. Wherever the spirits are raised, emotions follow, and an increase in positive emotion can only be a good thing. Have fun with magick; laugh, enjoy, and relish the emotions!

Lesson 25: Study Prompts and Questions

Understanding Magickal Ethics

- Briefly explain the importance of ethics considerations in magick. Why is it important to "do the right thing"?
- Offer two situations where magick *could* be used but, ethically, should *not* be.

Dos and Don'ts of Magick

- Should one's magickal potential be "revered," or is it just another tool to use at will, like knowing how to drive?
- Several situations were shown, explaining the dos and don'ts of magick. Can you offer two more?

Practicing Safe Spellcraft
- Explain the importance of keeping within one's safe level of expertise.
- In your own words, explain what a "magickal spill" is, how to take care of it, and how to avoid it in the first place.

All Work and No Play?
- What kind of hobbies could be incorporated into a Witch's magickal practice?
- Explain how laughter can be a useful tool in raising energy.

Lesson 25: Recommended Reading
- *Solitary Witch: The Ultimate Book of Shadows for the New Generation* by Silver RavenWolf
- *Voices from the Circle: The Heritage of Western Paganism* edited by Prudence Jones and Caitlin Matthews

LESSON 26
Ritual Principles and Etiquette

This lesson closely follows after the last one on magick and responsibility. This is the other side of the coin, if you like, on rituals and responsibility. We'll take a look at why we need rituals, what to expect, and what might be expected of you and take a peek at some things you should or should not do in a ritual. This is the first lesson in the rituals series. In the next four lessons, we'll take a closer look at how a Wiccan ritual unfolds and what it all means.

Why Ritual?

What, exactly, is a ritual? Why does the very term hold such deep mystery? Say the word *ritual,* and some people envision dark chambers, hooded robes, sinister incantations, and skulls dripping blood. But really, you can look at rituals in a couple of ways. You can see them either as an established or prescribed order of religious worship or a predetermined series of actions to accomplish a goal. With that in mind, a church's Sunday service is a ritual. Taking the same route to work every morning is a ritual. Even brushing your teeth or always using the same pattern when you mow the lawn are rituals. They are a connected series of actions, which together perform a specific purpose or intent.

Do we need rituals? Of course we do! They're a way of keeping everything in order, and all people have them. Many Witches, both solitaires and coven members, keep Craft rituals of their own as well. Going outside at midnight to honour the full moon is a common ritual, as is leaving a piece of one's meal outdoors for wild animals to find as thanks to the goddess. While many Christians say grace before a meal, Witches often trace a pentagram over the meal, either with a fingertip or merely with their line of sight.

In the Craft, rituals are an important part of worship. They generally follow a specific pattern, so the participants know what is expected of them. Witches attending a sabbat, for example, will have prescribed roles in the ritual procedure. Some have memorized lines they repeat at every ritual, others read from scripts, and others improvise the whole thing. All these ways are acceptable, but if the ritual is being performed in front of a public audience who may be unfamiliar with Witchcraft, memorized lines and orchestrated procedure will make the ritual easier to understand. Sabbats, esbats, handfastings (Pagan weddings), Wiccanings (rituals dedicating a newborn to the goddess), and wakes are all recognized and accepted rituals. Some covens hold other rituals as well, such as communal celebrations honouring everyone's pets and familiars or rituals honouring a Witch's advancement.

Ritual Leadership and Responsibility

As we've stated before, Witchcraft is not an "organized" religion. That's not to say it's a "disorganized" religion either, but it does not carry an established nationwide hierarchy. There is no single authority or prescribed litany. The Craft does have ranks and roles within the coven, but the High Priest and High Priestess are no closer to the god and goddess than anybody else—or any other living thing, for that matter. A squirrel or a whale or a pebble on the beach is as much a child of the goddess as any coven Priestess.

If that's true, then why does the Craft have Priests and Priestesses? What is expected of them? There are actually two ways to answer that question. Some will tell you that the High Priest and Priestess are the elders and the bearers of knowledge and wisdom. It is to them that you should turn to for answers, and it is their word that you should follow. Others feel that in the Craft, everyone is equal in the eyes of the gods. Therefore, every Witch who has attained first degree or an equivalent, accepted level of expertise is a Priest or Priestess, and coven leaders are given the distinction of "High" Priest or Priestess. There are roles and obligations, and the High Priest and Priestess do indeed oversee the ceremony, making sure everyone plays their parts and it all goes smoothly. Sometimes they have scripted lines they want the participants to read out, and sometimes the Priest and Priestess are happy if you ad lib your lines and put your own "spin" on it. That's fine; in a "free-form" religion, personal expression of worship is encouraged—within limits.

High Priests and Priestesses within the Craft have the responsibility of honouring the gods, keeping the Craft sacred, and teaching, with honesty and humility, those who wish to learn. Teaching is a two-way street, of course. The pupil should be as eager to learn as the mentor is to guide. Young Witches are advised to follow the teachings of their mentors and be respectful of their words and tutelage in coven, ritual, and everyday life.

A Look at Ritual Procedure

As I mentioned, participants in a ritual have specific roles and duties to perform. Let's examine them more closely here. We'll be looking at this again in a little bit, but here's a teaser of sorts.

The High Priest and Priestess lead the ritual, naturally, and other coven members have different roles to play as well. Many covens have a maiden, or Priestess in training, who either fills in for the Priestess or assists her in ritual. The Priest-apprentice is usually the summoner, and his role generally mirrors that of the maiden. At the start of most rituals, the maiden and summoner anoint the Priest and Priestess, symbolically cleansing them with oils and incense. A dab of oil on the forehead from the maiden and a body-cleansing or smudging with incense from the summoner are common practice. Then they anoint each other and take position at the eastern point of the ritual space. They anoint other coven members as each one enters the ritual circle.

The quarter-callers take their assigned positions upon entering, and other ritual participants file in and assemble around the circle wherever they feel comfortable.

The Priest and Priestess then invoke the Lord and Lady, and the ritual begins. The "body" of the ritual is where the primary magickal work takes place. Here the quarter-callers rejoin the ritual until called upon later.

When the ritual is complete, the Priest and Priestess thank and release the gods, the quarters-callers release the elements, and the ritual circle is dispersed.

It should be stressed that throughout the ritual, the High Priest and Priestess are generally the final arbiters; they have the final say on all matters. The other Witches should act in accordance with their will.

Dos and Don'ts in Ritual

Here we will discuss etiquette in ritual, protocols to be observed, and correct attitude and attire. If you have issues with the way the High Priest and Priestess run the ritual or the coven, consider withdrawing from participation. If you're asked to do something you have concerns about, such as speaking in public, snuffing a candle flame out with your fingers, or participating skyclad (not as many traditions do this anymore, but some do), these should be discussed and resolved beforehand. Of course, the most important aspect of coven etiquette and protocol is simply to show respect and use common sense.

Tips for the Priest and Priestess

Here are some tidbits of useful information that apply to the High Priest and Priestess:

Some People Are New at This

Don't assume that just because you've hosted a Mabon ritual every autumn for the last six years that everyone present has too. Everyone has a first time for doing something, and you did, too, way back when. Be patient with people who might not understand everything that's happening, and if they stick around to ask questions later, respect their curiosity.

Congregational Wicca

I'll admit, this one surprised me when I first encountered it. When I was starting out in the late '70s and early '80s, every Witch I met was eager to study with their elders, build up their Book of Shadows, and climb the degree ladder. So I was a little surprised when, around 2005 or so, I met Pagans at a ritual who had no interest in any of that. They just wanted to show up, join the circle, watch the Priest and Priestess officiate the ceremony, then go home. They were quite happy to be the congregation and had no desire to go beyond that. Some longtime Priests I've known looked down on them as if they lacked dedication. That attitude is unfair to the attendees and unfair to the ritual itself. Everyone encounters the goddess and the magick in their own way.

Be Mindful of the Weather

If the ritual is being held outdoors, keep aware of the weather. In some wintertime sabbats, heavy ritual garb, including thermal underwear and gloves, is not only recommended but often required. Likewise, if it looks like gale-force winds are predicted, don't hold the ritual outside. (And if such storm conditions are predicted in the area, invoke the element of air gently!)

Know Your Surroundings

This actually has two ramifications. One, become familiar with the location. Is it near a busy road? Are there stinging nettles or wasp nests nearby? Does the ground need to be raked first to clear it of sharp rocks or twigs?

Second, be aware of your neighbours. If you are performing skyclad, you don't want to hold the ritual in the parking lot of the local library. In any public ritual setting, people often become curious, and they could become intrusive. Many people, sadly, still have a deep mistrust of Witches and the Craft, and their misgivings must be taken into consideration. If the coven does hold public rituals, you might want to assign a nonparticipating member as ritual guardian to answer questions and act as security.

Be Mindful of People's Limitations and Their Possibilities
If you host an open ritual and someone attending has disabilities you hadn't counted on, don't make them feel marginalized. If a new participant is in a wheelchair, for example, don't assume to know what's best for them or "politely ignore" them. Let them decide what they can or can't do. It may surprise you!

Are Pets Involved?
Some covens like to invite pets into rituals. Invoking the element of air while holding a parrot is a wonderful visual, as is holding a cat while calling upon Bastet. Still, the element of chaos that pets can bring into ritual can easily get out of control. The maiden's dog decides to chase the Priest's cat, which leaps onto the altar, and … you get the idea. If pets are a part of ritual, keep them separated and leashed, or only invite them one at a time.

Tips for Participants or Attendees
These tips are for attendees and participants:

Speak Clearly
When speaking your lines, use a strong, clear voice. Make sure your words are easily understood. This makes the ritual easier to follow, and it shows respect to the gods and the spirits. Be attentive! Your participation in the ritual is important, otherwise you wouldn't have been asked to attend. Pay attention to what is going on; don't talk to your neighbour when somebody else is speaking. This isn't elementary school.

Don't Enter the Ritual Drunk
Obviously you shouldn't enter ritual under the influence of alcohol or mind-altering substances. Those could detract from your performance ability and endanger yourself and others. Alcohol might be served at some point during the ceremony, but even then it is served in moderation. (If—for any reason—you can't or don't wish to drink, you should say so. Everyone will understand.) Excessive use of such substances could make you clumsy, disoriented, and careless.

Try Not to Be Clumsy

Tripping over your own feet is bad; clumsiness can lead to accidents. Try not to burn yourself with a candle or fall headfirst into the cauldron. Many Witches take great pride in their ritual garb. Try not to drip wax or splash wine on them.

Many covens use a flaming cauldron during rituals, and fire-leaping is a popular ritual procedure, especially at Beltane or Yule. Clumsy or not, be careful, especially if you wear long flowing robes. Leaping over the fire is good; immolating oneself is bad.

Speaking of fire, two other considerations to mention: is there a crucible of incense burning on the altar? That's not an ashtray. And if the ritual bonfire is burning a bundle of blessed, consecrated wood gathered specifically for this ritual, don't toss your rubbish into it. If the bonfire is a sacred flame, somebody will surely let you know.

To Be Skyclad or Not to Be Skyclad

Some covens do still perform ritual skyclad, or nude. The preferred rule here is, "When in Rome…" However, if there are reasons you are not willing or cannot participate skyclad, discuss this before the event with the coven elders. They should be willing to accommodate your needs. If not, you might wish to find a different coven.

Avoid Interruptions

It is advisable to mute or turn off your phones before a ritual begins. If you are expecting an important phone call, you might want to delay the ritual until later or reschedule the ritual to another date if that's more convenient.

Be Mindful of Allergies

Many outdoor and some indoor rituals are plagued with the problem of allergies. Uncontrollable sneezing can interrupt any ritual. If medications cannot alleviate the problem, simply wait patiently and politely until the afflicted person regains their composure. This same guideline also applies to coughing. Wearing masks is perfectly acceptable.

Another bodily function that might come into play is flatulence. Sometimes the bowels simply have to have their say! Like sneezing and coughing, this is usually politely ignored, but if it's so rampant that the air is fouled, the Priestess should temporarily suspend the proceedings and give the person time to excuse themselves and make amends.

Keep Disputes Outside the Ritual

What if two ritual participants are fighting? For example, the coven herald and the south quarter-caller are husband and wife on the verge of divorce. In such cases, it is expected that they will be responsible enough to put their differences aside during ritual. It is neither the time nor the place for domestic grievances. If they cannot contain their hostility, the more even-keeled one is usually allowed to participate, and the hothead is given time to cool their heels.

Respect the Ritual Altar

Just because it's an open ritual, don't presume that anything on the altar is safe to handle. Many Witches are very protective of their ceremonial tools. Some have never been touched by anyone else since their consecration. Always ask first. If you don't know, don't touch.

How Sharp Is That?

We must not ignore athame safety. Many Witches like to keep their athames sharp, even if they never cut anything but air. Accidentally stabbing oneself during ritual or wounding the Priestess is generally regarded as a bad idea. Keep your wits about you when using your athame, and always keep it sheathed when not in use.

Lesson 26: Study Prompts and Questions

Why Ritual?

- Justify, in your own words, why we need and use rituals.
- Give two examples of nonreligious rituals.

Ritual Leadership and Responsibility

- Why should the coven honour the wishes of the High Priest and Priestess?
- List some of the duties other coven members perform during ritual.

A Look at Ritual Procedure

- Compare and contrast the role of a Priest or Priestess in Witchcraft with that of a Rabbi or a Christian Priest.
- List some of the ritual duties assigned to a Priestess of the Craft.

Dos and Don'ts in Ritual

- Why is etiquette so important in ritual?
- Give two examples of ritual faux pas.

Lesson 26: Recommended Reading

- *CovenCraft: Witchcraft for Three or More* by Amber K
- *Witch's Wheel of the Year: Rituals for Circles, Solitaries & Covens* by Jason Mankey

LESSON 27
Ritual Procedure: Setting the Stage

We continue our lessons with the first of a four-part series where we examine and analyze a common Wiccan ritual. Over the next four lessons, we'll watch as an imaginary coven prepares for and performs an esbat. We'll meet the coven members, see what they wear in ritual, and watch as they use magick and rites during the esbat in response to various hypothetical situations. We'll start with a look at the setup involved.

If you like, this four-lesson series on ritual progression can be combined into one or two sessions.

Fundamentals of Ritual

Within the Craft, rituals are primarily held for two purposes: to honour the gods and ancient spirits and observe the changing seasons of the year or to perform magickal work, such as healing, growth, or personal advancement. Dedicated Witches take ritual seriously. While there is much love, joy, and laughter in the Craft—even during ritual— it is always remembered that the gods and spirits deserve our love and honour.

Ritual work is a specific form of worship. It is a way of interacting with the Divine. In Christian church services, where the pastor gives a sermon and hymns are sung, homage is paid to the transcendent deity. In Craft rituals, the deity is an immanent part of the proceedings. Gods are welcomed into the circle and invited to participate in the festivities.

Within most traditions, a ritual can be divided into four parts:

1) Erecting the temple, where the circle is cast and the gods or spirits are invoked.
2) Working in ritual, where the intent or purpose of the ritual is performed.
3) Closing the ritual, where the spirits are thanked and dismissed.
4) Acting in accord, where the magick and purpose of the ritual is carried out into the world. (This is the part most easily forgotten; after a ritual is complete, many people lose touch with the magick that was raised.)

Over the next four lessons, we will examine that ritual in excruciating detail. I will use a formal-eclectic ritual, or a formally performed ritual in an eclectic style. Depending upon the tradition, there are myriad variations to ritual procedure and execution. The ritual studied here is loosely based on an Alexandrian esbat, meaning the coven borrows from the Alexandrian tradition. It's a lot like Gardnerian but with room for free-form interpretation and inspiration, and alterations were made by this particular coven. Through these lessons, each part is covered twice. It is first described in detail, then explained in *italics*.

The Fictional Covenstead

First, let's take a look at the fictional covenstead. This is where the coven meets, and it is usually the home of the High Priestess and Priest. It can move, of course. Sometimes the coven may hold ritual in a field or forest clearing, or it may rotate between different members' homes. A stationary covenstead, however, is usually the most advantageous.

Our fictional group, called Green Dragon Coven, meets at the home of the High Priestess and High Priest, Lady Morgaine and Laughing Tree, and the ritual area is in the basement of the house. Assorted posters, books, and bric-a-brac line the walls. A bead curtain hangs over the entrance to the stairs, and there is a nine-foot-wide circular straw mat on the floor. The altar is set up on a natural redwood slab coffee table. During downtime, the altar is against the wall, but for rituals it is moved to the center of the room. Unlike Christian services, where the Priest stands behind the pulpit and faces the congregation, the central altar is the hub of the wheel. Except during the invocation of the Lord and Lady, the Priest and Priestess move all around it.

Setting Up the Altar

For this full-moon esbat ritual, the altar is set up in this way: A ceramic statue of Cernunnos, adapted from the Gundestrup cauldron, is at the rear left of the altar. A silver statue of Artemis is at the rear right. Next to each of the statues is a taper candle, green for Cernunnos and white for Artemis, set in matching glass candleholders. In the middle of the altar, sitting on a large brass pentacle, is a stout pink candle that's four inches across. Next to the candle is a small geode filled with salt, a small white feather, a vial of oil, a hollow terra-cotta scarab beetle filled halfway with sand, a seashell containing spring water, and a book of matches. Next to the beetle there is a small charcoal disk and a little plastic pouch of resin incense.

Also on the altar near the Artemis statue is a silver chalice made in the shape of a dryad. Her upraised arms and branches hold the cup of the chalice. Next to that there is a small dish of dried flowers. In front of the Cernunnos statue is the coven athame. It has a twelve-inch-long, double-edged blade with a clear acrylic handle. Embedded within the handle is a large piece of tiger's eye. A small silver bell and an assortment of herbs and crystals are also on the altar. Lying on the floor under the altar is the coven sword. It's a replica of a medieval longsword.

At the edge of the straw mat there are four small tables. There is one at each of the cardinal compass points. These are miniature altars, and there's one for each of the elements. The east altar holds a fan made from pheasant feathers, a pewter statue of a faerie in flight, a tiny dutch windmill, some quartz crystals, and a white candle. The south altar holds a little statue of a red dragon, a small iron cauldron, a bundle of dried poinsettias, four pieces of red tiger's eye, and a red candle. The west altar holds a betta in a small glass fishbowl, a statue of a leaping dolphin, some seashells, a piece of blue agate, and a blue candle. The north altar holds a bonsai tree, an ivory carving of a stag, a large geode, two pieces of obsidian, and a dark green candle. Each elemental altar is about eighteen inches across and a foot high. These are usually against the walls of the room, but for ritual they are placed at the edge of the mat.

Why this setup?

The nine-foot straw mat on the floor is the sacred space area. Nine is relevant for two reasons. One, it is a multiple of three, and three is one of magick's "prime numbers." Two, a nine-foot circle is the most comfortable size for thirteen people, the traditional coven size, to stand around without feeling crowded. The altar does not need to be round, and a slab of redwood seems more natural and appealing for a nature-based faith.

The statue of Artemis, the Greek goddess of the moon and the hunt, is used by this coven for esbats. They keep other statues for other rituals, including Persephone for Imbolc and Freyja if a ritual demands a more forceful approach. Green Dragon Coven honours Cernunnos almost exclusively, although at times statues of Pan or Baphomet have been used. Some traditions insist that the god and goddess invoked at ritual be of the same pantheon. Others don't. Morgaine and Tree have no problem with mixing pantheons. The candles at the side of each statue are lit as that deity is invoked, symbolizing their active presence. Artemis's is white, for the moon, and Cernunnos's is green, for fertility and growth.

The large pink candle in the middle is the spirit candle; it is lit first, and all other candles used in the ritual are lit from it. Pink is used because it represents a synthesis of love, purity, and hope. The geode of salt represents earth, the seashell is water, the feather is air, and the incense represents fire. These are all used in the initial consecration and anointment part of the ritual. The terra-cotta beetle will hold the burning incense, which is both air and fire. Little charcoal discs or coins are readily available at most metaphysical supply shops, and some church suppliers offer similar forms of charcoal. Unlike cone or stick incense, crystalline, or "raw," incense won't burn without a charcoal base.

The dryad chalice represents the goddess, and the athame represents the god. All these things have their own purpose and significance during ritual. The various crystals scattered around the altar offer their own vibrations to the proceedings, and they add to the charm of the altar. The sword is used to mark or describe the circle. The four miniature altars will be used as the quarters are called. We'll examine the use of all these articles as the ritual progresses.

The Coven's Garb

Many people consider clothing to be an important part of ritual. As the saying goes, "The clothes make the man." Looking the part can do as much for the flow of the ritual as knowing one's lines and roles. Some covens insist that ritual garb be different from everyday wear—sort of like wearing one's "Sunday best" to church. Wearing ritual garb is a sign of respect, and the very process of changing clothes for an event puts you in a more focused mindset for that event. Here's a quick look at what each member of Green Dragon Coven chooses to wear and why.

Lady Morgaine, High Priestess

The High Priestess wears a bright yellow dress, a copper "Triple Goddess" crown, about three pounds of copper bracelets, a brass dragon necklace, and a coin belt that belly dancers wear. She likes the sunny yellow/copper look; she says that it makes her feel more magickal.

Many Witches like to wear lots and lots of jewelry during ritual, and there is a joke among Witches that one of the events at the imaginary Pagan Olympics is the "Jewelry Run." In it, you wear every single piece of jewelry you own and try to walk ten feet without falling over.

Laughing Tree, High Priest

The High Priest wears a silk black robe with a green dragon embroidered on the back, an enormous pewter pentagram necklace, and his personal athame, which he wears hanging from his cord. His crown is a green John Deere baseball cap with eight-inch fake antlers attached to it.

> *Not every tradition demands that the High Priest and Priestess wear crowns; it just happens that Morgaine and Laughing Tree like them. Laughing Tree wears his cord, which was presented to him upon assuming the title of High Priest, as a military general might wear medals of honour, and he feels that a John Deere baseball cap is ironically appropriate. A company that makes agricultural and farming machinery honours the Horned God and the Green Man. There's a deus ex machina joke in there somewhere. The antlers attached to it symbolize the presence of the god in the man.*

Jaguar, Morgaine's Maiden

Jaguar wears a bright tie-dyed toga and uses her cord as the belt. She wears a silver harem bracelet and a rose quartz diadem. Her bracelet, which consists of a bracelet and a ring with a chain between them, has a dragon medallion on the chain. Laughing Tree feels that every member of Green Dragon Coven should have a dragon somewhere on their ritual garb. Her diadem, which has a single amethyst jewel hanging over her third eye, represents her maiden status. It is sort of like a baby crown. Not all maidens wear diadems; Jaguar just likes it.

> *Is Jaguar the coven maiden or Morgaine's maiden? Technically she's both, but since she is learning directly from Morgaine—and not from the coven as a whole—she prefers to think of herself as maiden to Morgaine. Traditionally the maiden to a High Priestess is a female position, but in today's Wicca anyone can serve as maiden. A possible nonbinary term is squire.*

Wyvern, the Summoner

Wyvern wears a long, sleeveless beige tunic trimmed with green and silver brocade. He designed and made it himself after reading its description in a fantasy novel. He wears a sky blue sash around his waist and has wyverns (two-legged dragons) etched into the leather wristbands he wears. He wears two matching athames, which look like miniature swords, that are fifteen inches long. Each one has its own name.

> *Wyvern reads science fiction and fantasy voraciously, and his garb design is based on a character in a novel he's been reading. The twin athames are unusual, but Morgaine and Laughing Tree know how much the whole ensemble means to him.*

Cassandra

Cassandra wears a flowing gossamer black dress, a silver dragon's-head bracelet, a necklace of alternating tiger's eye and amethyst beads, and lots of rings. Sometimes Cassandra wears a stereotypical black pointy hat, completing the black-clad Witch look. Morgaine frowns upon her wearing it in ritual, however.

> *Cassandra is the only coven member who wears a long black dress, or the stereotypical witchy garb. She got the idea while visiting friends in Salem, Massachusetts. At the ritual she attended, the women wore black and the men wore brightly coloured clothes—a direct contrast to the professional corporate image. Her fondness for the hat reflects her view of Witchcraft. By wearing what the mundane world expects her to wear, she feels empowered simply by her appearance. In his* Discworld *series of books, Terry Pratchett referred to that as "headology."*

Crystal

Crystal wears a fiery red gown, heavy eyeliner, and several gold bracelets. She has a dragon tattooed on her left hip. She's also wearing wrist braces. As a corporate secretary, she suffers from carpal tunnel syndrome. The braces aren't exactly garb, but they are necessary, so they are allowed.

> *Crystal, a Sagittarius, loves the fire element and fiery symbolism. She favors her dragon tattoo, which she got when she joined the coven. Crystal says that it is "a part of me, all the time, not just something I wear when it's appropriate."*

RedWolf, the Ásatrú

RedWolf wears a long hauberk, or tunic, made of coarse gray wool, an amber necklace, and a Mjolnir or Thor's hammer talisman. There is a dragon engraved on the talisman. He also wears a shortsword inscribed with futhark. RedWolf wears a plastic horned Viking helmet he bought at a costume shop last Halloween.

Not all covens have members who practice Ásatrú. RedWolf is a member of Green Dragon Coven because he's a friend of Laughing Tree, and there aren't any Ásatrú groups in town. He follows his own version of the Craft, which is a blend of Ásatrú and Wiccan principles. He dresses in Norse garb, befitting his tradition. The plastic Viking helmet is just for show; real Vikings did not have horns on their helmets. The absurdity of the image reflects his lighthearted view of life.

OakBranch

OakBranch and his husband are nudists, so he prefers to work skyclad. He does wear a green jade dragon necklace, and he has a pentagram tattooed on his right arm. In outdoor or public rituals, he concedes to laws about indecent exposure and wears a Scottish kilt regimental style.

OakBranch feels that the best way to honour the gods is to greet them without any masks or disguises, such as clothing. Besides, this way he's always wearing his ritual garb under his everyday clothes. At forty-seven years old, he's still first degree, but he doesn't mind. He feels that he'll advance when, and if, the gods find him worthy.

Jason, the Coven Initiate

Jason has not yet put together a ritual garb, just as he has not yet found his magickal name. He improvises with a black-and-yellow pentagram T-shirt and green sweatpants. He wears his athame, which has a dragon image etched into the blade. For some people, this is perfectly acceptable ritual garb. Jason, however, wants to put together something more official looking and find his Craft name before he earns his first degree.

In Summary

Nobody's garb matches anyone else's, but that's okay. Each member has the right to self-expression in their ritual garb. Traditionally the ritual garb is the only thing worn; shoes, socks, and undergarments are not part of garb. Most Witches prefer loose clothing in ritual, and many feel that tight, restrictive items, such as neckties or bras, can impede the magickal flow.

Items like wristwatches are usually removed and phones are muted before ritual begins. A lot of Witches feel that anything technological does not belong in circle—except for pacemakers or artificial limbs, of course; those are okay. If you're reading your lines from a text on your phone or tablet, keep it with you too.

As this is an open esbat, there are two guests present: RedWolf's sister, Brianna, and OakBranch's husband, Ethan. They will stand outside the ritual circle and simply observe the proceedings. As a token of respect, both are barefoot but still in their normal clothes.

This brings us to the point where the ritual actually begins. In the next three lessons, we'll watch as the ritual unfolds.

Lesson 27: Study Prompts and Questions

Fundamentals of Ritual

- What is the purpose of ritual within the Craft?
- What is the difference between sabbats and esbats? Are they transcendent or immanent forms of worship? Explain.
- What are the four phases of a Wiccan ritual as described here?

Setting Up the Altar

- What shape should the altar be? Is it the same for every tradition?
- How important is the arrangement of the altar? Justify your answer.
- Briefly describe the items one can expect to find on a Witch's altar. Explain the significance of the items you list.

The Coven's Garb

- Why is ritual garb important?
- In the coven, Laughing Tree insists that everyone have a dragon image worked into their garb somewhere. Why is this important to him?

Lesson 27: Recommended Reading

- *The Art of Ritual* by Rachel Patterson
- *Witch's Wheel of the Year: Rituals for Circle, Solitaries & Covens* by Jason Mankey

LESSON 28
Ritual Procedure: Erecting the Temple

We continue our series on ritual participation and procedure as Green Dragon Coven goes through the process of erecting the temple. Again, each part of the ritual will be covered twice.

Grounding and Centering

Before ritual begins, the coveners observe quiet time. This is a brief period of solitary meditation and reflection. It is a time to slow down from the pace of the day and focus on the ritual to come. The coveners sit quietly for a few moments while the High Priestess and maiden make last-minute arrangements.

Lady Morgaine lights the spirit candle in the middle of the altar and burns some incense while Jaguar plays some soft music. After a few moments, when the room has settled, Morgaine rings the small bell once. Laughing Tree joins Morgaine at the altar, and the rest of the coveners assemble at the eastern gate. In this case, it is the doorway leading upstairs.

Quiet time is special to many Witches. It is a time of quiet reflection and meditation used to ground and center oneself. The term grounding and centering means settling down, finding that quiet center within, and focusing upon the ritual to come. The more people involved in a ritual, the longer the quiet time should be. Quiet time is also known as attunement; it is a period of becoming attuned to the task at hand.

Some covens don't use a spirit candle. To the members of Green Dragon, however, it represents the life and the pulse of the ritual. All other candles used in the ritual will be lit from the spirit candle to symbolize that all magick flows from one source.

There are many different kinds of incense available. Most metaphysical shops offer a wide range of incense blends, and some are created especially for sabbats and esbats, different spellworking, and so on. The right incense blend can make a real difference.

The soft music, which can be anything from Clannad to Loreena McKennitt, Faun, Kenny G, Brahms, or Chopin, sets the mood for the ritual. Bands like Necrophagia or Cannibal Corpse might be inappropriate. The ringing of the bell tells people when then the ritual is to begin. Even if your eyes are closed, you can hear the bell. You may need a second notification form if some of your coveners are hearing impaired.

All rituals begin in the east. It is the element of air, dawn, and gateways and new beginnings. The eastern point of the ritual space is known as the eastern gate.

Consecration and Anointment

Once the coven members are assembled, the ritual can begin. Normally the maiden and summoner join the High Priestess and High Priest at the altar for consecration and anointment. This time, however, Wyvern is absent, so OakBranch steps in to fulfill those duties. Jaguar takes the vial of oil, and OakBranch picks up the terra-cotta beetle and the feather.

With the vial of oil in her left hand, Jaguar turns to Morgaine. Morgaine stands still with her eyes closed and head slightly upraised. Jaguar dabs a little oil onto the index finger of her right hand and traces a small pentagram on Morgaine's forehead.

While doing this, she says, "Feel the healing touch of the Lady surging through you, washing away all negativity and fear. Let the spirit fill you."

Then she turns to Tree. He takes the same position that Morgaine did, and Jaguar anoints him in the same way with the same words.

The maiden begins the process of consecration by anointing the High Priestess and High Priest. She anoints the Priestess first, acknowledging her as the leader of the coven, followed by the High Priest. She holds the vial in her receptive hand, so she's able to apply the oil with her projective hand. The pentagram image she traced over the third eye (middle of the forehead) empowers the recipient; the third eye is marked because it's the gateway to the inner being.

As she receives the oil, the High Priestess envisions the oil flowing through her body and being, washing out negativity.

Be careful not to get any oil in the eyes. That can make a person go from anointed to annoyed. It's wise to check about oils beforehand, too, because some people may have allergic reactions to specific blends.

OakBranch then holds up the incense in his right hand and holds the feather in his left hand. That is his projective hand; OakBranch is left-handed. Morgaine stands before him, and OakBranch kneels before her. Starting at her left foot, he uses the feather to "spread" incense over her. He makes a brushing motion with the feather as he carries the incense up her left side, across her head, and down her right side.

As he does this, he says, "Feel the cleansing breath of the Lord surging over you, caressing away all the day's cares and worries. Let the spirit fill you."

He then repeats the process with Tree. After the High Priestess and High Priest are anointed, the maiden and summoner repeat the process upon each other, trading off with oil and incense.

As before, the High Priest and Priestess assume a receptive position, letting the incense flow over them and through them. You may notice that OakBranch started at the left foot, went up and over, and ended at the right foot. This means that the movement went widdershins, or counterclockwise. But remember that to the person being anointed, the process upon them is deosil. They are effectively stepping through a portal of incense.

Now, as Morgaine and Tree wait by the altar, Jaguar and OakBranch move to the eastern portal. One at a time, they anoint the remaining members of the coven. As each person is anointed, they step onto the straw mat and walk respectfully around the perimeter. Cassandra is first, then RedWolf, then Jason, and finally Crystal. Their roles as quarter-callers had been decided beforehand. Cassandra walks deosil all the way around the circle, stopping just to the right of the eastern gate. RedWolf follows, stopping by the north point. Jason follows RedWolf, stopping at west, and Crystal takes up the rear, stopping at south.

There is no change in the anointment process for the other coveners. Elders don't get special treatment.

Notice that every person enters the same way. From the eastern gate, they move deosil around the circle to predetermined positions. In the example here, there are very few participants. In fact, there are just enough to fill the roles prescribed. In rituals with more people, the quarter-callers would be anointed and welcomed into the ritual first, moving into position, before the other ritual participants are anointed and invited. In a ritual of fifty or five hundred people, this can take a little time. In those situations, a brazier that emits smoke is often placed on the ground, and people simply step over it and through the smoke.

Building Sacred Space

Once everyone has entered, Jaguar and OakBranch return to the altar. Jaguar puts down the oil and picks up the small geode of salt. Using her projective hand, she takes a pinch of salt and sprinkles it in a pentagram pattern into the seashell of water. Then she puts the geode down and picks up the seashell in her receptive hand. As the rest of the coveners watch, she walks from the altar to the eastern gate and the outside edge of the perimeter. She walks deosil slowly around the outside edge of the coven, gently sprinkling water onto the floor.

As Jaguar walks, she says, "Salt of purity, water of the sea, join together in harmony. For where thou art cast, let no harm or ill will last. So mote it be!"

Everyone present responds, saying, "So mote it be" in unison, as Jaguar returns to the altar.

The salt and water rite, used to consecrate the circle, is very old. It can be performed by either the High Priestess or the maiden. The rite banishes ill will and chaos from the circle, just as salt is used to purify food, and water is used to clean. In some covens, the rite is performed while standing at the altar, and the simple rite symbolically cleanses the entire area. Here, however, Morgaine feels that sprinkling water all around is more effective. And yes, what Jaguar is using is essentially Pagan holy water.

The call and response of "So mote it be" is used extensively in ritual at the closing of various actions. It's a way of bringing everyone's energy into the action. "So mote it be" is medieval English, meaning "So it must be."

OakBranch, still holding the terra-cotta beetle of incense and the feather, walks out to the eastern gate. As Jaguar had done, he walks deosil around the outside of the circle, using the feather to spread the incense.

As he goes, he says, "Sweet breath of air, spirit of fire bright, guard and protect our circle tonight. For where thou art cast, let no harm or ill will last. So mote it be!"

Everyone responds with "So mote it be" as OakBranch returns to the altar and puts the incense and feather down.

This is the counterpart to the salt and water rite. By using salt, water, air, and fire, all four material elements are used to consecrate the circle.

Now Tree picks up the coven sword. Moving to the eastern gate, he holds it out at a 45-degree angle, point down, and walks slowly deosil around the outside of the circle.

As he goes, he says, "Mighty Lord, gracious Lady, bless this blade that I may cast this circle. I call upon ye, oh powers of spirit, to bless and consecrate our rite, as a temple between the worlds. So mote it be!"

While everyone says, "So mote it be" in response, Tree holds the sword in a military salute position as he returns to the altar. He kneels down to lay the sword back under the altar.

The task of cutting, or marking, the circle frequently falls to the High Priest, summoner, or guardian; it used to be an exclusively male role. It was discussed whether OakBranch wanted to perform that rite in Wyvern's absence, but he deferred to Tree. Some covens use the athame, but Tree prefers the sword. It's long been a symbol of protection and guardianship, and he thinks it's only appropriate here. Besides, if the sword is known as the Master of the Five Elements, what better tool for the job?

This completes the task of creating sacred space. After Tree returns with the sword, Jaguar and OakBranch return to the perimeter of the circle.

Notice that because of the position of the quarter-callers, the symmetry of the circle will be unbalanced no matter where they stand. It's nice to have a symmetrical arrangement of people, but it's not imperative. Jaguar and OakBranch merely move deosil to wherever they feel most comfortable and stand at the edge of the circle.

Some traditions used to insist that the coven members stand in alternating gender, creating a male-female-male-female sequence. This arrangement was said to create a magickal battery, which enriched the power of the circle. Crowley first suggested it for that reason, and Gardner emphasized its importance. But many modern Witches feel that it's an incredibly outdated concept.

Calling the Quarters

Now that sacred space has been created with a perimeter, it is time to build the interior of the temple. This is done by calling upon the elements, or the four quarters, and it is the duty of the quarter-callers to invoke, or welcome, the four elements into the circle. Their presence adds to the magick of the proceedings, and they establish the four cornerstones of magick within the ritual space. You might think of them as the poles holding up a tent.

At a nod from Morgaine, Cassandra, at the eastern point, picks up the candle from the eastern miniature altar. She walks to the main altar, lights her candle from the spirit candle, and returns to her position. She places the candle upon the elemental altar and holds up her athame, pointing it east and up. Everyone else turns and faces the same way, pointing either with their athame or an open hand.

Cassandra says, "Greetings, guardians of the watchtowers of the east! Magnificent eagle, spirits of the new dawn, join us at our sacred rite! Be with us now; join us in our celebration of joy and worship! Hail, and welcome!"

Everyone responds with "Hail, and welcome!" They lower their arms and turn to face south.

> *The roles of quarter-callers were determined before the ritual began, so everyone knew where they would have to stand. When Cassandra carries her elemental candle to and from the altar, she does not have to walk the whole circle. Instead, she merely walks along a spoke. Raised hands and athames are a salute and a symbol of respect, as is the communal call of "Hail, and welcome!"*
>
> *Cassandra named a couple of elemental figures in her calling. Depending upon the element being called, a wide variety of animal spirits or animistic forces can be named. She also made reference to the watchtowers. Some covens use that word at every calling; others don't. The image of a fortress—a bastion of defense at the edge of reality—appeals to a lot of Witches.*

Now Crystal calls the southern quarter and the element of fire. She repeats Cassandra's procedure with the candle, then she raises her athame and says, "Welcome, spirits of the south! Magnificent phoenix, fires of inspiration and courage, and Mad Dog 20/20, join us at our sacred rite! Be with us now; join us in our celebration of joy and worship! Hail, and welcome!"

At the word *welcome*, Crystal draws a pentagram in the air with her athame, and everyone repeats, "Hail, and welcome!"

> *You'll notice a few differences here. Crystal did not use the same words as Cassandra. Some covens use identical callings, changing only the appropriate references, but Morgaine likes to let each person put their own "spin" on the calling. Crystal almost shouted her calling, using a loud, strong voice. Her reference to Mad Dog 20/20, a notorious alcoholic beverage, brought a chuckle from the coven. Some Witches might balk at using humor and comedic references in ritual, but Green Dragon sees nothing wrong with mixing humor with reverence. Of course the gods have a sense of humor; how else do you explain the platypus?!*
>
> *At the close of her calling, Crystal drew a pentagram deosil in the air with her athame, a visual blessing. Again, this is something that some Witches do, and others don't.*

Now it's Jason's turn. He's participated in rituals before, but this is his first time calling a quarter. Since he's unsure what to say, Jaguar wrote a small script for him.

He faces west and holds his script up as he calls out, "Great spirits of the west, dolphins, crashing waves, and soothing summer rains, join us in our rite. Bring to us your eternal wisdom; share with us your wash of emotion. Hail, and welcome!"

Everyone repeats, "Hail, and welcome!"

At a nudge from RedWolf, Jason grabs the candle and quickly lights it from the spirit candle.

> *Again, a different calling. Reading from a script is fine in some covens and frowned upon by others. Tree prefers not to use them but understands Jason's inexperience. Jason missed his cue to light the elemental candle, but that did not ruin the effect or his effort. The gods understand that humans are imperfect creatures.*

Finally, north must be called. As a Norseman, RedWolf always prefers to call north, even though the quarters are usually not called at all in Ásatrú ceremonies.

RedWolf lights the earth candle from the spirit candle, holds his shortsword high, and says, "Mighty elk! Proud winter wolf! Howling winds of the northern reaches! As Woden and Freyja be witness, I command you to attend our sacred rite! *Gothan daginn landveitter*! Hail, and welcome!"

He performs an intricate sword pattern in the air, a runic blessing, and sheathes his shortsword. Nobody repeats those motions or the Norse words he used, but they do say, "Hail, and welcome!"

RedWolf's calling is somewhat different from most. He adapted an Ásatrú rite to fit the quarter calling, naming two Norse gods in the process. This is rarely done but not generally forbidden. While the Norse gods won't be invoked into the circle, Tree has no problem with RedWolf calling upon Woden and Freyja. He thinks of them as honoured guests. The Norse words RedWolf used mean "Greetings, earth-spirits," and with his sword, he traced the runes for strength, partnership, and joy.

When it comes to the quarters, some Wiccans prefer to call them corners rather than quarters, referring to the "four corners of the earth" and the "four cornerstones of magick." The general consensus, however, is that they are quarters, not corners, for two reasons: One, since the four elements together compose the whole of the circle, each covers 25 percent, or a quarter, of the ritual space. The fifth element, spirit, is, of course, the altar itself. Two, where is a corner in a circle?

Invoking the Goddess and the God

Now that the circle is cast and the elements have been called, the gods must be welcomed. Morgaine and Tree stand together at the altar, facing east. The High Priestess calls the goddess before the High Priest calls the god, so Morgaine starts.

Standing with feet slightly apart, she lifts her arms up high with her hands open and palms up, and says, "Hail, mighty huntress of the silver bow! Lovely Artemis, be with us tonight. As we gather beneath your silvery light, teach us to read the subtle marks as we hunt the forests of our lives. Hail, and well met!"

She draws a circle in the air with her finger, then lights the goddess candle from the spirit candle as everyone repeats, "Hail, and well met!"

The position that Morgaine assumed is the "goddess position." It is used in invocations, evocations, and spellworking. By stretching out with her arms upraised and slightly apart and feet about three feet apart, Morgaine's stance opens her spirit and her chakras to receive the goddess. While she is not evoking the goddess here, the stance is essentially the same.

Morgaine wove a couple of Artemis's attributes into her calling. While the quarter callings ended with "Hail, and welcome," the goddess invocation ends with "Hail, and well met." It sounds more personal and respectful. We are talking about a goddess, after all.

Now Tree invokes Cernunnos. He assumes the same position that Morgaine did. Tree is quite fond of the antler-headed forest god, and his invocation reflects this: "Hail, mighty Horned God of the wild places! Noble Cernunnos, be with us this night! As we gather in your sacred grove, teach us to find the strength of the heart of the stag as we strive to overcome obstacles in our lives. Yo, 'Kern, get your smelly hide down here! Hail, and well met!"

There is a ripple of laughter as everyone says, "Hail, and well met!" and Tree lights the god candle from the spirit candle.

In some covens, his casual reference might be seen as blasphemous and could even get him banished from the coven. But as Tree sees it, Cernunnos is a partying, beer-drinking kind of god who would welcome the amiable mention.

Tree then looks around the gathering and says, "The circle is cast. We stand now in sacred space, in a place that is not a place, in a time that is not a time. Here, the Craft and the magick are all. So mote it be!"

Everyone responds with, "So mote it be!" as Morgaine rings the bell.

The phrase, "in a place that is not a place, in a time that is not a time" means that once sacred space has been established, the coven is no longer part of the mundane world. Sure, they are still standing in Morgaine and Tree's basement with Brianna and Ethan watching, but within the circle, they have entered a different spiritual dimension. Witches often notice that material sounds are less noticeable during ritual; car horns and outside sounds seem far away. Morgaine's bell signifies that the circle is cast, and the next phase of ritual can begin.

The temple is erected. In the next lesson, we'll examine some of the magickal workings performed in circle as the Green Dragon esbat continues.

Lesson 28: Study Prompts and Questions

Grounding and Centering

- Why do you think a period of quiet time, or attunement, would be important? How would you use that time?
- In your own words, explain what "grounding and centering" means.

Consecration and Anointment

- In the ritual described, the maiden anointed the coveners with oils, and the summoner cleansed them with incense. In your own words, explain the significance of each and why the maiden and the summoner performed these tasks.

Building Sacred Space

- Why was it important to walk clockwise around the circle?
- Explain the symbolism of the salt/water and air/fire consecrations.
- Why did the High Priest mark the circle with a sword if everyone already knows where the edge of the circle is?

Calling the Quarters

- In your own words, explain the significance of each of the four quarters as they relate to the ritual.
- Why are the quarters called in that particular sequence?
- Do you prefer the term *quarters* or *corners*? Explain and justify.

Invoking the Goddess and the God

- In your own words, explain why the gods are invited into ritual.
- If the gods are immanent, not transcendent, deities and already everywhere, why do they have to be invited into ritual?

Lesson 28: Recommended Reading

- *The Ultimate Guide to the Witch's Wheel of the Year: Rituals, Spells & Practices for Magical Sabbats, Holidays & Celebrations* by Anjou Keirnan
- *Voices from the Circle: The Heritage of Western Paganism* edited by Prudence Jones and Caitlin Matthews

LESSON 29
Ritual Procedure: Working in Ritual

In the last lesson, we watched as the members of Green Dragon Coven erected the temple, the first part of ritual procedure. Let's return now to watch as the esbat proceeds.

Statement of Purpose

With the temple erected and the circle cast, the main purpose of the ritual can commence.

Lady Morgaine looks around the coven and says, "We gather here to honour Artemis, daughter of the bright moon, and Cernunnos, Horned Lord of the forest, and to welcome the glow of the hunter's moon into our sacred circle. As the wheel turns and the days begin to grow shorter, we welcome the Lady of the silver bright moon and the Lord of the changing moon into our lives. On this esbat we recognize the wort moon. Litha is just past, and magick is abundant. Feel the vitality of the planet and the fullness of the moon as we work our magick tonight, and let the silver moon—even if she's not visible from this room—empower us all. Lammas, when the Lord gives of his own vitality to ensure the strength and survival of all livings things, approaches. Thanks are given them; we offer a moment of silence for personal reflection on the bounty of the gods."

Morgaine's statement sets the stage for the ritual. She allows a moment of silence for personal reflection and meditation. After about a minute, she rings the bell once, softly.

Laughing Tree then steps forward and says, "As regular visitors to our esbats know, we take this time to recognize the lunar cycle and honour the gods but also to honour the Divine within each other. We do this by offering support, counsel, and healing to our coven and to those whose lives we touch. Let no harm befall our family."

Everyone sits, and Tree and Morgaine spend a few minutes discussing coven business. They talk about upcoming events, coven finances, visiting friends and relatives, local politics, and the welfare of coven pets. Questions are asked and answered, and Crystal, the scribe, takes minutes.

This time of coven business and member support is often called family circle. Some covens don't include family circle in ritual, or they may hold similar events under a different name. Tree and Morgaine, however, feel that this time of working for the coven is an integral part of coven unity.

At this point, there is knocking on the front door of the house. Two knocks, then one, then three; this is the coven "key." Tree nods to Ethan, who is outside the sacred circle, and who then goes upstairs to answer the door. Many covens use key knocks as a kind of password. It's a safety device, and a way of knowing if the person at the door is a coven member.

Ethan comes back downstairs with Wyvern, the wayward summoner. He didn't have time to go home and get his garb, so he improvised with a loose renaissance festival shirt over his blue jeans. After removing his shoes, socks, phone, and watch, he's confronted at the eastern gate by Tree.

Tree holds the coven athame up, touching its point to Wyvern's chest, and asks, "Seeker of light, how would you enter this circle?"

"In perfect love and perfect trust," is Wyvern's response.

Tree replies, "That is good, for I say to you, it were better that you rush upon this blade than enter with fear or falsehood in your heart."

Wyvern bows, and Tree touches the flat of the blade to his own chest as a salute.

Using the athame, Tree cuts a magickal doorway in the wall of the circle. He goes from the floor at Wyvern's left foot, up and over his head, and down to his right foot. Wyvern steps through, and Tree closes the doorway by moving his athame in reverse, unmaking it.

Jaguar anoints Wyvern, performing both the summoner's and maiden's tasks to save time. Wyvern then walks deosil around the circle, stopping just to the right of Jason. Nobody admonishes him for being late; they're just happy he's there.

If Ethan or Brianna hadn't been outside the sacred circle and available to answer the door, one of the coven members would have cut a doorway to exit the sacred circle and gone upstairs to let Wyvern in. They would have brought Wyvern down to the eastern gate and then reentered the circle and closed the doorway behind them, leaving Wyvern to wait at the gate for Tree's challenge.

The challenge-and-reply is an excerpt of the initiation ritual, allowing the latecomer to declare his intentions. Tree was not going to attack Wyvern with the athame, nor was Wyvern going to impale himself on the blade. The athame is not a weapon. Notice that Tree cut Wyvern's doorway in the same pattern as Oak-Branch performed the incense cleansing—widdershins to the wielder, but deosil to the recipient. Should they have anointed him before he entered the sacred space? Maybe, but most people would not belabor the issue.

The movement and commotion at the eastern gate caused the elemental candle to blow out. Cassandra pauses briefly to light it from the spirit candle, but it goes out again. She tries to light it again, but Morgaine stops her, saying, "Let the wind spirits say what they may, we know that the candle has been lit."

Regaining the composure of the group, Tree asks if anyone has any requests for magickal work or healings.

Working with Magick

RedWolf steps forward and says, "I want to offer support for Jack, my roommate. He was arrested on Tuesday, hit with a DUI. He's under $800 bail; all I want is to offer him energy to get his head together."

Laughing Tree asks, "Do you have his permission to work magick for him?"

RedWolf nods, and Morgaine says, "Wolf, drunk driving is a very serious matter … he's not only risking his own safety but that of every other driver on the road with him. I can almost guarantee that any judgment will involve alcohol counselling, and he could lose his driver's license. Please tell Jack to spend less time communing with Dionysus and more with Athena. Let him know that he has the love and support of the coven, but any healing energy will only be performed when he's ready to accept it. No amount of healing will do any good unless he actually wants to be healed, otherwise you're just talking to a wall. We will, however, raise energy for a fair trial. It doesn't mean he'll get off easy, but it'll ensure the best results for everyone concerned."

Morgaine and Tree step back to join the circle, and everyone stands and joins hands.

Note that the first thing Tree did was to ascertain that permission had been granted to work magick. Part of the "harm none" principle is not to offer energy or magick—of any kind—without permission.

Morgaine asks Brianna, RedWolf's sister, to take a drum from the shelf and start a slow, rhythmic beat.

As the drum sounds, slowly at first, Morgaine says, "Everyone, visualize RedWolf's friend Jack. We know what he needs; we just have to see that he gets it. Together we'll raise energy for him. Focus on your center. Visualize a tiny spark in your heart chakra. Now energize it; bring it to life. Feel the spark moving around the circle, connecting heart to heart. See it spinning round the circle, coming back through you on the drumbeat."

As she starts to raise her hands, Morgaine motions to Brianna to increase the tempo. Everyone closes their eyes, focusing inward.

The drum beats faster.

Morgaine continues, "Feel your spark accelerating, growing in strength and vitality. As you send it around, see it growing from a single spark to a streak of light, zipping around, passing through you on the drumbeat."

The drum beats faster.

"Now you see everyone else's spark as well as they flow through you and around the circle. As the tempo increases, see them combining into a single glowing band of energy. Raise the power a couple of notches; keep it going, faster, brighter, higher, spinning through you."

The drum beats a rapid staccato rhythm, and everyone feels their arms raise as if lifted upon the spinning ring of energy. As the tempo increases, there is a palpable crackle of energy in the air. Ethan gasps. Even though he doesn't believe in magick, he feels it too.

Morgaine says, "As you focus the bright ribbon of energy, visualize it forming into a cone overhead, over the circle. Focus your energy into it—faster, brighter, higher. On my mark, see the energy speeding away to Jack to do its work. RedWolf, are you still focused on Jack?"

RedWolf says, "I am."

Everyone's arms are raised high, and Morgaine says, "Everyone focus … ready … ready … now!"

At her command, the drumbeat suddenly stops, and the group collectively envisions the bolt of energy streaking away to give Jack the guidance he needs. Everyone lowers their arms and relaxes.

One of the advantages of having visitors at a ritual is the possibility of musical accompaniment. Should the coven allow someone who's not actually a coven member to participate? Some might question it, but Tree and Morgaine welcome Brianna's "peanut gallery" participation. This was a simple power-raising exercise, using the most basic form of energy manipulation: rhythm. Notice that all through the power's raising, Morgaine constantly coached the coven, offering guidance and support. Even though they don't know who the presiding judge will be or when the trial will take place, the magick will know where and when to manifest. It was subconsciously programmed that way. If magick is raised and left unused, however, it can sour, causing headaches, negative reactions, or worse.

Crystal then raises her hand. Her carpal tunnel obviously causes some discomfort. "Can I get some healing for this?" she asks.

Morgaine asks her several questions about the duration of the symptoms, medical treatment, and so on to size up the situation.

After a short discussion, Morgaine and Tree decide to use a Witch's mill chant as a focused, immediate healing. Crystal kneels and lays her arms across the altar, and everyone else puts their projective hands on her shoulder.

Morgaine tells the coven, "This is a Witch's mill chant. I'll lead the chant; everyone join in on the last line for a vocalizing of energy. As the mill goes, visualize pulling cool healing energy up from the earth. See it flowing through you and into Crystal. Crystal, your job is to receive the healing light and let it fill you and your arms. See the carpal 'crud' flowing out of you through your hands, back into the earth. At the end of the chant, everyone seal the magick with a yell."

The Witch's mill is a popular group-oriented power-raising chant. If there are more people than the recipient has shoulder space for, then an outer ring of people can connect with an inner ring, like concentric circles.

Morgaine leads the chant:

> *Fire flame and Fire burn,*
> *Make the Mill of magic turn,*
> *Work the will for which we pray,*
> *Io Dio, Ha He Yay!*
> *Air breathe and Air blow,*
> *Make the Mill of magic go.*
> *Work the will for which we pray,*
> *Io Dio, Ha He Yay!*
> *Water heat and Water boil,*

Make the Mill of magic boil,
Work the will for which we pray,
Io Dio, Ha He Yay!
Earth without and Earth within,
Make the Mill of magic spin,
Work the will for which we pray,
Io Dio, Ha He Yay! [108]

The chant is repeated three times, and each time is faster and with more intensity. After the third round, Crystal nods, and everyone lets out a loud, raucous yell, visualizing the pains of her wrist pouring out as the healing energy flows through her. At the completion of the chant, everyone returns to the perimeter of the circle.

The Witch's mill is an excellent chant and a wonderful rhyme. All the elements are represented, and the last portion—"Io Dio, Ha He Yay!"—is a vocal toning used to center the magick. Keep in mind that magickal healing should never replace the care of a qualified physician. Magick can be used to enhance or hasten the healing process.

Earthing Excess Energy

Grounding and centering was used before ritual began to let everyone settle down from the day and clear their minds for ritual. Some covens will raise magick, ground it, and raise it again several times throughout the course of a single ritual, while others only ground and center once at the close of ritual.

After a period of magickal work and raising power, some people may feel somewhat disoriented, confused, or dizzy, and in extreme cases, some might experience nausea or mild hallucinations. Imagine riding a roller coaster and then feeling like you're still on the coaster hours later as you're driving home or cooking dinner. The members of Green Dragon Coven didn't go that far here, but they do feel slightly buzzy, so Tree suggests a period of grounding and centering. This is important for two reasons: one, keeping all that untapped energy bouncing around inside can cause reactions like irritability, nausea, or depression, and two, it lets you refocus on the world around you.

Different people do this in different ways.

---

108. Gray, *Magical Ritual Methods*, 215–16.

Cassandra sits quietly with her legs crossed and eyes closed. She's visualizing the energy flowing out of her and into the earth like bathwater going down the drain.

Crystal also sits with her legs crossed, but she holds her torso upright, arms reaching high overhead. She breathes deeply, letting each breath fill her entire being. With each breath, cool air flows in, and loose energy flows out.

Jaguar stands before the southern altar with her hands cupped over the red candle. Eyes closed, her arms twitch as she vigorously pumps energy down her arms and into the candle flame. This way, she reasons, her excess energy is being sent back into the universe to be used again.

OakBranch lies flat on his stomach with his arms and legs outstretched. He is letting the earth soak up his energy like a sponge.

Wyvern kneels, holding his athame with both hands, its point touching the floor. He visualizes energy flowing down the athame blade like a grounding rod.

RedWolf stands, holding a small quartz crystal in his hands. He focuses on it, sending his energy into the crystal. After the ritual, he will bury it near the roots of a favored tree. In this way, he is giving part of his essence back to Yggdrasil, the mythic Tree of Life of Norse lore.

Jason sits, petting Tree's pet dachshund. Pets, especially dogs, are wonderful for grounding. Just as a plant's photosynthesis turns carbon dioxide into oxygen, a dog takes in stress and gives back affection. Just don't overload the little guy.

Morgaine and Tree stand before the altar with their hands over the spirit candle. They are visualizing energy flowing down their arms and into the candle flame. It's very similar to Jaguar's method but less aggressive.

There are many different ways to purge excess energy; these are but a few. Remember, energy is mutable. It never really vanishes, like deleted data, but it can change form, be transferred from one item or person to another, or be released back into the ground. Each of the members of Green Dragon Coven releases energy in their own way, but the goal is the same—to clear their bodies and minds to be able to focus on the task at hand.

Use and Misuse of Magick

After settling down from the Witch's mill chant, Morgaine asks if there are any other magickal workings to be done. Tree mentions that a coven associate has a request. She opened a metaphysical shop and wants the coven to bless and charge a stone that will hang over the door to ensure good business.

Tree takes a piece of green tourmaline from the altar and hands it to Morgaine, saying, "Everyone take this stone as it comes around, and hold it for a couple of minutes, empowering it with prosperity and luck. Enhance it with your own energy, vitality, and spirit to bring Meredith's shop bountiful rewards."

Morgaine holds the crystal in both hands for a moment with her eyes closed. She puts it up to her third eye, kisses it, then hands it to Jaguar. Jaguar holds it a while, adding her own energy to it, before handing it to Wyvern, and so it goes on around the circle.

Meredith used to be part of Green Dragon Coven before moving cross-country. She has since opened a metaphysical shop and wants a coven blessing for the shop's success. Tree agreed, and the members of Green Dragon are charging a money-stone with luck, vitality, and prosperity. Unlike spells which have a time and place to "go off," the stone will continue to radiate luck for as long as Meredith keeps it "charged up." We'll discuss the magick and uses of stones and crystals in lesson 33.

A coven associate is one who has worked with the coven but is not an active member. Brianna, who practices as a solitaire, could be considered a coven associate, since she took a supporting role in the esbat. Ethan, however, could not. He is not a Witch, and he only came to the ritual at OakBranch's request. Very rarely is a non-Pagan recognized as a coven associate.

OakBranch suggests sending healing magick to a popular Hollywood celebrity. She'd been flying in a small plane with three other people when the plane crashed under mysterious circumstances. The celebrity was the only survivor and is recuperating in intensive care.

Morgaine steps in and explains why the coven won't help. They were not directly asked to; they don't have her permission to work magick for her. The celebrity in question may very well benefit from a magickal healing, but since she did not request it, none is performed. Magick can be used to heal, support, and guide, but it can be misused as well.

Sending magick to a person or place where it was not requested is a misuse of energy. This is as true for helping injured strangers as it is for putting a love spell on a friend. Part of knowing how to use magick is knowing when to use it. Likewise, a spell to help a small business or to manage one's finances is acceptable, but a spell to manipulate Wall Street or the European market is not.

There are no more magickal workings to perform, so Morgaine calls to close the circle. In the next lesson, we'll watch as the coven takes down the temple and closes the esbat.

Lesson 29: Study Prompts and Questions

Statement of Purpose
- Why do you think it's necessary to define the purpose of the ritual?
- Do you think this should be done for all rituals, including sabbats and esbats? Why or why not?
- When Wyvern arrived late to the circle, why did Tree challenge him that way?
- Do you think that "in perfect love and perfect trust" was the correct answer? Why? Or why not?

Working with Magick
- Do you agree with Morgaine's reason for not helping Jack directly? Explain.
- What was your impression of the Witch's mill rite?

Earthing Excess Energy
- Why do you think that raising energy and working with magick could have a disorienting effect on people?
- Why is getting rid of excess energy important?
- When you need to chill out quickly, what sort of things do you do?

Use and Misuse of Magick
- Name three valid uses of magick and three inappropriate uses. Justify each one.

Lesson 29: Recommended Reading
- *The Witch of the Forest's Guide to Natural Magick: Discover Your Magick. Connect with Your Inner & Outer World* by Lindsay Squire
- *Transformative Witchcraft: The Greater Mysteries* by Jason Mankey

Ritual Procedure: Closing the Ritual

Up to this point in the ritual series of lessons, we've watched as the members of Green Dragon Coven prepared the ritual space and performed various magickal workings. Now, in part four of the ritual series, we'll join them as they prepare to close the ritual and open the circle.

Before Saying Goodbye

Before taking down the temple, everyone participates in *hieros gamos* and cakes and ale. The coven members return to where they were when the temple was erected. Wyvern asks Brianna to hand him the tray of corn muffins and bottle of mead. Using his athame, Wyvern cuts a window in the circle, similar to the portal cut during his challenge, to accept them. He sets the tray on the altar and pours some mead into the altar chalice.

Laughing Tree and Lady Morgaine take their place at the altar. He picks up the chalice, and she picks up the athame.

Using both hands, she reverently dips the athame into the chalice, saying, "As the athame is to the Lord."

Tree responds with, "So the chalice is to the Lady."

Morgaine says, "Together they are the hieros gamos."

And Tree adds, "The sacred marriage, the union of opposites."

Morgaine and Tree kiss and lay down the chalice and the athame. This is a modern interpretation of the sacred marriage of the Lord and Lady, which some traditions observe with the Great Rite. The Great Rite can be interpreted as anything from a quick kiss between the Priest and Priestess to intercourse between lovers.

Note the role reversal in the act. The High Priest held the chalice, and High Priestess held the athame. This is symbolic of the balance between the Lord and Lady. Neither is complete without the other; indeed, each is part of the other. Their love is a circle, balanced and eternal.

Many covens use the same chalice for the heiros gamos and for cakes and ale; they feel that the ale has thus been consecrated. Others prefer to use a different one for sharing ale, saying that the one used for heiros gamos belongs only to the gods. Either way, the chalice(s) should already be on the altar.

The ceremony of cakes and ale gets its name from—drum roll, please—cakes and ale. Originally a Lammas rite, it was part of the harvest celebration. It's been adapted by many covens as a celebration of the bounty of the gods and is valid at any time of the year. It serves another purpose, as well: After raising energy and working with magick and grounding again, a little solid food in one's belly helps to refocus the body. It's another way of grounding.

Modern covens don't always specifically use cakes or ale, but the "cake" is always something baked, and the "ale" is usually a mild alcoholic beverage—assuming that everyone involved is of legal drinking age. Some covens serve pound cake, muffins, crumb cake, or even soft pretzels, and the ale can be anything from water to mead to whiskey. Some covens even serve chocolate chip cookies and milk.

Wyvern offers the tray of corn muffins to Morgaine with the words, "May you never hunger."

Morgaine accepts the tray, saying, "Thou art god."

After taking a muffin, Morgaine offers the tray to Tree, saying, "May you never hunger."

He takes the tray and responds with, "Thou art goddess."

While the tray of muffins is going around, Wyvern offers the mead to Morgaine, saying, "May you never thirst."

She responds with, "Thou art god."

Morgaine takes a sip of the mead, then passes the chalice to Tree.

The mead follows the muffins, going from person to person. The food, whatever it is, is offered by saying, "May you never hunger," and it is accepted with, "Thou art god" (or goddess, depending upon the provider). The drink follows the same pattern with the offering of, "May you never thirst."

Some covens stop after one revolution, while others let it keep going until there's nothing left. It's generally accepted, however, that the offering and acceptance lines are only used on the first pass. The summoner is often the one to start the process, and he offers it first to the High Priestess. This is symbolic of the young Lord providing for the Lady. It goes around the circle from person to person, so the summoner, of course, is the last to receive cakes and ale.

This coven has combined the hieros gamos and the celebration of cakes and ale into a single event, not unlike the blessing and passing of the communion wafer. Some covens perform them separately or use one but not the other. Note that the ale was passed around in the chalice from the altar, not just any old cup. Likewise, if the cake is to be cut, it is usually cut using the ritual athame. This way the Lord and Lady have an active role in providing for the Witches. If a Witch prefers to use their own chalice, that is acceptable; the provider can pour the ale into it from the bottle.

By offering food or drink, you are providing for the health and vitality of the recipient, and by accepting with the "Thou art god (goddess)" line, you are recognizing the divine spirit within the provider. The word god (or goddess) can be adjusted, depending upon the will and gender identity of the provider.

While the rite of cakes and ale is centuries old, the addition of "May you never thirst/hunger" and "Thou art god/goddess" was first introduced in the 1960s by the Church of All Worlds, a Pagan church that is recognized as a tradition all its own.

At this point, Medusa, one of Morgaine's cats, darts into the circle, almost knocking the south elemental altar over. Jaguar scoops her up, and Jason observes that there was never a portal cut to let her in. Technically this would be a breach in the circle, but Morgaine feels that when it comes to animals and small children, the circle wall is fluid. Many children and animals are drawn to the magickal vibrations, almost like moths to a flame. Can you honestly control how many ants walk across the circle in an outdoor ritual?

Finally, the coven is ready to close the ritual.

Divine Farewells

Morgaine assumes the goddess position again, as she did at the invocation of Artemis. This time she says, "Blessed Artemis, daughter of the silver moon, we thank you for your attendance at this ritual. Your compassion and your wisdom will be cherished always as your shining face ever guides us through our lives. Go if you must, stay if you will. Hail, and farewell!"

She snuffs out the goddess candle with her fingers as the coven responds with, "Hail, and farewell!"

With these words, Morgaine bids farewell to Artemis. Notice that she was thanked, and the line "Go if you must, stay if you will" allows the deity the option of staying without making any demands. Morgaine snuffed the candle out with her fingers rather than blowing it out. Some feel that blowing a candle out to extinguish it is disrespectful to the element of air.

Tree then assumes the god position and says, "Great Cernunnos, Forest Lord! We thank you for your presence at our esbat and your wisdom and your laughter and wish you well in your journeys. Great horned one, go if you must, stay if you will. Hail, and farewell!"

Tree snuffs out the god candle as the coven again responds with, "Hail, and farewell!" His release was very similar to Artemis's. Just as the goddess was invoked before the god, they are released in the same order.

Dismissing the Quarters

With everyone in the same place they were in at the circle's creation, Morgaine nods to Cassandra.

Cassandra raises her arms and says, "Hail, guardians of the watchtowers of the east! We thank you and honour you for your presence at our esbat. Go if you must, stay if you will. Hail, and farewell!"

Cassandra would snuff out the elemental candle, but since it went out during Wyvern's entrance, she doesn't have to. She holds it up, as a salute, as everyone repeats, "Hail, and farewell!"

While the invocations of the elements and the gods had different finishing lines, the line for dismissal is the same. There is no less respect when bidding farewell to close friends. Cassandra mentioned the watchtowers at both the invocation and the dismissal. A well-organized Witch, she likes to keep things consistent. The candle is usually left burning until the very end of the dismissal.

Now Crystal dismisses the element of fire.

She raises her athame and says, "Spirits of the south, thank you for your presence at our rite! Return ye now to your sacred places. Go if you must, stay if you will. Hail, and farewell!"

She again draws a pentagram in the air, then snuffs out the elemental candle as everyone repeats, "Hail, and farewell!"

Again, Crystal spoke loudly, almost shouting her dismissal, but did not use any funny references this time. She could have but merely chose not to.

Jason then turns to dismiss the element of water. Jaguar has a script ready for him, but he chooses to simply wing it, saying, "Hail, spirits of the water! Great whales, rivers, tears of the goddess. Thank you for being part of our esbat, for your time and compassion. Go if you must, stay if you will. Hail, and welcome—er, farewell."

Jason blushes as he snuffs out the candle. He's embarrassed but pleased to have said it on his own. Wyvern smiles and gives him a thumbs-up as everyone repeats, "Hail, and farewell!"

He goofed. But the spirits are forgiving; they know what he meant.

Now it's RedWolf's turn.

He draws his shortsword and holds it high, saying, "Spirits of the north! Great Woden, bright Freyja! We honour you as you depart for your snow-clad realm. Go if you must, stay if you will. Hail, and farewell!"

While the coven echoes his closing line, RedWolf draws the runes for opening and journey in the air before laying his sword's blade across the candle flame to snuff it out.

Again, RedWolf mentioned the Norse gods. While they were not specifically called to the esbat, their presence was felt. At least, as far as he's concerned they were.

Using a sword or athame to extinguish the candle is rare. Most Witches would not want to harm their blades that way, but RedWolf sees it as a salute to the heroes of Valhalla as well as a dismissal of the element.

Some covens dismiss deosil, going clockwise from east to north, and some dismiss going widdershins, or counterclockwise, starting at north and ending at east. Either way is acceptable; unlike a banishing, the widdershins dismissal is merely a symbolic closing of the door that was opened at the ritual's start.

There are also some that use cross-quarter callings for both invocation and dismissal. In the standard format, the quarter-caller, let's say east, stands at east and calls to the east, while everyone is behind them. In a cross-quarter calling, the western caller would call east, the southern caller would call north, and so on. This way, everyone else in the circle is an active part of the invocation. It's like the caller is saying, "I—and everyone else here—we all welcome you!"

Notice that of the five elements, only four were dismissed. The fifth, spirit, is always with us.

Opening the Circle

The gods were bid farewell, and the quarters were dismissed. All that remains is to open the circle. Tree again takes up the sword and walks deosil around the circle, saying, "Mighty Lord, gracious Lady! The ritual is done, the magick is away. The great powers are released. So mote it be!"

He returns to the altar and places the sword under it as everyone repeats, "So mote it be!"

Tree walked the circle deosil, unmaking the circle by following the path of the dismissal of the elements. If they had been dismissed widdershins, he would have walked that way. You shouldn't "cross the paths." It's not good to tangle one's closing.

Morgaine spreads her arms and says, "The rite is done, but the magick just begun! The circle is open but never broken. Merry meet, and merry part, and merry meet again!"

She snuffs out the spirit candle, officially ending the ritual, as the last three words—*merry meet again*—are joyously exclaimed by everyone all at the same time. Exuberant hugs follow, and Brianna and Ethan are invited to join in the celebration.

The ritual is over.

Acting in Accord

The rite is done, but the magick just begun. With these words, Morgaine reminds the coven that there is more to magick than just showing up for ritual. Witchcraft is not just something you "do" once a month when it's convenient. It is a philosophy, a lifestyle, and a commitment to the gods and the divinity within. Consider the rede and the Fourteen Principles of Wiccan Belief. Are those meant to be implemented only when it's convenient? Likewise, the magick and meaning of ritual should not be confined to the ritual itself.

Think of Crystal's carpal tunnel syndrome. The coven performed a magickal healing for her, the effects of which should stay with her long after the other Witches have gone home. Suppose that during ritual, the High Priest asks everyone to spend an hour that week picking up trash along the road; the Witches would be remiss if they did not comply. These are simple examples, but the importance of acting in accordance with the magick of ritual extends far beyond the material. Any Witch who participates in a ritual assumes the responsibility of following through on whatever rites were performed within circle, whether magickal or mundane.

The day after participating in a magickal ritual, write down your feelings about it, what happened, what it meant to you, and how you felt about it after a period of reflection. Your Book of Shadows is a good place for this. It may surprise you what has stayed with you!

Whatever the message of the ritual was, always keep it with you. Remember what you felt in circle and what was said. More than just the thought or the meaning—let the energy of the ritual become a part of you.

Lesson 30: Study Prompts and Questions

Before Saying Goodbye
- In your own words, explain the significance of the hieros gamos.
- What is the significance of the ceremony of cakes and ale?
- What do you think the lines "May you never hunger/thirst" and "Thou art god/goddess" mean?
- Do you agree that small children and animals do not need to observe portals in circle? Explain and justify.

Divine Farewells
- Why dismiss the gods if they are immanent deities? Do they have to go somewhere else?

Dismissing the Quarters
- Explain the purpose of dismissing the quarters.
- Would you go deosil or widdershins as you close the circle? Explain and justify.

Opening the Circle
- Should the path of the sword mirror the path of the elements? Justify your answer.
- What does the line "Merry meet, and merry part, and merry meet again" signify?

Acting in Accord
- In your own words, explain the importance of keeping the spirit of the ritual with you.

Lesson 30: Recommended Reading

- *Ancient Ways: Reclaiming the Pagan Tradition* by Pauline Campanelli
- *Eight Sabbats for Witches* by Janet and Stewart Farrar

LESSON 31
Rituals for the Solitary Witch

We spent the last few lessons watching as members of Green Dragon Coven performed an esbat ritual. That's great when you have plenty of people to fill the roles of Priest, Priestess, quarter-callers, and so on. But what if you don't have a coven to work with? What if you're a Solitary Witch or a Wiccan working alone? Do you have to do everything yourself? Well, naturally, yes. Let's see what's involved.

You Are Your Own Priest or Priestess

There are a lot of advantages to practicing as a solitaire. You can work your magick whenever you want; you don't have to coordinate your schedule with everyone else. You wake up at three in the morning, and you want to cast a circle? Go for it! You are your own boss.

As a Solitary Witch or Wiccan, you are responsible for your own behavior, the magick you raise, the spells you cast, and your relationship with the Divine. You are your own Priest or Priestess. You call the shots; you decide the nature of your worship and who you invoke during ritual. You work magick according to your own rules.

To some, this can build up such a barrier of apprehension that they resist the desire to move forward for fear of getting it wrong or offending the gods. Luckily there is a host of books, websites, social media communities, and other resources at your disposal. You may be solitary, but you don't have to live in a vacuum. My advice here is this: If you have a decision about what to say in a spell or how to invoke a deity, do a little research, and sit on it for a couple of days. Let the question settle in the back of your mind. The next time you think about it, your subconscious will have pushed the best answer to the surface. Go with that one.

Self-Initiation

Many covens have initiation rites, and as a solitary you can—if you want to—perform a ritual of self-initiation. It's not essential, but many feel that having done so gives them a stronger sense of awareness and self-worth.

A self-initiation ritual might go something like this:

- Prepare yourself mentally and physically. Clear your mind, relax, and take a shower or bath. This not only cleans you, it also refreshes and renews you.
- Using the process below, create sacred space. Yeah, we're jumping around a little bit. It's okay. You don't have to be initiated into the Craft to create your own Wiccan temple. Everyone's got to start somewhere.
  - Say something like, "I stand (or sit or kneel) before the gods and the spirits to dedicate and initiate myself as a Witch. What was is no more. What was is past. As a phoenix rises from its own ashes, I am born anew."
  - Blindfold yourself. You can just close your eyes for this part, but it's more significant if you have a physical item to remove from yourself.
  - Say something like, "I am reborn. I am awakened. I am one with the gods and the magick."
  - Remove the blindfold.
  - Say, "I am (your magickal name, if you have one, or your regular name), and I am part of the Craft of the Wise! So mote it be."

In lesson 11, Principles of Wiccan Belief, I wrote that calling oneself a Witch does not make a Witch, but neither does heredity itself or the collecting of titles, degrees, and initiations. Witches seek to control the forces within themselves that make life possible in order to live wisely and well, without harm to others, and in harmony with nature.

It's all well and good to call yourself a Witch, but you still have to mean it. I could say I'm a half-dragon, half-unicorn demigod from the planet Xerxes, but that doesn't mean I am one.

Once you've self-initiated, you still have to prove yourself as a child of the goddess.

Creating Your Own Sacred Space

You'll want your own sacred space, ritual area, or temple. Whatever you call it, it should be a place where you can be alone for a while. Many people set up an altar on top of the dresser in their bedroom. Some keep all their tools and such locked away in a safe place, and whenever they need them, they dig the box out and set everything up in front of them on the bed or on the floor. What's important is that it's yours, and everything has a special significance for you.

As a rule, you should have the following items available:

- Altar cloth or mat
- Goddess and/or god image or icon, such as statues or pictures
- Athame and/or wand
- Chalice
- Candle(s)
- Book of Shadows or a journal of some kind

It's also nice to have:

- Something representing the elemental symbols or colours
- Some crystals that resonate with you personally
- Other decorations that deepen your connection with spirit

Ritual Time

Whenever you want to use your sacred space—whether it's at an established altar or one you create as you need it—you should be able to give yourself some uninterrupted time alone, maybe half an hour to an hour. Close the door, settle your mind, and relax. Light some incense if you like. I find that it's best if you speak aloud what you are doing, even if you're alone. It makes the intention more valid, as opposed to just one thought in the flow of thoughts running through your mind. It's time to erect your temple. Put some soft music on if that helps.

- Say something like, "I connect with the spirits and the gods to work my will."
- Light a candle, which represents the living heart of your sacred space. (Okay, yes, *you* are the living heart of your sacred space, but this is a representation you can see and work with.)

- Imagine a circle manifesting around you. You can use your wand or athame to trace it out around you as you sit, you can stand and walk the circle, or you can just visually project it.
- Say, "I create this circle as a sanctuary between the worlds. Here I am one with the magick."
- Recognize the four elements, starting at east and going clockwise. You can verbally invoke each one, using lines similar to what Green Dragon used, or just mentally recognize their presence.
- Now invoke your deity or deities. If you use both a goddess and a god, it doesn't really matter who goes first as long as they're both recognized and welcomed into your circle.
- Say something like, "Beautiful Isis, goddess of life, I welcome you into my sacred space. Hail, and welcome." You can be as elaborate as you like. Do the same for both deities, using the appropriate name and appellations. Some people like to touch the icon, pick it up and kiss it, or just mentally recognize their presence when they do.
- With the elementals summoned and the gods invoked, say, "I create my world, my connection, my reality. I am in sacred space."

Unless it's just to create a sacred space for meditation, which is fine, many Solitary Witches and Wiccans use their temple as a place to work magick, whether consecrating items, casting spells, writing in their Book of Shadows or journal, or whatever. It's also a good place to practice a musical instrument, study, or just read.

Closing the Circle

Whether you used your sacred space for a rite of initiation, to meditate, or to work magick, you can't just open the door and leave the room. As we saw in lesson 25, if you leave the area "active," the magick can "sour," and when you reenter that area, it might make you feel disoriented or nauseous unless you've properly tidied up. You created the space by casting a circle, welcoming the elements, and invoking the deities, and you close the circle by unmaking it. When you've finished the work you were doing, go through the following process:

- Honour the deities you invoked, and thank them before releasing them. Say something like, "Blessed Isis, goddess of life and healing. Thank you for being part of my rite. Go if you must, stay if you will. Hail, and farewell." If you had lit a candle in her honour, extinguish it.

- Dismiss the elements. You can do this in the same order you summoned them (east, south, west, north) or in reverse order (north, west, south, east), thus unmaking the elemental pillars. Always be respectful; thank them for their presence.
- Now drop the circle. I usually envision it as a shimmering curtain of light around me that I see falling through the floor and vanishing. If you had lit a candle to start the rite, now is the time to safely extinguish it.
- Then say something like, "My rite is done, but the magick just begun. So mote it be."

Now you can open the door and leave your ritual area.

Working with Other Solitaries

If you work alone or with a group, you can still think of yourself as a Solitary Witch. You might be part of a grove, or you might belong to an online Wiccan group. Practicing as a Solitary Witch doesn't mean that you have to be alone *all* the time. You can meet others, cast a collective circle, and work magick together, or you can simply be part of a study group, sharing your knowledge and experience.

If you want to cast a circle and work magick together, is it necessary to elect a "designated High Priestess or Priest" from the group of Solitaries? You can, or you can work as a collective congregation. You could share copies of a prewritten rite in which everyone collectively summons the elements, invokes the goddess and the god, and closes the circle, as just described, when you're finished.

You could also lead a teaching circle, either online or in person, to help others develop a deeper understanding of Wicca and its myriad facets, or you could host an open circle for a sabbat or esbat rite. The possibilities are endless!

Lesson 31: Study Prompts and Questions

You Are Your Own Priest or Priestess
- What advantages are there to practicing as a Solitary Witch?
- What would some disadvantages be?
- Would you feel comfortable performing a self-initiation rite as presented?
- Read over the passage about calling oneself a Witch from the Principles of Wiccan Belief. Does that negate the legitimacy of self-initiating?

Creating Your Own Sacred Space
- Where would you feel comfortable setting up your temple or sanctuary?
- Do you think that Witches need to have expensive or flashy tools, or is anything all right?
- Using the described rite as a guide, write a circle-casting ritual of your own, using specific names and descriptions. (I used Isis as an example. Yours should include whomever you choose.)

Closing the Circle
- Why is it important to "take down" a circle?
- Would you perform the elemental dismissal in the order cast or reversed? Why?

Working with Other Solitaires
- Can Solitary Witches work together and still be considered solitary?
- What sort of exercises do you feel would be appropriate for a group of solitaires working together?

Lesson 31: Recommended Reading

- *Living Wicca: A Further Guide for the Solitary Practitioner* by Scott Cunningham
- *Solitary Witch: The Ultimate Book of Shadows for the New Generation* by Silver RavenWolf

LESSON 32
Working with Colours, Auras, and Chakras

We've studied the fundamentals of magickal theory, watched as a coven performed a basic esbat ritual, and discussed the ways a Solitary Witch might practice Witchcraft. Now, over the next few lessons, we'll dive deeper into the study of magick and spellcrafting and look at everything from colours and auras to stones and oils to the fine art of writing and casting a spell.

Colours have come up now and then—they were mentioned in lesson 19, Elements and Correspondences—and candles of specific colours were used on the altars during the Green Dragon Coven esbat. What do different colours signify? How are they used? Let's find out. We'll also have a look at auras and chakras.

Colours

Everyone has heard phrases like "green with envy" or "yellow-bellied coward." Why do we associate colours with emotions? Why do different colours have different magickal associations?

As we learned in lesson 22, thought and energy are just different mental or psychic energy wavelengths. Energy vibrates at different frequencies, and these frequencies evoke various results. Colours are our physical perception of light-energy vibrations. That's why different colour vibrations can produce different responses, which can sometimes manifest as emotions. For example, dark yellow is seen as a depressing colour, and dark blue implies authority. Both green and gold are seen as colours of wealth. Green implies growth and prosperity, which is why paper money is green in the United States, and gold, a variation of yellow, inspires imagination, wealth, and drive.

In magick, different colours are often used in spellcrafting to influence different results. Here's a list of the major colours and their magickal associations according to Western tradition.

Black

Black is the presence of the full spectrum of colour pigment. That's right—the presence of *all* colours. If you turn the lights off, the room is black. That's not the absence of colour but the absence of light waves. If you melt all your crayons together, you get black—and a big mess.

To some, its multihued quality makes black perfect for protective magick. To others, it represents the mysteries, the point from which all things are possible. Black can also represent the absorbing of energy, acceptance, anger, banishing, binding, challenges, determination, death and the afterlife, endings, justice, loss, release, breaking hexes, security, grief, negativity, magick, patience, persistence, rebirth, karma, secrets, spirituality, strength, and self-control. The element associated with the colour black is earth, and its planet is Pluto.

The term *black magick* is a misnomer. Magick, as we learned way back in the very first lesson, is a neutral force with no associated colour.

White

White is the absence of all colour and the universal symbol of peace and surrender. As the symbol of purity, it is used in healings and restorative magick. White also represents cleansing, protection, balance, clarity, divination, grounding and centering, guidance, knowing one's higher self, hope, innocence, optimism, spirituality, truth, and will power. The element associated with white is air, and its planet is the moon.

White magick? See the previous section.

Red

Often associated with blood or anger, red is the colour of life, passion, danger, and vitality. In magick, red is attributed to courage, cleansing, vitality, and invigoration. It also represents drastic change and the ability to "ride the storm out." Red can be used to promote courage, assertiveness, business ventures, creativity, energy, desire, love and romance, loyalty, motivation, passion, strength, power, survival, change, and overcoming obstacles. In China red is a colour of celebration and joy. Red, naturally, is associated with the element of fire, and its planet is Mars.

Pink

Pink takes all the passion and energy of red and tempers it with the purity of white, resulting in the colour of tenderness and affection. As a lighter shade of red, it also represents acceptance, affection, beauty, compassion, reconciliation, children, finding healing from abuse, fidelity, family, friendship, kindness, love, marriage, nurturing, passion, sensuality, and love. Pink can be associated with either fire or air, and its planet is Venus.

Orange

Orange is a warming, resuscitating colour. It is used in magick for spells of friendship and business partnerships. Orange is often seen as one of the colours of autumn and is used for digestive or stomach-related healings. It can be used to promote abundance, adaptability, ambition, celebration, confidence, creativity, courage, discipline, vital energy, independence, freedom, attaining one's goals, justice, money, positivity, pleasure, reconciliation, mental stimulation, strength, and travel. The element associated with orange is fire, and its planet is Jupiter.

Yellow

The colour of charm, exhilaration, and prosperity, yellow is associated with the seasons of spring and summer. It can also be used to stimulate a peaceful sleep. Magickally it is often used to charge or empower talismans and other magickal spell components. The colour yellow can be used for communication, friendships, learning new skills, happiness, intellect, inspiration, intuition, knowledge, wisdom, pleasure, stimulation, and travel. Conversely, yellow sometimes represents sickness, jealousy, or cowardice. Yellow is another air elemental colour, and its planet isn't a planet at all—it's the sun.

Green

Green is an earth colour and often associated with growth, prosperity, inherent strength, and perseverance. It's also a very soothing colour, relaxing without being tiring. Green can be used to represent abundance, acceptance, action, agriculture and farming, beauty, change, creativity, family, fertility, harmony, health and longevity, luck, the environment, nurturing, partnerships, peace, and prosperity. Green's association with envy is due to its growth aspect, which inspires awe and desire in others. Its elemental association and its planet are both the same thing—can you guess?

Blue

Blue can be a lazy, peaceful colour and a good shade for meditation. It's also used for healing and recuperation. Light blue is the colour of water and youth; dark blue represents wisdom and authority. The colour blue can also be used to promote honesty, trust, communication, dreamwork, sleep, tackling mental obstacles, wisdom, pregnancy, leadership, justice, advancing one's career, marriage and fidelity, interviews, and study. Some folklore accounts say that the colour blue is used to keep ghosts or malevolent spirits away. Blue is associated with the element of water, and its planet is Uranus.

Purple

The colour of psychic awareness, purple is an energy-raising and empowering colour. Magickally it is used in conjunction with invocations and meditations. It's somewhere between the creativity of red and the calming presence of blue, inspiring introspection. In magickal applications, purple can be used to represent astrology, authority, enlightenment, spiritual development, psychic awareness and protection, imagination, influence, independence, power, truth, wisdom, writing, overcoming one's fears or addictions, and managing one's emotions. Purple is also associated with mental awareness and teaching, which explains its use by many children's television characters. Its elemental correspondence is water, and its planet is Neptune.

Brown

Brown is the ultimate earth colour. It's soothing, deep-rooted, and reliable. Magickally brown represents material matters or concerns, endurance, hard work, animals, balance and harmony, courage, earthing or grounding, finding lost objects, stability, and material protection. Brown can, to some, represent sluggishness or immobility. Its element is earth, and its planet is also Earth.

Silver

The shining colour silver has long represented purity and reflection. It can also be used in spells for awareness, healing, intuition, divination, money and finance, psychic powers, discovering your hidden potential, fertility, feminine energy, stability, success, and the sea. Its element is water, and its planet is the moon.

Gold

Gold has a long history of representing wealth and prosperity. It can also represent abundance, fame and fortune, ambitions, money, positivity and positive growth, happiness, creativity, divination, power, influence, luxury, and masculine energy. Its element is earth, and its planet is the sun.

Gray

Gray, neither white nor black, is the essence of total neutrality and all things in balance. It can represent either harmony or stagnation. The element associated with gray is earth, and its planet is Saturn.

Blending Colours

Colours can be combined, of course, which blends the magickal correspondences. Pink, for example, could represent purity and strength, and aqua is growth through peace. Experiment with different colour combinations, and see if you can determine what the magickal correspondences would be.

Auras

Auras are energy waves vibrating from the body. Just as heat is a by-product of fire, aura emanations are a by-product of life energy. In the same way that body heat can be seen under ultraviolet light, auras can be seen as visible emanations of light and colour under certain conditions. The more activity going on or the more intense the emotion, the brighter the aura. For some, it is a low "hum," barely inches from the body. Others have a bright, active aura that's like a spinning wheel of colour. When fear or anger has a person in a negative frame of mind, the aura will be a dark colour and shrunken inward. If they are happy or energized, it will appear much brighter and radiating outwards.

Why can some people see auras and others cannot? Everyone has basic psychic ability. If you have any brain wave activity at all—if you can think and function—that's a psychic ability. Some people have odd abilities, such as being able to roll one's tongue or put both legs behind one's head. These are examples of unusual muscular flexibility. Enhanced psychic awareness is just another kind of flexibility. It's a limber "mental muscle," if you like. Enhanced psychic awareness is the ability to perceive bioelectric emanations. While the five senses are the normal ways of perceiving the outside world, some people have a "sixth sense," or an awareness beyond the physical senses. Perception of other people's psychic frequencies, the ability to see auras, or the ability to perceive mental activity as colour or even smell is a rare trait that some people do possess. For them, it's as normal as breathing. Some people can see vibrations without detecting specific colours, while others can feel the vibrations as a tingly or prickly sensation on the skin.

Aura Colour Associations

Here's a short list of what the aura colours mean.

White

White is the colour of the "perfect" aura, showing that you are balanced in mind, body, and spirit. This is, alas, rather hard to attain.

Red

Red stands for force, vigor, and energy. A dark red indicates a high temper. Red will also appear when the person is in an energetic, driven mood.

Orange

Orange shows thoughtfulness and consideration, but if it's tainted with brown, it indicates laziness.

Yellow

Yellow shows that a person is in good health and friendly. If the yellow is tinged with red or orange highlights, it indicates shyness.

Green

Green is a healing and relaxing colour and reveals that a person is being healed or is a healer. If the green is tinged with yellow, it indicates treachery and deceit.

Blue

Blue shows that a person is spirited, artistic, and selfless. A person with a lot of blue in their aura is usually dedicated to their work.

Indigo

Indigo is very prominent in spiritual people or those who are seeking answers.

Violet

Violet, like indigo, indicates spirituality or magickal awareness. If it is tainted with green, an unacknowledged personality conflict exists.

Seeing the Aura

Here's a fun way to see a person's aura. Have them stand in front of a white sheet or wall under a bright light. From about eight feet away, focus on a point on the wall about a foot above the person's head for approximately a minute. Then have the person move away from the wall, and look at where they were standing. You should see an outline where they stood in bright, varying colours. It's technically not an aura but a retinal "afterimage," but many people see different colours there.

While colours are the easiest way to perceive auras, they can manifest in many ways. Some people are said to have a negative aura, or "bad vibes," which can make them difficult to be around. Emotions, colours, and even sound and shadow are all ways one might perceive auras.

Chakras

Dating back more than three thousand years, the practice of working with the chakras started in early Hindu traditions. The word *chakra* translates to *wheel*, and the belief is that the body exists in two dimensions simultaneously, the physical body and the "subtle" or energy body. Healthy or open chakras spin with body energy, but they can become blocked. Chakra healing is a way of unblocking these vital energy centers within the body.

Study of the chakras dates back millennia, but Charles Leadbeater introduced a Western perspective of chakra work in the 1920s and added the colour spectrum to the practice.[109]

There are seven major, or vital, chakras and three minor. Located at integral points within the head, torso, spine, and limbs, the chakras correspond to focal points within both a person's physical self and energy self, or "etheric double."

What's an etheric double? Think of it this way: If you amplified the bioelectric energy of a living person to the physical range and separated it from the physical body, it would look like a nervous system "road map" of light and colour spanning the entire body with anchors at the ten chakra points. The etheric double, or energy self, is the "power grid" for the physical body.

The chakras, then, are the power plants of the body, and the body requires these bio-electric generators to function. They are the points at which energy can enter the body. To those who can read them, a chakra's colour or radiance defines both its clarity and the person's physical health, stamina, and well-being. The chakras can be perceived as proof positive of the link between body and spirit. If one's spirit is diminished, perhaps

---

109. Lochtefeld, *The Illustrated History of Hinduism*, 137.

by illness or depression, the effect is visible in the chakras and the etheric double, and the areas of the body governed by the chakras are indeed affected.

Working with the chakras requires the ability to focus on these energy points to cleanse, realign, or fine-tune them. If a person has a hard time communicating, for example, it is said their throat chakra is out of alignment, and a person who attracts negative energy has a blocked splenic chakra. Work on one's chakra involves meditating on that part of the body to become more in tune with it, washing out blocks, and realigning energy flows. It's kind of like being a chakra plumber.

The Chakras

The following lists of major and minor chakras define the location and area of effect for each of the chakras using these categories:

- *Chakra name:* Each chakra has a name related to its position. The numbering system goes from the ground up, but they are listed from the top down.
- *Body part:* This is the area of the body governed or managed by the chakra.
- *Location:* This is where the chakra is located within the body.
- *Focus:* This is the aspect of one's personality or spirit governed or managed by the chakra.
- *Colour:* This is the colour a healthy, balanced chakra is supposed to radiate to those trained in chakra therapy.
- *Balanced:* These are the benefits of a healthy, balanced chakra. If it is unbalanced, of course, the effect is diminished or opposite the balanced result.

The Major Chakras

There are seven major chakras. They are as follows:

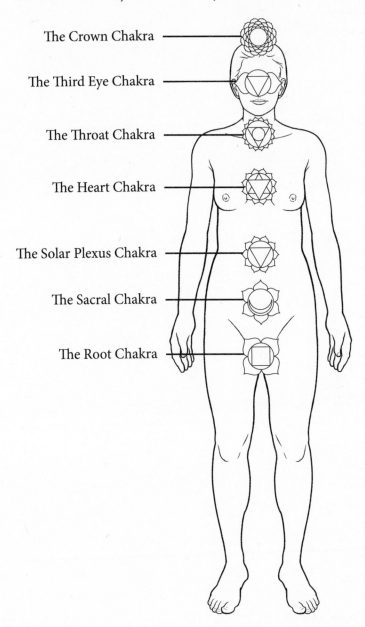

The Crown Chakra

The Third Eye Chakra

The Throat Chakra

The Heart Chakra

The Solar Plexus Chakra

The Sacral Chakra

The Root Chakra

Chakra Map

Seventh chakra: Crown
Name: Sahasrara
Body parts: Skull and brain
Location: Top of head
Focus: Spirituality
Colour: Violet
Balanced: Achieves goals

Sixth chakra: Third eye/forehead
Name: Ajna
Body part: Eyes
Location: Center of forehead
Focus: Intuition and wisdom
Colour: Indigo
Balanced: Charisma and psychic perception

Fifth chakra: Throat
Name: Vishuddha
Body parts: Mouth and throat
Location: Front of neck
Focus: Communication
Colour: Blue
Balanced: Good verbal skills

Fourth chakra: Heart
Name: Anahata
Body parts: Heart and lungs
Location: Center of chest
Focus: Love and relationships
Colour: Green
Balanced: Ability to love

Third chakra: Solar plexus
Name: Manipura
Body parts: Muscles and digestive system
Location: Upper abdomen

Focus: Willpower
Colour: Yellow
Balanced: Respect for self and others

Second chakra: Sacral or sexual
Name: Svadhishthana
Body parts: Womb and sex organs
Location: Lower abdomen
Focus: Emotions and sexuality
Colour: Orange
Balanced: Trust and creativity

First chakra: Root
Name: Muladhara
Body parts: Bones and joints
Location: Base of spine
Focus: Physical needs
Colour: Red
Balanced: Physical stamina

The Minor Chakras

There are three minor chakras. They are:

"A" chakra: Splenic
Body part: Waste matter
Location: Spleen
Focus: Purging negativity
Colour: Tan
Balanced: Internal vitality

"B" chakra: Hand
Body parts: Hands
Location: Hands
Focus: Touch and creativity
Colour: Aqua
Balanced: Artistic ability

"C" chakra: Foot
Body parts: Feet
Location: Feet
Focus: Grounding
Colour: Brown
Balanced: Balanced energy flow

Other Attributes

The chakras have other attributes as well, such as corresponding elements, zodiac signs, and Sanskrit names. Until recently, many people denied the effectiveness of holistic or homeopathic remedies such as acupuncture and herbal remedies, but the understanding of their effect is gaining ground in Western medicine, and an awareness of the chakras and chakra balancing is quickly gaining that same level of acceptance.

Specialists who are adept in chakra therapy can detect physical or emotional states of distress by analyzing the chakras and can offer remedies for those ailments. Chakra therapy often includes "rebalancing" a chakra, which often involves physical therapy, homeopathic remedies, and counselling.

Lesson 32: Study Prompts and Questions

Colours

- List some of the qualities attributed to each colour: black, white, red, pink, orange, yellow, green, purple, brown, gold, silver, and gray.

Auras

- Explain what auras are and what they mean.
- Define some of the qualities of the auras depending upon colour: red, orange, yellow, green, blue, indigo, and violet.

Chakras

- Explain what the chakras are, how they work, and how they can be used.
- Try to visualize the chakras as visible energy centers. Write down your results.
- Identify the ten chakras, and list some of their attributes.

Lesson 32: Recommended Reading

- *Chakra Healing: A Beginner's Guide to Self-Healing Techniques that Balance the Chakras* by Margarita Alcantara
- *Practical Color Magick* by Raymond Buckland

LESSON 33
Working with Stones and Crystals

Rocks! Everyone loves rocks. Many Witches have an assortment of stones on their altars, such as tiger's eye, amethyst, and rose quartz. Some carry a stone or two on them at all times, and they are very popular in jewelry. But the role that stones and crystals play in magick is one of the most widely known—and misunderstood—aspects of spellcrafting.

What are gemstones? How do they work? What do Witches do with them? Let's find out!

The Secrets of Stones

Stones come in three forms: sedimentary, igneous, and metamorphic. Sedimentary is particulates pressed together over millennia, igneous is cooled magma or lava, and metamorphic is the process by which thermal heat and pressure changes a stone's structure. All stones fall into one of these three categories. They undergo centuries of pressure, heating, and cooling and gradually form into mineral constructs of different shapes, colours, and densities. Salt crystals, for example, are always cubic. Trigonal quartz crystals appear six-sided, or hexagonal, like 3D snowflakes.

Are stones "alive"? They grow, they reproduce, they age, and they die, crumbling into dust. They do, indeed, feel and respond to emotion, though not always in the human spectrum. Stones, like all living things, pulse and vibrate at different frequencies. They give off emanations that all people, psychically adept or not, can tap into. (Have you ever held a magnet? That's a very *loud* stone.) If you hold a crystal in the palm of your receptive hand, you may feel it pulse or buzz like a fly held in your cupped palm. It may not be as obvious at first, but with time, practice, and exercise, you'll be able to feel it. Those vibrations trigger responses deep within the mind, which manifest in the desired results. That's why rose quartz triggers the emotion of love, and hematite is used in grounding and centering.

Some stones may be more subtle than others, but they all have something to say.

Rocks and Roles

For millennia, Witches, Druids, and other magickal healers and clairvoyants have used stones in their working and spellcrafting. Whether worked into jewelry, carried in pouches, or used in oracles and scrying tools, stones have long held an important role in the magickal "toolbox." But what stone does what? How do you know which one to use? Do different spells require different stones? Here's a (very small) chart of well-known gems, stones, and crystals and the traits attributed to them in magick.

Crystal/Stone	Magickal Traits
Agate	Health, love, and protection
Amber	Beauty, health, love, luck, and protection
Amethyst	Courage, health, and love
Aquamarine	Peace, psychic awareness, and purity
Aventurine	Enhanced psychic awareness
Azurite	Dreams, health, and psychic ability
Bloodstone	Health, prosperity, stamina, and success
Carnelian	Courage, peace, and sexual energy
Chalcedony	Peace, protection, and luck
Diamond	Courage, peace, protection, and spirituality
Emerald	Analytical thought and mental powers
Garnet	Empowerment, health, and protection
Geode	Concentrated power or magick and fertility
Green tourmaline	Financial prosperity and luck in business
Hematite	Grounding and health
Jade	Health, love, prosperity, and protection
Lapis lazuli	Health, love, and protection
Lodestone	Direction, guidance, and magnetism
Marble	Material success and protection
Moonstone	Divination, empowerment, and love
Obsidian	Divination, grounding, and peace
Onyx	Defense, protection, and reduced sexual desire
Opal	Beauty, luck, and past-life regression therapy
Pearl	Luck, protection, and success

Crystal/Stone	Magickal Traits
Quartz crystal	Astral projection, focused magickal power, and health
Red tourmaline	Physical strength and stamina
Rhodochrosite	Grounding, peace, and tranquility
Rose quartz	Love, luck, and spirituality
Ruby	Magickal power and protection from nightmares
Salt	Grounding, health, and protection
Sapphire	Health, peace, and prosperity
Sugilite	Heightened awareness, magickal power, and wisdom
Tiger's eye	Courage, divination, luck, and protection
Turquoise	Courage, friendship, love, and protection

Some people feel that amber, fossilized tree sap, is not really a stone at all and should be classified with plants. The general consensus, however, is that it works like a stone and should be classified as such.

Pearl is another tricky one. A pearl is formed when a grain of sand gets inside an oyster's shell, causing an irritant. The oyster isolates the grain of sand in a secretion that hardens, forming the pearl. The problem is that the oyster has to die for the pearl to be harvested, so many feel it is inappropriate for magickal use. "Cultured" pearls are harvested from oysters grown in tanks, similar in principle to farming livestock. How do you feel about working with pearl?

This is, of course, a very short list that merely outlines the most well-known stones or those most commonly used in magick. There are literally hundreds of crystals, gems, and semiprecious stones available for magickal use.

Cleansing Stones

Now let's take a look at how stones can be used. Here's a list of ideas, suggestions, and advice regarding the use of stones. The most important thing is that when you first get a stone it must be cleansed. Whether you receive it as a gift, purchase it from a metaphysical store, or find it on the ground, it carries energies from other people, other times. Remember, the average piece of quartz is millions of years old!

With Water

There are many ways to cleanse a stone, and here is one of the most common. Find a place outside where the stone will not be disturbed, and bury it in the ground for twenty-four hours. Then dig it back up, wash it off, and consecrate it. Excess vibrations will have been literally grounded, leaving the stone clean and pure.

Please note that some stones should not get wet. For example, malachite, a beautiful copper-based green stone, can actually leach toxins into the water. Here's a short chart showing stones that can be briefly submerged in water and those that can't.

Crystal/Stone	Magickal Traits
Agate	Okay to submerge
Amazonite	Not okay to submerge
Amber	Not
Aquamarine	Not
Aventurine	Okay
Black tournamine	Not
Calcite	Not
Citrine	Okay
Copper	Not
Desert rose	Not
Fluorite	Not
Gypsum	Not
Jasper	Okay
Kyanite	Not
Lapis lazuli	Not
Malachite	Not
Moonstone	Not
Opal	Not
Pyrite	Not
Quartz (all kinds)	Okay
Ruby	Not
Tiger's eye	Okay
Turquoise	Not

As a general rule, if the Mohs hardness scale of the stone is less than five, it's a softer stone, and it is more likely to be damaged in water. The closer to zero a stone is on the scale, the more sensitive it can be. Every stone has a listed Mohs hardness rating, and there are plenty of websites that will give you the Mohs scale, molecular information, regions the stones are found, and more.

Without Water

If you want to cleanse your stone without getting it wet, try this: get a shallow glass dish full of noniodized salt, and leave the stone in it overnight in the light of the moon. Prior energies will be washed out of it—the salt eliminates any preexisting influences, and moonlight energizes the stone's spirit.

Consecration

Once a stone has been cleansed, it should be consecrated. A consecration is a rite of dedication in which the stone is purified and rededicated to the service of the goddess and the god. Here's a simple consecration rite:

First, decide if the stone is for a particular spellworking, to be used as an altar piece, to be set into jewelry, or to be gifted to another. Choose which deity, if any, the stone is being dedicated to. Of course, it does not have to be dedicated to any particular deity at all.

Now erect your temple. You can use lesson 31's ritual to create sacred space as an example.

Light one candle, and place the stone on a small mirror in front of you between you and the candle. Concentrate on the purpose the candle will carry and say: "In this circle, I bring this stone (use the stone's name, or give it a magickal one if you like) to dedicate it to the service of the Lord and Lady. By my hand, I swear it shall never be used for harm nor any ill intent. My word is my vow. So mote it be!"

Close the circle.

You can, of course, use any variation of this rite that feels right for you. Remember, Witchcraft should echo what's in your soul, not what other people tell you.

Using Your Stones

Now that the stone is consecrated, it can be used. Here are a few pointers:

- Don't mix opposing stones in one use. For example, don't mix hematite, a grounding stone, with sugilite, an invigorating stone. The conflicting energies will drain each other like opposing magnetic polarities.

- Quartz is unique. Like a pawn in chess, it can assist any stone it's used with. Think of quartz as a kind of magickal battery. It's so simple in construction that its uses are infinite. It can be used and cleansed and used over and over again.

- Many stones will let you know when they are "done." For example, if a person has problems grounding and wears a hematite ring to help them focus, it will literally shatter and fall away when it is "full." (Unless, of course, it is cleansed on a regular basis.) Many Witches like to wear rings of red carnelian when courting a lover. If the ring shatters and breaks without provocation, it may be wise to seek a different partner.

- Stones can be used as oracles. For example, quartz, obsidian, and amber can be used in the same way a crystal ball is.

- Stones of the correct colour can be used as curative aids. Red garnet, for example, can assist a person with intestinal disorders. However, they should never replace the care of a qualified physician.

- Crystals can be worn, carried in a pocket, or kept in pouches as magickal tools to use throughout the day. They can also be worked into jewelry. Amber and rose quartz bracelets make excellent gifts for a loved one, and a green tourmaline amulet would be appropriate for a young professional.

- Staves and wands greatly benefit from the presence of stones. For example, a piece of amethyst at the end of a wand can do wonders for its magickal use.

You can't go wrong with stones; their uses are as limitless as your imagination.

Lesson 33: Study Prompts and Questions

The Secrets of Stones
- Explain how and why stones work.
- Give three examples of stones and their magickal properties.

Rocks and Roles
- Take any five stones from the list and explain how you would use them in your everyday life. Be descriptive.
- Do some research: name four stones not listed here and provide their magickal qualities.

Cleansing Stones
- Choose any five stones from this list and offer ways you would use them in magick or spells.
- Do stones have auras? Justify your answer.

Lesson 33: Recommended Reading
- *The Book of Crystal Spells: Magical Uses for Stones, Crystals, Minerals… and Even Sand* by Ember Grant
- *Crystals and Stones: A Complete Guide to their Healing Properties* by The Group of 5

LESSON 34
Working with Herbs and Plants

We spent some time looking at colours, auras, and stones. In this lesson we'll examine some well-known plants, their names through history, and their modern uses and applications. Since time immemorial, people have used plants in healing, vitality, psychic awareness, and other ways, but usually little attention is given to *why* they work. And that's actually very easy. Even more than stones, plants are alive; they're visibly active. They work in two ways: one, the inhaled vapor or ingested plant matter causes certain reactions, and two, the inherent vibratory frequency of molecular activity triggers responses within the psychic mind. The aromatic reaction is, of course, much more direct, and it can be perceived by anyone, even those who stubbornly deny the possibility of psychic activity.

Lately an increased awareness of herbal remedies has created a huge market in everything from Saint-John's-wort to hyssop to rose hips. While little plastic jars of herbal remedies are an excellent source, many Witches still like the visual appeal of sprigs of dried herbs hanging up around the kitchen and their sacred space.

Some Plants and Their Uses

Many people have heard that Saint-John's-wort can help alleviate depression, and chamomile soothes the nerves. But what other plants are there, and what do they do? Here's a short chart of plants, their fascinating magickal or medieval names, and their curative properties. Plants that are dangerous to ingest are noted as such. Never use a plant unless you're 100 percent certain you know what it is.

Plant Name	Magickal or Medieval Name	Uses or Applications
Aloe vera (*Aloe barbadensis*)	Medicine plant	Hang it in the home to prevent accidents, or wear it for sunburn.
Asafoetida (*Ferula assa-foetida*)	Devil's dung	Burn it or use as an oil extract to banish evil spirits.
Basil (*Ocimum basilicum*)	Witch's herb	Hang in the home to promote peace, or eat it to ease anxiety.
Catnip (*Nepeta cataria*)	Catmint	Brew it as tea for psychic awareness; it also intoxicates cats.
Chamomile (*Matricaria chamomilla*)	Ground-apple	Hang it in the home or use it as an oil extract to remove curses, or drink it as a tea to soothe the nerves.
Comfrey (*Symphytum*)	Blackwort	Wear it for safe travel, or drink it as tea for health.
Damiana (*Turnera diffusa*)	Damiana	Burn it or use it as an oil extract to increase psychic awareness, or drink it as tea to increase passion.
Echinacea (*Echinacea purpurea*)	Cone flower	Eat it or drink it as tea for strength and health.
Eyebright (*Euphrasia*)	Eyebright	Hang it in the home for honesty, or drink it as tea for memory.
Feverfew (*Tanacetum parthenium*)	Febrifuge	Drink it as a tea for a cold remedy, or wear it to reduce accidents.
Frankincense (*Boswellia serrata*)	Olibans	Burn it or use it as an oil extract to banish negativity.
Garlic (*Alllium sativum*)	Stinkweed	Eat it for health, or hang it in the home to ward off evil spirits.
Ginseng (*Panax ginseng*)	Wonder root	Burn it to banish evil spirits, or eat it for health.

Plant Name	Magickal or Medieval Name	Uses or Applications
Grape (*Vitis*)	Bacchus's eye	Eat it to promote passion.
High John the Conqueror (*Ipomoea purga*)	High John the Conqueror	Burn it for magickal success, or wear it for luck.
Kava (*Piper methysticum*)	Kava root	Hang in the home or use as an oil extract for protection, or drink it as tea for health.
Mandrake (*Mandragora officinarum*)	Brain thief	Hang it in the home or use as an oil extract for protection, or wear it to attract love. Just don't eat it!
Mistletoe (*Viscum album*)	Witch's broom	Burn it to banish evil, or hang it in the home to attract love. Just don't eat it!
Patchouli (*Pogostemon cablin*)	Puke-pot	Hang it in the home to attract money, or wear it to attract love.
Potato (*Solanum tuberosum*)	Leather jacket	Eat it for wealth, or wear it to alleviate toothaches.
Rowan (*Sorbus aucuparia*)	Witchwood	Hang it in the home for protection, or wear it to promote psychic awareness.
Sage (*Salvia officinalis*)	Sage	Burn it for clarity, eat it or use it as an oil extract for wisdom, or wear it to ward off evil spirits.
Saint-John's-wort (*Hypericum perforatum*)	Saint-John's-wort	Brew it as a tea to alleviate depression, or wear it for love. Just don't eat it raw!
Sandalwood (*Santalum album*)	Sandalwood	Burn it as incense for protection, or wear it for spiritual awareness.
Skullcap (*Scutellaria*)	Madweed	Hang it in the house to promote peace, or wear it for fidelity.

Plant Name	Magickal or Medieval Name	Uses or Applications
Valerian (*Valeriana officinalis*)	All-heal	Drink it as a tea for peace, use it as an oil extract, or wear it for love.
Yohimbe (*Corynanthe yohimbe*)	Black Venus	Eat it or drink it as a tea to promote sexual stamina. Using too much could cause hypertension or insomnia.

The Lore of Leaves

Plants, even more so than dogs, have been "humankind's best friend" throughout history. Druids have harvested mistletoe and rowan for millennia. Mistletoe's curative abilities and its aid in contraception, hunting skills, and enhanced psychic awareness did not go unnoticed, and rowan planted near a house was supposed to keep it safe from burglary. English sailors in the 1600s often carried limes and lemons aboard ships; the vitamin C prevented scurvy. That's why English people are called "Limeys."

But devil's dung? Brain thief? You've probably noticed that some plants have very amusing and poetic—and sometimes even scary—medieval names. Ever wonder why?

In medieval times, herb lore was an oral tradition, and many people knew the curative properties of plants. To remember what plants to look for, people used descriptions of how the plants might look, smell, or feel. Such descriptive names for plants and herbs made it easier to find them when foraging in the forest.[110]

Here's an excellent example of how the descriptive names of plants were used. In Shakespeare's *Macbeth*, the Weird Sisters (Three Witches) are seen brewing a mysterious potion. Their "old family recipe" includes: "Eye of newt and toe of frog, Wool of bat and tongue of dog, Adder's fork and blind-worm's sting, Lizard's leg and howlet's wing."[111]

Were they cooking up obscure body parts? Of course not! In the recipe, they were using the following:

- *Eye of newt:* Mustard seed
- *Toe of frog:* Buttercup
- *Wool of bat:* Holly leaves

---

110. Baker, *Discovering the Folklore of Plants*, 78.
111. Shakespeare, "Song of the Witches."

- *Tongue of dog:* Hound's-tongue
- *Adder's fork:* Adder's-tongue fern
- *Blind-worm's sting:* Knotweed
- *Lizard's leg:* Breastweed, or lizard's-tail
- *Howlet's wing:* Henbane

Note: This is not a recipe recommended for home brewing.

Sachets, Oils, and More

Often derived from plants, oils and incenses are an important part of the Craft. Used in spells, to enhance rituals, or just for the ambience, oils and incenses have countless applications. There are hundreds of recipes for oil blends and incenses. Let's examine a few here:

Sachets and Potpourri

One of the easiest applications of any plant for medicinal purpose is a sachet or potpourri blend. Simply hang the plant to dry without letting the leaves crush. Then grind the dried plant with a mortar and pestle and place the blended powder in a small bag— a sachet—that can be hung, worn, or carried.

A potpourri blend is simply dried leaves, flowers, and other plant parts heated in water to release the aroma. Potpourri blends can be enhanced with oils or empowered with crystals to heighten the effect. Just make sure not to let the water evaporate! Also remember that some stones might leech toxins into the blend. Always research before you use any stone or crystal in this way.

Sachet Blends

Some popular sachet blends include:

- *Anti-theft sachet:* Caraway, elder, garlic, juniper, and rosemary
- *Healing sachet:* Cayenne, cinnamon, ginger, rosemary, rose petals, rue, and sandalwood
- *Love sachet:* Baby's breath, carnation, orange peel, and rose petals
- *Protective sachet:* Angelica, cloves, dill, and marjoram
- *Wealth sachet:* Cinnamon, cinquefoil, clove, lemon balm, tonka bean, and vanilla bean

Oils

Oils can be used for anointing and consecrations, in perfumes or candle aroma, or as additions to other spellworkings for that extra touch.

To prepare an oil extract, cut a fresh sprig from a plant. (Remember the boleen? This is where you'd use it.) Place the carefully cleansed—not rinsed—plant in an airtight jar with a neutral carrier oil such as olive or jojoba, enough to cover the plant. Seal the jar, and leave it in the dark for twenty-four hours. Don't let light hit it; sunlight might bleach out the essence. After twenty-four hours have passed, replace the old plant with a new one, keeping the same oil. After three or four days of this, squeeze the oil through a cheesecloth, and keep it in another sealed, airtight container. Voilà! The oil can be stored for up to two years.

You can blend different oils for different applications, of course. Simply use an eye-dropper to ensure the exact amount of each blend. One last warning: Some blends might cause an allergic reaction or skin irritation. If this happens, you can try diluting them with more carrier oil. If you still get an unpleasant reaction, use a different recipe.

As always, research, read, collect, and experiment!

Oil Recipes

Here are a few simple oil recipes:

- *Anointing oil:* Cinnamon, myrtle, and rose
- *Courage oil:* Geranium, musk, and rose
- *Far-sight oil:* Acacia, anise, and cassia
- *Healing oil:* Carnation, rosemary, and sandalwood
- *Initiation oil:* Frankincense, myrrh, and sandalwood
- *Love oil:* Ambergris,* bergamot, clove, lavender, and musk
- *Money oil:* Cinnamon and patchouli
- *Moon oil:* Jasmine, lemon, rose, and sandalwood
- *Protection oil:* Dragon's blood, frankincense, and sandalwood
- *Purification oil:* Frankincense, myrrh, olive, and sandalwood
- *Sleep oil:* Mace and rose
- *Venus oil:* Ambergris, gardenia, violet, and wild rose

*Originally, ambergris was extracted from the scent gland of a whale; the whale had to be hunted and killed to retrieve it. This upsets many people, so modern synthetic ambergris is available. However, some perfume manufacturers still use organic ambergris; they just don't advertise it.

Incense

Many people use incense to create a soothing atmosphere, enhance psychic ability, or empower spellcrafting. There are three basic forms of incense: loose, or granular; cone, or pressed; and stick. Granular incense is burned over little charcoal "coins," or disks, in a shallow dish or censer. Cone, or pressed, incense can be burned on any heat-resistant surface. And stick incense can be burned anywhere and even carried. This lesson will focus on granular incense. Even though granular incense is the easiest to produce, making incense is still a little more complex than making oils.

Many incense blends begin with this popular base recipe:

- 6 parts powdered sandalwood (base element)
- 2 parts powdered benzoin or frankincense (binding element)
- 1 part ground orris root (to preserve the scent)
- 1 part saltpeter (for stability)

Add twenty drops of the essential oil desired. Remember to keep the benzoin to 20 percent of the total amount and saltpeter to 10 percent. These will help to slow the burning rate of the incense. A small kitchen scale might be helpful here. You can substitute ground leaves for the oils, or you can use oils in conjunction with them. You can use empowering elements such as crystal fragments as well. Blend the ingredients in your mortar and pestle. The mix will go from clumpy to gooey to grainy. Once it looks like slightly squishy grains, you're ready to go. It will burn easily over the charcoal, giving off a thick, heady smoke. Mixing your blends while in sacred space certainly couldn't hurt.

Incense Recipes

Here is a brief list of incense recipes:

- *Air (elemental) incense:* Lavender, neroli, and sandalwood
- *Consecration incense:* Aloe, mace, storax, and sandalwood
- *Divination incense:* Chicory, cinquefoil, and clove
- *Earth (elemental) incense:* Cypress oil, patchouli, pine, and salt
- *Fire (elemental) incense:* Dragon's blood, frankincense, musk, red sandalwood, and saffron
- *Full moon ritual incense:* Frankincense and sandalwood
- *Healing incense:* Cinnamon, myrrh, and saffron
- *House blessing incense:* Eucalyptus, myrrh, and nutmeg
- *Love incense:* Basil, bergamot, lavender, rose petals, and sandalwood
- *Meditation incense:* Acacia and sandalwood

- *Money incense:* Cinnamon, citron, clove, lemon balm, and nutmeg
- *Spirit (elemental) incense:* Benzoin, frankincense, myrrh, rosemary, and sandalwood
- *Water (elemental) incense:* Ambergris, benzoin, lotus oil, myrrh, and sandalwood

Notice that the specific quantities are not given. This is because not every supplier carries ingredients of identical strength, and you may wish to increase the influence of one ingredient over another. There are, of course, many more recipes than the ones included here, and you can find incense blends for different sabbats and esbats, for the signs of the zodiac, dedicated to assorted gods or goddesses, or for healing different ailments.

Keep a record—in your Book of Shadows, for instance—that lists the recipes, ingredients, sources, when you made each blend, the applications, and the results.

Lesson 34: Study Prompts and Questions

Some Plants and Their Uses
- Go beyond the lesson; research five plants not listed, and give their medieval name and their properties or applications.

The Lore of Leaves
- Why did medieval people give plants such descriptive names?

Sachets, Oils, and More
- Describe the way a sachet is prepared and used.
- Describe the way a potpourri blend is prepared and used.
- Describe the way essential oils are prepared and used.
- Describe the way granular incense is prepared and used.

Lesson 34: Recommended Reading

- *Discovering the Folklore of Plants* by Margaret Baker
- *The Magical Properties of Plants—and How to Find Them* by Tylluan Penry

LESSON 35
Amulets, Talismans, and Candle Magick

We'll continue our magickal studies by working with amulets, talismans, and candles, but before we begin, let's answer one quick question: what's the difference between an amulet and a talisman?

An amulet can be anything, though usually a natural item, worn or carried for luck. A stone, seashell, feather in your cap, or rabbit's foot can all be carried for luck (unless you're the rabbit, of course).

A talisman is very much like an amulet, but a talisman is created to bring about a specific result, not just "blanket luck." Talismans (not *talismen*) are usually human-made items, such as engraved jewelry. Have you seen the "lover's charm" necklaces where each person in a couple wears one half of a heart? Those are talismans.

Amulets

Amulets are possibly the oldest form of magickal paraphernalia. A Neolithic hunter wearing a necklace of bear claws, a pilot who keeps a feather in his cockpit for safe flying, or a Witch who wears a quartz crystal are all using amulets. They are usually naturally occurring objects empowered and charged for luck. Amulets are worn, carried, used as decorations around the house, or, if there are no laws against it in your area, suspended from your car's rearview mirror.

Examples of popular amulets include:

- Crystals or other stones
- Feathers
- Seashells
- Four-leaf clovers
- Mojo bags containing an assortment of charms.

311

Whatever your amulet, a simple ritual of consecration is recommended. Assemble the components to create your amulet, erect the temple, and create your amulet in a magickal environment. You can dedicate it to a specific deity or just enchant it "for luck." It's worth noting, though, that while "luck" is a rather broad term, you can have "focused luck" and use an amulet appropriate to the focus. Do you want luck with money? Green tourmaline or a sand dollar may be your friend. If you want luck in love, try a piece of garnet or rose quartz.

Within circle, cleanse all the components. Concentrate upon the intent and purpose; focus your mind on the intended function. Crafting the amulet in circle adds to a successful magickal empowerment. It's a good idea to complete the amulet in one go; stopping halfway through and picking it up again later could diminish its effectiveness. While making it, envision energy flowing into the piece. You have seen how manipulating energy works. Simply manipulate some of that into the piece you are working on. Once the amulet is crafted and empowered, it needs to be consecrated and charged. Announce its dedication and purpose to the gods, using the amulet's name if it has one, and charge the item using the correct magickal focus.

Complete the consecration and/or dedication of your amulet, and when you are ready, close the circle. Voilà! You have made an amulet.

Talismans

You could think of a talisman as a "complex amulet." Rather than just a stone carried for luck, a talisman is often inscribed with a message or symbolism for a specific purpose. You could make a talisman for personal protection at work, to keep burglars away from your car, or for long-term health.

Examples of talismans include:

- Medallions inscribed with magickal symbols
- Horseshoes (though generally not worn as jewelry)
- Pentacles
- Crosses, Mjolnir, or ankhs
- Poppets

Amulets and Talismans

Poppets, often associated with voodoo spells in popular culture, are not inherently evil. Neither is voodoo, for that matter. A poppet is simply a small doll made to represent an individual person. It is stuffed and contains items connected with the individual— a lock of hair or a photograph, for example. Pins used on poppets are usually black or white and used for healing. A white pin in the poppet's forehead might promote clarity of thought, and a black pin in the chest may be for banishing lung cancer.

As with an amulet, a Witch determines the use and purpose of the talisman before-hand, even writing a small rite before its construction. If it is being crafted for a particular person, be sure you have the express permission of your target before you start any magickal work. You must never work magick on someone without their understanding and consent. Also be sure your intent is clear and valid. Malicious or vengeful magick will only come back to harm you in the long run.

Before you begin crafting any amulet or talisman, do a little research, and determine what components would be best suited for the purpose. For example, if you are making a beaded talisman to soothe a child's nightmares, would you weave amethyst beads into it? Hematite? Obsidian?

Candle Magick

Working with candles can be a very rewarding endeavor, especially if you choose to cast your own wax. Candles can be used to light a room, empower a ritual, illuminate a situation, or assist in raising magick for spellcrafting. As with any magickal working, the candle will be more effective if it is created in circle.

Choosing Candles
Before beginning any work with candles and wax, there are choices and a few specifications to be aware of:

Colour
Colour magick was discussed in lesson 32. Refer to it to figure out what colour is appropriate for the spellworking. Be sure to use the correct colour of candle.

Scent
You can buy scented candles, although those are usually made with artificial perfumes, and natural scents are better. If you made some of the essential oils listed in lesson 34, by all means use those. You can either mix the oil into the wax when pouring the candle

or rub it on afterward. And here's a fun tip: If the candle is for a positive spell, such as luck or empowerment, rub the oil on deosil from the top going down. If the spell is for banishment, rub the oil on widdershins.

Decorations

Your candles can be decorated with crystals, gem fragments, seashells, or anything else you can come up with. Try mixing gem fragments into the poured wax. Just remember that some decorations could be flammable, and you are working with something that you're going to set on fire. It's best to err on the side of caution.

Making Your Own Candles

If you decide to cast your own candles, you should invest in a double boiler, a cooking thermometer, and a candle-making kit. Practice making candles and getting the hang of it before empowering your creations. You may choose to reuse wax from old castings. If you do, make sure it is cleansed of any old magick. To do this, melt the wax down first, pour it into a shallow dish, and let it set overnight, preferably in the moonlight. The moonlight will "bleach out" any old magickal resonances.

Size

Consider the amount of time the spell is intended to run. Is it going to be cast and completed within the circle, or will the spell run for several days? Let this determine the size of candle you wish to use. Votives and tea candles are good for a couple of hours, tapers are good for an evening or two, and large "tree stump" candles can last several weeks. (This is one of the nice things about candles—they can keep a spell alive while you are away.) Of course, if the spell is intended to run for several days, you need to be sure the candle will not go out, tip over, or in any way risk starting a fire.

Shape

Do you want to use a candle in a special shape? If the candle magick is for a particular person, you might use a figure-shaped candle. Candles in the shapes of animals, pentagrams, and many other items can be used. Check your favorite metaphysical or craft store or website to see what shapes are available—or create your own.

Safety

If there is an accident, is there a fire extinguisher or other fire suppression system (wet towels, sand, etc.) within reach? Be prepared for any emergencies.

Working with Candles

Now that we're all set, let's get busy. Erect a temple, if you want, then anoint the candle. To do this, keep the purpose or intent clearly in your mind, and hold the candle in your receptive hand. Using your projective hand, rub the appropriate oil onto the candle. If it's for an invocation or blessing, start at the bottom and rub in an upward deosil spiral. If it's for banishment, start at the top and rub deosil down. Some Witches prefer to rub widdershins down for a banishment, but others feel that's like rubbing the magick out of the candle.

Once it's anointed, set the candle in an appropriate place, usually on the altar, and light it with your projective hand. Many Witches use matches for this; some feel that using a lighter or other such tool seems like cheating.

While the candle is burning, visualize the magick flowing out of the flame and into the cosmos, fulfilling its task. Remember the "cone of power" raised in ritual? A candle is like a little cone of power all its own. Chanting or a recitation of the rite can help to maintain focus and intent. Of course, if it's a long-duration burning, focus on the intent at the outset, then let it do its work.

Once the spell is done, you can either let the candle burn itself out or extinguish it with your fingers or a candle snuffer. Blowing it out is said to disrespect the element of air.

If you initiate the spell within circle but want to leave the candle burning after the circle is over, try this: Instead of taking the circle down, visualize it shrinking as you mentally "gather it in." Focus it on the candle until all that's left of the circle is a little "spotlight" of magick. When closing the circle and dismissing the elements, you can leave the magickal spotlight burning to let the spell continue.

If you plan to leave the candle burning for a while, it's best not to leave it unsupervised. If you must, make sure it won't tip over, go out, or start another fire. If you can, leave it in the bathtub or the kitchen sink. Enough Witches were burned during the Inquisition; we don't need to go igniting anymore! If you're really unsure, you can indeed snuff the candle out, relight it later, and crank the magick up again.

Some store-bought candles, such as novena prayer candles, are made specifically to burn for several days. They're made inside tall glass holders, which keep the flame safe from breezes or curious fingers, and should anything tip the glass over, the flame will simply put itself out. The glass may be hot to the touch, though.

Candles really are effective magickal tools; they are a visible, material representation of the magick at work. Whether purchased or hand-made, candles represent the life of the spell, and the simple flame is a warm, friendly reminder of the presence of spiritual forces all around us.

Lesson 35: Study Prompts and Questions

Amulets

- What is the difference between an amulet and a talisman?
- List five examples of magickal amulets.
- Using any one item from the list you just wrote, describe the process used to find, cleanse, fashion, consecrate, empower, and use the amulet.
- Consider a "focused luck" amulet. What specific item would you recommend to promote luck in finding a job or buying a car?

Talismans

- List five examples of magickal talismans.
- Using any one item from the list you just made, describe the process used to find, cleanse, fashion, consecrate, empower, and use the talisman.

Candle Magick

- What magickal properties do candles possess?
- Explain how a candle is anointed and cleansed before use.
- Write a simple candle ritual. Include erecting the temple, anointing and empowering the candle, and closing the circle.

Lesson 35: Recommended Reading

- *Exploring Candle Magick: Candles, Spells, Charms, Rituals, and Divinations* by Patricia Telesco
- *Practical Candleburning Rituals: Spells & Rituals for Every Purpose* by Raymond Buckland

The Art of Spellcrafting

Now that we've discussed magickal theory, ritual procedure, and spell components, let's put it all together. In this lesson, we'll examine the fundamentals of spellcrafting from preparation to performance. But before we go any further, let's establish exactly what a spell is:

> *A spell is a sequence of words or actions that is intended to change a situation or cause an event to occur.*

Compare this definition with my own example, which compares prayer, spells, and meditation:

> **A prayer is *talking to God*, meditation is *listening to God*, and spells are *working with God*.**

There are essentially two classes of spells: thaumaturgic and theurgic, and these spells often employ a wide range of magickal components to assist the Witch in their work.

Spells can, it's true, be malevolent or benign, created to harm or to heal. But if you've been paying any attention at all, you know that harmful spells are unethical and should be avoided. Besides, Witches who work unethical magick run the risk of being bitten in the butt by the Threefold Law.

Different Types of Spells

Besides the definitions thaumaturgic and theurgic, there are many different ways to define a spell. In lesson 24, I discussed such spell classifications as abjuration and necromancy. As a rule, however, most Witches are more concerned with the spell's purpose than its classification. Knowing that a protection spell is abjuration rather than necromancy is useful to bring the spell into focus, but it is not as vital as its intent.

The spell definitions most used by Witches include:

Banishment

These are spells in which the target is kept away from the subject. Banishment spells can be directed at people, or a Witch might use banishment to overcome an addiction, such as gambling or alcoholism.

Binding

Binding spells differ from banishments in that the spell target is restricted but not over-powered. As was stated in the lesson 25, Magick and Responsibility, binding spells are a form of defensive action—"Lest in self-defense it be"—so the rede is not compromised.

Blessing

Spells of blessing need no explanation. Theurgic in nature, these spells bestow favor or luck upon the target.

Charging

While not really "spells," these are used to charge or empower material objects, such as a Witch's magickal tools.

Clarity

Spells for clarity offer a clearer look at a situation or aid the Witch in viewing something or someone without bias.

Healing

Here's another spell that needs no explanation. Healing is used to accelerate or enhance (but not replace) the physical or emotional recuperative process.

Protection

Protection spells, of course, are used to protect the target from harm, whether material, magickal, or psychological.

Sympathetic

This term actually covers a wide range of applications. Sympathetic magick, a centuries-old process, is the use of icons or images that represent the actual target. For example, if a person is injured, healing energy is sent via a photograph of that person. The use of locks of hair, fingernails, and other "body parts" in sympathetic magick creates an immediate, direct sympathetic bond with the target.

Function or Spell?

Observant students will notice that invocation, evocation, and divination were not included in this list. The act of drawing down, welcoming spirits into a magickal setting, or the practice of divinatory arts are not so much spells as "functions." Activities such as charging or empowering something can be seen as both a spell and a function. Review the definition of a spell at the start of this lesson.

Black Magick, White Magick, and Hexes

Let's quickly address the terms *black magick*, *white magick*, and *hexes*. Way back in the very first lesson of Wicca 101, we learned that magick is a neutral force with no colour. To call magick used for harm *black magick* is incorrect. Besides, the term could also be construed to have racist implications. Magick, just to reiterate, is a neutral force like electricity. What's important is how the magick is used or applied.

The word *hex* has two possible meanings. *Hexen*, in German, simply means "Witches," and *hexe* means "Witch." But that itself comes from the old Germanic word *hagzissa*, or "hag." A *hex*, by definition, can be a Witch or any spell performed by a Witch, older woman, wisewoman, or crone. Hexes, like any sphere of magick, can be used for purposes malevolent or benign, but the generally negative connotation mirrors the typical public view of Witches as a whole. Mundane perspectives aside, hexes and hexcraft are a viable, positive form of magick.

Philosophies of Spellcrafting

There are four primary schools of thought regarding the fundamentals of spellcrafting, and they are ways to address how a spell is composed. These could be described as "simple versus complex," "recipe," "fuzzy logic," and the "four cornerstone" philosophies. We'll examine these one at a time.

Simple versus Complex

A simple spell is a series of words or motions quickly performed. The magick is raised, the spell is performed, and the Witch goes on about their business. For example, if the Witch suffers from chronic allergies, a quick banishment spell is used to drive away or suppress the sneezing fits. To do this, the Witch might envision the allergy-causing pollen as a cloud of dust around them. They inscribe a simple circle in the air in front of them and visualize the dust or pollen being swept into it. The Witch then draws a banishing pentagram over the circle and mentally and physically pushes it away. A spell of this kind could be performed in seconds. Simple spells are generally thaumaturgic, not theurgic, in nature.

A complex spell more closely resembles a formal ritual. The temple is erected, quarters are called, and the appropriate deities are (usually) invoked. The body of the spell is performed within the temple, and the magick is released to perform its task. We'll examine the composition of a complex spell in detail a little later.

Recipe

A spell could be compared to a recipe, and it can be as personalized as the Witch or recipient prefers. Look at it this way: You collect ingredients, mix them together, cook them up, and end with a finished product. Of course, not everyone likes their meals prepared the same way. Do you put pickle relish in your tuna fish salad or a splash of beer in your macaroni and cheese? Do you prefer vegan alternatives to meat? The meal is essentially the same either way, but different preparations appeal to different people. Likewise, the details of a spell's composition and performance can be as varied as the Witch desires. Is it a simple or complex spell? Do you use tarot cards or the futhark or invoke Nike or Freyja? These are all possibilities to consider when writing your spell. Different spell components can be substituted as well. Do you prefer amethyst or agate? If your power animal is a cougar, would you invoke its strength when working magick to heal a friend's parakeet?

Fuzzy Logic

There are many different ways to put a spell together, but many older books give specific formulas for spell construction, imploring that the formula be followed to the letter. Time of day, lunar phase, verbal recitation—they all must be exactly right to get the desired effect. Many modern Witches, however, ascribe to the theory that a spell is like "fuzzy logic." As long as the intent is true and the energy is there, the spell will work. A good spell should still be carefully written and plotted out, but it does not need to be exactly the same every time. The magick will know what to do.

Consider this: if you were to perform a healing spell on a friend's pet, you'd know the basics before you start, but would you cast identical spells for an angelfish, a tarantula, and an Alaskan malamute? Just as no two situations are identical, one can argue that no two spells should be identical. Every situation has different details, such as the gender and age of the target, the availability and cost of components, and so on. These factors are why so many modern books on the Craft have lists of correspondences and substitutions.

The Four Cornerstones of a Spell

Many Witches feel that the elements of a spell should mirror the four cornerstones of magick, or the Witch's pyramid. That way, all four elements—plus spirit—would be represented, creating a well-rounded, solid spell. In this aspect of spellcrafting, the cornerstones are represented in this way:

- *Somatic (air):* Like the pentagram described in the simple spell or the runic pattern that RedWolf used at the Green Dragon esbat, the somatic elements are manipulations of the hand (or athame or wand) through the air. These movements breathe life into the spell.
- *Luminary (fire):* Candles are an integral part of many Witches' spell-working. The type and colour of candle used can enhance the spell's success, and the candle flame, of course, represents the beating heart of the spell.
- *Verbal (water):* The spoken word is the emotion of the spell. You could just think or whisper it, but putting sound and voice to the spell gives it more feeling. A spell spoken out loud has more "oomph."
- *Material (earth):* The material components of a spell give it something to stand on and carry it through the casting. Herbs, crystals, and consecrated talismans are all examples of material substances used in spells.
- *Spirit (spirit):* This, of course, is the magick itself—the power raised in the casting of the spell. Without spirit, without magick, you're just wasting your time.

Spell Composition

How is a spell "composed"? That's actually quite easy. It involves two parts, setup and scripting, with several steps within each part.

Setup

Spell setup consists of the following steps:

Identify the Situation

Examine the situation from all known angles, taking into account ethical considerations, the personal conditions of the target or subject, and the time frame involved. This could require counselling and discussion with the intended recipient of the spell.

Consider Your Options

Are there any nonmagickal ways to resolve the situation? What could be done to improve things? Would your input have the desired effect, or would it only make things worse? Do you have enough experience and know-how to craft the desired spell?

Check Your Resources

If you've performed a similar spell before, can you refer back to it for pointers? (Remember, you may not want to replicate the spell exactly; conditions could have changed.) Do you have the components necessary, or could you gather them effectively?

Prepare the Components

This step assumes that there are necessary spell components that weren't readily available. Preparations might include mixing the correct oils, making incense, crafting talismans, or gathering herbs.

Scripting

Spell scripting consists of the following steps:

Prepare a Draft of the Spell

This is not always necessary; oft-repeated spells, such as healings, could be performed from memory. Still, some situations do require a script or at least a dry run to ensure that the spell will be as effective as possible. This is a good time to consider which deities to call upon or what chants or incantations to use.

Double-Check

Again, this is not always necessary, but as in many professions, the rule of thumb is "measure twice, cut once" just to make sure.

Write the Spell

This is the finished copy—the entire spell in black and white—ready to be cast. Some Witches are content to type spells up on a computer and simply print them out, while others prefer to write them on specially made parchment with handcrafted inks. Dove's Blood and Dragon's Blood are two examples of popular inks for this purpose.

Rehearse the Spell

Spells that involve the cooperation and commitment of several people can lose their effectiveness if the people are not clear on what exactly is required of them. Rehearsing a spell, just like rehearsing a play, ensures that everyone is on the same page. (How do you rehearse a spell without casting it? Easy! Don't light the candles, and don't raise any magick; just pretend you are.)

Spell Composition Example

Remember Crystal from the esbat? She mentioned that her carpal tunnel syndrome was causing her some discomfort and asked the coven for a healing spell. The Witch's mill that was performed offered her temporary relief, but the pain has returned. Lady Morgaine decides to compose a spell specifically for Crystal's healing. Using the spell composition method, Morgaine takes the following steps:

1) Identify the situation. Morgaine does not know much about carpal tunnel syndrome, so she researches it on reliable websites and asks her physician about it to learn as much as she can about treatments and conditions. She asks Crystal to describe how it feels from the inside, and she visits Crystal's working environment.

2) Consider your options. After examining the situation, Morgaine concludes that she can indeed compose a spell to help Crystal's condition.

3) Check your resources. Going to her magickal medicine cabinet, Morgaine pulls out a couple of books with spells that she can adapt to the task at hand. She also roots through her herbal supply to find helpful remedies.

4) Prepare the components. Following her research, Morgaine prepares an oil made from willow, orange, and sandalwood extracts. She also makes a couple of "bracelets" from wrapped willow leaves.

5) Prepare a draft of the spell. Morgaine puts together an outline of the spell process, jotting down notes that she will weave into the finished product. After a couple of revisions, she's ready to write the final script.

6) Double-check. Yep, did that.

7) Write the spell. With all the pieces in place, Morgaine writes the spell out in full. This will be a "complex" spell performed in a ritual format with both theurgic and thaumaturgic elements. The final script includes everything from creating sacred space to closing the circle. Being fond of the medieval look, Morgaine types the script on her computer with a calligraphic lettering font and prints it on parchment-style paper. When it's all over, she'll give a copy to Crystal to keep in her Book of Shadows.

8) Rehearse the spell. Morgaine and Crystal meet at the covenstead for a dry run of the spell.

Lesson 36: Study Prompts and Questions

Different Types of Spells

- Write the supplied definition of a spell, and paraphrase it in your own words.
- How does a spell differ from a prayer?
- Can Witches cast harmful spells? Should they? Explain.
- Identify and define the eight types of spells.

Philosophies of Spellcrafting

- Briefly explain the following four concepts or philosophies of spellcrafting: simple versus complex, recipe, fuzzy logic, and the four cornerstones.
- Compare and contrast simple versus complex spells with theurgy versus thaumaturgy.
- Compare and contrast the four cornerstones of a spell with the four cornerstones of magick. Be sure to include elemental references.

Spell Composition
- What are the two parts of spell composition?
- List and identify the eight possible steps in composing a complex spell.

Lesson 36: Recommended Reading
- *Magick in Theory and Practice* by Aleister Crowley
- *The Witch's Book of Spellcraft: A Practical Guide to Connecting with the Magick of Candles, Crystals, Plants & Herbs* by Jason Mankey, Matt Cavalli, Amanda Lynn, and Ari Mankey

LESSON 37
The Art of Spellcasting

In the last lesson, we examined the fundamentals and philosophies of spellcrafting and discussed the basic steps involved in spell composition. Now let's continue from crafting to the casting of the spell.

Making Magick

Just as there are steps involved in crafting a spell, there are steps involved in casting it. There are, as we saw earlier, two types of spells: simple and complex. In the following sections, we'll look at both.

Create Sacred Space (Simple)

You can simply create an "internal temple" where the body itself is the consecrated area. This encompasses the body, spirit, mind, and magick. Adept Witches often feel that the four elements are always present, so recognizing them and erecting the temple can be performed in the space of a few heartbeats. This process is known as bringing one's "magickal self" into focus.

Create Sacred Space (Complex)

Here the Witch collects the necessary components, centers themself or the collective group, and begins to focus on the spell about to be cast. This is similar to the "erecting the temple" phase of a ritual, complete with calling the quarters.

Perform the Spell (Simple)

Remember the allergy-banishing example from the last lesson? Performing a simple spell can be as basic as a hand motion or a quick visualization as long as the magick backing it up is there.

Perform the Spell (Complex)

While it is the most prominent part of casting a spell, this is not the most important part. Every aspect of the spell, from inspiration to follow-through, holds equal importance. Still, this is the step where the spell is brought to life. Words are spoken, components are used, and the spell is made whole. We'll discuss this in detail again very soon.

Release the Spell (Simple or Complex)

This is the same in both simple and complex spells. In either case, the magick has to be directed effectively to be any good.

Having raised the energy and performed the spell, the Witch must now do something with it. Just like the final "oomph" in the energy raising at the esbat, this is where the magick is directed and sent out and the spell is closed. Many spells go wrong at this point. Despite all the planning and beautiful recitation, if the magick is not effectively directed, it will just sit and wither. This could be compared to telling a joke but forgetting the punch line.

Follow Through (Simple)

Since many simple spells are performed quickly, following through can be as easy as checking in on the progress from time to time. If it's warranted, you might wish to repeat the spell or begin planning a more complex approach.

Follow Through (Complex)

Once the spell has been effectively raised, performed, and released, the Witch should now follow up on its progress. Is it being used effectively? Enchanting a piece of red tourmaline with healing energy for an injured friend is wonderful, but it does no good if he leaves it in the bathroom. A spell for clarity sent to an alcoholic is a waste of time if all it does is make her levelheaded enough to go buy more beer. Spell follow-through actually begins before the spell is even cast to ensure that the spell's recipient knows what to do. This is similar to being told by your doctor what medication to use, when, and how much and then simply forgetting to follow their orders. In some cases, a follow-up magickal counselling could be recommended.

Magick in Detail

Let's go back and examine some aspects of the spellcasting in greater detail. Using Lady Morgaine's spell for Crystal's carpal tunnel syndrome, we'll go through the four parts of spellcasting one at a time.

Create Sacred Space

Morgaine and Crystal meet for the spell. With all the spell components in place, Morgaine prepares to bring the spell to life. Before lighting the first candle, she grounds and centers herself, and Crystal does the same. Since this is a spell for Crystal, Morgaine lets her call the quarters as she likes while Morgaine lights the spirit candle, casts the circle, and invokes the deities.

Perform the Spell

Okay, down to business. The components are ready, the spell is written, and sacred space has been prepared. Together the two Witches raise a cone of power. Morgaine recites the spell, and at the appropriate times, she massages her oil blend into Crystal's wrists and visualizes drawing the pain out of them as if pulling a clog from a drain. She takes the bracelets she'd made and wraps them around Crystal's wrists. While she does this, Crystal focuses on realigning her hand chakra, envisioning the chakra colour going from a turbulent reddish-brown colour to a clear blue. With the spell now cast, Morgaine prepares to release it.

Release the Spell

In some spells, such as the power raising for RedWolf's friend, the magick is raised, focused, and directed at a distant target. Here, however, Crystal's healing is immediate. The energy is focused and concentrated by the cone of power and released into her wrists as the spell progresses. Still, even here, the final release is a valid part of the spell procedure. The magick is "locked in" where it will remain, continuing the healing process.

Follow Through

For the next few days, Crystal reports on her condition, telling Morgaine of any changes that may have occurred. She does not abandon her prescribed medical treatment of the carpal tunnel; the spell was intended to assist and enhance the medical care, not replace it. The spell is a success—Crystal shows a marked, rapid improvement in her flexibility and tension. Even her physician is impressed. Morgaine and Crystal each keep a copy of the spell, so they can refer back to it should the need arise.

Analysis of a Spell

Here's the text from Morgaine's Book of Shadows for Crystal's healing spell.

Spell for Crystal (Carpal Tunnel)

Preparations

- Essential oil blend of sandalwood, orange, and willow (SOW oil)
- Bracelets made from wrapped willow leaves, consecrated with SOW oil
- Statues of Brigid and Sirona
- Candles

Casting

- Light spirit candle—create sacred space

Invocations of the Gods

Say: *I welcome and call upon you, blessed Brigid, mighty mother, bearer of riches, bringer of bounty. By leaf, flower, and fruit, by life, love, and hearth, I welcome you to assist she who seeks your aid. Hail, and welcome!*

Light candle to Brigid.

Say: *Wise Sirona, lady of the healing touch and the sacred word, teacher, healer, bringer of life, love, and mirth, I welcome you to assist she who seeks your aid. Hail, and welcome!*

Light candle to Sirona.

Say: *Great spirits, welcome! Your daughter Crystal seeks your aid. Allow the power of healing to enter her, let the cool pure water flow in, and may the pain and tension flee!*

Procedure

Massage SOW oil into Crystal's wrists.

Say: *Breath of sandalwood, ease away the tension; fire of orange, burn away the pain; strength of willow, bring the healing to fruition; spirit of magick, let only health remain.*

Using a massage technique, pull the tension out of Crystal's wrists, and send it into the spirit candle.

After massaging the oil into Crystal's wrists, focus on the healing magick using Starhawk's Changes chant. Wrap the bracelets around her wrists.

While both continue the chant, wrap the willow bracelets around Crystal's wrists.

Maintain the cone of power until Crystal decides it's time to close the spell.

Farewells to the Gods

Say: *Blessed Brigid, lady of the forge of magick, we thank you for your assistance here tonight. We ask that you continue to lend healing energy to our sister Crystal as she continues her recovery. Go if you must, stay if you will. Hail, and farewell.*

Extinguish Brigid's candle.

Say: *Strong Sirona, goddess of healing, we thank you for your guidance here tonight. We ask that your healing song carry our sister Crystal on her path to recovery. Go if you must, stay if you will. Hail, and farewell!*

Extinguish Sirona's candle.

Say: *The spell is open but never broken. Let the magick live on.*

With these words, the spell is complete. Morgaine will continue to monitor Crystal's progress to ensure that the magick keeps. As you can see, this spell resembles a modified ritual. Some ritual elements, such as the hieros gamos, have been omitted as this is only a healing spell and not a full ritual procedure.

Lesson 37: Study Prompts and Questions

Making Magick

- List and identify the steps involved in casting a spell.
- Explain the similarities and differences between a simple and a complex spell.

Magick in Detail

- Think of a simple spell you've seen performed in ritual, read about in a book, or seen in a movie. Break it down into the four parts, and explain how it was performed.
- Do the same thing for a complex spell.

Analysis of a Spell

- Write two spells, one simple and one complex. You may choose from the following situations or create one of your own.
    - Helping a friend recover from a car accident.
    - Helping a coven member deal with reoccurring nightmares from childhood.

> ‣ Cleaning up "spilled magick."
> ‣ Getting a promotion at work.
> ‣ Working with a group of Witches to help a local business stay open.

Lesson 37: Recommended Reading

- *Spellcrafting: Strengthen the Power of Your Craft by Creating and Casting Your Own Unique Spells* by Arin Murphy-Hiscock
- *The Witch's Book of Spellcraft: A Practical Guide to Connecting with the Magick of Candles, Crystals, Plants & Herbs* by Jason Mankey, Matt Cavalli, Amanda Lynn, and Ari Mankey

LESSON 38
Wards, Shields, and Protection

"You're writing a book on teaching Witchcraft?" the young Pagan asked. "Are you gonna do a section on defense against the dark arts like in *Harry Potter*?"

Yes, I am, and here it is. In this lesson, I'll spend time discussing one very important aspect of magick—how to protect yourself, your home, and your loved ones.

Do I Need Protecting?

During the years of the Inquisition, it was dangerous—often fatal—to be accused of being a Witch. Anyone who was accused, whether they practiced Witchcraft or not, was immediately suspect.

"But that was then," you say. "People are smarter now, aren't they?"

Well, yes and no. The laws have changed; in the United States and the United Kingdom, it is no longer illegal to practice Witchcraft, and many Western governments do recognize Wicca as a legitimate religion. Unfortunately what's written in the law books doesn't always reflect how people think. There are indeed people who were raised believing that Witches are evil servants of Satan, and no force in the world is going to convince them otherwise. It is an unfortunate truth that what people do not understand, they fear. And what they fear, they destroy. This was true in the ancient world, it was true in the Middle Ages, and it is true today.

Modern Witches are still at risk of persecution by the ignorant and the closed-minded, but we also have to be wary of possible psychic or magickal attacks from unethical Witches, malevolent spirits, or simple negative or chaotic energy. One of the drawbacks of being psychically and magickally aware is the awareness of more unseen forces than the mundane world is willing to acknowledge.

The most obvious threat is that of fear itself. People who fear Witches due to ignorance or misinformation can spread that fear, making other people feel nervous or paranoid about Witches. This can lead to action against Witches and their families such as Wiccan children being removed from school or taken from their families. Witches also run the risk of losing their jobs if supervisors or other authority figures believe the rumors and allegations.

Another risk is psychic attacks from other Witches. This is rare, but it does happen. If a Witch feels that their position in a coven is at risk, they might try to dissuade the one they perceive as a threat by psychic or magickal means.

Yet another danger is negative energy. There are some people out there who are so full of negative or chaotic energy that they are simply difficult to be around. These individuals could disrupt a Witch's psychic awareness, causing disjointed thoughts, lack of concentration, or nausea. Some people like this are just mean, angry, and unhappy people who wear their negativity like a cloak. Others are just so chaotic that their mere presence makes it hard to focus or concentrate.

One should also consider negativity in inanimate objects. Imagine you are on a long road trip and stop at a hotel for the night. Opening the door of the hotel room, you get a strong psychic image of a brutal murder that happened in the room twenty-five years ago. Psychically blind people might not be aware of anything wrong, but the psychic impressions left in the room make it impossible for you to sleep there. Short of changing rooms, what would you do? The following section includes examples of the different forms of magickal defense and protections available to Witches.

Protection Spells

Basic protection spells are actually very easy, and with a little research, you could write an effective one. A Witch could carry a protective amulet or talisman or perform a protective asperging on themselves on a regular basis. If the Witch wears a pentagram necklace or ring, they might keep it charged on the altar when they're not wearing it (assuming that they occasionally take it off). When moving into a new house, apartment, or room, it is always wise to cleanse it. Not *clean*, but *cleanse*. Cleaning a house involves mops, soapy water, and so on. Cleansing a house is a different matter, more of a magickal effort.

To begin, the Witch sweeps out every room and sweeps all the dust—and the negativity—right out the front door. Then the Witch performs an asperging of the house. The consecration phase from the Green Dragon esbat is an excellent example of an asperging. The Witch walks through the house and blesses and consecrates every room and portal, including doors, windows, mirrors, fireplaces, electrical outlets, telephone jacks, dryer vents, and so on with earth and water, fire and air—just like erecting a temple. At each location mentioned above, the Witch sprinkles the area with salted water, saying:

Salt of purity, water of the sea,
Join together in harmony.
For where thou art cast,
Let no harm or ill will last.
So mote it be!

The Witch then consecrates the same spots with burning incense, saying:

Sweet breath of air, spirit of fire bright,
Guard and protect our home outright.
For where thou art cast,
Let no harm or ill will last.
So mote it be!

As you can see, this procedure is almost identical to anointing a person. Only this time it's for portals in a home. Of course, you know not to spray water into the electrical outlets, right? If possible, the Witch should walk around the entire outside of the building, laying down a circle of salt as another protective measure. It's often wise to refresh the salt regularly, and a Witch may do so at full moons, for example. Be careful not to pour too much salt. Consider the effect it may have on the soil, in drainage areas, or on slugs. They're important too.

Of course, if the Witch lives in a multifamily building or an apartment complex, they cannot do this without the consent of all the other tenants who share the building. Whenever a Witch moves, they should leave the broom they used to sweep at the old house. That way they're leaving all its old negativity there. New house, new broom.

Suppose a Witch is moving into a new neighbourhood where they do not feel entirely welcome. The verbal part of a protection spell might go something like this:

Blessed Minerva,
Goddess of protection and wisdom,
I beg your aid.
Keep safe our home and hearth,
Watch over all those who live here,

And let enter only those who would be welcome.
Lady Minerva, this I do ask of thee.

They may wish to enhance the protective spell with amulets around the house. Sprigs of rowan or small bundles of ethically sourced sage hung over doors and windows will add to the effect, and many Witches hang a small decorated wicker broom over the main entrance into the home. Little pentagrams charged with protective energy and hung over the door or placed under the welcome mat can't hurt either.

If you don't want to go through the process of erecting a temple when blessing a house, you can simply draw a small pentagram or protective rune at each portal with the incantation of:

Love within, harm without; let no ill will linger about.

Wards

Unlike a basic protection spell, a ward is a magickal shield or barrier placed around a person or an area. Wards can be placed to protect against individuals, intruders, or magickal attacks.

Let's say Stephanie Windsong is separated from her abusive husband, and a divorce is in the works. He keeps harassing her with abusive phone calls at three in the morning, driving past her house, and so on. Since they were married for several years, he knows exactly how to upset her. She could work magick against him to keep him away, such as banishment or binding spells, but this time she wants to ward and protect the house. She goes about setting up a ward over the front door, which will magickally secure the whole house.

Stephanie erects a temple and uses that magickal environment to assemble the components needed. She grinds up some sandalwood incense with her mortar and pestle and blends it with consecrated water and a little white glue, making sort of a thin, almost invisible watery paint. She also charges a small round mirror, enchanting it to deflect malevolent attacks. Using the sandalwood mixture, she paints a large pentagram on the outside of her door and writes the words *love within, harm without, let no malice linger about* around it in Theban script. She hangs the small mirror in the center of the pentagram, so her husband's negativity will reflect back onto him. When the sandalwood paint mixture dries, it will be invisible, but the magick will remain. Stephanie enhances the effect by visualizing the entire ward as a big stained glass window with the light of her magick shining out. Wards of this nature can be recharged with just a thought. Naturally the more experienced and confident the Witch, the stronger the ward will be.

Wards can be placed over any portal or protected area; a ward over your car can protect it from being broken into. Note that wards, just like protective spells, can be either thaumaturgic or theurgic. If you should ever need to take down a ward, it's done similar to the way spilled magick is cleaned up.

Another useful ward is to take four iron nails—they have to be iron—and bury them at the four corners of the property. As you're doing so, imagine a massive canopy, like a big top circus tent, coming into place over the building. The iron deflects magick and defends the area.

You could also make a Witch bottle. These are fun. A Witch bottle is a countermagickal device or trap that draws negativity toward it and away from the area being protected. To make a Witch bottle, you must first get an old glass bottle or jar with a tight, waterproof lid. Collect broken glass, rusty nails, bent staples, whatever—they just need to be nasty, sharp things. Place them in the bottle along with some of your own urine. (Yes, collect some pee, and pour it in there. To avoid any chance of injury or splashing, don't have to pee right into the bottle.) Don't put any hair or fingernail clippings in the bottle. Only use urine—stuff your body is getting rid of. Once all that nasty stuff is sealed in the little bottle, bury it somewhere *away* from your property, preferably near running water or a crossroads. Negativity directed toward you will be drawn toward the negativity in the bottle and away from you.

Personal Shields

There are essentially two types of personal shields: physical and manifest. A physical shield is an amulet or talisman carried or worn by a person. That pentagram necklace you wear is a physical shield, for example. They can be charged, consecrated, and empowered before wearing if you so desire. Manifest shields are magickally created by the individual. Very empathetically aware—and thus vulnerable—Witches often create them before entering difficult situations, such as meeting an aggressive or hostile person, dealing with a "psychic vampire" or energy leech, or going to the shopping mall on Black Friday.

Here's an example of a simple manifest shield. Start by visualizing a cone of power extending around and above you. Now change the cone into a sphere of shimmering silvery-blue light that totally encompasses you. Now "solidify" it in your mind with the mirrored surface on the outside. Negative energies or attacks will rebound off the surface and return to the attacker. With a little practice, creating manifest shields like this can become as easy as a thought, and they will become stronger as your experience, proficiency, and confidence grow. Manifest shields can also be tailored, like wards, to defend against specific assaults.

Witch Wars

In today's Pagan society you have a wide range of people with different temperaments and goals, and they don't always see eye to eye. Disagreements lead to hostility, silly accusations are posted on social media, and suddenly you have a "Witch war" on your hands. Witch wars are an unfortunate—and thankfully rare—occurrence in a magickally aware and presumably supportive community. A coven member is publicly chastised, for example, suffers an emotional breakdown, and starts bad-mouthing the other coven members. Other people hear the rumors, word spreads, emails are sent, and it goes from there. Egos flare, accusations are made, and before you know it, there's a Witch war going on.

In a worst-case scenario, a vindictive Witch starts casting spells against those they consider their enemies, which triggers a chain reaction within the local Craft community. Victims of a magickal attack might find themselves disoriented or unable to focus, getting into fights with loved ones for no reason or behaving irrationally at work. This is where defensive magick would come into play. If magick is used in a Witch war, the best course of action is to recognize the source of the problem and set up wards against future attacks. If you find yourself drawn into a Witch war, for any reason, it is best to never take the offensive. Those who use magick to attack others are in direct violation of the rede and will soon find a karmic debt waiting to be repaid. They also run the risk of being outcast themselves. Remember, the Threefold Law does not take sides. For those on the defensive, all you really need is to keep a level head about you, set up whatever wards or manifest any shields you feel are necessary, and wait for it to blow over. Some Witches might urge you to take "retaliatory justice" and cast spells of entrapment against the aggressors, but such actions are not recommended. In the matter of magickal attacks, the best offense is a good defense. Thankfully Witch wars are quite rare, nonviolent occurrences. They're usually more of a war of words, egos, and posturing than anything else. While they almost never spill over into the mundane world, they can be psychically damaging to all involved. The easiest way to avoid a Witch war is to simply not get involved in one. Don't believe everything you hear, and don't get drawn into taking sides. Let the pouty Witches have their spat; it'll likely blow over in a couple of weeks.

If friendships are jeopardized in such occurrences, they're at least a good way to determine who your real friends are and who you can rely on both magickally and socially.

Lesson 38: Study Prompts and Questions

Do I Need Protecting?
- List a few of the hazards—magickal and mundane—that a modern Witch might occasionally face.
- Name a few deities one might call upon for protection.

Protection Spells
- Give an example of a house blessing. Write an original one if you like.
- Offer examples of two other types of protective spells and how they could be used.

Wards
- Explain the difference between a ward and a protective spell.
- Give three examples of where a ward might be used.
- Think of a situation where you might use a ward, and describe how you would create and empower it.

Personal Shields
- What is the difference between physical and manifest shields?
- How do personal shields differ from protection spells?
- Explain the process used in creating a simple manifest shield.

Witch Wars
- Why do you think some Witches would act against their covens or violate the rede or the Ardanes?
- Describe what you think is the best course of action if you feel you are the victim of a magickal or psychic attack.

Lesson 38: Recommended Reading
- *Protection and Reversal Magick: A Witch's Defense Manual* by Jason Miller
- *The Truth about Witchcraft Today* by Scott Cunningham

LESSON 39
The Future of the Craft

We've come a long way since our ancestors wondered about the movement of the stars and experimented with herbs and such. And we've come a long way since so many people were tortured or killed for the alleged crime of Witchcraft. And we've come a long way since you started reading this book! Now, as we close out Wicca 102, we'll take a look at where Witchcraft is going—now and tomorrow.

Out of the Broom Closet

Today, as we stand on the brink of tomorrow, we need to reexamine where history has brought us. We should never forget the horrible price that so many paid for the desire to simply live. Many were persecuted for their beliefs or lifestyles; in some parts of the world, this is true even today. But now, in the twenty-first century and moving forward, the world is gradually changing. The New Age fascination of the 1970s, '80s, and '90s brought people closer to concepts like herbalism, reincarnation, crystal magick, astral travel, and alternate forms of spirituality, and with more and more television shows and movies featuring Witches as regular characters, the outlandish notion that Witches are "ordinary people" seems a little more normal every day.

Still, precautions must be taken. Newspapers occasionally report incidents such as a young girl who wore a pentagram to school and was expelled for hexing a teacher, parents whose children were taken from them under accusations of evil Witchcraft and devil worship, and people who lost their jobs because their coworkers didn't agree with their religious beliefs.

What is a modern Witch to do? Do the Ardanes and the rede still apply or don't they? How should we act? What if we're confronted about our beliefs? Sometimes keeping a low profile is necessary for survival. What you do when you go to church—however you envision your church—is your business and yours alone.

But if a friend should happen to ask about that funny star you wear or why the kids are talking about esbats and goddesses and athames, don't be secretive. After centuries of bad press, many people still have gross misconceptions about the Craft. Too many people still believe that Witchcraft is synonymous with evil and devil worship, and the only way to change this is to educate them on the true nature of the Craft.

Here's a quote from a small-business management newsletter that I find applicable:

> *Some bosses make a practice of holding back information, telling employees only the minimum facts they need to do their job. That's a serious mistake, because ignorance of the facts causes gossip, misunderstandings and needless hostility. The smartest policy is to tell employees everything you can, keep them so well supplied with correct information that rumors don't have a chance to get a foothold. Intelligent managers know that when information stops, rumors start.*[112]

This attitude can well be applied to Witchcraft. For centuries people have been told that Witchcraft is evil and mysterious, and as long as Witches keep the Craft a secret, those people will keep on believing it. They'll have no reason to think otherwise—especially if you avoid the question or act in a shady or suspicious manner. With that knowledge, there are two factors to consider regarding how you might present the Craft to others. First, do you feel safe sharing it with others, or does the idea rub you the wrong way? Second, what are your surroundings like? If you live in an area where people might be more amiable to "alternate faiths," by all means share and share well. If you live in a more conservative area, it might be wise to keep your pentagram safely tucked away under your shirt. Some people simply refuse to accept new ideas, no matter how much beneficial information you are willing to provide.

Books, Magazines, Websites, and Social Media

Speaking of information, one should be aware of misinformation. There are literally hundreds of books, movies, and websites available that make ludicrous claims regarding Witches and the Craft. When looking for information on the Craft, be sure to avoid the "Witch-crap" titles. Any book that claims to teach you absolutely everything about Witchcraft in ninety-eight pages is probably crap. A book that tells you how to become filthy rich overnight using spells is probably crap. A movie that describes Witches as

---

112. "Soundings #8," 2.

lesbian servants of Lucifer is definitely crap. "Learn how to become a warlock today, and you'll grow a giant penis!" Uh-huh, sure.

Here's an easy rule of thumb when choosing a source on Witchcraft. If you are unfamiliar with the author, do a little research. See what else the author has written; read some reviews online.

Do a quick web search for Witchcraft-related sites or blogs, and you will find that they generally fall into one of four categories: those written by legitimate Witches to promote the Craft; those written by historians to put the Craft into a historical, theological context; those written by religious fanatics and naysayers who deride the Craft as a tool of evil; and those written by wannabe Pagans who make vast, outlandish claims about the Craft and their own magickal prowess. As with books and magazines, be selective, and don't believe everything you read.

Pagan Festivals, Conferences, and Pagan Pride Days

Thirty, even twenty years ago, if you tried to join a coven, you might have been met with secrecy and suspicion, and you would have assumed that was just the way it was "supposed to be." In some covens, that is still the case today. In general, however, the attitude is changing. You may find a whole new perspective and be welcomed into open classes, parties, meetings, and even a minor ritual or two. Witches of old had to be more secretive to avoid persecution, but today's Pagan society is different. This is thanks—in no small part—to the growth and popularity of Pagan conferences and festivals.

A conference can be anything from an evening lecture on a college campus to a weekend or weeklong event with speakers, workshops, rituals, vendors, and concerts. Pagan conferences offer the attendees an opportunity to meet others of a like mind, attend workshops and discussions on a variety of topics related to Paganism, and meet authors or celebrities.

Pagan Pride Day festivals are a much smaller but no less vital affair. Pagan Pride Day, or PPD, is an international organization that supports one- or two-day festivals, usually outside at a local public park, where members of different Pagan communities within a city or region can meet. The other purpose of PPD is outreach. It is written into the PPD charter that festivals under the PPD banner should be open to the public so everyone can encounter the Craft and meet Witches and Wiccans local to them. Another function of PPD is charity. The usual price of admission is a food donation to a local homeless shelter or food bank.

A modern Pagan festival is a meeting of many people—Witches, Druids, ceremonial magicians, animists, and more—that usually takes place in a three- to five-day camping environment. There are classes, workshops, open rituals, merchants, drum circles, sing-alongs, kids' activities, and a feeling of togetherness that would have been impossible only fifty years ago. A modern festival welcomes people from dozens of different paths and traditions to grow and learn from each other. Like conferences, Pagan festivals allow Pagans to be themselves, but here they can create self-governing microcommunities for the duration of the event.

There used to be some concern, though, over whether or not such festivals were really healthy for the Craft. One side claimed that they provided an excellent forum for growth and learning and that the "clan" feeling one gets is vital to the renaissance of the Craft.

The opposing view, mostly from older, more established traditions, was that a melting-pot environment would only weaken the power of the Craft. They believed that too many people from too many different traditions could not hope to work together with any focused result. With the availability of so many open gatherings, fewer people are willing to work on developing a coven identity, and as a result, "the coven is losing its magick," as Witchcraft author Margot Adler wrote.[113]

Many feel, however, that the individual rewards of a festival or communal outdoor gathering outweigh the risks of magickal "bleaching." As Adler also wrote:

> *To go out walking and not have the fears of ravenous glances, cat-calls, come-ons or other unasked-for advances. To feel the wind, sun, air and water on my naked body without feeling vulnerable to physical attack. To be able to sing and chant loudly with the power of my lungs. To dance and move with the strength of all the muscles of my body. To feel that I can be whoever I am with total acceptance and unselfconsciousness—and to have that feel as natural as breathing!*[114]

That is what many Witches look for in modern festivals. They don't look forward to just the workshops and rituals and merchants but the reaffirmation of self as a vital and dynamic part of nature, the world, and the goddess.

---

113. Adler, *Drawing Down the Moon*, 429.
114. Adler, *Drawing Down the Moon*, 427.

Event Etiquette

If you do decide to attend a Pagan festival, there are, of course, a few ground rules to observe. Think of a self-governing city of five hundred to two thousand people composed entirely of Witches and Pagans. As with any "sudden community," there are guidelines to follow:

- Tolerance and respect are the order of the day. As trite as it sounds, treat others the way you'd want them to treat you.
- Don't be rude or abusive; there's no need for it.
- If you aren't sure of someone's preferred pronouns, it's all right to ask. Simply say, "What are your preferred pronouns?" You can then show them the respect of using the correct pronouns.
- Don't assume that everyone you see wishes to be hugged. Simply ask them if they hug or open your arms as an invitation. If you're rejected, no big deal.
- If you're camping in a tent, bring a rake to clear the ground before you set up your tent. You'll thank me at 3:19 a.m.
- If someone is skyclad, don't gawk. Some large outdoor festivals allow nudity, some don't. It's a personal choice to be skyclad or partially so. Respect people's identity.
- Don't take pictures without asking first. This applies everywhere.
- Don't bring a screaming toddler to a lecture. Another no-brainer, really. Infants can't always express themselves discreetly, which isn't their fault, and you may have to work around that.
- If you have to leave a talk, leave quietly. No big fuss. People will understand.
- Merchants really don't appreciate haggling. If an item has a sticker on it saying twenty-nine dollars, and you think it's worth less, it still costs twenty-nine dollars.
- If the organizers need volunteers, raise your hand. Big events are almost always shorthanded, and every volunteer is very much appreciated.
- If you're attending a workshop, bring your own pen and paper to write on. Really, it's wise to carry a notebook—or some sort of recording device, if they allow that—to any lecture or workshop you attend. And a pen.

- If there's a meal plan offered, bring your own plate, cup, and silverware. The event planners don't always know how many they might need. A lot of historical reenactment groups do this, and it's just a good idea. Plus, it saves a ton of waste.
- If there's a ritual bonfire, it's not a trash can. There's probably a stack of wood that goes in the fire, which may or may not have been consecrated beforehand. Paper cups and cigarette butts don't belong in it.
- If there's a drum circle going on and you see an unattended drum just sitting there, don't assume it's free to play. Many people's drums are as sacred to them as their chalice and athame.
- You might be getting back to nature, but you still need to bathe. No, really. Even Pagans have noses.
- Drink plenty of water. Wear sunscreen—and hard-soled shoes. Trust me.
- Be respectful of the land, and try to leave it cleaner than it was when you arrived.
- Don't be alarmed if you see people in flamboyant or eccentric garb— or none at all. Don't stare, and treat everyone, including yourself, with respect both physically and spiritually.
- Remember that for many people this isn't just a vacation. It's a spiritual retreat and an affirmation of self.

Witchcraft Now and Tomorrow

What does the future hold for today's Witches? Where are we going? If the events of yesterday and today are any indication of the evolution of the Craft, it is developing into a vibrant, powerful force.

The grip of monotheism on Western consciousness is weakening as more and more alternative forms of spirituality enter the mainstream. With a growing interest in herbal and homeopathic healing and therapy and an increased awareness of personal spirituality, the world becomes an easier place for a Witch to live just about every day.

The struggle is by no means over yet, though; centuries of bad press and suspicion are not buried overnight, and public opinion is an ornery beast. It is one not easily subdued. We will probably not—in our lifetimes, at least—see the Craft as widely accepted as Christianity, and remember, it took five hundred years for Christianity to develop into a major world power. Of course, becoming a major world power is not the goal of the Craft and never was.

German philosopher Arthur Schopenhauer once said, "To truth only a brief celebration of victory is allowed between the two long periods during which it is condemned as paradoxical, or disparaged as trivial," which has been simplified to the following well-known phrase: "All truths go through three stages. First, they are ridiculed. Then, they are violently opposed. Finally, they are accepted as being self-evident."[115]

All Witches want is to be accepted as equals and to be able to live and worship openly and without fear. The belief that Earth is a living, viable organism and that all living things are part of an interconnected whole is really a simple and ancient ideal, and it is one that we strive to nurture and encourage for the good of all living things.

For Witches everywhere, the fight against persecution and suspicion—the fight for recognition—is not yet won, but an age of enlightenment draws closer with every new day.

Use your magick and your talents to the best of your ability. Work with one another, and love, honour, and respect each other, and you'll be amazed at what you can accomplish!

Lesson 39: Study Prompts and Questions

Out of the Broom Closet

- Do you feel that modern Witchcraft is gaining in acceptance and recognition? Why or why not?
- Do you feel comfortable with the idea of sharing your spirituality with others? Explain.

Pagan Festivals, Conferences, and Pagan Pride Days

- What Pagan events have you heard about? Which one(s) have you attended?
- If you have attended a Pagan festival, briefly describe the experience and how it affected you.
- Do you feel that multifaith festivals are weakening our magickal focus and intent, or are they beneficial to the Craft? Explain and justify.

---

115. Schopenhauer, *The World as Will and Representation*, xvii.

Witchcraft Now and Tomorrow

- Offer examples, either positive or negative, that you may have seen that demonstrate an increased public awareness of Witchcraft.
- "All truths go through three stages. First, they are ridiculed. Then, they are violently opposed. Finally, they are accepted as being self-evident." Analyze this pattern as it applies to the history of the Craft and offer examples.
- Do you feel that the rede or the Ardanes are valid in today's covens? Justify your conclusion.

Lesson 39: Recommended Reading

- *Drawing Down the Moon: Witches, Druids, Goddess-Worshippers, and Other Pagans in America Today* by Margot Adler
- *Witchcraft Today—60 Years On* edited by Trevor Greenfield

APPENDIX 1
Teacher's Resource Material

If you are using these lessons in a classroom environment for a group of students, here are some optional activities that you may find useful. They were designed to urge the students to apply critical thinking or creativity to their studies and deepen their understanding of the subject matter. Not every lesson was designed with additional activities, but you may use them as you wish.

Wicca 101: The History, Philosophy, and Ethics of Witchcraft

Lesson 2:
The History of the Craft: From the Birth of Religion to the Ancient Empires
Activity
Research and write an essay about one of the facets of early religion described in this lesson. Discuss society, geography, names, and forms of worship.

Lesson 3:
The History of the Craft: The Dark Ages and the Inquisition
Classroom Module
Hold a mock trial. Appoint students as judges, inquisitors, and accused Witches. Take notes of how the trial unfolds and discuss how the class reacted to the trial and the judgment.

Lesson 5:
Facets of Spirituality and Divinity
Classroom Module 1
Create a "divine debate team." Argue the benefits and failings of each aspect discussed in this lesson.

Classroom Module 2

Discuss these philosophies and give examples of each.

- Monotheism: There is only one god—one divine creator—who governs over all. Transcendent or immanent, all began with the One.
- Polytheism: Different aspects of life are governed by different deities. In Hawaiʻi, for example, Pele is the goddess of volcanoes, but she does not govern animals; they are the domain of Kamapuaʻa, the beast god, who is seen as a large white pig.
- Animism: Every aspect of nature, seen and unseen, is possessed of an individual spirit. An animist looks at a spiral of dust and twigs caught in a small windstorm. "Look," they say, "the wind spirits are active today!"
- Western pantheism: All the gods are worthy of respect and honour. It doesn't matter if it's Jehovah, Baphomet, Zeus, Pele, Venus, or Amaterasu; gods are gods, and they deserve equal praise. This could also be compared to henotheism, discussed in lesson 3.
- Eastern pantheism: All that we know is an expression of the ultimate mystery. "Just as we are words in the song of God," I once told a friend, "so is the rainbow like the dreaming of the storm."

Lesson 6:
The Many Faces of the Goddess

Activity

Write a report on any chosen goddess. Include her culture, birth, and history, and describe the ways in which she was (or is) traditionally worshipped.

Classroom Module

Pick a historical or literary figure, and discuss which goddesses were guiding them at different times during their life. (You know the Christian parable about footprints in the sand? This exercise is like that but with different goddesses stepping in as needed.)

Lesson 7:
The Many Faces of the God

Activity

Write a report on any chosen god. Include his culture, birth, and history, and describe the ways in which he was (or is) traditionally worshipped.

Lesson 8:
Charges of the Goddess and the God
Activity
Write an original charge to a goddess or god of your choice.

Lesson 9:
The Wheel of the Year and the Eight Sabbats
Activity
Pick a season and examine various customs or folkways associated with that season.

Lesson 10:
The Esbats and Other Lunar Mysteries
Activity
Keep a journal with you. For one full month, be aware of the moon's phases, and write how the phases affect your life magickally and materially.

Lesson 11:
Principles of Wiccan Belief
Classroom Module
In previous lessons, we discussed the differences in perspectives between Wicca and the Old Craft. Debate the message of the Fourteen Principles of Wiccan Belief as it relates to either side.

Lesson 12:
The Wiccan Rede, Ethics, and the Magickal Life
Classroom Module
Let the students recount ethical situations they have encountered. Debate the best course of action using the Craft's view of ethics.

Lesson 14:
Witchcraft and Sacred Sex
Activity
Research and write a brief essay on one of these topics: the *Kama Sutra*, tantric sex, or holistic sensuality. Explain how they relate to Craft philosophy, and offer examples of practice or principle.

Lesson 15:
Life, Death, and Beyond
Activity

Research another culture's concept of the afterlife, and write a brief essay about it.

Lesson 16:
The Web, the Wheel, and the Way
Activity

The very first study question in Wicca 101 was: "What does the word *Witch* mean to you?" Now that you've completed this lesson, answer it again.

Wicca 102: Inside the Coven, the Meaning of Ritual, and Magickal Theory

Lesson 18:
The Laws of the Craft

This lesson is shorter than most, but if you are using it in a classroom teaching environment, the discussions may go on for a while.

Classroom Module

Debate the following situations. Try to determine what the most beneficial course of action would be using the Ardanes as your guide.

- Two coven members are getting divorced. Both want to attend the Yule sabbat, but neither wants the other to attend. How and what should the elders decide?
- A coven member has threatened the maiden with blackmail if she does not sleep with him. He has threatened to expose her at work, which could jeopardize her career. What should she or the coven as a whole do?
- A young coven member gets permission to invite his friend to attend an esbat. The friend tells her parents about the coven, and they, in turn, call the police to report satanic activities at the covenstead. Was the young Witch or the friend acting in the coven's best interests? What should be done when—or if—the police arrive?
- The High Priest is engaged to be married. Unfortunately the coven feels that his fiancée wants him to choose between the Craft and marriage.

She denies this, but her actions say otherwise. What and how should the elders decide?

Lesson 19:
Elements and Correspondences
Classroom Module

We know that the elemental positions are based on the perceptions of Western European and British geography. Get a large wall-sized atlas, and let each student show on the atlas where they were born. Would the elemental positions be different?

Lesson 20:
Magickal Signs and Symbols
Activity

Research five more magickal symbols than the ones provided in this lesson, and provide an illustration, definition, and magickal significance for each.

Lesson 21:
The Tools of the Craft
Class Module

Debate the legitimacy of "traditional" Witch's tools as perceived by modern media.

- Is the athame a ritual tool or weapon?
- Is the black, pointy hat an icon of evil or a cone of power?

Suggest other tools and their meanings.

Lesson 23:
The Four Cornerstones of Magick
Classroom Module

Discuss with the class how these other scenarios could benefit from the application of the concepts of to know, to will, to believe, and to keep silent.

- You want to convince your boss to adopt your new marketing strategy to sell a product.
- You are determined to overcome your fear of spiders.
- You are trying to come to grips with the fact that you have a gambling addiction and figure out how to handle it.

Lesson 24:
The Many Faces of Magick
Classroom Module

Discuss which form of magick applies to the following situations:

- A Witch performs a spell to summon her departed grandmother's spirit into ritual.
- A Witch agrees to a blind date and chooses to enhance his appeal with magick.
- Fearing attacks from a vindictive ex-spouse, a Witch places protective magick around her house.
- During a full moon esbat, a young Witch calls down Hecate to make the ritual more powerful.
- The coven performs a group ritual to help heal a young Witch who was overwhelmed by Hecate; she'd bitten off more than she could chew.

Lesson 25:
Magick and Responsibility
Activity

Chances are you've seen public service announcements on television or social media where celebrities talk about safety, teenagers and drugs, and so on. Write and/or perform an imaginary PSA about the safe use of magick.

Lesson 27:
Ritual Procedure: Setting the Stage
Activity

Different styles of garb were discussed in the lesson. You don't have to copy anyone else's garb; try to create your own. Describe or sketch the garb you would like to wear.

Lesson 30:
Ritual Procedure: Closing the Ritual
Activity

Attend or observe a ceremonial ritual from another faith. Write a comparison between that and a Craft ritual.

The Ritual in Review

This is a review of the esbat procedure from lessons 27 to 30 that is designed for an interactive classroom setting. It is entirely optional. If you feel that the class does not need it, proceed to the next lesson. The study questions at the end of this section, however, are highly recommended.

Part 1: Setting the Stage

- Many Witches and covens keep a special altar or temple area reserved for magickal working. The magickal library and ritual supplies are often kept there. Discuss with the class why a special, reserved area is important.
- Before ritual, the temple area is prepared, the altar is set, and incense is lit. Challenge the class to define the uses of each item on the altar and the significance of incense and appropriate music.
- Various forms of ritual wear were discussed in the lesson. Invite students to describe their ideal ritual garb and the significance behind the components.

Part 2: Erecting the Temple

- Prior to ritual, the coven observed a period of attunement, or quiet time. Discuss with the students the importance of this period of meditation.
- The ritual begins with the maiden and summoner anointing and cleansing the High Priestess (HPS) and High Priest (HP) with oils and incense. Allow the students to discuss the significance of this procedure.
- The HPS and HP wait while the maiden and summoner repeat the process of anointing and cleansing for participants as they enter ritual space. Discuss the meaning of this and the significance of entering from the east.
- After everyone has entered the circle, the area is cleansed and purified with salt and water and air and fire. Again, discuss the significance of these actions. Why is it not purified before people enter?
- The HP then walks the circle perimeter deosil with a sword to cast the sacred circle. Allow the class to discuss what this means.
- The elements are then invoked in a deosil pattern starting with east. Invite the students to explain the meaning of the elements and the significance of the pattern in which they are invoked.

- Now the HPS invokes the goddess, and the HP invokes the god. Discuss the importance of this invocation, and allow the students to debate which deities would be appropriate at various sabbats and esbats.

Part 3: *Working in Ritual*

- The "body" of the ritual begins with a statement of purpose, during which the meaning of the ritual is explained and coven business is discussed. Allow the students to explain the significance of the statement of purpose.
- During the esbat, there was an interruption involving Wyvern, who had to answer Laughing Tree's challenge. Allow the students to debate the implication of the challenge and the significance of both the question and the answer.
- A Witch's mill was performed using a rhyming chant to build a power-base of energy. Discuss with the students how words can be transformed into energy and from energy into magick. Allow the students to explain how a chant can be used.
- After the magickal workings, the coven members took time to ground and center. Discuss with the students the significance of this action and its effect.
- A stone was charged to be used by someone not present at the ritual. Allow the students to explain how magick can be put "into" something.
- OakBranch suggested sending healing to a stranger, but his offer was declined. Discuss the importance of getting permission before any magickal work.

Part 4: *Closing the Ritual*

- Next the HPS and HP performed the hieros gamos. Engage the class in a discussion of the significance of this act and its origins.
- The coven members participated in the ceremony of cakes and ale. Discuss the significance of the ceremony, and allow the students to suggest different forms of "cakes" and "ale."
- The HPS and HP then bid farewell to the deities, snuffing out their candles in the process. Discuss the importance of treating gods with honour and respect.

- Following the departure of the deities, the elements were dismissed. Discuss the significance of allowing the elements to depart. Let students debate whether this should be performed deosil or widdershins.
- The HP then uses the sword to take down the circle. Discuss the meaning of this action and the direction used.
- Following the ritual, it is important to follow through with what was performed in ritual. Allow the students to discuss the significance of "acting in accord."

Part 5: Rituals Formal and Informal

This was a formal ritual, so what's in an informal ritual? What can be modified or omitted? Some covens keep the ritual area consecrated at all times, so that does not need to be repeated. The statement of purpose can be modified or omitted, as can the cleansing and the ceremony of cakes and ale. The only parts that are of prime importance are the invocations and dismissals and the magickal working itself.

If time is short, sections can, of course, overlap. For example, the hieros gamos and the ceremony of cakes and ale can be concurrent assuming, of course, that they do not involve the same chalice.

If a Witch is working solitary, naturally they do everything, from consecration to dismissal, themselves. Since this is a private ceremony, the Witch can modify the ritual as they see fit as long as neither the significance nor the meaning are compromised.

Study Questions Part 1: Ritual Procedure

- Arrange these ritual components in the correct order and identify who is responsible for performing each task.

Task	Order	Performed By
Invoke east	_____	_____
Anoint with oil	_____	_____
Hieros gamos	_____	_____
Cast circle with sword	_____	_____
Walk deosil into circle	_____	_____
Grounding and centering	_____	_____

Task	Order	Performed By
Bid farewell to the goddess		
Ceremony of cakes and ale		
Release the circle		
Invoke north		
Bid farewell to the god		
Attunement		
Cleanse with incense		
Dismiss west		
Set the altar		
Welcome the god		
Salt and water consecration		
Dismiss north		
Statement of purpose		
Magickal working		
Invoke south		
Dismiss south		
Dimiss east		
Welcome the goddess		
Invoke west		
Fire and air consecration		
Get into garb		

- List four possible magickal workings that could be performed within ritual.
- If your group was pressed for time while performing a ritual, what modifications do you think would be appropriate?

Study Questions Part 2: Write a Ritual
- Create a ritual of your own. Specify whether it is an esbat, sabbat, or private ceremony. Include full invocations for the elements and the goddess and the god as well as consecrations. The inclusion of magickal workings within ritual is optional. Use as many pages as necessary.

Lesson 34:
Working with Herbs and Plants
Classroom Module 1

Bring some everyday leaves to class. Give them descriptive names of your own, and see if other people can identify them using only the names you created.

Classroom Module 2

Using the list provided in this lesson, create an original herbal blend of your own, and explain its use or application.

Lesson 37:
The Art of Spellcasting
Classroom Module

Take a moment to review the definition of a spell provided at the beginning of lesson 36, and compare it with the performance of both simple and complex spells.

Lesson 38:
Wards, Shields, and Protection
Classroom Module

Invite the students to suggest other simple house blessings or forms of personal protective magick.

Lesson 39:
The Future of the Craft
Activity

Do you think a nature-oriented religion could survive in space? Could you hold esbats on the moon or sabbats in a colony on Mars? Explain.

APPENDIX 2
Final Exams

This appendix includes a final exam for Wicca 101 and Wicca 102. Each test is divided into six parts: multiple choice, true or false, fill in the blanks, question and answer, a glossary of terms, and essay questions. The Wicca 102 exam will also include additional exercises. Answers for the tests can be found at the end of the appendix.

Wicca 101

Welcome to the final exam in Wicca 101. Allow approximately ninety minutes for the full test.

Part 1: Multiple Choice

While there may appear to be more than one correct answer, choose the one you feel is most accurate.

1. Religion and worship exist because: _____
    (a) they offer humans a way of communicating with the gods.
    (b) the gods demand obedience.
    (c) they establish a relationship between humans and the mysteries of life.
    (d) they seemed like a good idea at the time.

2. Immanent divinity is: _____
    (a) where the gods are an integral part of the world.
    (b) where the gods rule from a distance.
    (c) where the gods play Skee-Ball with the world.
    (d) none of the above

3. Monotheism is the belief that: _____
    (a) there are many gods who govern different aspects of life.
    (b) there is only one god and one goddess.
    (c) there is only one deity who governs all things.
    (d) God has a very contagious disease.

4. Western pantheism is the belief that: _____
    (a) everything we know comes from God.
    (b) all deific pantheons exist and should be honoured.
    (c) life is an extension of a transcendent deity.
    (d) all life originated in a frying pan.

5. Creation myths exist because: _____
    (a) some people need more than just a scientific analysis of life.
    (b) early humans wanted a spiritual explanation for their origin.
    (c) people want to "flesh out" the legends of the gods.
    (d) the idea of a stork carrying a baby planet just seemed too hokey.

6. The deity origin myth in which he or she is born from fire is called: _____
    (a) astral.
    (b) parthenogenic.
    (c) elemental.
    (d) a three-alarm warning in the maternity ward.

7. Thealogy, as opposed to theology, is: _____
    (a) the study of the New Testament.
    (b) the study of the whole of spirituality.
    (c) the study of goddesses.
    (d) bad spelling.

8. The Earth Mother is often visualized as: _____
    (a) a large, green-haired pregnant woman.
    (b) a tree with many breasts.
    (c) the cynosure of feminist divinity.
    (d) a really mean mother.

9. The three aspects of the Triple Goddess are: _____
    (a) Maiden, Mother, and Crone.
    (b) Maiden, Mother, and Warrior.
    (c) Maiden, Moon, and Crone.
    (d) Vanilla, Chocolate, and Strawberry.

10. The Oak and Holly Kings represent: _____
    (a) Yule and Litha.
    (b) rivals for the goddess's affection.
    (c) the dueling forces of summer and winter.
    (d) two cards in the tarot deck.

11. The Horned God is said to have no father because: _____
    (a) he is a product of parthenogenic birth.
    (b) he slew his own father at Litha.
    (c) he is his own father.
    (d) he couldn't find his birth certificate.

12. The Charge of the Goddess is: _____
    (a) a way of communicating with the deity.
    (b) a combination of prayer, invocation, and divine promise.
    (c) a poem devoted to the goddess.
    (d) her credit card bill.

13. Early humans molded clay images of goddesses because: _____
    (a) they wanted to see what they looked like.
    (b) they wanted an artifact for ritual.
    (c) they wanted to create a physical representation of the Divine.
    (d) they really wanted a Chia Pet.

14. The Fourteen Principles of Wiccan Belief were created because: _____
    (a) there was a need to create a foundation for new traditions.
    (b) there was a need to reestablish a link with the old path.
    (c) there was a need to justify American Witchcraft as a valid faith.
    (d) there was a need to establish a basic code for modern Wicca.

15. Sacred sexuality is: _____
    (a) sex in ritual.
    (b) the divine aspect of sensuality.
    (c) harnessing sexual energy for magickal means.
    (d) Wiccan orgies.

16. Why was the King James Version of the Bible commissioned? _____
    (a) The authors disagreed with the original version.
    (b) The authors wanted to rewrite the book in English.
    (c) The authors wanted to justify their political agenda.
    (d) The authors thought it would be a valid use of the Gutenberg press.

17. The Inquisition was started because: _____
    (a) the pope wanted a reason to punish non-Christians.
    (b) it was a way of putting the "fear of God" into people.
    (c) there were just too many people to convert them all.
    (d) it was thought that any act against the church was an act of treason.

18. In what way did the anti-Witchcraft laws change in the 1700s? _____
    (a) Witchcraft laws were repealed in England.
    (b) Witches were seen as common criminals and charlatans.
    (c) Witches were tried in a regular court, not the Inquisition.
    (d) Witches were temporarily turned into newts.

19. Margaret Murray theorized that modern Witchcraft was: _____
    (a) derived from ancient spiritual customs.
    (b) invented by Gerald Gardner.
    (c) inspired by the Druids and shamans.
    (d) invented by Satan to fool good Christians.

20. Dorothy Clutterbuck was: _____
    (a) hanged in Salem in 1692.
    (b) a popular Wiccan author.
    (c) Gerald Gardner's High Priestess.
    (d) the name of a Witch's familiar in the 1500s.

Part 2: True or False

_____ 1. Gerald Gardner invented the world *Wicce*.

_____ 2. Kali is the Hindu goddess of death and rebirth.

_____ 3. Polytheism is the belief that one god can be worshipped in many different ways.

_____ 4. Amaterasu is a principal Japanese sun god.

_____ 5. The Craft demands that you abandon all other faiths.

_____ 6. The full moon is a representation of the Mother Goddess.

_____ 7. The full moon in February is known as the chaste moon.

_____ 8. A coven is a magickal family or worship group.

_____ 9. The King James Bible was written in 1198.

_____ 10. Witches should not sell love potions for profit.

_____ 11. Hecate is the Greek goddess of midnight.

_____ 12. Witches believe that good Witches reincarnate and bad Witches don't.

_____ 13. Triskaidekaphobia is the fear of thirteen.

_____ 14. In the Wiccan creation myth, the god started out female.

_____ 15. Gardnerian is the oldest Wiccan tradition.

_____ 16. All Wiccans are vegetarians.

_____ 17. The *Malleus Maleficarum* was used to condemn Witches.

_____ 18. *Wyrd* is another word for *magick*.

_____ 19. The Wiccan Rede is the law of the Witches.

_____ 20. If you kiss a Witch on the full moon, you'll turn into one (a Witch, not a full moon).

Part 3: Fill in the Blanks

1. Bide the _____ law ye must,
   In _____ love and perfect _____.
   Eight words the Wiccan _____ fulfill;
   An harm ye _____, do what ye _____
   Lest in _____-_____ it be,
   Ever mind the Rule of _____:
   What ye _____ out comes back to thee.
   _____ this with _____ and heart,
   And _____ ye meet and merry ye _____.

2. A Witch is a person of any _____ who follows an ancient
   _____-oriented _____. Witches view the planet as
   a _____, and honour her with seasonal celebrations known as
   _____.

3. The eight sabbats:
   _____, on October 31, is the start of the _____ of the Year.
   Ostara, held on _____, is known as _____ by the Christian church.
   The Summer Solstice, held on _____, is also called _____.
   Imbolc, also called _____ or _____, is on _____.
   Yule, observed on _____, is also called the _____.
   Mabon, or the _____ _____, is held on _____.
   Lughnassadh, a harvest _____, is held on the _____ of August.
   The sabbat held around May 1 is _____.

4. In 1486 Heinrich Kraemer and James Sprenger wrote the _____
   _____. The book gave evidence and testimony that Witches worshipped
   _____ and helped to fuel the anti-Witchcraft hysteria.

5. Matthew Hopkins was a self-appointed _____ _____ who
   worked in England in the 1600s.

Part 4: Question and Answer

1) How do esbats differ from sabbats?
2) What did Thomas Aquinas propose?
3) Explain the legend of the Oak and Holly Kings.
4) Name four Maiden Goddesses and list the aspects of life they govern.
5) Name four Mother Goddesses and list the aspects of life they govern.
6) Name four Crone Goddesses and list the aspects of life they govern.
7) Name four god archetypes and briefly describe each one.
8) How do Wiccans differ from Witches?
9) What is a blue moon? Why is it important?
10) Briefly explain the concept of the *wyrd*.
11) Explain the difference between Eastern and Western pantheism.

Part 5: A Witch's Dictionary

Define the following words or phrases:

- Anthropomorphic birth
- Astral birth
- Burning Times
- Charge of the Goddess
- Goddess
- Knights Templar
- Magick
- Pagan
- Parthenogenic birth
- Priest
- Priestess
- Sabbats
- Skyclad
- Threefold Law
- Wiccan
- Witch

Part 6: Essay Questions

1) Explain the cycle of the sabbats as they relate to the goddess and the god.
2) Explain why the Inquisition was created and how it affected people's notions about Witchcraft.
3) Define the Witch's view of ethics as they relate to modern-day worship.
4) Write your feelings about Witchcraft as a whole.

Wicca 102

Welcome to the final exam in Wicca 102. Allow approximately two to three hours for the full test. The fact that you are taking this test means that you have completed a yearlong study of Witchcraft and are (hopefully) close to receiving your first-degree initiation. Congratulations!

Part 1: Multiple Choice

While there may appear to be more than one correct answer to many questions, choose the one that you feel is the most accurate.

1. What was the original purpose of a coven? _____
    (a) To establish a sense of camaraderie.
    (b) For mutual strength and support.
    (c) To allow Witches a chance to study together.
    (d) So they could all wear matching outfits and look cool.

2. The Ardanes were created to: _____
    (a) offer guidance and support to the coven.
    (b) let the coven members know what's going on.
    (c) create a political agenda by which to run the coven.
    (d) give the High Priestess a legal standpoint in coven affairs.

3. The word of the High Priestess is: _____
    (a) inviolate law.
    (b) to be honoured with respect.
    (c) the word of the goddess.
    (d) shrill and screeching.

4. The elements are assigned specific positions because: _____
    (a) that's where they were perceived by early Europeans.
    (b) the gods drew lots and that's what came up.
    (c) Gerald Gardner said so.
    (d) they've just always been that way.

5. Divination can be best described as: _____
    (a) a way of honouring the Divine.
    (b) one of many forms of spellcasting.
    (c) the art of predicting future events.
    (d) a way of locating magickal objects.

6. Music is used during ritual to: _____
    (a) keep everyone on the same beat.
    (b) set the mood before any magickal work begins.
    (c) drown out the noise so neighbours won't get nosy.
    (d) enhance the magickal working.

7. The chakras can be best described as: _____
    (a) a popular singing group from the 1960s.
    (b) a way of mapping the human nervous system.
    (c) energy centers within the body.
    (d) places in the body where the aura emanates.

8. The auras are: _____
    (a) a way of determining one's mood or mental state.
    (b) energy rays emanating from the body.
    (c) colours attributed to emotion.
    (d) those funky lights at the North Pole.

9. The pentagram represents: _____
    (a) the Canadian rock band Rush.
    (b) Satan!
    (c) the most commonly occurring number in nature.
    (d) the five elements.

10. Athames are customarily made from metal because: _____
    (a) sacrificial blood is harder to wipe off a wooden blade.
    (b) magick is better channeled through a conductive material.
    (c) metal represents the union of the five elements.
    (d) all of the above

11. The coven summoner is also known as the: _____
    (a) Priest's apprentice.
    (b) lackey.
    (c) coven gofer.
    (d) all of the above

12. The four cornerstones of magick are: _____
    (a) to believe, to will, to know, and to respect.
    (b) to keep silent, to will, to know, and to believe.
    (c) to desire, to believe, to will, and to consecrate.
    (d) air, fire, water, and earth.

13. The number *thirteen* is important because: _____
    (a) lots of people suffer from triskaidekaphobia.
    (b) a coven of thirteen members is the most powerful in size.
    (c) it's the number of Jesus and his disciples.
    (d) it's the number of moons in a calendar year.

14. Magick can be described as: _____
    (a) spells, incantations, and enchantments.
    (b) anything a Witch does to alter their surroundings.
    (c) the psychic ability to redirect natural forces.
    (d) the art of manipulating energy.

15. Who is responsible for taking notes at coven meetings? _____
    (a) archivist
    (b) scribe
    (c) squire
    (d) Whoever has the most legible handwriting.

16. Gods can be described scientifically as: _____
    (a) They can't. Gods exist beyond scientific understanding.
    (b) mass hallucinations.
    (c) beings found at the end of enlightenment.
    (d) manifest, cooperative focused will.

17. Pagan festivals are good places to: _____
     (a) associate with other Witches and Pagans.
     (b) meet fun, interesting new people.
     (c) forget where your tent is.
     (d) avoid.

18. The necessary components for a base incense recipe are: _____
     (a) frankincense, sandalwood, benzoin, saltpeter, and essential oil.
     (b) benzoin, orris root, lemon balm, and essential oil.
     (c) some foul-smelling crud, charcoal, and a match.
     (d) orris root, saltpeter, benzoin, sandalwood, and essential oil.

19. The four components in the cornerstone philosophy of spellcasting are: _____
     (a) verbal, somatic, material, and luminary.
     (b) somatic, aural, material, and ethereal.
     (c) verbal, evocative, luminary, and ethereal.
     (d) luminary, somatic, ethereal, and verbal.

20. "Coming out of the broom closet" refers to: _____
     (a) gay and lesbian Witches.
     (b) trying to locate one's ritual garb.
     (c) publicly announcing oneself as a Witch.
     (d) putting away your antiquated flying device and buying a vacuum cleaner.

Part 2: True or False

_____ 1. A group of Solitary Witches can work together and still be considered "solitaires."

_____ 2. A Witch should always work to protect the rede, even at the cost of their own safety.

_____ 3. The High Priest and High Priestess of a coven should be a married couple.

_____ 4. Discussing coven details with another coven is punishable by banishment from the Craft.

_____ 5. Consecrating a Witch's tool is best performed under the full moon.

_____ 6. A Witch's athame should never be used for harm.

_____ 7. *Boleen* is another word for *athame*.

_____ 8. Playing prerecorded music is not acceptable in outdoor rituals.

_____ 9. Only the High Priest is allowed to question the High Priestess's decisions during ritual.

_____ 10. Ritual garb must never be worn outside of ritual.

_____ 11. The deities invoked during theurgic spellcasting must be from the same pantheon.

_____ 12. Spells must never be performed without the permission of the recipient or a qualified representative.

_____ 13. Spell procedure should be fully rehearsed before spellcasting.

_____ 14. Reusing partially burned candles is allowed.

_____ 15. Never attempt any new spells on the dark moon.

_____ 16. Never use your consecrated tarot deck for entertainment purposes.

_____ 17. Pagan Pride Day festivals don't have an admission fee.

_____ 18. Talismans have one purpose; amulets have many.

_____ 19. All Witches are vegetarians.

_____ 20. Not all coven members are human.

Part 3: Fill in the Blanks

1. The pentagram is one of the oldest _____ symbols in human history. Its _____-pointed shape can be found in all areas of nature, from the starfish to the sand _____ to the cross-cut core of an _____.

2. While thought by the _____ Church to represent _____, the pentagram is really a simple representation of_____. Its five points represent the five _____ (_____, _____, _____, _____, and _____) enclosed in the endless wheel of unity.

3. A _____ is a short knife, usually with a curved _____, and used for harvesting herbs.

4. A _____ is a thick, wooden rod, usually as tall as the wearer. It can be decorated with runes, carvings, or crystals.

5. Everyone uses _____. Witches burn them for _____ purposes, to honour the gods, or just for _____.

6. Deosil is the _____ direction, and _____ is counterclockwise.

7. A _____ is a large pot, usually metallic. One ritual use is for _____. Another is a communal _____ pot.

8. Often used to signal the start of ritual, a _____ is usually silver or copper.

9. _____ quartz is a stone frequently used to attract love.

10. The _____, normally a wooden stick, is the same length as the user's _____. Many Witches keep several for different _____.

11. Hematite is a popular _____ used for _____.

12. Sabbats can be moved to the closest available _____ except for _____ which is always held on October _____.

13. The _____ is a length of rope or cord as long as the owner's
    _____ plus _____. It is usually presented to the Witch upon
    _____.

14. A _____ is a small metal incense burner often swung from a chain.

15. There are _____ vital energy centers in the body known as the
    _____.

16. The _____ is a double-edged blade usually with a dark
    _____. While some Witches use it for _____ purposes, it is
    never used as a _____.

17. The practice of letting excess _____ drain out of the body is also
    known as _____ and _____.

18. The hieros _____ is the ritualistic _____ of the Lady and the
    Lord.

19. The period of silence before a ritual begins is known as _____ or
    _____ _____.

20. If the High Priest and Priestess are unable to lead a ritual, it is performed by the
    _____ and _____.

21. The _____ of _____ is a Witch's personal diary, notebook,
    _____, etc.

22. When a Witch dies, they are said to travel to _____.

23. The five forms of deity origin myths are _____, _____,
    _____, _____ and _____.

24. A _____ is a personalized drinking vessel. Every Witch should have
    one.

Part 4: Question and Answer

1) Explain why the sword is called the Master of the Five Elements.
2) Explain how a candle is cleansed and anointed before use.
3) Explain the difference between physical and manifest shields.
4) List some of the duties assigned to the maiden of the coven.
5) List some of the duties assigned to the summoner of the coven.
6) When can a High Priestess call herself a Witch Queen?
7) What is the difference between simple and complex spells?
8) How do esbats differ from sabbats?
9) What are the four phases of a common Wiccan ritual?
10) Explain the difference between reality, energy, and magick.

Part 5: A Witch's Dictionary

Define the following terms:

- Abjuration
- Altar
- Alteration
- Amulet
- Ankh
- Archivist
- Ardanes
- Attunement
- Bard
- Chakras
- Conjuration
- Coven
- Cowan
- Deosil
- Divination
- Elements
- Ethics
- Evocation
- Festivals
- Grounding and centering

- Grove
- Hexagram
- High Priest
- High Priestess
- Incantation
- Invocation
- Magick
- Maiden
- Potpourri
- Pursewarden
- Ritual
- Solitaire
- Spell
- Spiritual reality
- Summoner
- Talisman
- Thaumaturgy
- Theurgy
- Warlock
- Widdershins
- Witch

Part 6: Essay Questions

1) Explain the correlation between magick and consensual reality.
2) In your own words, explain how or why a spell "works."
3) Describe the complete process of crafting a spell.
4) Explain the process used to cleanse, consecrate, and anoint a person entering ritual.
5) Explain the importance of ethical responsibility in magick.
6) What does the inverted pentagram symbolize? Who uses it and why?
7) Briefly explain the process used in creating a ward.
8) What plant(s) would you recommend to a person wishing to alleviate depression?

9) Write an invocation to any one of the following deities:
   Athena, Brigit, Quan Yin, Cthulhu, or Hecate.
   Be sure to include some mention of their sphere of authority.

10) Complete the following sentence: "I am a Witch because…"

Part 7: Additional Exercises

Describe the magickal or medicinal uses of the following plants, and explain how they might be used:

- Aloe
- Damiana
- Mandrake
- Patchouli
- Valerian

Draw a simple altar, and label the items on it.

On the following list, assign the different items or concepts to one of the five elements, picking whichever seems best to you. It's okay if some fall into more than one category.
   Use a—air, f—fire, w—water, e—earth, and s—spirit.

volcanoes ( )	storms ( )	gravel ( )	west ( )	whispers ( )
quartz crystals ( )	north ( )	light ( )	tigers ( )	computers ( )
flowers ( )	south ( )	YouTube ( )	bones ( )	blue ( )
gasoline ( )	brooms ( )	butter ( )	tickling ( )	sapphires ( )
bacteria ( )	green ( )	jellyfish ( )	ants ( )	money ( )
ice ( )	thought ( )	camping ( )	poetry ( )	dreams ( )
east ( )	blood ( )	swords ( )	beer ( )	questions ( )
singing ( )	tests ( )	crayons ( )	sex ( )	coffee ( )

Wicca 101 Answers

Multiple Choice

1: c	2: a	3: c	4: b	5: b	6: c	7: b	8: a	9: a	10: c
11: c	12: b	13: c	14: d	15: b	16: c	17: d	18: c	19: a	20: c

True/False

1: T	2: T	3: F	4: F	5: F	6: T	7: T	8: T	9: F	10: T
11: T	12: F	13: T	14: T	15: T	16: F	17: T	18: F	19: F	20: F

Fill in the Blanks

1) Wiccan; perfect; trust; Rede; none; will; self; defense; Three; send ; Follow; mind; merry; part
2) gender; nature; spirituality; goddess; sabbats
3) Samhain; Wheel; March 31; Easter; June 21; Litha; Oimelc; Candlemas; February 2; December 21; Winter Solstice; Harvest Festival; September 21; festival; second; Beltane
4) *Malleus Maleficarum*; Satan
5) Witchfinder General

Wicca 102 Answers

Multiple Choice

1: b	2: a	3: b	4: a	5: c	6: d	7: b	8: b	9: d	10: b, c
11: a	12: b	13: d	14: d	15: b, d	16: d	17: a	18: d	19: a	20: c

True/False

1: F	2: F	3: F	4: F	5: T	6: T	7: F	8: F	9: F	10: F
11: F	12: T	13: F	14: T	15: F	16: T	17: F	18: F	19: F	20: T

Fill in the Blanks

1) spiritual; five; dollar; apple
2) Christian; Satan; nature; elements; air; fire; water; earth; spirit
3) boleen; blade
4) staff

5) candles; many; ambience

6) clockwise, widdershins

7) cauldron; renewal; cooking

8) bell

9) Rose

10) wand; forearm; purposes

11) stone; grounding

12) date; Samhain; 31

13) cingulum; height; girth; initiation

14) thurible

15) seven (or ten); chakras

16) athame; handle; ritual; weapon

17) energy; grounding; centering

18) gamos; union

19) attunement; quiet time

20) maiden; summoner (or whoever is available)

21) Book; Shadows; journal

22) Summerland

23) anthropomorphic; astral; elemental; extraction; parthenogenic

24) chalice

APPENDIX 3
Rituals

The following are three full rituals. There's one for dedication, one for initiation, and one for consecration. They can be adapted as needed.

Ritual of Dedication

Following completion of the Wicca 101 section, students are encouraged to participate in a Ritual of Dedication. This is a very informal, nonmagickal ritual, and it is more a mere ceremony of recognition than anything else. No quarters are called, nor is a temple erected; it doesn't even need an altar, although a simple altar dedicated to the Lord and Lady does make a nice touch. It can be performed on an individual basis, or the entire class can participate as a group.

The Significance of Dedication

The Ritual of Dedication serves two purposes. It recognizes that each student has successfully completed the Wicca 101 section and reaffirms that the student is ready to delve into the Wicca 102 portion. If any student is still unsure whether they want to continue their study of the Craft, this is the time to bow out gracefully. If the instructor feels that any student is not ready to progress, this is the time to gently dismiss them from the class or encourage them to take a break from the studies.

During the ritual, each student is offered a gift or token, which indicates that the student is recognized and honoured as a dedicant of the goddess. It might be a simple stone pendant or a small herbal sachet.

Becoming a dedicant of the Craft should not be taken lightly; it is a bold step along a new path. This ritual is the stepping-stone into the world of the Craft. No longer is the student an observer, but the student becomes an active participant in the Craft of the Wise. The subject matter in Wicca 101 was objective, merely a study of the history and philosophy of the Craft. The classes offered in Wicca 102 are naturally more involved, and more hands-on experience is offered. The Ardanes are discussed, ritual procedure is studied, and the students learn the fine art of spellcrafting.

The Ritual of Dedication

Allow everyone to settle down before the ceremony commences. When you're ready, let everyone form a circle, joining hands. The High Priest and High Priestess stand in the center of the circle.

High Priestess: *We gather today before the Lord and the Lady to witness the dedication of our friend(s) to the study of the Craft of the Wise.*

The summoner escorts the dedicant to the center of the circle to stand before the High Priest and Priestess. If there is more than one, the following process is repeated for each participant.

High Priestess: *Have you come before us to learn the secrets of the Craft of the Wise, the ways of the Old Religion?*

Dedicant: *I have.*

High Priestess: *Know ye that the hand of the goddess will be upon you, and nothing that she touches comes away unchanged. Are you ready to begin?*

Dedicant: *I am.*

High Priest: *Do you swear to live by the Wiccan Rede and to use the knowledge you will gain only where none may be harmed?*

Dedicant: *I do so swear.*

High Priestess: *To these you must also swear: never to reveal the magickal names of your fellow dedicants or what you will have learned to those who might use this knowledge for ill. Do you swear to keep this knowledge within the grove* (or circle, class, or coven, whichever applies)?

Dedicant: *I do so swear.*

High Priest: *Do you also swear to study diligently and to honour the Lord and Lady by your dedication for as long as you are one with us?*

Dedicant: *I do so swear.*

High Priestess: *By what name would you be known, while in our circle?*

Dedicant: *I would be known as _____.*

The individual offers a magickal name if one has been chosen. Otherwise, mundane names are fine.

High Priestess: *Then repeat after me:*

> *I, (name), swear that as a dedicant of the Old Religion, I shall study the lore of the Craft with diligence and humility, and in perfect love and perfect trust. I shall not betray this knowledge, nor shall I show any disrespect to my elders nor to the gods.*

The dedicant repeats the oath.

High Priest: *And to you, we present this token, and invite you to proceed in your studies of the Old Religion. Hail, and welcome!*

The dedicant is presented with a small token of recognition.

High Priestess: *Hail, and welcome, (name).*

They exchange hugs, handshakes, kisses, etc.

This is a *very* informal ritual—more akin to a fraternity initiation than a magickal working—but the significance of the ritual should not be overlooked. Its theatrical dialogue reflects some of the customs of the older traditions of the Craft. You may, of course, write or perform a different dedication ritual altogether, but some form of rite of passage is strongly recommended.

Ritual of Initiation

The dedicant Witches have finally completed the entire Wicca 101 and 102 courses and have filled their brains with knowledge, their hearts with wonder, and their spirits with enlightenment. The only thing left is to initiate them as real Witches. Congratulations!

The Significance of Initiation

Why do we need the initiation? We know these new Witches are good enough; they've exhibited all the knowledge and wisdom one could ask for and show great promise. They're intelligent, eager, and ready to be turned loose on the world. Do they need initiating?

Well, yes. Whereas the Ritual of Dedication was essentially a formality, the Ritual of Initiation is much more than that. The initiation actually serves several purposes mundane, divine, and sublime. It is a rite of passage, something often found missing in today's industrial society. For many young adults, there is no single event in which they can announce to the world: "I have arrived." I believe part of the reason so many youths feel estranged from family and authority figures is that they are subconsciously seeking a form of recognition and awareness—a declaration of self. In the Jewish culture, the bar or bat mitzvah is a formal recognition of adulthood. College graduation serves a similar purpose, but that is merely a stepping-stone to greater responsibility. Some teenagers find self-worth and personal gratitude in getting their driver's license. But many of these are seen as mere substitutions for something with deeper meaning. Whether the about-to-be-initiated Witch is eighteen, twenty-eight, or seventy-eight, the feeling is the same. A formal process of initiation gives them that spotlight; it is their fifteen minutes of fame and a time to be recognized and accepted by elders and peers as having "made it."

This ritual also brings about subtle changes within the Witch. What were once vague concepts or ideas become more substantial, and the Witch feels a sense of greater confidence and awareness. They feel more attuned to the harmonies of the world, both within and without. This is another aspect of the rite of passage, and it is similar to the changes within the Scarecrow, the Tin Man, and the Cowardly Lion in the Land of Oz. The process of initiation awakens what may have been lying dormant within the Witch, waiting to be summoned.

On a deeper level, the ritual opens a gateway between the inner self and the magickal realm; there is a synergy between self and spirit that may have only been glimpsed before. Many elders who perform initiations feel that the initiate is completely open to the wisdom of the gods and that during the ritual they become wiser, stronger, and more empowered than the elders themselves.

Initiates sometimes report seeing psychic or clairvoyant visions or discovering a clarity of wisdom and awareness that they had previously thought unattainable.

Considering all these aspects of the initiation process, two things become clear: one, that for those who are ready to receive the initiation, it is a time of spiritual and personal rebirth and reawakening, and two, it is all the more obvious that one should not initiate anyone who is not deemed ready. Carefully consider the merits, challenges, and ramifications of the initiation process before you agree to formally welcome anyone into the Craft of the Wise.

The Ritual of Initiation

It used to be that the initiation was a private, secret affair closed to everyone but the initiate and the coven. Nowadays, however, friends and loved ones are often invited to witness and share in the event.

Erecting the Temple

Before the ritual begins, the initiate is blindfolded and bound with their hands tied behind the back. They are told to wait a little distance away from the temple or sacred space, so they can neither hear nor see what is happening. This signifies that the initiate is at the mercy of both the coven and the gods. The symbolic surrender is a test of both courage and humility. It is perceived by some as being similar to the Fool card in the tarot's major arcana.

Period of Quiet Time, or Attunement

The period of attunement is especially poignant for the initiate themselves. They are about to experience a fundamental change in their perception of the Craft.

Casting the Circle

The process of asperging and anointing and consecrating with oils and incense is performed as usual. The initiate does not receive consecration until later.

Calling the Quarters

If there are certain aspects of the elements that the initiate favors, it is appropriate to mention those during the callings. If there are aspects that the High Priest or Priestess feels the initiate could benefit from, those may likewise be invoked.

Invocation of the Goddess and God

Similarly if the initiate has specific deities that they favor, by all means use those. If not, you might use the "coven standard" or choose deities of wisdom, rebirth, and so on.

The Initiation

The summoner steps out of the circle and gently leads the initiate to the perimeter of the circle. There they stand in silence until called upon to enter the circle. The summoner then reenters the circle, and the High Priest silently hands him an athame. It can either be the one used for regular coven business or, if the elders feel that such a gift is appropriate, one that will be presented to the initiate later.

High Priest: *Listen to the words of the Great Mother. She who of old has been called Artemis, Astarte, Dione, Melusine, Cerridwen, Diana, and by many other names.*

High Priestess: *Whenever you have need of anything, once in the month, and better it be when the moon is full, then shall ye assemble in some secret place to adore the spirit of me, who am queen of all the wise. You shall be free from slavery, and as a sign that ye be free, you shall be naked in your rites. Sing, dance, feast, make music, and love, all in my praise. For mine is the ecstasy of the spirit, but mine also is joy on Earth. My law is love unto all beings. Mine is the secret door that opens upon the land of youth, and mine is the cup of the wine of life. That is the cauldron of Cerridwen. That is the Holy Grail of immortality. I give the knowledge of the spirit eternal and beyond death. I give peace, freedom, and reunion with those who have gone before. Nor do I demand aught in sacrifice, for behold, I am the mother of all things, and my love is poured out upon the earth.*

High Priest: *Hear now the words of the star goddess, the dust of whose feet are the hosts of heaven, whose body encircles the universe.*

High Priestess: *I, who am the beauty of the green earth and the white moon among the stars, do call upon your souls. Arise and come unto me. For I am the soul of nature that gives life to the universe. From me all things proceed, and unto me they must return. Let my worship be in the heart that rejoiceth, for behold—all acts of love and pleasure are my rituals. Let there be beauty and strength, power and compassion, honour and humility, mirth and reverence within you. And you who seek to know me, know that thy seeking and yearning will avail thee not, unless thou knowest this mystery: that if that which you seek you findest not within* *thee, you will never find it without, for behold—I have been with thee from the beginning, and I am that which is attained at the end of desire.*[116]

A version of the Charge of the Goddess is recited at almost every initiation. Here the goddess is speaking through the High Priestess to the initiate alone. Note that the High Priest recites the invocation part of the charge, and the body is recited by the High Priestess.

Summoner: *You who stand on the threshold between the world of humanity and the realms of the ancient ones, have you the courage to proceed?*

Initiate: *I do.*

Summoner: *That is good, for truly I say to you, it were better that you should rush upon this blade and perish* (touches athame point to initiate's chest) *than to make the attempt with fear or falsehood in your heart. Yet still, we await the passwords.*

Initiate: *I have two: perfect love and perfect trust.*

Summoner: *All who have these are doubly welcome in this circle. Now I pass you through the veil.*

The summoner cuts a portal to admit the initiate and guides them to stand before the altar to receive the Five-Fold Blessing. Traditionally if the initiate is female, the High Priest performs the blessings. If it is a male initiate, the High Priestess takes over. This is not necessarily true today.

High Priest/ess: *Blessed be thy feet, which have brought thee in these ways.* (Kisses the initiate's feet.) *Blessed be thy knees, which kneel before the sacred altar.* (Kisses the initiate's knees.) *Blessed be thy navel, which links us all to the goddess.* (Kisses the initiate's navel.) *Blessed be thy breast, formed in beauty and strength.* (Kisses the initiate's chest.) *Blessed be thy lips, that shall speak the sacred names.* (Kisses the initiate's lips or cheek.)

High Priest/ess: *Now we take your measure; this cord shall represent you and you alone.*

---

116. K, *CovenCraft*, 430.

If the High Priest performed the blessing, the High Priestess takes the measure or vice versa. A length of cord, usually silver or green, is used to take the initiate's measure. The cord is initially thirteen feet long, which is one of the prime magickal numbers. First, the initiate is measured from the head to foot, then around the chest, making the total length about eight to nine feet. Any excess is cut off. The measured cord and the excess piece are set upon the altar until later.

Some traditions measure the person's arm span as well. The discarded piece is often kept at the covenstead, creating a magickal link between the Witch and the coven.

High Priest/ess: *By what name would ye be known within this coven?*

Initiate: *I am to be called* (gives chosen name, magickal or otherwise).

This is the first time that the initiate's magickal name is uttered aloud within this ritual. Names, as we have seen before, hold power, and the initiate is the first to speak it, empowering themselves with the name.

High Priest/ess: *Are you prepared to swear fealty to the Craft and to this coven?*

Initiate: *I am.*

High Priest/ess: *Then repeat after me:*

> *I, (Initiate's name),*
> *In the presence of the Lady and of the Lord and of the guardians and spirits of old,*
> *Do freely and solemnly swear that I will ever be true to the Craft of the Wise,*
> *That I shall follow the Rede to the best of my ability,*
> *That I will never reveal the secrets of the Craft except to a person well-prepared,*
> *And that I will aid and protect my brothers and sisters of the Craft.*
> *All this I swear by my hope of a future life,*
> *And may my tools break and turn against me if I should break this, my solemn oath.*

Whoever performed the blessing also performs the oath. If a magickal name had been chosen specifically for the initiation, it should not be uttered until that moment. Unlike much of the Craft, the wording of the oath is unchanged as much is as known since Gardner's initiation. The full weight, risk, and responsibility of a follower of the Old Religion is upon the initiate. The oath-giver continues with the consecration.

High Priest/ess: *I mark you with this triple sign.*

Traditionally the High Priest/ess takes a magickal oil, usually initiation or consecration oil, and, with the index and middle fingers of the projective hand, dabs it at the initiate's third eye, left nipple, and right nipple (or close). Some traditions would anoint the nipples and the throat. Others simply draw a pentagram or a triangle over the third eye chakra.

High Priest/ess: *I anoint you with the sacred wine.*

The process is repeated with consecrated wine. Wine has long been considered a magickal gift—the fermented grape was transformed from a simple fruit into a bringer of higher wisdom.

High Priest/ess: *I consecrate you with a kiss.* (Kisses the initiate in the same places.) *By this sign and these marks shall you be recognized as a Witch by all who have eyes to see and hearts to love.*

The summoner now removes the bindings and the blindfold, so the High Priest and High Priestess are the first people the initiate sees upon opening their eyes.

Summoner: *Before the gods and spirits of old, I present* (Initiate's name) *and Witch!*

Now the initiate is presented with gifts. In some traditions they receive a new set of magickal tools, or the existing ones are presented again now that the initiate is fully qualified to use them. In other traditions the High Priestess presents a token of the goddess, such as a jewel or a seashell, and the High Priest presents a token of the god, such as a deer antler or a staff. In all cases the initiate also receives the measure.

Closing the Temple
And there was much rejoicing!

The Ritual of Initiation is far more formal than the Ritual of Dedication, and it should be. The initiate is now a full-fledged Witch and ready to take their rightful place among the Craft of the Wise.

Ritual of Consecration

The following is merely one example of a consecration ritual. There are as many different consecration rites as there are facets of the Craft. Feel free to use this one as is, to modify it to your preference, or to write something completely different.

The Significance of Consecration

A Witch's magickal tools are sacred items and a material link between the Witch, the magick, and the spirit realms. Through the act of consecration, a connection is established between the item, the Witch, and the magick, forging a bond that should not be compromised. While the magick does not need tools, a Witch often needs a material point or focus to "hang the magick on." While this is true, it should also be remembered that the consecrated magickal tools have a spiritual essence in their own right, which should be honoured and respected. The presence of the consecrated tools enhances and empowers the magickal abilities of the Witch, not unlike the presence of a familiar.

This is one of the reasons that a Witch's consecrated items should not be handled in ritual by another. They are magickally attuned to the one person alone, and to handle them seems almost a violation of privacy. Some Witches admit to having felt violated, almost as a form of psychic assault, if their altar or magickal tools are handled or misused—either in ignorance or with malicious intent.

A Witch's consecrated tools, or any other dedicated magickal items, are treated with respect and courtesy. The Witch feels a sense of reverence toward their magickal tools and an almost maternal sense of pride. Consecrating one's tools serves another purpose as well. If, for any reason, a consecrated item is stolen, the thief will suffer much hardship and discomfort until the item is returned to its rightful owner.

The Ritual of Consecration

Consecration rites are usually solitary endeavors as the Witch is consecrating personal items. A group might be involved if the consecrated item will be used by all of the coven. Such items could be a chalice or sword.

Period of Attunement

Perform as taught in Wicca 102.

Erect the Temple

Perform as taught in Wicca 102.

The Consecration

The act of consecration consists of two phases: elemental consecration and divine consecration. As with the process of erecting the temple, the elemental phase is first.

Using your receptive hand, pick up the item to be consecrated. For the purpose of this demonstration, we are consecrating an athame.

Wave the athame gently through a chosen incense and say: *Breath of air, powers of the east, I dedicate this, my sacred blade, to your service. May the spirits bless and consecrate my athame.*

Instead of saying what the item is, you may wish to personalize it with a magickal name, such as Excalibur or Moonblade.

Next, pass the athame gently through the candle flame, and say: *Fires of passion, powers of the south, I dedicate this, my sacred blade, to your service. May the spirits bless and consecrate my athame.*

If the item is something flammable, such as your Book of Shadows, merely go *near* the flame, not through it.

Next, pour a few drops of water on the athame, and say: *Waters of life, powers of the west, I dedicate this, my sacred blade, to your service. May the spirits bless and consecrate my athame.*

If the item is something that could be harmed or damaged by water, such as a deck of tarot cards, merely dip your finger in the water and rub a little along the item's edge. If you feel comfortable immersing the item completely, go for it! But be mindful of the makeup of the water. If you consecrate your athame in the Atlantic Ocean, for example, be sure to rinse it off in fresh water afterward, so the salt water won't corrode the metal.

Finally, pour a few salt crystals over the athame, and say: *Salt of the earth, powers of the north, I dedicate this, my sacred blade, to your service. May the spirits bless and consecrate my athame.*

You're not consecrating a slug, are you? Good. Onward.

Now for the divine consecration.

Hold the athame in both hands, high over your head, and say: *O, wise Artemis! O, great Cernunnos! I dedicate this, my sacred blade, to your service. May you bless and consecrate my athame that it may work in your service, in perfect love and perfect trust, for the good of all. So mote it be.*

Hold the athame aloft for a few heartbeats, then draw it down, kiss it, and place it upon the altar.

Close the Ritual
Perform as taught in Wicca 102.

Again, this is merely one example of a simple consecration ritual. You can be as elaborate as you like and substitute whatever deities or elemental figures that you feel are appropriate. You don't have to go through the entire ritual process for each and every item either. If you are consecrating your entire regalia, erect the temple once and consecrate each item individually within the sacred space.

Recommended Reading

Ancient & Shining Ones by D. J. Conway

Ancient Ways: Reclaiming the Pagan Tradition by Pauline Campanelli

Animal Speak: The Spiritual & Magical Powers of Creatures Great & Small by Ted Andrews

Aradia, or the Gospel of Witches by Charles Leland

The Art of Ritual by Rachel Patterson

The Art of Sexual Ecstasy: The Path of Sacred Sexuality for Western Lovers by Margot Anand

Blood and Mistletoe: The History of the Druids in Britain by Ronald Hutton

The Book of Crystal Spells: Magical Uses for Stones, Crystals, Minerals … and Even Sand by Ember Grant

The Book of Runes: A Handbook for the Use of an Ancient Oracle: The Viking Runes by Ralph Blum

Buckland's Complete Book of Witchcraft by Raymond Buckland

Bulfinch's Mythology by Thomas Bulfinch

Chakra Healing: A Beginner's Guide to Self-Healing Techniques that Balance the Chakras by Margarita Alcantara

The Chalice and the Blade: Our History, Our Future by Riane Eisler

The Complete Book of Incense, Oils & Brews by Scott Cunningham

CovenCraft: Witchcraft for Three or More by Amber K

Creative Visualization: Use the Power of Your Imagination to Create What You Want in Your Life by Shakti Gawain

Crystals and Stones: A Complete Guide to Their Healing Properties by The Group of 5

Cunningham's Encyclopedia of Crystal, Gem & Metal Magic by Scott Cunningham

Cunningham's Encyclopedia of Magical Herbs by Scott Cunningham

Discovering the Folklore of Plants by Margaret Baker

Drawing Down the Moon: Witches, Druids, Goddess-Worshippers, and Other Pagans in America Today by Margot Adler

Eight Sabbats for Witches by Janet Farrar and Stewart Farrar

Elemental Witchcraft: A Guide to Living a Magickal Life through the Elements by Heron Michelle

The Encyclopedia of Witchcraft and Demonology by Hope Rossell Robbins

Encyclopedia of Witches and Witchcraft by Rosemary Ellen Guiley

Exploring Candle Magick: Candles, Spells, Charms, Rituals, and Divinations by Patricia Telesco

Futhark: A Handbook of Rune Magick by Edred Thorsson

Gaia: A New Look at Life on Earth by James Lovelock

The Great Cosmic Mother: Rediscovering the Religion of the Earth by Monica Sjöö and Barbara Mor

The Great Secret, or, Occultism Unveiled by Éliphas Lévi

The Hero with a Thousand Faces by Joseph Campbell

A History of Pagan Europe by Prudence Jones and Nigel Pennick

A History of Witchcraft: Sorcereres, Heretics & Pagans by Jeffrey B. Russell and Brooks Alexander

Living, Loving & Learning by Leo F. Buscaglia

Living Wicca: A Further Guide for the Solitary Practitioner by Scott Cunningham

The Mabinogion translated by Gwyn Jones and Thomas Jones

The Magical History of Britain by Martin Wall

The Magical Household: Spells & Rituals for the Home by Scott Cunningham and David Harrington

The Magical Properties of Plants—and How to Find Them by Tylluan Penry

Magical Rites from Crystal Well by Ed Fitch

The Magical World of the Anglo-Saxons by Tylluan Penry

The Magician's Companion: A Practical and Encyclopedic Guide to Magical and Religious Symbolism by Bill Whitcomb

Magick in Theory and Practice by Aleister Crowley

The Malleus Maleficarum of Heinrich Kramer and James Sprenger edited by Montague Summers

Many Moons: The Myth and Magic, Fact and Fantasy of Our Nearest Heavenly Body by Diana Brueton

The Masks of God by Joseph Campbell

Mastering Witchcraft: A Practical Guide for Witches, Warlocks, and Covens by Paul Huson

Moon Magic: A Handbook of Lunar Cycles, Lore, and Mystical Energies by Aurora Kane

The New Book of Goddesses and Heroines by Patricia Monaghan

A New Wiccan Book of the Law: A Manual for the Guidance of Groves, Covens & Individuals by Lady Galadriel

The Pagan Book on Living and Dying: Practical Rituals, Prayers, Blessings, and Meditations on Crossing Over by Starhawk, M. Macha NightMare, and The Reclaiming Collective

Paganism: An Introduction to Earth-Centered Religions by Joyce Higginbotham and River Higginbotham

Paganism: An Introductory Guide: Pagan Holidays, Beliefs, Gods and Goddesses, Symbols, Rituals, Practices, and Much More! by Riley Star

Pagans and Christians by Robin Lane Fox

The Pagan's Muse: World of Ritual, Invocation, and Inspiration edited by Jane Raebrun

The Power of Myth by Joseph Campbell and Bill Moyers

Practical Candleburning Rituals: Spells & Rituals for Every Purpose by Raymond Buckland

Practical Color Magick by Raymond Buckland

Protection & Reversal Magick: A Witch's Defense Manual by Jason Miller

Real Magic: An Introductory Treatise on the Basic Principles of Yellow Magic by Philip Emmons Isaac Bonewits

The Rede of the Wiccae: Adriana Porter, Gwen Thompson, and the Birth of a Tradition of Witchcraft by Robert Mathiesen and Theitic

Solitary Witch: The Ultimate Book of Shadows for the New Generation by Silver RavenWolf

The Song of Eve: Mythology and Symbols of the Goddess by Manuela Dunn Mascetti

Spellcrafting: Strengthen the Power of Your Craft by Creating and Casting Your Own Unique Spells by Arin Murphy-Hiscock

The Spiral Dance by R. Garcia y Robertson

Stranger in a Strange Land by Robert A. Heinlein

Symbols of the Occult: A Directory of Over 500 Signs, Symbols, and Icons by Eric Chaline

Transformative Witchcraft: The Greater Mysteries by Jason Mankey

True Magick: A Beginner's Guide by Amber K

The Truth about Witchcraft Today by Scott Cunningham

The Twelve Faces of the Goddess: Transform Your Life with Astrology, Magick, and the Sacred Feminine by Danielle Blackwood

The Ultimate Guide to the Witch's Wheel of the Year: Rituals, Spells & Practices for Magical Sabbats, Holidays & Celebrations by Anjou Kierman

The Urban Pagan: Magical Living in a 9-to-5 World by Patricia Telesco

Voices from the Circle: The Heritage of Western Paganism edited by Prudence Jones and Caitlin Matthews

West County Wicca: A Journal of the Old Religion by Rhiannon Ryall

When, Why … If: An Ethics Workbook by Robin Wood

The Wicca Source Book: A Complete Guide for the Modern Witch by Gerina Dunwich

Witchcraft for Tomorrow by Doreen Valiente

Witchcraft Today—60 Years On edited by Trevor Greenfield

Witchcraft Today, Book One: The Modern Craft Movement by Chas S. Clifton

Witchcraze: A New History of the European Witch Hunts by Anne Llewellyn Barstow

The Witches' God by Janet Farrar and Stewart Farrar

The Witches' Way: Principles, Rituals, and Beliefs of Modern Witchcraft by Janet Farrar and Stewart Farrar

The Witch of the Forest's Guide to Natural Magick: Discover Your Magick. Connect with Your Inner & Outer World by Lindsay Squire

The Witch's Altar: The Craft, Lore & Magick of Sacred Space by Jason Mankey and Laura Tempest Zakroff

The Witch's Book of Spellcraft: A Practical Guide to Connecting with the Magick of Candles, Crystals, Plants & Herbs by Jason Mankey, Matt Cavalli, Amanda Lynn, and Ari Mankey

The Witch's Guide to Manifestation: Witchcraft for the Life You Want by Mystic Dylan

Witch's Wheel of the Year: Rituals for Circles, Solitaries & Covens by Jason Mankey

The Woman's Dictionary of Symbols and Sacred Objects by Barbara G. Walker

The Woman's Encyclopedia of Myths and Secrets by Barbara G. Walker

Wylundt's Book of Incense by Steven R. Smith

Glossary

This is a list of words and phrases used frequently in Wicca and Witchcraft. You'll encounter them in this book and elsewhere, so here are some helpful definitions.

air: In many Wiccan or Witchcraft traditions, air is the element that corresponds to east, communication, thought, and new beginnings. See also *elements*.

altar: The focal point of a Witch or Wiccan's place of worship. It's usually a flat surface and holds their athame, chalice, and other magickal tools.

amulet: An object worn or carried, usually for protection. See also *talisman*.

animism: The belief that all aspects of nature are alive and interconnected and that everything has an inherent spirit.

apostasy: The conscious decision to turn away from or renounce one's established faith or religion. In some countries, apostasy is still considered a capital offense. See also *Burning Times*.

Aradia, or the Gospel of the Witches: A short book written by Charles Leland, first published in 1899, that describes the rituals and practices of Pagan Witches in Tuscany, Italy.

Ardanes: The Laws of the Craft originally written by Gerald Gardner. It has been rewritten many times. See also *Laws of the Craft*.

aspect: A form, facet, manifestation, or personality of a deity that bears its own name, personality, and appearance. Persephone, for example, is a Maiden aspect of the goddess, and Hecate is a Crone aspect.

asperger: A ritual tool used to sprinkle water, usually for purification or blessing. It might be a perforated metal dish or sphere or a bundle of leaves dipped in water.

athame: A tool that resembles a knife used by many Wiccans and Witches to channel energy. Some use their athame for cutting things in a ritual or magickal environment, others don't. Athames used to traditionally have a decorated black handle. The athame is traditionally a masculine-aspect item. See also *boleen (or boline)*.

attunement: An activity that brings one's mind, psyche, and spirit into focus prior to ritual.

bell: In some traditions, a bell is rung to start ritual or welcome the spirits. It is usually a small copper or silver hand bell.

Beltane: One of the eight sabbats, Beltane is usually observed on May 1. Beltane is a fire festival, celebrating the growing vitality of the natural world.

besom: An antiquated name for a broom. A besom is a broom that has been consecrated for use in ritual, such as sweeping away negative energies.

black moon: The second new moon in a single month. See *blue moon*.

blessed be: An all-purpose greeting used by Wiccans and Witches. It can be a greeting, an exclamation, or an oath.

blue moon: The second full moon in a single month. See *black moon*.

boleen (or boline): A small knife, usually white-handled, used to cut herbs or carve items for magickal use. The traditional boline has a crescent moon shape and is sharpened on the inside edge. See also *athame*.

Book of Shadows (BOS): A personal journal, diary, scrapbook, or archive kept by a Wiccan or Witch. It might contain spell lists, ritual transcripts, recipes, pictures, and so on. Some keep the contents of their BOS secret; others share the information freely. Books of Shadows are often decorated to reflect the personality of their owner. See also *grimoire*.

Burning Times: A period in history between approximately 1200 and 1700 CE when many people were tried and executed for alleged crimes, such as Witchcraft, heresy, homosexuality, or apostasy. Exact figures are unknown, but it is believed to be between twenty thousand and sixty thousand victims. See also *apostasy*.

cakes and ale: The practice of sharing nourishment and drink during ritual. It can refer to the part of ritual in which they are served or to the items themselves.

candle: Candles are frequently used in magick and ritual to signify the presence of spirit, to open or close a ritual ceremony, or to help you find your way. Some Wiccans and Witches make their own candles, adding herbs or oils to the wax. Candles can also be engraved for spellwork.

casting the circle: The process by which a ritual space is created. See also *circle*.

cauldron: A large vessel, usually iron, which can represent the mysteries or the womb of the goddess or the mystery beyond the veil. Cauldrons can be used as part of a "casting away" ritual, to hold sacred fire or water, or even to cook in over a fire.

chakras: The focal points of the energy field of the human body. There are traditionally seven major and three minor chakras, each representing energy centers within the body. Cleaning or aligning the chakras is frequently used as part of a healing process.

chalice: A cup or wine glass used in ritual. It might hold consecrated water or wine that is shared in ritual. The chalice is traditionally a female-aspect item.

Charge of the Goddess: A written passage frequently regarded as Wiccan liturgy, which denotes the connection between the goddess and the reader. One of the most common versions was written by Doreen Valiente in 1964 and based on input from Gerald Gardner.

circle: The practice of working magick together (we were in circle); a term for a small group of Wiccan or Witches (we are a circle); and the act of creating a ritual space (cast a circle). See also *casting the circle*.

cleansing: A process, often magickal in nature, of ridding a person or an object of unwanted or excess energies or influences.

cone of power: The energy raised in ritual is visualized as a cone with the magick at the peak released to fulfill its purpose.

consecration: The process of welcoming a person into ritual, usually by dabbing a drop of oil on the forehead or having them step through a stream of incense smoke. It also refers to the process of cleansing and dedicating one's ritual tools. See also *ritual tools*.

cord: Also known as a girdle or cingulum, a cord is a measured length of rope or similar material. Cords of specific colours can be used to denote rank within a coven, or cords can be used in spellwork that involves the tying or untying of knots.

correspondences: A list of symbolic equivalents used in magick. For example, north corresponds to the element of earth, which corresponds to foundation and stability.

coven: A group of Witches who gather to celebrate their faith and work magick. Covens can be any size of three or more and are usually led by a High Priest and/or High Priestess. Covens are usually autonomous and self-governing groups.

cowan: A term rarely used anymore, it refers to anyone who is not Pagan, Wiccan, or Witch.

Craft: Another term for Witchcraft.

crystal ball: A clear sphere, usually of crystal or glass, used in divination. A person using a crystal ball doesn't as much "see" anything in it but uses it as a way to focus their attention inward.

dedicant: A noninitiated student of Wicca. Also sometimes known as neophyte, seeker, student, or candidate.

dedication: A procedure, usually in ritual, when a Wiccan or Witch formally declares their intention to practice the religion of Wicca or Witchcraft.

degrees: Levels of initiation or experience used in some Wiccan or Witchcraft traditions. Most traditions that use degrees have a three-tiered system.

deosil: Clockwise, or "sunwise." When casting a circle or working positive magick, it is customary to move in a deosil direction. See also *widdershins*.

divination: The art or practice of foreseeing trends or discovering hidden knowledge by using tools such as tarot cards or runes.

Drawing Down the Moon: A process in ritual usually performed by the High Priestess in which the essence of the goddess is channeled into her.

drum: A musical instrument used by many Pagans, Wiccans, Witches, and groups for entertainment or trance work. There are many styles of drums available, and the style is usually up to the individual.

earth: In many Wiccan or Witchcraft traditions, it is the element corresponding to the north, foundation, stability, and material prosperity. See also *elements*.

earthing: The practice of releasing excess energy raised in magick or ritual after the spellworking is completed. See also *grounding and centering*.

elder: A person recognized as having the experience and wisdom necessary to serve as teacher, counselor, or leader within the Wiccan or Witch community.

elements: The five classes of energy recognized by many Witches and Wiccans. They are air, fire, water, earth, and spirit. See also the listing for each element.

energy: A magickal field that permeates all living things. Also the resonance or vibration of that field.

equinox: The period of the year when the day and night are of equal length. The Spring Equinox is traditionally on Ostara, March 21, and the Autumn Equinox is on Mabon, September 21. See also *solstice*.

esbat: A gathering of Witches or Wiccans to celebrate the phases of the moon, to hold ritual, or merely to socialize. See also *sabbat*.

familiar: An animal companion believed to assist in magickal workings, such as a pet whose presence makes the Wiccan or Witch feel more capable. The concept of a familiar was often used during the Inquisition as evidence of a Witch's alleged evil work.

fire: In many Wiccan or Witchcraft traditions, fire is the element corresponding to south, creativity, passion, determination, and sexuality. See also *elements*.

full moon: The lunar phase when the moon is brightest. It is often regarded as the time to work magick for healing, abundance, or prosperity. Also mentioned in the Charge of the Goddess as the most opportune time to gather.

garb: A Wiccan's or Witch's clothes that are worn specifically while in a ritual, a circle, or while working magick. Garb usually consists of a robe, tabard, or loose clothing decorated as the individual desires. See also *regalia*.

god: To some, *god* is interchangeable with the name of a divine entity. To many Pagans, *god* refers to the masculine aspect of divinity, such as the Horned God. See *goddess*.

goddess: The feminine personification of deity. Also known as the Lady. In Wicca she is frequently visualized in three aspects: the Maiden, Mother, and Crone. See *god*.

grimoire: An antiquated term for a book, usually containing magickal information. See also *Book of Shadows (BOS)*.

grounding and centering: The process of calming one's energies down after a magickal working. Also refers to the connection established between a Wiccan or Witch and the earth. See also *earthing*.

grove: A group of Pagans, Wiccans, or Witches often regarded as the "outer court" of a coven. A grove may or may not have a Priest or Priestess in charge.

healing: The process of restoring health, vitality, or focus, often by magickal means. Magickal healing, however, should never replace medical care but work in conjunction with it.

Heathen: Within the magickal community, a Heathen is one who follows the Norse tradition. To the layperson, *heathen* can refer to anyone who is uneducated, uncivilized, or lacking religious focus.

henotheism: The philosophy of being accepting or welcoming of faiths, religions, or deities other than your own.

High Priest: A High Priest, or HP, is the leader of a coven or magickal group. They are usually third degree and can be ordained clergy, although ordination is not a requirement in most traditions. The role is traditionally held by a male.

High Priestess: In many traditions, the High Priestess, or HPS, is the formal leader of a coven or magickal group. The HPS is often female, and as with High Priest, the position is usually third degree.

Imbolc: One of the eight sabbats, usually held on February 2. It is also known as Oimelc or Candlemas and celebrates the reawakening of the world as winter's cold begins to recede.

immanence: The belief that deity exists everywhere—within all things and all people. See also *transcendence*.

initiation: The procedure of making a person a formal member of a coven.

karma: A spiritual concept of cause and effect. Karma is the philosophy that one's behavior in one lifetime will affect the luck or bearing in subsequent incarnations. Karma is not, contrary to popular belief, "instant justice."

Lammas: A harvest festival, usually held on August 2. It is often regarded as synonymous with Lughnassadh, even though they are separate events. See also *Lughnassadh*.

Laws of the Craft: A collection of rules on behavior and practice within Witchcraft. The rules were first written by Gerald Gardner, who claimed to have received them from a much earlier source. See also *Ardanes*.

Litha: Also called midsummer, Litha is one of the eight sabbats and is usually held on June 21. Litha celebrates the height of power of the natural world and often acknowledges the union of the Lord and Lady. See also *Lord and Lady*.

Lord and Lady: Refers to the archetypal god and goddess—the principal divinities in the Wiccan faith. The Lord and Lady may also be known by specific names, such as Cernunnos and Artemis.

Lughnassadh: One of the eight sabbats. It is known as the festival of the first harvest and usually held on August 2. See also *Lammas*.

Mabon: One of the eight sabbats, it corresponds with the Autumn Equinox. Usually held on September 21, it is known as the festival of the second harvest.

magick: The art or science of changing reality by intent and willpower. Also refers to the psychic direction or awareness of energies. *Magick* is spelled with a *k* to differentiate it from magic, sleight of hand, or parlor games.

maiden: A coven role or position, traditionally held by a woman, as a "Priestess in training." The individual often assists the HPS in ritual functions.

monotheism: The belief in only one god, or the belief that there is only one god.

moon: The symbol of the Triple Goddess, in which the three phases of waxing, full, and waning are reflected in the Maiden, Mother, and Crone.

mortar and pestle: The bowl and grinder seen in many pharmacy signs. These are frequently used to prepare herbs for spellwork.

occult: Essentially "secret knowledge." It refers to any metaphysical or magickal knowledge or experience. Traditionally it referred to mysterious or unknown practices.

Ostara: One of the eight sabbats, it is usually held on March 21. Ostara is observed in conjunction with the Spring Equinox.

Pagan: One who follows any nature-oriented belief, religion, or spirituality.

pantheism: The philosophy or belief that deity can be perceived of a collective of many individuals. It can be further divided into Eastern pantheism and the belief that the world (or universe) is derived from a transcendent deity, and Western pantheism and the belief that deity can have many different identities.

pendulum: A pendulum is a weight on the end of a chain or cord that acts as a scrying or divination tool. By asking a question and studying the pendulum's movement, one can determine the possible answer to a question.

pentacle: A dish or disk engraved with a pentagram. The pentacle is often the centerpiece of one's altar.

pentagram: Possibly the most common symbol of Wicca or Witchcraft, a pentagram is a five-pointed star enclosed in a circle. It represents the five elements within the encompassing wheel of life.

perfect love and perfect trust: A Wiccan ideal and philosophy that one should give and receive with equal honesty, openness, and willingness.

polarity: One of the fundamental concepts in Wicca that everything exists in a balance of opposite polarities, such as male/female, night/day, life/death, etc. Within ritual, sexual polarity, or the idea that certain roles could only be held by certain genders, used to be far more important than it is today.

polytheism: The philosophy that one can believe in many gods.

power: Energy drawn from natural sources or from one's own intent.

quarters: The four quarters are the cornerstones of a ritual environment. The quarters are called at the start of a ritual and dismissed at the conclusion.

regalia: The collective term for a Wiccan's or Witch's garb and accoutrements. A High Priest's regalia, for example, may include a robe, an antler headdress, a staff and an athame, and other tools. See also *garb*.

reincarnation: The belief that an individual soul or spirit can inhabit many lives, lifetimes, or bodies. Most Wiccans and Witches believe in the concept of reincarnation.

religion: The structured practice of observance of, worship of, or belief in a divine, supernatural, or spiritual essence or entity(ies). If religion is the structured practice of worship, then spirituality is the awareness of that entity. See also *spirituality*.

ritual: A series of steps or procedures in worship, celebration, or activity. The term usually refers to an event held at sabbats and esbats.

ritual tools: Implements used in magickal work or ritual. A Witch's tools, including the athame and chalice, are usually consecrated by and for the individual. See also *consecration*.

runes: Letters or stones used in Norse futhark divination. Each letter or image has its own significance or meaning. Also, though a less common definition, a rune can be a symbol or promise shared between individuals.

sabbat: One of eight days of special observance in Wicca and Witchcraft, which together compose the Wheel of the Year. A sabbat may refer to the day or the ritual, ceremony, or observance on that day. The eight sabbats are Samhain, Yule, Imbolc, Ostara, Beltane, Litha, Lughnassadh or Lammas, and Mabon. See also *esbat*.

salt: In ritual, salt is a symbolic element of earth and a cleansing or purifying material, especially when mixed with water.

Samhain: One of the eight sabbats, it is traditionally held on October 31. Samhain is the festival of the third harvest and honours the sacrifice of the Pagan god as the world prepares for winter. Memorials for departed loved ones are often held at Samhain. It also corresponds with the popular holiday of Halloween.

scourge: A bound collection of strands of fabric or leaves used in ritual purification. It might also refer to the purification process or the item itself. It used to be that a scourge was used on dedicants as part of their initiation process.

skyclad: Meaning naked, or "wearing only sky." Skyclad ritual participation used to be very common, sometimes required, but now it is only voluntary, if observed at all.

solstice: The longest day/shortest night or its opposite. The solstices are the Winter Solstice on December 21 and the Summer Solstice on June 21. See also *equinox*.

spell: A series of words, actions, or processes performed to accomplish a magickal task or desired result. A spell may be simple or complex and may be performed alone or in a coven or group of Witches.

spirit: The invisible, intangible essence of a being's life energy, separate from the material form of a living being. It could be comparable to a soul. It is also the universal life force of which we are but one small part.

spirituality: The belief in spirit as a universal life essence, the belief in supernatural forces, or the practice working with supernatural forces. See also *religion*.

staff: Part of a Witch's regalia, a staff is a length of wood that is usually as long as the bearer is tall.

Summerland: The Wiccan concept of afterlife, Summerland is that place where spirits rest between incarnations. It is often also seen as the eternal home of the Lord and Lady.

summoner: A coven role usually assigned to a "Priest in training." The role used to be exclusively male, like the Priest, but that gender assignment is less strict today.

sword: Part of a Witch's regalia, or it may be held by a coven. The sword is regarded as the "Master of the Five Elements" because it is forged from earth, heated in fire, cooled in water, wielded in air, and guided by spirit.

talisman: Usually a constructed magickal object, such as a silver pentagram necklace. Talismans can have many purposes but are usually worn as protective symbols. See also *amulet*.

tarot: A deck of seventy-eight cards. Each card has a specific meaning, although the images can be very different from deck to deck. The tarot deck is a very popular divinatory tool, and many Wiccans and Witches use or read tarot cards regularly.

thaumaturgy: A field of magick or spellwork in which the Wiccan or Witch draws power into the spell themselves. See also *theurgy*.

theurgy: A field of magick or spellwork in which the Wiccan or Witch calls upon the Divine to assist in or empower the working. See also *thaumaturgy*.

Threefold Law: The philosophy that what you send out, whether positive or negative, will return threefold.

thurible: An incense burner used in ritual purification. A standard thurible is usually metal and hangs from one chain but sometimes three.

tradition: A path, denomination, or belief system within Wicca or Witchcraft used as a foundation of principle. Gardnerian and Alexandrian are two examples of a tradition.

transcendence: The philosophy that a deity is separate from the world. It also describes a period in which one's consciousness is temporarily separate from the physical world. See also *immanence*.

wand: A small stick, usually the length of a person's forearm, used to assist in magick or spellwork. It is usually seen as an element of air. Some people decorate wands to specific purposes or intentions.

warlock: May refer to an outcast former coven member or, sometimes, a male Witch or Wiccan.

water: In many Wiccan or Witchcraft traditions, water is the element that corresponds to west. It is the realm of emotions, memories, and dreams. See also *elements*.

Wheel of the Year: The cycle of eight sabbats, which correspond to the four seasons.

Wicca or Wiccan: A nature-oriented religion that honours the goddess and the god and their relationship with the world. It is also known as the Old Religion.

Wiccan Rede: The ethical core of Wicca. It is a short verse and summoned up in the eight words: *An ye harm none, do what thou will.*

widdershins: Counterclockwise direction used in spells of banishment or reduction. See also *deosil*.

Witch: One who practices Witchcraft. A Witch can be of any gender.

Witchcraft: Part religion, part philosophy, and part lifestyle, Witchcraft is the practice and observance of honouring the god and goddess and of working magick. Also known as the Old Religion, the Craft, or the Craft of the Wise.

Witch's pyramid: A symbolic depiction of the four states of awareness that correspond to the elements. The four sides of the pyramid are to know, to will, to believe, and to keep silent.

Yule: One of the eight sabbats, it is usually held on December 21. It is also the date of the Winter Solstice. Traditional Yule celebrations observe the turning of the wheel as the god is reborn and the days begin to grow longer.

Bibliography

Abbott, Geoffrey. *Execution: The Guillotine, the Pendulum, the Thousand Cuts, the Spanish Donkey, and 66 Other Ways of Putting Someone to Death*. New York: St. Martin's Press, 2006.

"Abjuration of the Realm Law and Legal Definition." US Legal. Accessed October 19, 2022. https://definitions.uslegal.com/a/abjuration-of-the-realm/.

Adler, Margot. *Drawing Down the Moon: Witches, Druids, Goddess-Worshippers, and Other Pagans in America Today*. New York: Penguin Books, 1997.

Aquinas, Thomas. "Question 11, Article 3." In *Summa Theologica*, translated by Fathers of the English Dominican Province. Accessed October 24, 2022. https://gbt.org/summa.html.

Baker, Margaret. *Discovering the Folklore of Plants*. London: Bloomsbury Publishing, 2008.

Balter, Michael. "The Seeds of Civilization." *Smithsonian Magazine*. May 2005.

Barber, Malcolm. *The New Knighthood: A History of the Order of the Temple*. Cambridge: Cambridge University Press, 1995.

———. *The Trial of the Templars*. Cambridge: Cambridge University Press, 2006.

Barnard, Alan. *Genesis of Symbolic Thought*. Cambridge: Cambridge University Press, 2012.

Barrett, Francis. *The Magus*. London: Adansonia Publishing, 2013.

Barstow, Anne Llewellyn. *Witchcraze: A New History of the European Witch Hunts*. San Francisco: Pandora, 1994.

Bates, Brian. *The Way of Wyrd: Tales of an Anglo-Saxon Sorcerer*. New York: Berkley Books, 1988.

Batty, Miles. *Teaching Witchcraft: A Guide for Teachers and Students of the Old Religion.* Longview, TX: Three Moons Media, 2006.

Brugmann, Birte. "Migration and Endogenous Change." In *The Oxford Handbook of Anglo-Saxon Archaeology*, edited by Helena Hamerow, David A. Hinton, and Sally Crawford, 30–45. Oxford: Oxford University Press, 2011.

Burman, Edward. *The Templars: Knights of God.* Rochester, VA: Destiny Books, 1986.

Cantrell, Gary. *Wiccan Beliefs & Practices: With Rituals for Solitaries & Covens.* St. Paul, MN: Llewellyn Publications, 2001.

Chambers, Robert. *Domestic Annals of Scotland: From the Reformation to the Revolution.* London: W. & R. Chambers, 1859.

Clifton, Chas S. *Witchcraft Today, Book One: The Modern Craft Movement.* St. Paul, MN: Llewellyn Publications, 1996.

"Classical Greek Culture." Khan Academy. https://www.khanacademy.org/humanities /world-history/ancient-medieval/classical-greece/a/greek-culture.

Cohen, Elizabeth. "Can You Imagine Cancer Away?" *CNN*, March 3, 2011. http://edition .cnn.com/2011/HEALTH/03/03/ep.seidler.cancer.mind.body/.

"Constantine." *Christianity Today*, 1998. https://www.christianitytoday.com/history /people/rulers/constantine.html.

Crowley, Aleister. *The Book of the Law.* York Beach, ME: Weiser Books, 1976.

———. *The Equinox.* Vol. 3, no. 10. Edited by Hymenaeus Beta X. York Beach, ME: Weiser Books, 1990.

———. *Magick in Theory and Practice.* New York: Castle Books, 1992.

Cunliffe, Barry, ed. *The Oxford Illustrated History of Prehistoric Europe.* Oxford, United Kingdom: Oxford University Press, 2001.

Cunningham, Scott. *Earth Power: Techniques of Natural Magic.* St. Paul, MN: Llewellyn Publications, 1983.

Cunningham, Stanley B. *Reclaiming Moral Agency: The Moral Philosophy of Albert the Great.* Washington, DC: The Catholic University of America Press, 2008.

Davies, Owen. *Witchcraft, Magic, and Culture 1736–1951.* Manchester, United Kingdom: Manchester University Press, 1999.

Davies, Owen, and Willem de Blécourt, eds. *Beyond the Witch Trials: Witchcraft and Magic in Enlightenment Europe.* Manchester, United Kingdom: Manchester University Press, 2004.

Demos, John Putnam. *Entertaining Satan: Witchcraft and the Culture of Early New England.* Oxford, United Kingdom: Oxford University Press, 1983.

Detienne, Marcel. *The Gardens of Adonis: Spices in Greek Mythology.* Translated by Janet Lloyd. Princeton, NJ: Princeton University Press, 1994.

Doyle White, Ethan. "The Meaning of 'Wicca'": A Study in Etymology, History, and Pagan Politics." *The Pomegranate: The International Journal of Pagan Studies* 12, no. 2 (2011): 185–207. https://journal.equinoxpub.com/POM/article/view/3186.

Duignan, Brian. "Enlightenment." Britannica. Updated September 21, 2022. https://www.britannica.com/event/Enlightenment-European-history.

The Editors of Encyclopaedia Britannica. "Druids." Britannica. Updated August 31, 2022. https://www.britannica.com/topic/Druid.

———. "First Council of Nicaea." Britannica. Updated September 20, 2022. https://www.britannica.com/event/First-Council-of-Nicaea-325.

Esler, Philip, ed. *The Early Christian World.* London: Routledge, 2017.

"Excerpts from Chief Seattle's Famous Speech to President Franklin Pierce." Children of the Earth United. https://www.childrenoftheearth.org/chief_seattle.htm.

Furey, Robert. *Joy of Kindness.* New York: Crossroad, 1993.

Gardner, Gerald. "The Old Laws." In *The Gardnerian Book of Shadows.* Sacred Texts. https://www.sacred-texts.com/pag/gbos/gbos38.htm.

Gibbons, Lois Oliphant, ed. *George Lincoln Burr: His Life by Roland H. Bainton; Selections from His Writings.* Ithaca, NY: Cornell University Press, 1943.

Gray, William G. *Magical Ritual Methods.* York Beach, ME: Samuel Weiser, 1980. https://poderesunidosstudio.files.wordpress.com/2009/12/william-g-gray-magical-ritual-methods.pdf.

Greenfield, Trevor, ed. *Witchcraft Today—60 Years On.* Winchester, United Kingdom: Moon Books, 2014.

Halsall, Paul. "Medieval Sourcebook: Witchcraft Documents [15th Century]." Internet Medieval Source Book. Accessed October 24, 2022. https://sourcebooks.fordham .edu/source/witches1.asp.

"Herbert Daniel Dettmer, Appellee, v. Robert Landon, Director of Corrections, Appellant, 799 F.2d 929 (4th Cir. 1986)." JUSTIA US Law. https://law.justia.com/cases /federal/appellate-courts/F2/799/929/117777/.

"History of Christmas." Did You Know? Accessed October 24, 2022. https://didyouknow. org/christmas/history/.

Huskinson, Janet, ed. *Experiencing Rome: Culture, Identity, and Power in the Roman Empire*. London: Routledge, 2000.

Huson, Paul. *Mastering Witchcraft: A Practical Guide for Witches, Warlocks, and Covens*. New York: Putnam, 1970.

Huss, Boaz, Marco Pasi, and Kocku von Stuckrad. "Introduction. Kabbalah and Modernity." In *Kabbalah and Modernity: Interpretations, Transformations, Adaptations*, edited by Boaz Huss, 1–12. Leiden, Netherlands, 2010.

Hutton, Ronald. *Blood and Mistletoe: The History of the Druids in Britain*. London: Yale University Press, 2009.

———. *The Triumph of the Moon: A History of Modern Pagan Witchcraft*. Oxford: Oxford University Press, London, 2001.

K, Amber. *CovenCraft: Witchcraft for Three or More*. St. Paul, MN: Llewellyn Publications, St. Paul, MN, 1998.

Kamen, Henry. *The Spanish Inquisition: A Historical Revision*. New Haven, CT: Yale University Press, 1999.

Kark, Chris. "Archaeologists from Stanford Find an 8,000-Year-Old 'Goddess Figurine' in Central Turkey." *Stanford News*. September 29, 2016. https://news.stanford .edu/2016/09/29/archaeologists-find-8000-year-old-goddess-figurine-central-turkey/.

Kipling, Rudyard. *Puck of Pook's Hill*. London: Macmillian, 1906.

Kondratiev, Alexei. "Thou Shalt Not Suffer a Witch to Live: An Enquiry into Biblical Mistranslation." *Enchante*, 18 (1994): 11–15.

Leach, Edmund Ronald. "Kingship and Divinity: The Unpublished Frazer Lecture, Oxford, 28 October 1982." *HAU: Journal of Ethnographic Theory* 1, no. 1 (2011): 279–98.

Lee, John Alan. *Colours of Love: An Exploration of the Ways of Loving.* Toronto: New Press, 1973.

Lochtefeld, James. *The Illustrated Encyclopedia of Hinduism: A–M.* New York: Rosen Publishing Group, 2002.

Lovelock, James. *The Vanishing Face of Gaia: A Final Warning.* New York: Basic Books, 2009.

MacMullen, Ramsay. *Christianity and Paganism in the Fourth to Eighth Centuries.* New Haven, CT: Yale University Press, 1997.

Mallory, J. P., and D. Q. Adams, eds. *Encyclopedia of Indo-European Culture.* Chicago: Fitzroy Dearborn, 1997.

Mango, Cyril, ed. *The Oxford History of Byzantium.* Oxford: Oxford University Press, 2002.

Mark, Joshua J. "Religion in the Ancient World." World History Encyclopedia. March 23, 2018. https://www.worldhistory.org/religion/.

Mathiesen, Robert. "Charles G. Leland and the Witches of Italy: The Origin of Aradia." In *Aradia or the Gospel of Witches: A New Translation*, edited by Mario Pazzaglini and Dina Pazzaglini, 25–57. Blaine, WA: Phoenix Publishing, 1998.

Mishkov, Aleksandar. "Wicca—Fastest Growing Religion of the 20th Century." Documentary Tube. Accessed October 19, 2022. https://www.documentarytube.com /articles/wicca-fastest-growing-religion-of-the-20th-century.

Moura, Ann. *Grimoire of the Green Witch: A Complete Book of Shadows.* St. Paul, MN: Llewellyn Publications, 2003.

Myth Woodling. "FAQ: What Is the Summerland? Do You Think It Is a Real Place?" Jester Bear. Published March 23, 2014. http://www.jesterbear.com/Wicca/FAQ summerland.html.

Narr, Karl J. "Prehistoric Religion." Encyclopedia Britannica. Updated April 21, 2021. https://www.britannica.com/topic/prehistoric-religion.

Noble, Catherine. "From Fact to Fallacy: The Evolution of Margaret Alice Murray's Witch-Cult." *The Pomegranate: The International Journal of Pagan Studies* 7, no. 1 (2015): 5–26. https://doi.org/10.1558/pome.v7i1.5.

Pennington, Kenneth J. "Innocent III." Britannica. Updated July 12, 2022. https://www.britannica.com/topic/Vergentis-in-senium.

Piggot, Stuart. *William Stukeley: An Eighteenth-Century Antiquary*. London: Thames and Hudson, 1985.

Price, Neil. *The Viking Way: Religion and War in Late Iron Age Scandinavia*. Uppsala, Sweden: Department of Archaeology and Ancient History, 2002.

Rapley, Robert. *A Case of Witchcraft: The Trial of Urbain Grandier*. Manchester: Manchester University Press, 1998.

Relton, Herbert Maurice. *Studies in Christian Doctrine*. London: Macmillan, 1960.

Ridley, Ronald T. Akhenaten: A Historian's View. Cairo: The American University in Cairo Press, 2019.

Robb, John, Renzo Bigazzi, Luca Lazzarini, Caterina Scarsini, and Fiorenza Sonego. "Social "Status" and Biological "Status": A Comparison of Grave Goods and Skeletal Indicators from Pontecagnano." *American Journal of Physical Anthropology* Vol. 115, 3 (2001), 213–222. https://doi.org/10.1002/ajpa.1076.

Robbins, Rossell Hope. *The Encyclopedia of Witchcraft and Demonology*. New York: Crown Publishers, 1959.

Román, Rachel. "Season of the Jewitch: The Occultists Reviving Jewish Witchcraft and Folklore." The Times of Israel. October 30, 2021. https://www.timesofisrael.com/season-of-the-jewitch-the-occultists-reviving-jewish-witchcraft-and-folklore/.

Schopenhauer, Arthur. *The World as Will and Representation*. Vol. 1, translated by F. E. J. Payne. New York: Dover Publications, 1969.

Shakespeare, William. "Song of the Witches: 'Double, Double Toil and Trouble.'" Poetry Foundation. https://www.poetryfoundation.org/poems/43189/song-of-the-witches-double-double-toil-and-trouble.

"Soundings #8." Rockville, MD: Dorothy Davis, 1988.

Southern, Pat. *The Roman Empire: From Severus to Constantine*. London: Routledge, 2001.

Starhawk. *The Spiral Dance: A Rebirth of the Ancient Religion of the Goddess*. San Francisco: Harper & Row, 1989.

Steiner, Rudolf. *Knowledge of the Higher Worlds and Its Attainment*. East Sussex, United Kingdom: Rudolf Steiner Press, 1947.

Stourton, Edward. *John Paul II: Man of History*. London: Hodder & Stoughton, 2006.

Sturluson, Snorri. *EDDA*. Translated and edited by Anthony Faulkes. London: Everyman Press, 1995.

Summers, Montague, trans. *The Malleus Maleficarum of Heinrich Kramer and James Sprenger*. Mineola, NY: Dover Publications, 1928.

Sutin, Lawrence. *Do What Thou Wilt: A Life of Aleister Crowley*. New York: St. Martin's Press, 2000.

Thomas, Ben. "Eating People Is Wrong—But It's Also Widespread and Sacred." *Anthropology Magazine*. April 20, 2017.

Thompson, Gwen. *The Wiccan Rede*. The Witches' Almanac, 1975.

Tylor, Edward Burnett. *Primitive Culture: The Origins of Culture*. New York: Henry Holt, 1877.

Valiente, Doreen. "The Charge of the Goddess." Berkshire, United Kingdom: The Doreen Valiente Foundation. https://www.doreenvaliente.com/Doreen-Valiente-Doreen _Valiente_Poetry-11.php.

———. *The Wiccan Rede*. Berkshire, United Kingdom: The Doreen Valiente Foundation, 1964.

Vawr, Taliesin Enion, Rhuddlwm ap Gawr, and Merridden Gawr. *The Word: Welsh Witchcraft, the Grail of Immortality, and the Sacred Keys*. Lincoln, NE: iUniverse, 2002.

Welch, Lew. *Ring of Bone: Collected Poems of Lew Welch*. Edited by Donald Allen. San Francisco: Grey Fox, 1979.

Welch, Marin. "Pre-Christian Practices in the Anglo-Saxon World." In *The Oxford Handbook of the Archaeology of Ritual and Religion*, edited by Anders Andrén, 863–876. Oxford: Oxford University Press, 2011.

Whitcomb, Bill. *The Magician's Companion: A Practical and Encyclopedic Guide to Magical and Religious Symbolism*. St. Paul, MN: Llewellyn Publications, 1993.

Wille, John J. "Evidence for Pentagonal Symmetry in Living and Model Cellular Systems." *Natural Science* 3 (2011): 866–883. https://doi.org/10.4236/ns.2011.310112.

Zell-Ravenheart, Oberon, and Morning Glory Zell-Ravenheart. *Creating Circles & Ceremonies: Rituals for All Seasons and Reasons*. Newburyport, MA: New Page Books, 2006.

To Write to the Author

If you wish to contact the author or would like more information about this book, please write to the author in care of Llewellyn Worldwide Ltd. and we will forward your request. Both the author and the publisher appreciate hearing from you and learning of your enjoyment of this book and how it has helped you. Llewellyn Worldwide Ltd. cannot guarantee that every letter written to the author can be answered, but all will be forwarded. Please write to:

Miles Batty
℅ Llewellyn Worldwide
2143 Wooddale Drive
Woodbury, MN 55125-2989
Please enclose a self-addressed stamped envelope for reply,
or $1.00 to cover costs. If outside the U.S.A., enclose
an international postal reply coupon.

Many of Llewellyn's authors have websites with additional information and resources. For more information, please visit our website at http://www.llewellyn .com.